Windows® XP

FOR

DUMMIES®

by Andy Rathbone

WILEY

Wiley Publishing, Inc.

Windows® XP For Dummies®

Published by
Wiley Publishing, Inc.
909 Third Avenue
New York, NY 10022
www.wiley.com

Copyright © 2001 Wiley Publishing, Inc., Indianapolis, Indiana

Published simultaneously in Canada

For general information on our other products and services or to obtain technical support, please contact our Customer Care Department within the U.S. at 800-762-2974, outside the U.S. at 317-572-3993, or fax 317-572-4002.

Wiley also publishes its books in a variety of electronic formats. Some content that appears in print may not be available in electronic books.

Library of Congress Cataloging-in-Publication Data:

Library of Congress Control Number: 2001092737

ISBN: 0-7645-0893-8

Manufactured in the United States of America

17 16 15 14 13 12 11

1B/TR/QT/QU/IN

About the Author

Andy Rathbone started geeking around with computers in 1985 when he bought a boxy CP/M Kaypro 2X with lime-green letters. Like other budding nerds, he soon began playing with null-modem adapters, dialing up computer bulletin boards, and working part-time at Radio Shack.

In between playing computer games, he served as editor of the *Daily Aztec* newspaper at San Diego State University. After graduating with a comparative literature degree, he went to work for a bizarre underground coffee-table magazine that sort of disappeared.

Andy began combining his two main interests, words and computers, by selling articles to a local computer magazine. During the next few years, he started ghostwriting computer books for more-famous computer authors, as well as writing several hundred articles about computers for technoid publications like *Supercomputing Review, CompuServe Magazine, ID Systems, DataPro,* and *Shareware.*

In 1992, Andy and *DOS For Dummies* author/legend Dan Gookin teamed up to write *PCs For Dummies.* Andy subsequently wrote the award-winning *Windows For Dummies* series, *Upgrading & Fixing PCs For Dummies, MP3 For Dummies,* and many other *For Dummies* books.

Today, he has more than 15 million copies of his books in print, which have been translated into more than 30 languages.

Andy lives with his most-excellent wife, Tina, and their cat in Southern California. He wants a new LCD panel monitor for his main computer, but then the cat wouldn't have anyplace to sleep. Feel free to drop by his Web site at www.andyrathbone.com.

Dedication

To my wife, parents, sister, and cat.

Author's Acknowledgments

Special thanks to Dan and Sandy Gookin, Matt Wagner, the Kleskes, the Tragesers, Steve Hayes, Nicole Haims, Kim Darosett, and Jerelind Charles.

Publisher's Acknowledgments

We're proud of this book; please send us your comments through our online registration form located at www.dummies.com/register/.

Some of the people who helped bring this book to market include the following:

Acquisitions, Editorial, and Media Development

Senior Project Editor: Nicole Haims
  (Previous Edition: Darren Meiss)

Senior Acquisitions Editor: Steve Hayes

Senior Copy Editor: Kim Darosett

Copy Editor: Jerelind Charles

Technical Editor: Lee Musick

Editorial Manager: Leah Cameron

Permissions Editors: Carmen Krikorian, Laura Moss

Media Development Coordinator: Marisa Pearman

Media Development Supervisor: Richard Graves

Editorial Assistant: Jean Rogers

Production

Project Coordinator: Dale White

Layout and Graphics: Joyce Haughey, Brian Massey, Barry Offringa, Jill Piscitelli, Heather Pope, Jacque Schneider, Betty Schulte, Julie Trippetti, Jeremey Unger

Proofreaders: TECHBOOKS Production Services

Indexer: Maro Riofrancos

Special Help: Teresa Artman, Amy Pettinella, Rebecca Senninger, Diana Conover

Publishing and Editorial for Technology Dummies
  Richard Swadley, Vice President and Executive Group Publisher
  Andy Cummings, Vice President and Publisher
  Mary C. Corder, Editorial Director

Publishing for Consumer Dummies
  Diane Graves Steele, Vice President and Publisher
  Joyce Pepple, Acquisitions Director

Composition Services
  Gerry Fahey, Vice President of Production Services
  Debbie Stailey, Director of Composition Services

Contents at a Glance

Introduction *1*

Part 1: Bare-Bones Windows XP Stuff *7*

Chapter 1: What Is Windows XP? 9

Chapter 2: Ignore This Chapter on Computer Parts 15

Chapter 3: Windows XP Stuff Everybody Thinks You Already Know 39

Part 11: Making Windows XP Do Something *59*

Chapter 4: Starting Windows XP 61

Chapter 5: Field Guide to Buttons, Bars, Boxes, Folders, and Files 75

Chapter 6: Moving Windows Around 97

Chapter 7: I Can't Find It! 103

Chapter 8: That "Cut and Paste" Stuff (Moving Around Words, Pictures, and Sounds) 115

Chapter 9: Sharing It All on the Network 125

Part 111: Using Windows XP Applications (And Surfing the Web) *145*

Chapter 10: Your Desktop, Start Button, and Taskbar (And Free Programs) 147

Chapter 11: That Scary My Computer Program 181

Chapter 12: Cruising the Web, Sending E-Mail, and Using Newsgroups 209

Chapter 13: Sound! Movies! Media Player! 239

Part 1V: Help! *268*

Chapter 14: Customizing Windows XP (Fiddling with the Control Panel) 269

Chapter 15: The Case of the Broken Window 301

Chapter 16: Figuring Out Those Annoying Pop-Up Messages 311

Chapter 17: Help on the Windows XP Help System 327

Part V: The Part of Tens *340*

Chapter 18: Ten Exciting New Windows XP Features 341

Chapter 19: Ten Aggravating Things about Windows XP (And How to Fix Them) 349

Chapter 20: Ten (Or So) Windows XP Icons and What They Do 355
Chapter 21: Ten Most Frequently Asked Windows Questions................................359

Appendix: Glossary *367*

Index *373*

Cartoons at a Glance

By Rich Tennant

"Jeez–I thought the Registry just defined the background on the screen."

page 7

"Yes, Unicenter has an automated 'Help' function. Why?"

page 59

Gee, Richard, you'll have to show me where on the toolbar you found an icon labeled "Overkill".

page 267

"This is amazing. You can stop looking for Derek. According to an MSN search I did, he's hiding behind the dryer in the basement."

page 145

"Well, that's the third one in as many clicks. I'm sure it's just a coincidence, still, don't use the 'Launcher' again until I've had a look at it."

page 339

Cartoon Information:
Fax: 978-546-7747
E-Mail: richtennant@the5thwave.com
World Wide Web: www.the5thwave.com

Table of Contents

Introduction 1

  About This Book 1

  How to Use This Book 2

  And What about You? 3

  How This Book Is Organized 3

      Part I: Bare-Bones Windows XP Stuff 3

      Part II: Making Windows XP Do Something 4

      Part III: Using Windows XP Applications

        (And Surfing the Web) 4

      Part IV: Help! 4

      Part V: The Part of Tens 4

  Icons Used in This Book 5

  Where to Go from Here 6

Part 1: Bare-Bones Windows XP Stuff 7

  Chapter 1: What Is Windows XP? 9

    What Are Windows and Windows XP? 9

    What Does Windows Do? 11

    How Does Windows XP Affect My Older Programs? 13

    Should I Bother Using Windows XP? 13

    Bracing Yourself (And Your Computer) for Windows XP 14

  Chapter 2: Ignore This Chapter on Computer Parts 15

    The Computer 15

    The Microprocessor (CPU) 17

    Disks and Disk Drives 17

      Floppy disks 18

      Compact discs (CD-ROM drive stuff) 18

      DVD discs 20

      Iomega drives 20

      Hard disks 20

      What does write-protected mean? 21

    The Mouse and That Double-Click Stuff 22

    Video Cards and Monitors 25

    Keyboards 26

      Groups of keys 26

      More key principles 28

    Modems and the Internet 30

    Printers 32

    Networks 32

    Sound Cards (Making Barfing Noises) 33

    Ports 33

    Parts Required by Windows XP 35

**Chapter 3: Windows XP Stuff Everybody
Thinks You Already Know 39**

Activation 39
Backing Up a Disk 40
Clicking 41
The Cursor 42
Defaults (And the Any Key) 43
Desktop (And Changing Its Background) 43
Double-Clicking 44
Dragging and Dropping 44
Drivers 45
Files 45
Folders (Directories) 46
Graphical User Interfaces 47
Hardware and Software 47
Icons 48
The Internet 48
Kilobytes, Megabytes, and So On 49
Loading, Running, Executing, and Launching 50
Memory 51
The Mouse 51
Networks 52
Pointers/Arrows 53
Plug and Play 53
Quitting or Exiting 54
Save Command 54
Save As Command 55
ScanDisk 55
Shortcuts 56
Temp Files 57
The Windows 57
The World Wide Web 57

Part II: Making Windows XP Do Something 59

Chapter 4: Starting Windows XP 61

Logging On to Windows XP 62
    It wants me to enter a password! 63
    Starting your favorite program with the Start button 64
Pull-Down Menus 67
    Loading a file 68
    Putting two programs on-screen simultaneously 70
Printing Your Work 71
Saving Your Work 72
Logging Off of Windows XP 72

Chapter 5: Field Guide to Buttons, Bars, Boxes, Folders, and Files . . . 75

A Typical Window 76
Bars 77
    Moving windows with the title bar 77
    Bossing around windows with the menu bar 78

Moving inside your window with the scroll bar 79
Switching windows with the taskbar 81
Borders 81
The Button Family 82
Sending commands with command buttons 82
Choosing between option buttons 84
Changing a window's size with Minimize and Maximize buttons 85
The Useless Control-Menu Button 86
Filling Out Bothersome Forms in Dialog Boxes 87
Typing into text boxes 87
Choosing options from list boxes 88
Drop-down list boxes 89
Check boxes 90
Sliding controls 91
Just Tell Me How to Open a File! 92
Hey! When Do I Click, and When Do I Double-Click? 94
When Do I Use the Left Mouse Button, and
When Do I Use the Right One? 95

Chapter 6: Moving Windows Around **97**
Moving a Window to the Top of the Pile 97
Moving a Window from Here to There 98
Making a Window Bigger or Smaller 99
Making a Window Fill the Whole Screen 101

Chapter 7: I Can't Find It! **103**
Finding Lost Windows on the Desktop 103
Plucking a lost window from the Task Manager 104
Tiling and cascading windows (The "deal all
the windows in front of me" approach) 105
Finding Lost Files, Folders, Music, Photos, Videos,
People, or Computers 106
Finding any lost files or folders 108
Finding lost pictures, music, or video 111
Finding lost documents 112
Finding computers or people 112
Searching the Internet 113

**Chapter 8: That "Cut and Paste" Stuff (Moving Around Words,
Pictures, and Sounds)** **115**
Examining the Cut and Paste Concept (And Copy, Too) 116
Highlighting the Important Stuff 117
Cutting, Copying, or Deleting What You Highlighted 118
Cutting the information 119
Copying the information 120
Deleting the information 120
Finding out more about cutting, copying, and deleting 121
Pasting Information into Another Window 121
Leaving Scraps on the Desktop Deliberately 122

Chapter 9: Sharing It All on the Network **125**

Fiddling with User Accounts 126
  Changing a user account's picture 127
  Switching quickly between users 129
  Creating, deleting, or changing a user account 130
Skip the Rest of This Unless You Have or Want a Network 131
  Can I get in trouble for looking into the wrong computer? 133
  How do I access other networked computers? 134
  Sharing your own computer's stuff with the network 135
  Sharing a printer on the network 136
How Do I Create My Own Computer Network? 138
  Buying a network's parts 138
  Installing the network's parts 140
Letting the Network Setup Wizard Set Up Your Network 141

Part III: Using Windows XP Applications
(And Surfing the Web) **145**

Chapter 10: Your Desktop, Start Button, and Taskbar
(And *Free* Programs) **147**

Rolling Objects along the Windows XP Desktop 148
  Arranging icons on the desktop 150
  Using the Recycle Bin 151
  Making a shortcut 152
  Uh, what's the difference between a shortcut and
    the actual program? 155
  Shutting down Windows XP 155
The Way-Cool Taskbar 157
  Shrinking windows to the taskbar and retrieving them 158
  Clicking the taskbar's sensitive areas 159
  Customizing the taskbar 161
Controlling the Printer 164
The Start Button's Reason to Live 165
  Starting a program from the Start button 166
  Adding a program's icon to the Start menu 167
  Making Windows start programs automatically 168
The Start Menu's Free Programs 169
  The Start menu's first-tier programs 169
  The Start menu's All Programs area 170
My Version of Windows XP Doesn't Have
  the Right Freebie Programs! 178

Chapter 11: That Scary My Computer Program **181**

Why Is the My Computer Program So Frightening? 182
Getting the Lowdown on Folders 185
Peering into Your Drives and Folders 186
  Seeing the files on a disk drive 186
  Seeing what's inside folders 188
Loading a Program or File 189

Deleting and Undeleting Files, Folders, and Icons 190
Getting rid of a file or folder 190
How to undelete a file 191
Copying or Moving a File, Folder, or Icon 193
Selecting More Than One File or Folder 195
Renaming a File, Folder, or Icon 196
Using Legal Folder Names and Filenames 197
Copying a Complete Floppy Disk 198
Creating a Folder 199
Seeing More Information about Files and Folders 200
What's That Windows Explorer Thing? 203
How Do I Make the Network Work? 204
Making My Computer and Windows Explorer List Missing Files 207
Formatting a Disk 207

**Chapter 12: Cruising the Web, Sending E-Mail, and
Using Newsgroups 209**
What's the Difference between the Internet, the
World Wide Web, and a Web Browser? 210
Who Can Use the Internet and World Wide Web? 211
What's an ISP, and Do I Need One? 213
What Do I Need to Access the World Wide Web? 213
Setting Up Your Internet Account with the
Internet Connection Wizard 214
What Is a Web Browser? 218
How Do I Navigate the Web with Internet Explorer? 219
What's a home page? 219
How do I move from Web page to Web page? 221
How can I revisit my favorite places? 222
What's an index or search engine? 222
But How Do I Do This? 224
I can't get it to install! 225
How do I install the firewall? 225
I keep getting busy signals! 226
The Web page says it needs [insert name of
weird plug-in thing here]! 226
How do I copy a picture from the Internet? 227
Little boxes keep popping up on the Web pages! 227
Managing E-Mail with Outlook Express 228
Setting up Outlook Express 6.0 to send and receive e-mail 229
Getting ready to send e-mail 231
Composing a letter 231
Reading a received letter 233
What does the News area do? 236
Finding and reading a newsgroup 237

Chapter 13: Sound! Movies! Media Player! 239
Understanding Media Player 240
Using Media Guide to Find Videos, Music, and
Movie Trailers on the Internet 242
Finding and Playing Internet Radio Stations 244

Finding Media on Your Computer and Putting It into
the Media Library 247
Creating Playlists 248
Playing CDs 248
Playing DVDs 250
Playing MP3s and WMAs 251
Creating WMAs or MP3s 253
Storing Files in Your My Music and Shared Music Folders 255
Playing Videos 256
Moving Music or Video to an MP3 Player or Pocket PC 257
Burning Your Own CDs 259
Adding Skins to Media Player 261
Fixing Media Player Muckups 262
It just doesn't work! 263
Does it have to be so huge? 263
Bizarre Multimedia Words 264

Part IV: Help! *267*

**Chapter 14: Customizing Windows XP
(Fiddling with the Control Panel)** **269**
Finding the Right Control Panel Option 270
Appearance and Themes 276
Changing the display's background, screen saver,
and resolution 276
Making Windows display folders differently 282
Adjusting your taskbar and Start menu 283
Viewing your computer's fonts 284
Network and Internet Connections 285
Add or Remove Programs 286
Removing programs 286
Installing a new program 287
Adding or removing Windows components 287
Sounds, Speech, and Audio Devices 288
Changing Windows' volume and playing with its sounds 288
Letting Windows talk to you 290
Performance and Maintenance 290
Seeing information about your computer 290
Turning on or off visual effects 291
Freeing up space on your hard disk 291
Rearranging your hard disk to speed it up (defragmenting) 292
Other Performance and Maintenance icons 293
Printers and Other Hardware 293
Adding new hardware 293
Fiddling with printers and faxes 294
Game controllers 296
Scanners and cameras 296
Making Windows XP recognize your double-click 297
Phone and modem options 298
User Accounts 298

Date, Time, Language, and Regional Options 299
Regional and language options 299
Setting the computer's date and time 299

Chapter 15: The Case of the Broken Window 301

Restoring Calm with System Restore 301
My Mouse Doesn't Work Right 303
Making Older Programs Run under Windows XP 303
It Says I Need To Be an Administrator! 304
I'm Stuck in Menu Land 305
Keeping Windows Up-to-Date 305
All My Desktop Icons Vanished 306
I'm Supposed to Install a New Driver 306
His Version of Windows XP Has More Programs Than Mine! 307
I Clicked the Wrong Button (But Haven't Lifted My Finger Yet) 307
My Computer Is Frozen Up Solid 308
The Printer Isn't Working Right 308
My Double-Clicks Are Now Single Clicks! 309

Chapter 16: Figuring Out Those Annoying Pop-Up Messages 311

Access Is Denied 312
AutoComplete 312
Click Here to Activate Now 313
Connect To 314
Error Connecting To 314
File Name Warning 315
Found New Hardware 316
Hiding Your Inactive Notification Icons 316
If You Remove This File, You Will No Longer Be Able to
Run This Program 317
Missing Shortcut 318
New Programs Installed 318
New Updates Are Ready to Install 319
Open with 320
Privacy Alert — Saving Cookies 321
Rename 322
Safe to Remove Hardware 322
Stay Current with Automatic Updates 323
There Are Unused Icons on Your Desktop 323
When You Send Information to the Internet 324
You Have Files Waiting to Be Written to the CD 325

Chapter 17: Help on the Windows XP Help System 327

Get Me Some Help, and Fast! 327
Press F1 328
Click the right mouse button on the confusing part 328
Choose Help from the main menu 329
Sending in the Troubleshooters 329
Search — letting Windows do the work 331
Consulting a Program's Built-In Computer Guru 331
Finding Help for your exact problem 334
Using Windows Help and Support Center 335

Part V: The Part of Tens 339

Chapter 18: Ten Exciting New Windows XP Features 341
Way Cool Folders 342
Remote Assistance 343
Burning (Writing Information onto) CDs 344
Files and Settings Transfer Wizard 344
User Accounts 345
Increased Stability 345
Built-in Firewall against Internet Hackers 346
Automatically Sets Clock 347
Windows XP Must Be Activated 347
Making Windows XP Run Like Your Old Version of Windows 347

Chapter 19: Ten Aggravating Things about Windows XP
(And How to Fix Them) 349
How Do I Change the Volume? 349
What Version of Windows Do I Have? 350
I Want to Click Instead of Double-Click (Or Vice Versa)! 350
My Bar Full of Buttons Just Fell Off! 351
Keeping Track of All Those Windows Is Too Hard 352
The Taskbar Keeps Disappearing! 352
My Print Screen Key Doesn't Work 353
Lining Up Two Windows on the Screen Is Too Hard 353
The Folder Lists the Wrong Stuff on My Floppy Disk 354
It Won't Let Me Do Something Unless I'm An Administrator! 354

Chapter 20: Ten (Or So) Windows XP Icons and What They Do 355

Chapter 21: Ten Most Frequently Asked Windows Questions 359
How Do I Remember All the Stuff I Can Do to a File? 359
Should I Upgrade to the Windows XP Home or Professional Version? ...361
How Do I Add a Picture of My Face to My User Account? 361
Why Can't Windows XP Play My DVDs? 362
Why Can't Windows XP Create MP3 Files? 363
How Do I Get Rid of the Welcome Screen? 363
How Can I See Previews of My Pictures? 364
How Can I Make All My Web Pages Open in a Full-Screen Window? 365
What Will I Miss If I Don't Use the Internet with Windows XP? 365

Appendix: Glossary 367

Index 373

Introduction

· ·

*W*elcome to *Windows XP For Dummies!*

This book boils down to this simple fact: Some people want to be Windows wizards. They love interacting with dialog boxes. While sitting in front of their computers, they randomly press keys on their keyboards, hoping to stumble onto a hidden, undocumented feature. They memorize long strings of computer commands while washing their hair. Some don't even wash their hair.

And you? Well, you're no dummy, that's for sure. In fact, you're much more developed than most computer nerds. You can make casual conversation with a neighbor without mumbling about ordering pizzas over the Internet, for example. But when it comes to Windows and computers, the fascination just isn't there. You just want to get your work done, stop, and relax for a while. You have no intention of changing, and there's nothing wrong with that.

That's where this book comes in handy. It won't try to turn you into a Windows wizard, but you'll pick up a few chunks of useful computing information while reading it. Instead of becoming a Windows XP expert, you'll know just enough to get by quickly, cleanly, and with a minimum of pain so that you can move on to the more pleasant things in life.

About This Book

Don't try to read this book in one sitting; there's no need. Instead, treat this book like a dictionary or an encyclopedia. Turn to the page with the information you need and say, "Ah, so that's what they're talking about." Then put down the book and move on.

Don't bother trying to remember all the Windows XP buzzwords, such as "Select the menu item from the drop-down list box." Leave that stuff for the computer gurus. In fact, if anything technical comes up in a chapter, a road sign warns you well in advance. That way, you can either slow down to read it or speed on around it.

You won't find any fancy computer jargon in this book. Instead, you'll find subjects like these, discussed in plain old English:

  ✔ Why did they choose a weird name like "Windows XP"?

  ✔ Finding the file you saved or downloaded yesterday

✔ Moving those little windows around on the screen with the mouse

✔ Making Windows XP run like your older versions of Windows

✔ Starting and closing programs by clicking the mouse button

✔ Making Windows XP work again when it's misbehaving

There's nothing to memorize and nothing to learn. Just turn to the right page, read the brief explanation, and get back to work. Unlike other books, this one enables you to bypass the technical hoopla and still get your work done.

How to Use This Book

Something in Windows XP will eventually leave you scratching your head. No other program brings so many buttons, bars, and babble to the screen. When something in Windows XP has you stumped, use this book as a reference. Look for the troublesome topic in this book's table of contents or index. The table of contents lists chapter and section titles and page numbers. The index lists topics and page numbers. Page through the table of contents or index to the spot that deals with that particular bit of computer obscurity, read only what you have to, close the book, and apply what you've read.

If you're feeling spunky and want to learn something, read a little further. You can find a few completely voluntary extra details or some cross-references to check out. There's no pressure, though. You won't be forced to learn anything that you don't want to or that you simply don't have time for.

If you have to type something into the computer, you'll see easy-to-follow text like this:

www.vw.com

In the preceding example, you type the cryptic string of letters www.vw.com and then press the keyboard's Enter key. Typing words into a computer can be confusing, so a description of what you're supposed to type usually follows. That way, you can type the words exactly as they're supposed to be typed.

Whenever I describe a message or information that you see on-screen, I present it this way:

```
This is a message on-screen.
```

This book doesn't wimp out by saying, "For further information, consult your manual." Windows XP doesn't even *come* with a manual. You won't find information about running specific Windows software packages, such as Microsoft Office. Windows XP is complicated enough on its own! Luckily, other *For Dummies* books mercifully explain most popular software packages.

Don't feel abandoned, though. This book covers Windows in plenty of detail for you to get the job done. Plus, if you have questions or comments about *Windows XP For Dummies,* feel free to drop me a line on my Web site at www.andyrathbone.com.

Finally, keep in mind that this book is a *reference.* It's not designed to teach you how to use Windows XP like an expert, heaven forbid. Instead, this book dishes out enough bite-sized chunks of information so that you don't *have* to learn Windows.

When you're ready for some more-advanced Windows XP information, pick up a copy of *Windows XP Secrets.* Written by Curt Simmons, the thick book leads you safely through some of the Windows XP program's more tumultuous ground.

And What about You?

Well, chances are that you have a computer. You have Windows XP or are thinking about picking up a copy. You know what *you* want to do with your computer. The problem lies in making the *computer* do what you want it to do. You've gotten by one way or another, hopefully with the help of a computer guru — either a friend at the office, somebody down the street, or your fourth-grader. Unfortunately, though, that computer guru isn't always around. This book can be a substitute during your times of need. Keep a doughnut or Pokémon card nearby, however, just in case you need a quick bribe.

How This Book Is Organized

The information in this book has been well sifted. This book contains five parts, and I divided each part into chapters relating to the part's theme. With an even finer knife, I divided each chapter into short sections to help you figure out a bit of Windows XP's weirdness. Sometimes, you may find what you're looking for in a small, boxed tip. Other times, you may need to cruise through an entire section or chapter. It's up to you and the particular task at hand.

Here are the categories (the envelope, please):

Part 1: Bare-Bones Windows XP Stuff

This book starts out with the basics. You find out how to turn on your computer and how to examine your computer's parts and what Windows XP does to them. It explains all the Windows XP stuff that everybody thinks that you already know. It explains the new features in Windows XP, separating the wheat from the chaff while leaving out any thick, technical oatmeal. You discover whether your computer has enough oomph to run Windows XP. And you end this part (with great relief) by turning off your computer.

Part II: Making Windows XP Do Something

Windows XP leaps onto the screen with a snappy beat and overly excited videos. But how do you make the darn thing do something *useful?* Here, you find ways to overcome the frustratingly playful tendencies of Windows XP and force it to sweep leaves off the driveway or empty the dishwasher.

Part III: Using Windows XP Applications (And Surfing the Web)

Windows XP comes with bunches of exciting free programs. Finding and starting the programs, however, is quite a chore. This part dissects the Windows XP backbone: Its annoying "Welcome" screen and User Name buttons, the mammoth Start button menu that hides all the important stuff, and your computer's desktop — the background your running programs rest upon.

This part of the book explains how to store your files so you can find them again. It shows how to send e-mail and play with that World Wide Web thing everyone talks about. Turn here for information on playing music CDs and MP3s and movies. As a bonus, you discover why your computer screen looks like a blinking billboard for Microsoft products. (And how to turn those ads off.)

Part IV: Help!

Although glass doesn't shatter when Windows XP crashes, it still hurts. In this part, you find some soothing salves for the most painful irritations. Plus, you find ways to unleash the Windows XP program's wise new team of powerful Troubleshooting Wizards. Imagine: A computer that can finally wave a wand and fix itself!

Part V: The Part of Tens

Everybody loves lists (except during tax time). This part contains lists of Windows-related trivia — ten aggravating things about Windows XP (and how to fix them), ten confusing Windows XP icons and what they mean, ten ways to make Windows XP start working again, and other shoulder-rubbing solutions for tense problems.

Icons Used in This Book

Already seen Windows? Then you've probably noticed its *icons,* which are little pictures for starting various programs. The icons in this book fit right in. They're even a little easier to figure out:

Watch out! This signpost warns you that pointless technical information is coming around the bend. Swerve away from this icon, and you'll be safe from the awful technical drivel.

This icon alerts you about juicy information that makes computing easier: A tried and true method for keeping the cat from sleeping on top of the monitor, for instance.

Don't forget to remember these important points. (Or at least dog-ear the pages so that you can look them up again a few days later.)

The computer won't explode while you're performing the delicate operations associated with this icon. Still, wearing gloves and proceeding with caution is a good idea when this icon is near.

Already familiar with Windows Me, Windows 98, or another version of Windows? This icon marks information that can ease your transition from old to new.

Some PCs may vary

If Windows XP came already installed on your PC, be forewarned: PC manufacturers love to customize their PCs' versions of Windows. Some toss in oodles of extra software; some simply toss an America Online icon onto the desktop. Still other manufacturers strip Windows XP of some of its programs. If you think your version of Windows XP lacks some features, check out Chapter 15. It describes what to do if somebody else's version of Windows has more fun stuff than your own.

Where to Go from Here

Now, you're ready for action. Give the pages a quick flip and maybe scan through a few sections that you know you'll need later. Please remember, this is *your* book — your weapon against the computer criminals who've inflicted this whole complicated computer concept on you. So pretend you're back in grade school, and you can't get caught: Circle any paragraphs you find useful, highlight key concepts, cover up the technical drivel with sticky notes, and draw gothic gargoyles in the margins next to the complicated stuff.

The more you mark up your book, the easier it will be for you to find all the good stuff again.

Getting great Windows XP information online

The geeks at Microsoft are always complicating their products in the name of perfection, and Windows XP is no exception. Fortunately, several online resources help you fight back.

My Web site, www.andyrathbone.com, contains tips on using Windows XP, as well as any corrections made to this book after it went to print.

The site also carries links to the publisher's site, Dummies.com (www.dummies.com), which provides a way to sign up for daily For Dummies eTips sent by e-mail. While you're there, drop by the Windows XP Resource Center for additional information about Windows XP.

Part I
Bare-Bones
Windows XP Stuff

The 5th Wave   By Rich Tennant

"Jeez—I thought the Registry just
defined the background on the screen."

In this part . . .

Most people are dragged into Windows XP without a choice. Their new computer probably came with a version of Windows XP already installed; or maybe you had Windows XP installed at the office, where everyone has to learn it except for Jerry, who moved over to the Art Department and got his own Macintosh; or perhaps the latest version of your favorite program requires Windows XP, so you've had to learn to live with the darn thing.

No matter how you were introduced, you can adjust to Windows XP, just like you eventually learned to live comfortably with that funky college roommate who kept leaving hair clogs in the shower.

Whatever your situation, this part keeps things safe and sane, with the water flowing smoothly. If you're new to computers, the first chapter answers the question you've been afraid to ask around the lunchroom: "Just what is this Windows XP thing, anyway?"

Chapter 1

What Is Windows XP?

In This Chapter

▶ Understanding what Windows XP is and what it does

▶ Finding out how Windows XP affects your current programs

▶ Deciding whether you should upgrade to Windows XP

*O*ne way or another, you've probably already heard about Windows, created by the Microsoft company and owned by one of the richest men in the world. Windows posters line the walls of computer stores. Everybody who's anybody talks breezily about Windows, the Internet, and the World Wide Web. Weird code words, such as www.vw.com, stare out cryptically from magazines, newspapers, bus stops, and blimps.

To help you play catch-up in the world of Windows, this chapter fills you in on the basics of the newest version of Windows, called *Windows XP.* The chapter discusses what Windows XP is and what it can do. This chapter also shows how Windows XP works with older Windows programs you may have on your shelf.

Because Windows XP comes preinstalled on most new computers, this chapter also answers that question nagging away at owners of older computers: Should I bother upgrading to Windows XP?

What Are Windows and Windows XP?

Windows is just another piece of software, like the zillions of others lining the store shelves. But it's not a program in the normal sense — something that lets you write letters or lets your coworkers play Bozark the Destroyer over the office network after everybody else goes home. Rather, Windows controls the way you work with your computer.

Years ago, computers looked like typewriters connected to TV sets. Just as on a typewriter, people typed letters and numbers onto the computer's keyboard. The computer listened and then placed those letters and numbers onto the screen. But it was ever-so-boring.

The method was boring because only computer engineers used computers. Nobody expected normal people to use computers — especially not in their offices, their dens, or even in their kitchens. Windows changed all that in several ways.

- Windows software dumps the typewriter analogy and updates the *look* of computers. Windows replaces the old-style words and numbers with colorful pictures and fun buttons. It's fun and flashy, like a Versace necktie.

- Windows XP is the most powerful of Microsoft's Windows software — software that's been updated many times since starting to breathe in January 1985. XP is short for *Experience,* but Microsoft calls it Windows XP to make it sound hip, as if Jimi Hendrix would have used it.

- Programmer types say Windows software is big enough and powerful enough to be called an *operating system.* That's because Windows "operates" your computer. Other programs tell Windows what to do, and Windows makes your computer carry out those commands.

- Microsoft built Windows XP on the shoulders of Windows 2000, an older but powerful version of Windows designed for business users. That means Windows XP is much more difficult to crash than Windows Me or Windows 98. Unfortunately, it also means Windows XP is more difficult for beginners to use.

What version of Windows XP do I need?

Windows XP comes in two basic versions: Windows XP Home and Windows XP Professional. Chances are, you'll use Windows XP Home, the version designed for homes and small businesses. Like its predecessor, Windows Me, Windows XP Home supports networking, modem sharing, and other fancy tricks. You can install Windows XP Home over Windows 98 and Windows Me (but not Windows 95, Windows NT, or Windows 2000).

Larger businesses need the more advanced version, Windows XP Professional, to handle their more powerful computing needs. It includes ho-hum things, such as corporate security, advanced group policy settings, roaming user profiles, Kerberos Extended Errors facility, and other indigestible buzzwords. The Professional version can be installed over Windows 98, Windows Me, Windows NT 4.0, Windows 2000, and Windows XP Home.

Strangely enough, Windows XP Professional works better on laptops than Windows XP Home does. The Professional version contains better battery-management features and works better with wireless Internet connections.

Microsoft also sells Windows XP Server edition, but nobody needs that version — except people who take advanced computer courses that explain *why* they need it.

What Does Windows Do?

Like the mother with the whistle in the lunch court, Windows controls all the parts of your computer. You turn on your computer, start Windows, and start running programs. Each program runs in its own little *window* on-screen, as shown in Figure 1-1. Yet Windows keeps things safe, even if the programs start throwing food at each other.

Windows gets its name from all the cute little windows it places on your monitor. Each window shows information, such as a picture, a program that you're running, or a baffling technical reprimand. You can put several windows on-screen at the same time and jump from window to window, visiting different programs. You can even enlarge a window to fill the entire screen.

Some people say that colorful windows, pictures, and music make Windows easier to use; others say that Windows is a little too artsy. To write a letter in Windows XP, for example, do you select the picture of the notepad, the ballpoint pen, or the folder marked Communications?

✔ A computer environment that uses little pictures and symbols is called a *graphical user interface,* or *GUI.* (It's pronounced *gooey,* believe it or not.) Pictures require more computing horsepower than letters and numbers, so Windows XP requires a relatively powerful computer. (You can find a list of the requirements in Chapter 2.)

✔ When the word *Windows* starts with a capital letter, it refers to the Windows program. When the word *windows* starts with a lowercase letter, it refers to windows you see on-screen. When the word *Windows* ends with the letters *XP,* it refers to the latest version of the Windows software, Windows XP.

✔ Because Windows uses graphics, it's much easier to use than to describe. To tell someone how to view the next page in a Windows document you say, "Click in the vertical scroll bar beneath the scroll box." Those directions sound weird, but after you've done it, you'll say, "Oh, is that all? Golly!" (Plus, you can still press the PgDn key in Windows. You don't have to "click in the vertical scroll bar beneath the scroll box" if you don't want to.)

✔ With Windows XP, your desktop doesn't have to look like a typewritten page *or* a desktop. It can look like an Internet Web page, as shown in Figure 1-2. (You can find more about Web pages and the Internet in Chapter 12.) In fact, the chameleon-like Windows XP can run like a Web page, resemble earlier Windows versions, or let you customize it to your own fancy, which introduces many more ways for things to go wrong.

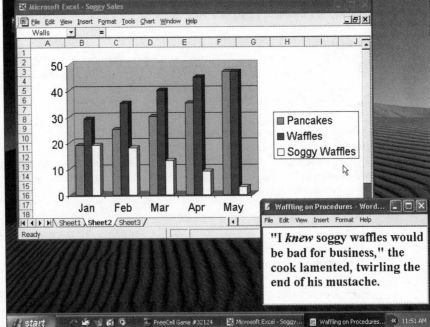

Figure 1-1:
Programs
run inside
little
windows
on the
Windows XP
desktop.

Figure 1-2:
Windows XP
enables
Web surfers
to fill their
desktops
with pages
from the
Internet.

How Does Windows XP Affect My Older Programs?

Windows XP can still run most of your older Windows programs, thank goodness. So after upgrading to Windows XP, you won't have to buy expensive new software immediately. It runs almost any program that worked under Windows Me, Windows 98, and Windows 95.

✔ Because Windows XP is based on the big-business-based Windows NT and Windows 2000 software, Windows XP runs most of those types of programs as well.

✔ You can't install Windows XP on your five-year-old computer and expect it to run well. Windows XP is a big operating system for a big computer. You'll probably have to buy a new computer or add bigger shoulders to your older one. (In computer language, "big shoulders" translates to a faster CPU chip, more memory, a larger hard drive, and a CD-ROM drive.) Unfortunately, adding bigger shoulders often costs more than buying a new PC. (Chapter 2 explains what type of computer Windows XP demands.)

✔ Windows XP prefers *Plug and Play* hardware. That means that it prefers devices that come on PCI cards. If your computer uses mostly ISA cards, you'll probably want a new computer.

✔ If one of your older programs has trouble running or installing on Windows XP, use the Compatibility Mode described in Chapter 15.

✔ When people say that Windows XP is *backward compatible,* they just mean that it can run software that was written for older versions of Windows. (Don't even think about running Macintosh software, though.)

Should I Bother Using Windows XP?

Windows users are elbowing each other nervously by the water cooler and whispering the Big Question: Why bother buying Windows XP, going through the hassle of installing it, and learning all its new features?

Well, many people are just stuck with it: Windows XP comes preinstalled on most new computers. Other people prefer Windows XP for its sturdiness. Microsoft took its strong business version of Windows, tweaked it, and called it Windows XP. That means it's better for running networks. Better yet, it won't crash as often. If one program stops working, you simply shut down that program. Your computer will keep running, as will your other programs.

Basically, the upgrade question boils down to this answer: If your computer crashes a lot when using your current version of Windows, it may be time to upgrade. But if you're happy with your current computer setup, don't bother. After all, why buy new tires if your old ones still have some life left?

Bracing Yourself (And Your Computer) for Windows XP

With Windows, everything happens at the same time. Its many different parts run around like hamsters with an open cage door. Programs cover up each other on-screen. They overlap corners, hiding each other's important parts. Occasionally, they simply disappear.

Be prepared for a bit of frustration when things don't behave properly. You may be tempted to stand up, bellow, and toss a nearby stapler across the room. After that, calmly pick up this book, find the trouble spot listed in the index, and turn to the page with the answer.

- Windows software may be accommodating, but that can cause problems, too. For example, Windows XP often offers more than three different ways for you to perform the same computing task. Don't bother memorizing each command. Just choose one method that works for you and stick with it. For example, Andrew and Deirdre Kleske use scissors to cut their freshly delivered pizza into slices. It stupefies most of their houseguests, but it gets the job done.

- Windows XP runs best on a powerful new computer with the key words *Pentium III, Pentium 4, AMD Athlon,* or *testosterone* somewhere in the description. Look for as much *RAM* (random access memory) and as many *gigabytes* as you can afford. You can find the detailed rundown of the Windows XP finicky computer requirements in Chapter 2.

What's the Windows XP Service Pack?

Windows XP Service Pack 1 repairs many of Windows XP's flaws. To see if your computer has the Service Pack installed, click the Start button, right-click My Computer and choose Properties. Look for the line, "Service Pack," in the System entry.

If yours doesn't say "Service Pack," download it from Windows Update (listed near the top of the Start menu's All Programs area). It may also be ordered on a CD from Microsoft at www.microsoft.com. More information about the Service Pack awaits near the end of Chapter 15.

Chapter 2

Ignore This Chapter on Computer Parts

. . . .

In This Chapter

▶ Finding out the names for the gizmos and gadgets on your computer

▶ Understanding what all those things do

▶ Finding out what stuff your computer needs in order to use Windows XP

. . . .

*T*his chapter introduces computer gizmos and gadgets. Go ahead and ignore it. Who cares what all your PC gadgetry is called? Unless your PC's beeping at you like a car alarm (or not beeping when it's supposed to beep), don't bother messing with it. Just dog-ear the top of this page, say, "So, that's where all that stuff is explained," and keep going.

In Windows XP, you just press the buttons. Windows XP does the dirty work, scooting over to the right part of your computer and kick-starting the action. In case Windows XP stubs a toe, this chapter explains where you may need to put the bandages. And, as always, the foulest-smelling technical chunks are clearly marked; just hold your nose while stepping over them gingerly.

The Computer

The computer is that box, usually beige, with all the cables poking out its back. Officially, it probably answers to one of two names: IBM (often called *True Blue* when people try to dump their old ones in the classifieds) or an *IBM compatible* or *clone*.

Today, most people just call their computers *PCs* because that's what IBM called its first *personal computer* back in 1981. In fact, IBM's first PC started this whole personal computing craze, although some people lay the blame on video games.

The concept of a small computer that could be pecked on in an office or den caught on well with the average Joe, and IBM made gobs of money — so much money, in fact, that other companies immediately ripped off the IBM design. They cloned, or copied, IBM's handiwork to make a computer that worked just like it. These computers, made by companies such as Dell, Gateway, and others, are compatible with IBM's own PC. They can all use the same software as an IBM PC without spitting up.

IBM-compatible computers generally cost less than IBM's official brand of PCs, and they usually work just as well (or better) than IBM's own line of computers. In fact, more people own compatibles than own IBM's own line of personal computers.

✔ Windows XP runs equally well on IBM-compatible computers and on IBM's own brand of computers; the key word is *IBM*. Computers from other planets, like the Macintosh, don't run Windows XP, but their owners don't care. They just smile pleasantly when you try to figure out how to create a Windows XP *file association.*

✔ Okay, so a Macintosh *can* run some versions of Windows software, but they require special (and expensive) Windows-emulating software. (Head for www.connectix.com.) These days, you're probably better off sticking with either a Mac or a PC — don't try to interbreed their brands of software.

✔ As other companies built compatible computers, they strayed from the original IBM design. They added sound, color, and dozens of exciting new internal parts. Luckily, Windows XP usually identifies what computer parts it's dealing with, so it knows what tone of voice to use when speaking with them.

✔ Laptop and notebook computers can run Windows XP with no problems — as long as they buy a separate version of Windows XP for each of them. (That's because Windows XP includes Microsoft's irritating new copy-protection scheme called *Activation;* it's covered in Chapter 3.)

✔ Different brands of computers often tweak Windows subtly, adding different programs and sticking extra buttons on their keyboards. Don't be surprised to see some slight differences between the instructions in this book and the computer in front of you.

✔ Palmtops and other handheld computers can't run Windows XP. They use an itty-bitty version of Windows called Windows CE. (Windows CE Version 3.0 powers Microsoft's new Pocket PCs, designed to compete with the Palm handhelds.)

The Microprocessor (CPU)

The computer's brain is a chunk of silicon buried deep inside the computer's case. Over the years, the CPU has grown from the size of a cracker to a mammoth chocolate bar. This flat computer chip is the *microprocessor,* but nerds tend to call it a *central processing unit,* or *CPU.* (You may have seen flashy microprocessor TV commercials that say "Intel Inside." Intel is a leading CPU developer.)

The computer's microprocessor determines how quickly and powerfully the computer can toss information around. Windows XP isn't happy unless it rides on a Pentium III microprocessor or an even faster one. You can also use Intel's speedier Pentium 4 and Itanium microprocessors, as well as a speedy AMD Athlon. Yep, if you're looking to use Windows XP, you'll probably want a new computer.

- A microprocessor is the current evolution of the gadget that powered those little 1970s pocket calculators. It performs all the computer's background calculations, from juggling spreadsheets to swapping dirty jokes through office e-mail.

- Microprocessors are described by several numbers. Generally, the bigger the numbers, the faster and more powerful the chip.

- Don't know what microprocessor lives inside your computer? Right-click on the Start menu's My Computer button and choose Properties from the pop-up menu. When the System Properties window appears, the processor's name appears near the bottom. If the numbers still look confusing, Intel offers free software to identify your Intel CPU at www.intel.com.

- Don't be afraid to buy a fast AMD Athlon microprocessor for your new computer. It's just as fast, cheaper, and just as good as Intel's. (Disclosure: I have stock in Intel, but I'm considering a trade to AMD.)

- CPU manufacturers assign several numbers to their chips. Intel usually places a number after the chip's name: Pentium II, Pentium III, and Pentium 4. A CPU's processing speed is measured in *megahertz,* or *MHz.* The *cache* size (pronounced "cash") is measured in *kilobytes,* like 512K. When comparing microprocessors, just remember that the bigger the number, the faster Windows performs.

Disks and Disk Drives

The computer's *disk drive,* that thin slot in its front side, is like the drawer at the bank's drive-up teller window. That disk drive enables you to send and retrieve information from the computer. Instead of making you drop information into a cashier's drawer, the computer makes you send and receive your information from disks. The most popular types — the floppy disk, the compact disc, the DVD, the Zip disk, and the hard disk — appear in the next five sections.

Not sure what kilobyte (K), megabyte (MB), and gigabyte (GB) mean? Head for that section in Chapter 3.

Floppy disks

You can shove anything that's flat into a floppy drive, but the computer recognizes only one thing: *floppy disks.* Things get a little weird here, so hang on tight. See, by some bizarre bit of mechanical wizardry, computers store information on disks as a stream of magnetic impulses.

A disk drive spits those little magnetic impulses onto the floppy disk for safe storage. The drive can slurp the information back up, too. You just push the disk into the disk drive and tell Windows whether to spit or slurp information. That's known as *copy to* or *copy from* in computer parlance.

Floppy disks are sturdy 3½-inch squares that are losing popularity in favor of the compact disc, or CD, which I describe in the next section.

> ✔ A disk drive automatically grabs the 3½-inch disk when you push it in far enough. You hear it *clunk,* and the disk sinks down into the drive. If it doesn't, you're putting it in the wrong way. (The disk's silver edge goes in first, with the little round silver thing in the middle facing down.) To retrieve the disk, push the button protruding from around the drive's slot and then grab the disk when the drive kicks it out.

> ✔ Computer stores sell blank floppy disks so that you can copy your work onto them. Unless your new box of blank disks has the words *preformatted* or *IBM formatted,* you can't use the disks straight out of the box. They must be *formatted* first. I cover this merry little chore in Chapter 11.

> ✔ Computers love to *copy* things. When you're copying a file from one disk to another, you aren't *moving* the file. You're just placing a copy of that file onto that other disk. (Of course, you can *move* the files over there, if you want, as I describe in Chapter 11.)

Compact discs (CD-ROM drive stuff)

Computer technicians snapped up compact disc technology pretty quickly when they realized that the shiny discs store music in the form of numbers. Today, most companies sell their programs and information on compact discs. A single compact disc holds more information than hundreds of floppy disks.

To use a disc, your computer needs its own compact disc drive. The CD player with your stereo won't cut it. (The CD player with your computer will play music, however, provided your PC has speakers.)

CDs enter your computer in a more dignified way than a floppy disk. Push a button on your compact disc drive, and the drive spits out a little platter. Place the CD on the platter, label side up, and push the little button again. The computer grabs the CD, ready for action. (If the button's too hard to reach, just nudge the platter, and it'll retreat.)

- ✔ For years, you couldn't copy files onto a compact disc — you could only read information from it. Only the people at the CD factory could copy files to CDs, and that's because they had a whoppingly expensive machine. Now, many cheap compact disc drives let you read *and* copy files and music to your own discs. In fact, copyright attorneys are holding international conferences to make sure that nobody can create copies of their favorite Pearl Jam albums and give them to their friends.

- ✔ Windows XP comes with software for writing information to blank CDs. To create copies of your favorite Pearl Jam albums, head for Chapter 13.

- ✔ A CD that stores information until it's full is known as a CD-R. A CD that can read, write, erase, and then write more information is called a CD-RW. Naturally, the CD-RW discs cost much more than their limited cousins.

- ✔ Compact disc is spelled with a *c* to confuse people accustomed to seeing disk ending with a *k*.

- ✔ Multimedia computers need a sound card as well as a compact drive; the drive alone isn't enough to make music. This requirement is the computer industry's special way of making people spend more money. (Most of today's computers come with a built-in CD-ROM drive and sound card.)

- ✔ Windows XP's Media Player can play MP3 files — tiny files containing songs from your CDs. For the latest information about MP3, pick up my book, *MP3 For Dummies,* 2nd Edition, published by Wiley Publishing, Inc.

- ✔ The latest compact disc drives play both CDs and *DVD discs* — the discs with movies on them. DVD players get their own section coming up next.

- ✔ To copy files to a blank CD, insert the blank CD into your writable CD drive. Next, select the file or files you'd like to copy (described in Chapter 11). Right-click the selected file or files, choose Send To, and select your CD drive from the pop-up list. Finally, click the little CD icon that appears in your screen's bottom right corner, and follow the directions.

DVD discs

Although it's hard to tell the difference between a DVD disc and a compact disc by looking, the computer certainly knows. A DVD disc can hold up to 25 times more information than a CD — enough information to hold an entire movie in several languages and extra perks, such as a director's voiceover explaining why a certain actress giggled during certain shots.

DVD drives cost a bit more, but they play back music CDs as well as DVDs (the kind you rent or buy in video stores). Most DVD drives can't write to CDs, though, although writeable DVD drives are starting to appear on souped-up multimedia PCs.

DVD drives are great for computer nerds who love watching movies on a 15-inch computer monitor with tiny speakers. Nearly everybody else prefers watching DVDs on their living room TV or home theater.

Although nearly every sound card works with a DVD player, only special DVD-compatible sound cards can play the extra *surround sound* stored on a DVD.

Iomega drives

Tired of the huge void between floppies and CDs, the Iomega company introduced a popular new breed of disks and drives more than a decade ago. Their robotic-sounding Zip disks caught on quickly, letting users stuff 100MB of data onto a disk resembling a little plastic coaster.

Today's Zip disks hold up to 750MB of information, yet the Zip drives still read the 100MB disks of yesteryear.

To store even *more* data, the company's branched out into the portable hard drive market. Plug a portable hard drive into your computer's FireWire or USB 2.0 port, and dump your data onto it for a quick backup.

- ✔ Like many other electronic gadgets these days, Iomega's portable drives look sort of like Sony Walkmans.
- ✔ Zip disks and portable hard drives provide an easy way to move data from the office to home and back — if you're forced to even consider such a thing.

Hard disks

Not every computer has a compact disc drive, Iomega drive, or even a floppy drive, but just about everybody has a hard disk: little spinning donuts inside the computer that can hold thousands of times more information than floppy disks. Hard disks are also much quicker at reading and writing information. (They're a great deal quieter, too, thank goodness.)

Windows XP insists on a hard disk because it's such a huge program. It grabs more than a gigabyte of space for itself.

✔ The point? Buy the largest hard disk you can afford. A 20GB drive certainly isn't excessive.

✔ If a program has a lot of *multimedia* — sounds, graphics, or movies — you need an even bigger hard disk or perhaps a second one. That type of information eats up the most space on a hard disk.

What does write-protected mean?

Write protection is supposed to be a helpful safety feature, but most people discover it through an abrupt bit of computer rudeness: Windows XP stops them short with the threatening message shown in Figure 2-1 while they are trying to copy a file to a floppy disk or CD.

Figure 2-1:
Windows XP
sends an
error
message
if a disk
is write-
protected.

A *write-protected disk* has simply been tweaked so that nobody can copy to it or delete the files it contains. Write protection is a simple procedure, surprisingly enough, requiring no government registration. You can write-protect and unwrite-protect disks in the privacy of your own home.

✔ To write-protect a 3½-inch floppy disk, look for a tiny black sliding tab in a square hole in the disk's corner. Slide the tab with a pencil or your thumbnail so that the hole is uncovered. The disk is now write-protected.

✔ To remove the write protection on a 3½-inch floppy disk, slide the little black plastic thingy so that the hole is covered up.

✔ All CDs come write-protected. That's why you must use Windows XP's special CD writing tool that prepares the CD and writes the information. (Copying information to a CD is covered in Chapter 18.)

✔ If you encounter the write-protect error shown in Figure 2-1, wait until the floppy drive stops making noise. Remove the disk, unwrite-protect the disk, and put it back in the drive. Then repeat what you were doing before you were so rudely interrupted.

✔ Write-protection messages are different than Access Denied messages. If Windows XP denies you access to something, head to Chapter 9 to understand its reasoning for your slap in the face.

The Mouse and That Double-Click Stuff

The *mouse* is that rounded plastic thing that looks like a child's toy. Marketing people thought that the word *mouse* sounded like fun, so the name stuck. Actually, think of your mouse as your electronic finger, because you use it in Windows to point at stuff on-screen.

Most mice have little rollers, or mouse balls, embedded in their bellies. (Where were the animal-rights people?) When you push the mouse across your desktop, the ball rubs against electronic sensor gizmos. The gizmos record the mouse's movements and send the information down the mouse's tail, which connects to the back of the computer.

Disk do's and doughnuts

✔ Do label your disks so that you know what's on them. (You can write on the top side of compact discs with a permanent felt-tip pen.)

✔ Do at least make a valiant effort to peel off a floppy disk's old label before sticking on a new one. (After a while, those stacks of old labels make the disk too fat to fit into the drive.)

✔ Do feel free to write on the label after it has been placed on the disk.

✔ Do not write on the disk's sleeve instead of the label. Disks always end up in each other's sleeves, leading to mistaken identities and faux pas.

✔ Do copy important files from your hard disk to floppy disks or compact discs on a regular basis. (This routine is called *backing up* in computer lingo.)

✔ Do not leave floppy disks lying in the sun.

✔ Do not place 3½-inch disks next to magnets. Don't place them next to magnets disguised as paper clip holders, either, or next to other common magnetized desktop items, such as older telephones.

✔ Do handle compact discs and DVDs by their edges, not their surfaces. Keep the backside of the discs as clean as possible, and place them in their cases when you're not using them. Don't use them for coasters unless they're in their cases.

As you move the mouse across your desktop's rubber mousepad, you see an *arrow,* or *pointer,* move simultaneously across the computer screen. Here's where your electronic finger comes in: When the arrow points at a picture of a button on-screen, you press and release, or *click,* the left button on the mouse. The Windows button is selected, just as if you'd pressed it with your finger. It's a cool bit of 3-D computer graphics that makes you want to click buttons again and again.

- ✔ You control just about everything in Windows XP by pointing at it with the mouse and clicking the mouse button. (The mouse pitches in with a helpful clicking noise when you press its button.) Sometimes you need to click twice in rapid succession. The last sections in Chapter 5 explain mouse-click mechanics.

- ✔ The plural of mouse is *mice,* just like the ones cats chew on. It's not *mouses.*

- ✔ Some laptops come with a *touch pad* — a little square thing for you to slide your finger over. As you move the tip of your finger across the pad, you move the mouse pointer across the screen. Other laptops, like IBM's suave black ThinkPads, have a *TrackPoint,* a little pencil eraser that sticks up out of the keyboard, wedged above the B key and below the G and H. Just push the eraser in the direction you want the mouse to move, and the mouse pointer scurries.

- ✔ Microsoft's IntelliMouse has what looks like a tiny waterwheel protruding from the mouse's neck. By slowly rolling the waterwheel back and forth with your index finger, you can scroll up or down in your current work, line by line. Fun! Plus, pushing down once on the waterwheel creates an automatic double-click, depending on how the mouse is set up.

- ✔ Not all mice roll atop balls. Some use little light sensors to track their movement. Dave Chapman sent me a letter about his optical mouse that worked intermittently. A replacement mouse worked similarly, sometimes behaving properly, other times uncontrollably. The problem worsened as spring approached. At his wits' end, he noticed his computer-illiterate wife sitting at the desk, holding a piece of printer paper over the mouse as she worked. "You won't believe this," she said. "But when the sun shines in the window and onto the mouse, it won't work." Dave fixed the mouse by pulling down the window shade when he worked.

The mouse arrow changes shape, depending on what it's pointing at in Windows XP. When it changes shape, you know that it's ready to perform a new task. Table 2-1 is a handy reference for the different uniforms the mouse pointer wears for different jobs.

Don't worry about memorizing all the various shapes that the pointer takes on. The pointer changes shape automatically at the appropriate times. I describe the shapes here so that you won't think that your pointer's goofing off when it changes shape.

Table 2-1   The Various Shapes of the Mouse Pointer

Shape	What It Points At	What to Do when You See It
↖	Just about anything	Use this pointer for moving from place to place on-screen. Then click to bring that place to Windows' attention.
✛	A single window	Uh-oh. You've somehow selected the annoying size or move option from the Control menu. Pressing the keyboard's little arrow keys now make the current window bigger or smaller. Press Enter when you finish, or press Esc if you want to get away from this uncomfortable bit of weirdness.
↕	The top or bottom edge of a window	Hold down the mouse button and move the mouse back and forth to make the window grow taller or shorter. Let go when you like the window's new size.
↔	The left or right side of a window	Hold down the mouse button and move the mouse back and forth to make the window fatter or skinnier. Let go when you like the window's new size.
↘	The corner of a window	Hold down the mouse button and move the mouse anywhere to make the window fat, skinny, tall, or short. Let go when you're through playing.
I	A program or box that accepts text (this pointer is called an *I-beam*)	Put the pointer where you want words to appear, click the button, and start typing the letters or numbers. This only works in areas that accept words, though, like word processors or forms.
☝	A word with a hidden meaning in Windows or the Internet	Click the mouse, and Windows XP trots out some more helpful information about that particular subject.
⌛	Nothing (Windows is busy ignoring you)	Move the mouse in wild circles and watch the hourglass spin around until Windows catches up and lets you do something constructive. The hourglass often appears when you are loading files or copying stuff to a floppy disk.
↖⌛	Anything	Keep working. This pointer means that Windows XP is doing something in the background, so it may work a little more slowly.

Shape	What It Points At	What to Do when You See It
⌖?	Anything	By clicking the little question mark found in the top-right corner of some boxes, you create this pointer. Click confusing on-screen areas for helpful informational handouts.
⊘	Something forbidden	Press the Esc key, let go of the mouse button, and start over. (You're trying to drag something to a place where it doesn't belong.)

Video Cards and Monitors

The *monitor* is the thing you stare at all day until you go home to watch TV. The front of the monitor, called the *screen* or *display*, is where all the Windows XP action takes place. The screen is where you can watch the windows as they bump around, cover each other up, and generally behave like nine people eyeing a recently delivered eight-slice pizza.

Monitors have *two* cords so they won't be mistaken for a mouse. One cord plugs into the electrical outlet; the other heads for the *video card*, a special piece of electronics poking out from the computer's back. The computer tells the video card what it's doing; the card translates the events into graphics information and shoots the pictures up the cable into the monitor, where they appear on-screen.

What do I install on my laptop computer?

Microsoft designed Windows XP Professional, not Windows XP Home, to run on laptop or notebook computers. The Professional version works better with battery-driven computers and offers more wireless Internet connection options.

Laptops should be beefed up with the following in order to run Windows XP Professional:

✔ A separate copy of Windows XP. Remember, each copy of Windows XP may be installed on only a single computer. No longer can you install the same copy on both your desktop and laptop computers.

✔ 600 MHz or faster processor with 128MB RAM

✔ 20GB ATA/66 hard drive

✔ 8MB AGP graphics adapter and 3D hardware acceleration

✔ DVD player or CD-RW/DVD player

✔ Built-in speakers

✔ Built-in 56K modem

✔ Two USB ports

✔ Port replicator for easy connection to external keyboard, mouse, and monitor

✔ Like herbivores and cellulose-digesting gut microorganisms, monitors and video cards depend upon each other. Neither can function without the other. In fact, your monitor only displays pictures as nicely as your video card can dish them out. Also, LCD monitors require special cards capable of feeding them the right signals.

✔ Unlike other parts of the computer, the video card and monitor don't require any special care and feeding. Just wipe the dust off the screen every once in a while. (And at least *try* to keep the cat off the monitor.)

✔ Spray plain old glass cleaner on a rag and then wipe off the dust with the newly dampened rag. If you spray glass cleaner directly on the screen, it drips down into the monitor's casing, annoying the trolls who sleep under the bridge.

✔ Some glass cleaners contain alcohol, which can cloud the antiglare screens found on some fancy new monitors. When in doubt, check your monitor's manual to see if glass cleaner is allowed. My Nanao monitor came with its own special rag for wiping off the glass.

✔ When Windows XP first installs itself on your computer, it interrogates the video card and monitor until they reveal their brand name and orientation. Windows XP almost always gets the correct answer from them and sets itself up automatically so that everything works fine the first time.

✔ Windows XP may be dominating, but it's accommodating, too. It can handle a wide variety of monitors and cards. In fact, most monitors and cards can switch to different *modes,* putting more or fewer colors on-screen and shrinking the text so that you can cram more information onto the screen. Windows XP enables you to play around with all sorts of different video settings, if you're in that sort of mood. (If you are, check out Chapter 14.)

Keyboards

Computer keyboards look pretty much like typewriter keyboards with a few dark growths around the perimeter. In the center lie the familiar white typewriter keys. The grayish keys with obtuse code words live along the outside edges. They're described next.

Groups of keys

Obtuse code-word sorters divvy those outside-edge keys into key groups:

Function keys: These keys either sit along the top of the keyboard in one long row or clump together in two short rows along the keyboard's left side.

Function keys boss around programs. For example, you can press F1 to demand help whenever you're stumped in Windows XP.

Numeric keypad: Zippy-fingered bankers like this thingy: a square, calculator-like pad of numbers along the right edge of most keyboards. (You might have to press a key called Num Lock above those numbers, though, before they'll work. Otherwise, they're *cursor-control keys,* which I describe next.)

Cursor-control keys: If you *haven't* pressed the magical Num Lock key, the keys on that square, calculator-like pad of numbers are usually the cursor-control keys. These keys have little arrows that show which direction the cursor moves on-screen. (The arrowless 5 key doesn't do anything except try to overcome its low self-esteem.) Some keyboards have a second set of cursor-control keys next to the numeric keypad. Both sets do the same thing. Additional cursor-control keys are Home, End, PgUp, and PgDn (or Page Up and Page Down). To move down a page in a word-processing program, for example, you press the PgDn key.

Pressing the cursor keys doesn't move the little mouse-pointer arrow around on the screen. Instead, cursor keys control your position inside a program, letting you type information in the right place.

The Windows key: Eager to make money from selling keyboards *and* software, Microsoft came out with a bold new design: the Microsoft Natural Keyboard, which includes special *Windows* keys. (The keys, which straddle your spacebar, boast a little Windows icon like the icon on your Start button.) Pressing the Windows key opens the Start menu, which can be done at the click of a mouse, anyway. Ho hum. A little key next to the Windows key — the one with the little mouse pointer and menu — quickly opens menus. Table 2-2 shows more things the Windows key can do — if you can remember them.

Table 2-2	Windows Key Shortcuts
To Do This	*Press This*
Display Windows XP Help	\<Windows Key>+F1
Display the Start menu	\<Windows Key>
Cycle through the taskbar's buttons	\<Windows Key>+Tab
Display Windows Explorer	\<Windows Key>+E
Find files	\<Windows Key>+F
Find other computers on the network	Ctrl+\<Windows Key>+F
Minimize or restore all windows	\<Windows Key>+D
Undo minimize all windows	Shift+\<Windows Key>+M

Ignore these awful graphics terms

Some people describe their monitors as "boxy" or "covered with cat hair"; others use the following strange scientific terms:

✔ **Pixel:** A pixel is a fancy name for an individual dot on-screen. Everything on-screen is made up of bunches of dots, or pixels. Each pixel can be a different shade or color, which creates the image. (Squint up close, and you may be able to make out an individual pixel.) If your thin new LCD monitor has a tiny dot that doesn't match the colors on the rest of your screen, that pixel is "out." Complain, loudly, when you first take it out of the box. It occasionally results in a replacement.

✔ **Resolution:** The resolution is the number of pixels on a screen — specifically, the number of pixels across (horizontal) and down (vertical). More pixels mean greater resolution: smaller letters and more information packed onto the same-sized screen.

People with small monitors usually use 800 x 600 resolution. People with normal-to-larger-sized monitors often switch to 1024 x 768 resolution so that they can fit more windows on-screen.

✔ **Color:** This term describes the number of colors the card and monitor display on-screen. Today's speedy video cards can easily display Windows XP in millions of colors.

✔ **Mode:** A predetermined combination of pixels, resolution, and colors is described as a graphics _mode._ Right out of the box, Windows XP uses a mode that works for just about everybody. You don't need to know any of this stuff. If you're feeling particularly modular, however, you can change the Windows XP graphics modes after reading the "Appearance and Themes" section of Chapter 14.

More key principles

These keyboard keys may sound confusing, but Windows still makes you use them a lot:

Shift: Just as on a typewriter, this key creates uppercase letters or the symbols %#@$ — the traditional G-rated swear words.

Alt: Watch out for this one! When you press Alt (which stands for _Alternate_), Windows does one of two bothersome things: It moves the cursor to the little menus at the top of the current window, or it underlines a single letter in your menus. To go back to normal, press Alt again.

Num Lock: Pressing this key toggles your numeric keypad (described in the preceding section) from displaying numbers to controlling the cursor.

Ctrl: This key (which stands for _Control_) works like the Shift key, but it's for weird computer combinations. For example, holding down the Ctrl key while pressing Esc (described next) brings up the Windows XP Start menu.

Esc: This key (which stands for *Escape*) was a pipe dream of the computer's creators. They added Esc as an escape hatch from malfunctioning computers. By pressing Esc, the user was supposed to be able to escape from whatever inner turmoil the computer was currently going through. Esc doesn't always work that way, but give it a try. It sometimes enables you to escape when you're trapped in a menu or a dastardly dialog box. (Those traps are described in Chapter 5.)

Scroll Lock: This one's too weird to bother with. Ignore it. (It's no relation to a *scroll bar,* either.) If a little keyboard light glows next to your Scroll Lock key, press the Scroll Lock key to turn it off. (The key's often labeled Scrl Lk or something equally obnoxious.)

Delete: Press the Delete key (sometimes labeled Del), and the unlucky character sitting to the *right* of the cursor disappears. Any highlighted information disappears as well. Poof.

Backspace: Press the Backspace key, and the unlucky character to the *left* of the cursor disappears. The Backspace key is on the top row, near the right side of the keyboard; it has a left-pointing arrow on it. Oh, and the Backspace key deletes any highlighted information, too.

If you've goofed, hold down Alt and press the Backspace key. This action undoes your last mistake in most Windows XP programs. (Holding down Ctrl and pressing Z does the same thing.)

Insert: Pressing Insert (sometimes labeled Ins) puts you in Insert mode. As you type, any existing words are scooted to the right, letting you add stuff. The opposite of Insert mode is Overwrite mode, where everything you type replaces any text in its way. Press Insert to toggle between these two modes.

Ugly disclaimer: Some Windows XP programs — Notepad, for example — are always in Insert mode. There's simply no way to move to Overwrite mode, no matter how hard you pound the Insert key.

Enter: This key works pretty much like a typewriter's Return key, but with a big exception: Don't press Enter at the end of each line when typing documents. A word processor can sense when you're about to type off the edge of the screen. It herds your words down to the next line automatically. So just press Enter at the end of each paragraph.

You'll also want to press Enter when Windows XP asks you to type something — the name of a file, for example, or the number of pages you want to print — into a special box. (Clicking a nearby OK button often performs the same task.)

Caps Lock: If you've mastered the Shift Lock key on a typewriter, you'll be pleased to find no surprises here. (Okay, there's one surprise: Caps Lock affects only your letters. It has no effect on punctuation symbols or the numbers along the top row.)

Tab: There are no surprises here, either, except that Tab is equal to five spaces in some word processors and eight spaces in others. Still, other word processors enable you to set Tab to whatever number you want. Plus, a startling Tab Tip follows.

Press Tab to move from one box to the next when filling out a form in Windows XP. (Sometimes these forms are called *dialog boxes.*)

PrtScrn/SysRq: Press this key, and Windows snaps a picture of your desktop, ready to be pasted into a graphics program like Paint. Hold down Alt and press PrtScrn, and Windows snaps a picture of only the currently active window. Use the Paste function, described in Chapter 8, to copy the snapped picture to another program. (SysRq doesn't do anything.)

Ctrl+Alt+Delete: Pressing all three of these keys at the same time brings up the Windows XP Task Manager. Described in Chapter 7, the Task Manager lets you switch from window to window and oust any misbehaving programs.

✔ If you don't own a mouse or a trackball, you can control Windows XP exclusively with a keyboard. But it's awkward, like when Darth Vader tries to floss his back molars.

✔ The Scroll Lock and Pause/Break keys don't do anything worthwhile in Windows. However, if you hold down the Windows key and press Break, Windows' System Properties window appears, displaying lots of technical mish-mash about your computer.

✔ Finally, some keyboards come with special keys installed by the manufacturer. My Gateway's keyboard lets me adjust the sound, log on to the Internet, control my CD or DVD, or make the computer go to sleep. Information about these keys lives in my computer's Control Panel under an icon named Multi-function Keyboard.

Modems and the Internet

I admit it. I used my modem the other night to order Thai food from the restaurant across town. How? My wife and I dialed up Food.com (www.food.com) through the Internet, chose our items from the on-screen menu, and punched in our address and phone number. An hour or so later, we stuffed ourselves with Mee Krob and other unpronounceable bits of yumminess.

Modems are little mechanical gadgets that translate a computer's information into squealing sounds that can be sent and received over plain, ordinary phone lines. We clicked the check box next to Mee Krob on our computer, a modem at the credit card company tabulated the whole process, and the electric registers started ringing.

Most new computers include built-in modems for dialing up the Internet's World Wide Web. In fact, if you bought a new computer, you probably already have all the parts you need to jump on the Internet bandwagon. Windows XP comes with the software you need to power those parts: Internet Explorer.

With Internet Explorer, you can browse the Web, or blanket your desktop with Web pages, as shown in Figure 2-2. Elaborate Web site art will fill your desktop like posters along the walls of Parisian streets.

✔ Even if you already have a modem and Internet Explorer, you must pay monthly fees to an Internet service provider (ISP). The ISP gives you a special name and password that let you access the Internet.

✔ Chapter 12 covers the Internet and the Web. It doesn't say what Mee Krob tastes like, though.

✔ The computers on both ends of the phone lines need modems in order to talk to each other. Luckily, most online services have hundreds, or even thousands, of modems for your computer's modem to talk to over the phone lines.

✔ Some speedy modems don't use phone lines — they ride on special cables installed by your cable TV company or phone company.

✔ Internet access is two-way — you can talk to other people, and they can talk to you. To filter out evil people who take advantage of this and try to break into your computer, Windows XP includes a *firewall.* Chapter 12 shows how to install it.

✔ Your computer doesn't have a modem? You'll find complete installation instructions in one of my other books, *Upgrading and Fixing PCs For Dummies,* 5th Edition (IDG Books Worldwide, Inc.).

Figure 2-2:
Windows XP
enables you
to spread
Web pages
across your
desktop.

Printers

Realizing that the paperless office still lies several years down the road, Microsoft made sure that Windows XP can shake hands and send friendly smoke signals to hundreds of different types of printers. In fact, Windows XP often recognizes new printers as soon as you plug their cables into your computer.

If Windows XP doesn't notice your efforts, Chapter 14 shows you how to choose the name and manufacturer of your printer from Windows XP's massive list. Windows checks its dossiers, finds your printer information, and immediately begins speaking to it in its native language.

That's all there is to it — unless, of course, your printer happens to be one of the several hundred printers *left off* the Windows XP master list. In that case, cross your fingers that your printer's manufacturer is still in business. You may need to get a *driver* from the manufacturer (see Chapter 15) before your prose can hit the printed page.

✔ Printers must be turned on before Windows XP can print to them. (You'd be surprised how easily you can forget this little fact.)

✔ Windows XP prints in a *WYSIWYG* (What You See Is What You Get) format, which means that what you see on-screen is reasonably close to what you'll see on the printed page.

Networks

Networks connect PCs so that people can share information. They can all send stuff to a single printer, for example, share a modem, or send messages to each other asking whether Marilyn has passed out the paychecks yet.

Some networks are relatively small — less than five computers in a home or small office, for example. Other networks span the world. In fact, the Internet runs on a huge computer network that sprawls through nearly every country.

✔ Microsoft created Windows XP on the shoulders of its Big Business version of Windows. That means Windows XP handles networks with finesse and delicacy. That also means it offers dozens of bothersome, difficult-to-understand details about local area connections and user names. Chapter 9 holds the full scoop.

✔ Windows XP Home version contains enough networking gusto that it lets several different computers share a single printer, modem, and files. Windows XP Professional version adds more-advanced networking features that placate system administrators. Home and small-business users will do fine with Windows XP Home version.

Sound Cards (Making Barfing Noises)

For years, PC owners looked enviously at Macintosh owners — especially when their Macs ejected a disk. The Macintosh would simultaneously eject a floppy disk from its drive and make a cute barfing sound. Macs come with sound built in; they can barf, giggle, and make *really* disgusting noises that I won't mention here.

But the tight shirts at IBM decided there was no place for sound on a Serious Business Machine. The industry soon wised up, however, and now nearly every PC comes with a sound card. Plug a pair of speakers into the sound cards speaker outlet, and the accounting department's computers can barf as loudly as the ones in the art department down the hall.

- ✔ A sound card looks just like a video card. In fact, all cards look alike: long green or brown flat things that nestle into long flat slots inside the computer. Speakers plug into sound cards like monitors plug into video cards, only the speakers have smaller plugs.

- ✔ Although most new computers come with sound cards already installed, most companies constantly release new software for making them work better. (Chapter 15's section on installing a new driver can help knock a miscreant sound card back into action.)

- ✔ Windows XP comes with a wide variety of noises, but it doesn't have any barf noises. Windows Media Player, described in Chapter 13, lets you listen to music CDs, Internet radio stations, DVD soundtracks, MP3 files, and just about anything else that makes sounds.

- ✔ The latest, fanciest computers come with DVD drives, special sound cards, software, and extra speakers so that you can hear *surround sound* when watching DVD movies. Better clear off your desk for the big woofer and extra speakers that go with it.

- ✔ Just like the Macintosh, Windows enables you to assign cool sounds to various Windows XP functions. For example, you can make your computer scream louder than you do when it crashes. For more information, refer to the section in Chapter 14 on making cool sounds with multimedia.

Ports

The back of your computer contains lots of connections for pushing out and pulling in information. The deeper you fall into the Windows lifestyle, the more likely you'll hear the following words bantered about. Plus, when something falls out of the back of your computer, Table 2-3 shows you where it should plug back in.

Table 2-3	What Part Plugs into What Port?	
This Port . . .	*. . . Looks Like This . . .*	*. . . And Accepts This*
Keyboard	New Style	Your keyboard. (Some laptops let a mouse plug into the new style keyboard ports, too.)
Mouse		Your mouse. (Known as a PS/2 port, some laptops also let a keyboard plug into it.)
Video		Your monitor's smallest cable. (The monitor's biggest cable plugs into the power outlet.)
Serial (COM)	Old Style (Pre-1994) / New Style	External modems.
Parallel (LPT)		Your printer.
USB		Universal Serial Bus (USB) gadgets. (Used by digital cameras, gamepads, printers, MP3 players, and more.)
Sound		A sound card has at least three of these ports for these tiny plugs: one for headphones, one for the microphone, and the other for an external sound source like a radio, tape recorder, camcorder, TV card, and so on.
Cable TV		TV cards accept your TV cable here; some cable modems use an identical port.
Telephone		Run a telephone line from the wall to here on a modem. (The modem's second jack lets you plug in the telephone. Look closely for a label.)
Network		Networks use one of two connector styles. 10BaseT looks like a telephone line, but slightly thicker. Thin Coax is a rounded metal cup that pushes over a rounded metal cylinder.

Parts Required by Windows XP

Table 2-4 compares what Windows XP asks for on the side of the box with what you *really* need before it will work well.

Table 2-4	What Windows XP Requires	
Requirements Politely Touted by Microsoft	*What You Really Want*	*Why?*
A Pentium 300 MHz microprocessor	A Pentium III or Athlon running at 500 MHz	While at the store, compare Windows XP running on different Pentium III computers. The faster the computer, the less time you spend waiting for Windows XP to do something exciting.
64MB of memory (RAM)	At least 128MB of memory	Windows XP crawls across the screen with only 64MB and moves much more comfortably with 128MB. RAM is cheap; if you plan to run programs like Microsoft Office and multimedia tools, quickly bump that to 256MB or more.
2GB of free hard disk space	At least 20GB	A full installation of Windows XP could consume an entire gigabyte; Windows programs quickly rope off their own sections of the hard drive, too. Plus, all that sound and video you're going to be grabbing off the Internet and your digital camera will take up a whole lotta space. Don't be afraid to buy a hard disk that's 40GB (40 gigabytes) or larger so your computer will be useful for a long time.

(continued)

Table 2-4 *(continued)*

Requirements Politely Touted by Microsoft	What You Really Want	Why?
A 3½-inch high-density disk drive	Not needed for installing or using Windows XP	However, an occasional Windows program still comes packaged on high-density, 3½-inch floppy disks. Plus, floppy disks are a handy way to move your files to other computers.
Color SVGA card	Same	For viewing videos, look for these qualifications on the video card box or the computer specifications sheet: 32MB or more of memory, AGP support, motion compensation support for DVD playback, and support for DVI, S-Video, and composite video output.
12x or faster CD-ROM or DVD drive	Same	You'll want a CD-ROM drive to install Windows XP. (A DVD drive can read normal CDs, so it'll work fine.) For the first time, Windows XP supports drives that write to CDs as well.
Internet access	56K modem or faster	Windows XP relies extensively on Internet communication for everything from product registration, automatic updates, off-site computer fix-ups, and game playing. The faster your modem, the less time you'll spend twiddling your thumbs.
Any PS/2-compatible mouse	Same	Microsoft makes some darn good mice, with much better warranties than Microsoft's software. I prefer the IntelliMouse — the kind with the little spinning wheel on its back.
A 15-inch monitor or larger	An LCD monitor	The bigger your monitor, the bigger your desktop: Your windows won't overlap so much. Unfortunately, super-large LCD monitors are super-expensive.

Other computer parts you'll probably need

Can your computer handle the requirements in Table 2-4? Unfortunately, there's more. Windows XP will work at its most basic level with that type of muscle, but it needs more before it will reach full capacity.

For instance, in order to hear anything from your computer, you need a sound card and amplified stereo speakers with a subwoofer. (If you choose USB speakers, your computer needs USB ports.) Headphones are great for late-night listening.

Planning on connecting several computers with a network so they can share files, printers, and a modem? You'll need a network adapter card for each computer, as well as their corresponding cables, which I explain in Chapter 9.

To watch TV on your monitor, you need a compatible TV tuner card. (Check your cable TV connection, too. Most TV tuner cards don't pick up much without cable TV.)

Planning on watching DVDs? Then you'll need your own DVD-playing software before Windows XP's Media Player will be able to show the DVDs. Yes, it's weird, and it's covered in Chapter 13.

To dump pictures from your digital video camcorder into Windows XP's Movie Maker, you need an IEEE 1394 (FireWire) port.

Chapter 3

Windows XP Stuff Everybody Thinks You Already Know

In This Chapter

▶ Explanations of the strange terms used in Windows XP

▶ Information on where to look for more details on these strange terms

*W*hen Microsoft Windows first hit the market in 1985, it failed miserably. Windows' weak attempts at fancy graphics choked the equally weak computers of the day. Even when it did run, Windows was slow, awkward, and downright ugly.

Today's powerful computers easily whip Windows into shape. After 15 years on the market, Windows has turned into a trendy bestseller that's preinstalled on nearly every new PC.

Because Windows has been around for so long, a lot of people have had a head start. Many kids learned about Windows in grade school. Even today's major corporations seem to take it for granted that you can successfully navigate their Web pages.

To help you catch up, this chapter is a tourist's guidebook to those weird Windows words that everybody else thinks you already know.

Activation

Here's a big secret: You don't really own Windows XP. Even when you buy Windows at the store, or it comes preinstalled on your new computer, it's not yours. No, the fine print says that only *Microsoft* owns Windows. You only own a license — permission — to run Windows on your computer. Worse than that, you're only granted permission to run Windows on a single computer.

In the past, many people bought one version of Windows — one for their desktop computer and one for their laptop. And why not? They either used their desktop computer or their laptop — they never used them both at the same time.

Windows XP changes that with its new Activation feature. When you install Windows XP, an annoying window pops up, asking you to "activate" your version of Windows. When you click the Activate button, Windows XP takes a "picture" of your computer's components, links them to the serial number on your copy of Windows XP, and sends that information to Microsoft over the Internet.

Then, if you or anybody else ever tries to install that same version of Windows on a different computer, Windows XP says you're using somebody else's version of Windows XP, and it won't work.

✔ Okay, what happens if you don't bother to "activate" a copy of Windows XP? It simply stops working after 30 days. The new Activation feature ensures that each copy of Windows XP will only work on a single computer. Even if Windows XP came preinstalled on your new computer, you can't take the bundled Windows XP CD and install it on another computer.

✔ No Internet connection? Then you must call Microsoft's toll-free number, talk to a customer service representative, and activate your copy of Windows by typing in a 25-number password.

✔ If Windows XP came pre-installed on your new computer, the computer manufacturer probably activated Windows XP for you. (If Windows XP doesn't constantly nag you to activate it, then it's probably already been activated.)

✔ If you upgrade your computer — adding lots of new parts — Windows XP might think it's been installed on a new computer and stop working. The solution? You must call Microsoft's toll-free number and convince those folks that you're not trying to steal their software.

✔ Welcome to Windows XP!

Backing Up a Disk

Computers store *bunches* of files on their hard drives. And that multitude of files can be a problem. When the computer's hard drive eventually dies (nothing lives forever), it takes all your files down with it. Pffffft. Nothing left.

Computer users who don't like anguished *pffffft* sounds *back up* their hard drives religiously. They do so in three main ways.

Some people copy all their files from the hard disk to a bunch of floppy disks or CDs. Although backup programs make this task easier, it's still a time-consuming chore. Who wants to spend half an hour backing up computer files *after* finishing work?

Other people buy a *tape backup* unit. This special computerized tape recorder either lives inside your computer like a floppy disk or plugs into the computer's rear. Either way, the gizmo tape-records all the information on your hard disk. Then, when your hard disk dies, you still have all your files. The faithful tape backup unit plays back all your information onto the new hard drive. No scrounging for floppy disks.

Finally, some people buy special *cartridge* storage units. These mechanisms work like hard drives you can slide in and out of your computer. Iomega's Jaz drives, for example, can store up to 2GB (gigabytes) of information on a single cartridge. (The Peerless cartridges hold 10 or 20GBs.) A single cartridge is much easier to store than hundreds of floppies. (More information about Iomega's drives lurks in Chapter 2.)

- ✔ Don't use old backup programs with Windows XP. Unless the backup software specifically states that it's compatible with Windows XP, the backup might not be reliable. (Windows XP Professional comes with a simple backup program included; Windows XP Home does not.)

- ✔ The average cost of a backup unit runs from $150–$400, depending on the size of your computer's hard drive. Some people back up their work every day, using a new tape or backup disk for each day of the week. If they discover on Thursday that last Monday's report had all the best stuff, they can pop Monday's backup into the unit and grab the report.

- ✔ Windows XP lets you copy files to CDs, which hold around 600MB. To copy a file to a writable CD drive, put a writable CD in your computer's writable CD drive. Then right-click on the file you want to copy, choose Send To, and select your writeable CD drive from the menu.

Clicking

Computers make plenty of clicking sounds, but one click counts the most: the one that occurs when you press a button on a mouse. You'll find yourself clicking the mouse hundreds of times in Windows XP. For example, to push the on-screen button marked Push Me, you move the mouse across your desk until the little on-screen arrow rests over the Push Me button, and then click the mouse button.

- ✔ When you hear people say, "Press the button on the mouse," they leave out an important detail: *Release* the button after you press it. Press the button with your index finger and release it, just as you press a button on an elevator.

- Most mice have 2 buttons; some have 3, and some esoteric models for traffic engineers have more than 12. Windows XP listens mostly to clicks coming from the button on the *left* side of your mouse. It's the one under your index finger if you're right-handed. (Windows XP also lets left-handed folks swap their left and right mouse button controls.) The Windows XP Control Panel, covered in Chapter 14, lets you tweak many mouse settings.

- Windows XP listens to clicks coming from both the left *and* right buttons on your mouse. In fact, if you're ever confused about what you can do with something in Windows, right-click on it. A little menu appears, listing the things you can do with that confusing thingy.

- Don't confuse a *click* with a *double-click*. For more rodent details, see the sections "The Mouse," "Double-Clicking," and "Pointers/Arrows," later in this chapter. The insatiably curious can find even more mouse stuff in Chapter 2, including the Microsoft IntelliMouse with the little spinning wheel doohickey.

The Cursor

Typewriters have a little mechanical arm that strikes the page, creating the desired letter. Computers don't have little mechanical arms (except in science fiction movies), so they have *cursors:* little blinking lines that show where that next letter will appear in the text. You can distinguish between the cursor and the mouse pointer with one look: Cursors always blink steadily; mouse pointers never blink.

For more information, check out the section "Pointers/Arrows" in this chapter or Table 2-1 in Chapter 2. Or, keep reading the neatly aligned items in the following list:

- Cursors appear only when Windows XP is ready for you to type text, numbers, or symbols — usually when you write letters or reports or fill out forms.

- The cursor and the mouse pointer are different things that perform different tasks. When you start typing, text appears at the cursor's location, not at the pointer's location.

- You can move the cursor to a new place in the document by using the keyboard's *cursor-control keys* (the keys with little arrows). Or you can point to a spot with the mouse pointer and click the button. The cursor leaps to that new spot.

- Filling out a form? Here's a trick for the lazy: Press Tab after filling out each blank. At each press, the Tab key kicks the cursor to the next line on the form. Pressing Tab saves a lot of pointing and clicking to get the cursor to the right place. Hold down Shift while pressing Tab to move in reverse.

Defaults (And the Any Key)

Finally, a computer term that you can safely ignore. Clap your hands and square dance with a neighbor! Here's the lowdown on the, er, hoedown: Some programs present a terse list of inexplicable choices and casually suggest that you select the only option that's not listed: the *default option*.

Don't chew your tongue in despair. Just press Enter.

Those wily programmers have predetermined what option works best for 99 percent of the people using the program. So, if people just press Enter, the program automatically makes the right choice and moves on to the next complicated question.

- The default option is similar to the oft-mentioned *Any key* because neither of them appears on your keyboard (or on anybody else's, either — no matter how much money they paid).

- *Default* can also be taken to mean *standard option* or *what to select when you're completely stumped.* For example, strangers riding together in elevators stare at their shoes by default.

- When a program says to press any key, simply press the spacebar. (The Shift keys don't do the trick, by the way.)

Desktop (And Changing Its Background)

To keep from reverting to revolting computer terms, Windows XP uses familiar office lingo. For example, all the action in Windows XP takes place on the Windows XP desktop. The *desktop* is the background area of the screen where all the windows pile up. To jazz things up, Windows covers the desktop with pretty pictures known as the background. (Earlier versions called it *wallpaper.*)

Windows XP's standard desktop background shows a *Teletubbies*-green hillside. Not into *Teletubbies*? Windows XP comes with several arty pictures you can use as replacement backgrounds (and Chapter 10 can help you hang them up).

You can customize the background to fit your own personality: pictures of kittens, for example, or centipedes. You can draw your own background with the built-in Windows XP Paint program, which saves your work in one of the special background formats.

Internet Explorer and other Internet browsers let you automatically grab any picture you find on a Web site and turn it into your desktop's background. Right-click on the cool picture and choose the Set As Background option.

Double-Clicking

Windows XP places a great significance on something pretty simple: pressing a button on the mouse and releasing it. Pressing and releasing the button once is known as a *click*. Pressing and releasing the button twice in rapid succession is a *double-click*.

Windows XP watches carefully to see whether you've clicked or double-clicked its more sensitive parts. The two actions are completely different. Clicking usually selects something. Double-clicking usually makes something jump into action. I clarify this confusion at the end of Chapter 5.

   ✔ A double-click can take some practice to master, even if you have fingers. If you click too slowly, Windows XP thinks that you're simply clicking twice — not double-clicking. Try clicking a little faster next time, and Windows XP will probably catch on.

   ✔ Can't click fast enough for Windows XP to tell the difference between a mere click and a rapid-fire double-click? Grab the office computer guru and say that you need to have your Control Panel called up and your clicks fixed. If the guru is at the computer store, tiptoe to the "Mouse" section in Chapter 14, where I discuss the Windows Control Panel.

Dragging and Dropping

Although the term *drag and drop* sounds as if it's straight out of a *Sopranos* episode, it's really a nonviolent mouse trick in Windows XP. Dragging and dropping is a way of moving something — say, a picture of an egg — from one part of your screen to another.

To *drag*, put the mouse pointer over the egg and *hold down* the left or right mouse button. (I prefer the right mouse button.) As you move the mouse across your desk, the pointer drags the egg across the screen. Put the pointer/egg where you want it and release the mouse button. The egg *drops,* uncracked.

   ✔ Big Tip Dept.: If you hold down the *right* mouse button while dragging, Windows XP tosses a little menu in your face when you let go, asking if you're sure that you want to move that egg across the screen. Always hold down your right mouse button when dragging.

   ✔ For more mouse fun, see the sections, "Clicking," "Double-Clicking," "The Mouse," and "Pointers/Arrows" in this chapter and, if you're not yet weak at the knees, the information on the parts of your computer in Chapter 2.

✔ Started dragging something and realized in midstream that you're dragging the wrong thing? Breathe deeply like a yoga instructor and press Esc. Then let go of your mouse button. Whew! (If you've dragged with your right mouse button and already let go of the button, there's another option: Choose Cancel from the pop-up menu.)

Drivers

Although Windows XP performs plenty of work, it hires help when necessary. When Windows XP needs to talk to unfamiliar parts of your computer, it lets special *drivers* do the translating. A driver is a piece of software that enables Windows XP to communicate with parts of your computer.

Hundreds of computer companies sell computer attachables, from printers to sound cards to sprinkler systems. Microsoft requires these companies to write drivers for their products so that Windows XP knows the polite way to address them.

✔ Sometimes computer nerds say that your *mouse driver* is all messed up. They're not talking about your swerving hand movements. They're talking about the piece of software that helps Windows XP talk and listen to the mouse.

✔ Computer products often require new, improved drivers. The best way to get these new drivers is from the Web, usually on the Web site of the company that made the gadget. Sometimes, the Microsoft Web page itself will have the proper driver, too.

✔ No Internet connection? If you send a begging letter to the company that made your mouse, the company may mail you a new, updated driver on a floppy disk. Occasionally, you can get these new drivers from the wild-haired teenager who sold you your computer. Find a computer guru to install the driver, however, or check out the section on installing drivers in Chapter 15.

✔ The All Programs area of Windows XP's Start menu lists a program called Automatic Update. Described in Chapter 15, the program dials Microsoft's Windows Update Web site. There, a stethoscope examines your computer and inserts software to keep Windows up to date. It occasionally offers updated drivers, as well.

Files

A *file* is a collection of information in a form that the computer can play with. A *program file* contains instructions telling the computer to do something useful, like adding up the number of quarters the kids spent on SweeTARTS last month. A *data file* contains information you've created, like a picture of an obelisk you drew in the Windows XP Paint program.

- ✔ Files can't be touched or handled; they're invisible, unearthly things. Somebody figured out how to store files as little magnetic impulses on a round piece of specially coated plastic, or *disk.* (Yep, these are the disks I cover in Chapter 2.)

- ✔ A file is referred to by its *filename.* Windows lets you call files by a descriptive phrase, as long as it doesn't total more than 255 characters.

- ✔ Many filenames have optional *extensions* of up to three letters that usually refer to the program that created them. For example, the Windows XP Paint program automatically saves files with the extension BMP. Microsoft realized that most people don't care about file extensions, so Windows XP normally hides them when it's displaying filenames.

- ✔ Filenames have more rules and regulations than the Jacuzzi at the condo's clubhouse. For more information than you'll ever want to know about filenames, flip to Chapter 11.

Folders (Directories)

Nobody would ever confuse a computer with an office. Yet, Windows XP tries awfully hard to extend the common office metaphor to your computer. Your monitor's screen, for instance, is called a *desktop.* And, just like an office, Windows XP stores your files in *folders.*

No matter how hard Windows tries, though, storing files is never as easy. You can't just open a file drawer and slide in last year's tax returns. Trying to maneuver files into folders in Windows is like trying to snag the stuffed bear using the crane machine at the fair.

Because files and folders are such painful experiences, they're explained fully in Chapter 11. In the meantime, just think of folders as separate work areas to keep files organized. Different folders hold different projects; you move from folder to folder as you work on different things with your computer.

- ✔ A file cabinet's Vegetables folder could have an Asparagus folder nested inside it for organizing material further. In fact, most folders contain several other folders in order to organize information even more. You need to be pretty fastidious around computers; that's the easiest way of finding your work again.

- ✔ Technically, a folder in a folder is a nested *subfolder* that keeps related files from getting lost. For example, you can have folders for Steamed Asparagus and Raw Asparagus in the Asparagus folder, which lives in the Vegetables folder.

Graphical User Interfaces

The way people communicate with computers is called an *interface*. For example, the *Enterprise*'s computer used a *verbal interface*. Captain Kirk just told it what to do.

Windows XP uses a *graphical user interface*. People talk to the computer through *graphical symbols,* or pictures. A graphical user interface works kind of like travel kiosks at airports — you select some little button symbols right on the screen to find out which hotels offer free airport shuttles.

✔ A graphical user interface is called a *GUI,* pronounced "gooey," as in "Huey, Dewey, Louie, and GUI."

✔ Despite what you read in the Microsoft full-page ads, Windows XP isn't the only GUI for a personal computer. The Apple Macintosh has used a graphical user interface for years.

✔ You'll eventually hear people raving about an operating system called Linux (usually pronounced LINE-uhx, after Linus, the operating system's creator). Programmers and computer tweakers love Linux, but this new operating system can't run nearly as many programs as Windows. Don't buy a new PC with Linux installed unless you're an advanced computer user or married to a friendly one.

✔ The little graphical symbols or buttons in a graphical user interface are called *icons.* Chapter 20 displays most of Windows' built-in icons and what they mean.

✔ When combined with other software, like Microsoft Word XP, Windows XP can talk to us using its built-in speech generator. (Check out the Control Panel's Speech button for a preview.)

Hardware and Software

Alert! Alert! Fasten your seat belt so that you don't slump forward when reading about these two particularly boring terms: hardware and software.

Your CD player is *hardware;* so are the stereo amplifier, speakers, and batteries in the boom box. By itself, the CD player doesn't do anything but hum. It needs music to disturb the neighbors. The music is the *software,* or the information processed by the CD player.

✔ Now you can unfasten your seat belt and relax for a bit. Computer *hardware* refers to anything you can touch, including hard things like a printer, a monitor, disks, and disk drives.

✔ *Software* is the ethereal stuff that makes the hardware do something fun. A piece of software is called a *program*. Programs come on disks or CDs, or they can be copied to your computer from the Internet.

✔ When somber technical nerds (STNs) say, "It must be a hardware problem," they mean that something must be wrong with the computer itself: its disk drive, keyboard, or central processing unit (CPU). When they say, "It must be a software problem," they mean that something is wrong with the program you're trying to run.

Here's how to earn points with your computer gurus: When they ask you the riddle, "How many programmers does it take to change a light bulb?" pretend that you don't know this answer: "None; that's a hardware problem."

Icons

An *icon* is a little picture, like the one in the margin. Windows XP fills the screen with little pictures, or icons. You choose among them to make Windows XP do different things. For example, you'd choose the Printer icon, the little picture of the printer, to make your computer print something. Icons are just fancy names for cute buttons.

✔ Windows XP relies on icons for nearly everything from opening files to releasing the winged monkeys.

✔ Some icons have explanatory titles, like Open File or Terrorize Dorothy. Others make you guess; for example, the Little Juggling Man icon opens the network mail system.

✔ For more icon stuff, see the section "Graphical User Interfaces," earlier in this chapter.

The Internet

In the late 1960s, the U.S. government worried that enemies could drop bombs on its main cluster of Department of Defense computers, quickly turning circuits into slosh. So, the scientists moved the computers away from each other, connecting them globally with high-speed phone lines and a unique system of information forwarding.

If a computer in San Diego blew up, for example, the data chain from surrounding computers wouldn't simply stop there. The other computers would automatically reroute their information to other computers in the network, and everybody would still have e-mail waiting the next morning (except for the folks in San Diego, of course).

With this sprawling chain of new networks running automatically in the background, enemies no longer have a single target to destroy. The system has proven quite durable, and thousands of other networks have hopped on for a ride. Many academic institutions climbed aboard as well, helping the system grow to gigantic proportions. Now known as the *Internet,* the information chain's built-in independence keeps it uncontrollable, uncensored, and rampantly random in quality.

Anybody can use the Internet and its trendy World Wide Web to sample the information strewn about the globe. Windows XP includes most of the tools you need to jump aboard.

- In fact, Windows XP relies heavily on the Internet. It includes software for cruising the Web, watching video clips, listening to worldwide Internet radio stations, and downloading software.

- There's one problem. In order to use Windows XP's tools and visit the Web, you need to sign up with an Internet service provider (ISP). These businesses usually charge a monthly fee, just like any other utility company.

- For more Internet fun, see Chapter 12.

Kilobytes, Megabytes, and So On

Figuring out the size of a real file folder is easy: Just look at the thickness of the papers stuffed in and around it. But computer files are invisible, so their size is measured in bytes (which is pronounced like what Dracula does).

A *byte* is pretty much like a character or letter in a word. For example, the word *sodium-free* contains 11 bytes. (The hyphen counts as a byte.) Computer nerds picked up the metric system much more quickly than the rest of us, so bytes are measured in kilos (1,000), megas (1,000,000), and gigas (way huge).

A page of double-spaced text in Notepad is about 1,000 bytes, known as 1 kilobyte, which is often abbreviated as 1K. Approximately 1,000 of those kilobytes is a megabyte, or 1MB. About 1,000 megabytes is a gigabyte, which brings us to your computer's sales slip: Most new hard drives sold today are 20GB (gigabytes) or larger.

- Just about all floppy disks these days can hold 1.44MB. Today's programs are huge, so they usually come on compact discs, which hold more than 600MB.

- All files are measured in bytes, regardless of whether they contain text. For example, the green hillside background that Windows XP often places on the desktop takes up 1,440,054 bytes. (For information on placing backgrounds on your desktop, see Chapter 10.)

✔ A page of double-spaced text in Notepad takes up about 1K, but that same page in Microsoft Word consumes much more space. That's because Word sticks in lots more information: the font size, the author's name, bookmarks, spell-check results, and just about anything else you can think of.

✔ The Windows XP My Computer and Explorer programs tell you how many bytes each of your files consumes. To find out more, check out the information in Chapter 11. (*Hint for anxious users:* Right-click on any file's name and choose Properties from the menu that pops up; you will find more information about a file than you want to know.)

One kilobyte doesn't *really* equal 1,000 bytes. That would be too easy. Instead, this byte stuff is based on the number two. (Computers love mathematical details, especially when a two is involved.) One kilobyte is really 1,024 bytes, which is two raised to the 10th power, or 2^{10}. That means the 1,440,054-byte green hillside background adds up to 1.37MB. For more byte-size information, see Table 3-1.

Table 3-1	Ultra-Precise Details from the Slide-Rule Crowd		
Term	*Abbreviation*	*Rough Size*	*Ultra-Precise Size*
Byte	byte	1 byte	1 byte
Kilobyte	K or KB	1,000 bytes	1,024 bytes
Megabyte	M or MB	1,000 kilobytes	1,048,576 bytes
Gigabyte	G or GB	1,000 megabytes	1,073,741,824 bytes

Loading, Running, Executing, and Launching

Files are yanked from a file cabinet and placed onto a desk for easy reference. On a computer, files are *loaded* from a disk and placed into the computer's memory so that you can do important stuff with them. You can't work with a file or program until it has been loaded into the computer's memory.

When you *run, execute,* or *launch* a program, you're merely starting it up so that you can use it. *Load* means pretty much the same thing, but some people fine-tune its meaning to describe when a program file brings in a data file.

Picture lovers can start programs by double-clicking pictures — icons — on the Windows XP desktop. Word-oriented people can start programs by double-clicking names in a list with My Computer (although those programs let you double-click icons, too, if you prefer).

Memory

Whoa! How did this complicated memory stuff creep in here? Luckily, it all boils down to one key sentence:

The more memory a computer has available, the more pleasantly Windows XP behaves.

- Memory is measured in bytes, just like a file. The computer at the garage sale probably came with 640 kilobytes, or 640K, of memory. Last year's computer models usually came with at least 64MB of memory. Today's computers often come with at least 128MB of memory installed.

- Windows XP requires computers to have at least 128 megabytes, or 128MB, of memory, or it won't even bother to come out of the box.

Memory and hard disk space are both measured in bytes, but they're two different things: *Memory* is what the computer uses for quick, on-the-fly calculations when programs are up and running on-screen. *Hard disk space* is what the computer uses to store unused files and programs.

Everybody's computer contains much more hard disk space than memory because hard disks — also known as *hard drives* — are so much cheaper. Also, a hard disk remembers things even when the computer is turned off. A computer's memory, on the other hand, is washed completely clean whenever someone turns it off or pokes its reset button.

Not sure about all that kilobyte and megabyte stuff? Skip a few pages back to the "Kilobytes, Megabytes, and So On" section.

The Mouse

A *mouse* is a smooth little plastic thing with a tail coming out of its head. Most mice rest on a little roller, or *ball*. The tail plugs into the back of the PC. When you push the mouse across your desk, the mouse sends its current location through its tail to the PC. By moving the mouse around on the desk, you move a corresponding arrow across the screen.

Multitasking and task switching

Windows XP can run two or more programs at the same time, but computer nerds take overly tedious steps to describe the process. So skip this section because you'll never need to know it.

Even though the words *task switching* and *multitasking* often have an exclamation point in computer ads, there's nothing really exciting about them.

When you run two programs, yet switch back and forth between them, you're task switching. For example, if Jeff calls while you're reading a book, you put down the book and talk to Jeff. You are task switching: stopping one task and starting another. The process is similar to running your word processor and then stopping to look up a phone number in your handy business card database program.

But when you run two programs simultaneously, you're multitasking. For example, if you continue reading your book while listening to Jeff talk about the Natural History Museum's new Grecian urns, you're multitasking: performing two tasks at the same time. In Windows XP, multitasking can be playing a solitaire game or adding a huge spreadsheet while you're downloading a file in the background and watching the stock ticker on the Internet.

These two concepts differ only subtly, and yet computer nerds make a big deal out of the difference. Everybody else shrugs and says, "So what?"

You can wiggle the mouse in circles and watch the arrow make spirals. Or, to be practical, you can position the on-screen arrow over an on-screen button and click the mouse button to boss Windows XP around. (Refer to the sections "Clicking," "Double-Clicking," and "Pointers/Arrows," and, if you haven't run out of steam, turn to Chapter 2 for information on the parts of your computer.)

Networks

Networks connect PCs so that people can share equipment and information. Every computer on the network can send stuff to one printer, for example, or people can send messages back and forth talking about Jane's new hairstyle.

You, as a Windows XP beginner, are safely absolved from knowing anything about networks. Leave network stuff to that poor person in charge.

- ✔ Unless you're working on a computer in an office, you probably won't have to worry about networks. If you find yourself worrying about them, Chapter 9 holds the answers, including how to set one up in your own home or office.

- ✔ For information about dial-up networks, like connecting to the Internet through the Windows XP Internet Explorer, head for Chapter 12.

Pointers/Arrows

This idea sounds easy at first. When you roll the mouse around on your desk, you see a little arrow move around on-screen. That arrow is your *pointer*, and it is also called an *arrow*. (Almost everything in Windows XP has at least two names.)

The pointer serves as your *electronic index finger*. Instead of pushing an on-screen button with your finger, you move the pointer over that button and click the left button on the mouse.

So what's the hard part? Well, that pointer doesn't always stay an arrow. Depending on where the pointer is located on the Windows XP screen, it can turn into a straight line, a two-headed arrow, a four-sided arrow, an hourglass, a little pillar, or a zillion other things. Each of the symbols makes the mouse do something slightly different. Luckily, I cover these and other arrowheads in Chapter 2.

Plug and Play

Historically, installing new computer devices has required substantial technical expertise to configure and load hardware and software. Basically, that means that only geeks could figure out how to fix their computers and add new gadgets to them.

So, a bunch of computer vendors hunched together around a table and came up with *Plug and Play* — a way for Windows XP to set up new gadgets for your computer automatically, with little or no human intervention. You plug in your latest gadget, and Windows XP "interviews" it, checking to see what special settings it needs. Then Windows XP automatically flips the right switches.

Because Windows XP keeps track of which switches are flipped, none of the parts argues over who got the best settings. Better yet, users don't have to do anything but plug the darn thing into their computers and flip the On switch.

- ✔ Of course, the process couldn't be *that* simple. Only gadgets that say "Plug and Play" on the box allow for this automatic switch flipping. With the others, you probably need to flip the switches yourself. (But at least they still work when the right switches are flipped.)

- ✔ Some people call Plug and Play "PnP." Other, more skeptical, people refer to Plug and Play as "Plug and Pray." Windows XP can't recognize everything, particularly older computer parts.

- ✔ For the best chance of success, install only new gadgets that say *Plug and Play* and *Windows XP compatible* on the box. And never install a second gadget before you're sure the first gadget is working correctly.

Quitting or Exiting

When you're ready to throw in the computing towel and head for greener pastures, you need to stop, or quit, any programs you've been using. The terms *quit* and *exit* mean pretty much the same thing: making the current program on-screen stop running so that you can go away and do something a little more rewarding.

 Luckily, exiting Windows XP programs is fairly easy because all of them are supposed to use the same special exit command. You simply click the little X in the upper-right corner of the program's window. (You'll find an example in the margin.)

 Never quit a program by just flicking off your computer's power switch. Doing so can foul up your computer's innards. Instead, you must leave the program responsibly so that it has time to perform its housekeeping chores before it shuts down.

- When you press Alt+F4 or click the little X in the upper-right corner, the program asks whether you want to save any changes you've made to the file. Normally, you click the button that says something like, "Yes, by all means, save the work I've spent the last three hours trying to create." (If you've muffed things up horribly, click the No button. Windows XP disregards any work you've done and lets you start over from scratch.)

- If, by some broad stretch of your fingers, you press Alt+F4 by accident, click the button that says Cancel, and the program pretends that you never tried to leave it. You can continue as if nothing happened.

- Windows XP still lets you close most Windows programs by double-clicking the icons in their uppermost left corners. However, it's usually easier to single-click the X in the program's uppermost *right* corner. But either action tells the program that you want to close it down.

 - Save your work before exiting a program or turning off your computer. Computers aren't always smart enough to save it automatically.

Save Command

Save means to send the work you've just created on your computer to a disk for safekeeping. Unless you specifically save your work, your computer thinks that you've just been fiddling around for the past four hours. You need to specifically tell the computer to save your work before it will safely store the work on a disk.

Thanks to Microsoft's snapping leather whips, all Windows XP programs use the same Save command, no matter what company wrote them. Press and release the Alt, F, and S keys in any Windows XP program, and the computer saves your work.

If you're saving something for the first time, Windows XP asks you to think up a filename for the work and pick a folder to stuff the new file into. Luckily, I cover this stuff in Chapter 4.

- ✔ You can save files to a hard disk or a floppy disk; some people save files on Zip drives or on writable compact discs. (Check out Chapter 2 for more drive specifics.) Or if you're working in a networked office, you can often save files onto other computers.

- ✔ If you prefer using the mouse to save files, click the word *File* from the row of words along the top of the program. After a menu drops down, choose Save. Some programs even have a little picture of a floppy disk along their top edge; clicking the picture saves the file.

- ✔ Choose descriptive filenames for your work. Windows XP gives you 255 characters to work with, so a file named *June Report on Squeegee Sales* is easier to relocate than one named *Stuff*.

- ✔ Some programs, such as Microsoft Word for Windows, have an *autosave* feature that automatically saves your work every five minutes or so.

Save As Command

Huh? Save as *what*? A chemical compound? Naw, the Save As command just gives you a chance to save your work with a different name and in a different location.

Suppose that you open the Random Musings file in your Miscellaneous Stuff directory and change a few sentences around. You want to save the changes, but you don't want to lose the original stuff. So you select Save As and type the new name, *Additional Random Musings*.

- ✔ The Save As command is identical to the Save command when you're first trying to save something new: You can choose a fresh name and location for your work.

- ✔ The world's biggest clams can weigh up to 500 pounds.

ScanDisk

When previous Windows versions crashed, a program called ScanDisk quickly searched for hard drive errors. Windows XP no longer crashes as often, and it no longer includes ScanDisk. It uses ChkDsk, instead.

To check a hard drive for suspected errors, open My Computer from your Start menu, and right-click the suspect drive. Choose Properties, and then click the Tools tab of the Properties window. Click the Check Now button to seek and repair hard drive errors.

Shortcuts

The shortcut concept is familiar to most people: Why bother walking around the block to get to school when a shortcut through Mr. McGurdy's backyard can get you there twice as fast?

It's the same with Windows XP. Instead of wading through a bunch of menus to get somewhere, you can create a shortcut and assign an icon to it. Then, when you double-click the shortcut icon, Windows XP immediately takes you to that location.

You can create a shortcut to the letter you're currently working on, for example, and leave the shortcut icon sitting on your desktop within easy reach. Double-click the letter's shortcut icon, and Windows XP automatically wades through your computer's folders and files, grabs the word processor, and throws your letter onto the screen.

A *shortcut* is simply a push button that loads a file or program. You can even make shortcuts for accessing your printer or a favorite folder.

To create a desktop shortcut to a special file, folder, or program, open My Computer (or Explorer) and right-click on your coveted item's icon. Choose Send To from the pop-up menu, and select Desktop (Create Shortcut). A shortcut to that item appears on your desktop. Fun!

✔ Internet-crazy Windows XP even lets you create shortcuts to your favorite spots on the Internet and sprinkle them around your desktop for easy access. Just point at the icon next to the Internet site's address in Internet Explorer and drag it to the desktop.

✔ The ever-helpful Start button automatically makes shortcuts to the programs you use most often. Click the Start button, and you see shortcuts waiting for you. To adjust the number of listed shortcuts, right-click on the Start button, click Properties, click the Start Menu tab, and click the Customize button. That lets you adjust the number of stored shortcuts from 0 to 30. (Hit the Clear button to wipe the list clean and start over.)

✔ A shortcut isn't a program. It's a push button that starts a program. If you delete a shortcut, you haven't deleted the program; you've just removed a button that pointed to that program. You can still access the program through My Computer or Windows Explorer.

Temp Files

Like children who don't put away the peanut butter jar, Windows XP also leaves things lying around. They're called *temp files* — secret files that Windows XP creates to store stuff in while it's running. Windows XP normally deletes them automatically when you leave the program. It occasionally forgets, however, and leaves them cluttering up your hard drive. Stern lectures leave very little impression.

✔ Temp files usually (but not always) end with the letters TMP. Filenames resemble words, such as `~DOCOD37.TMP`, `~WRI3FOE.TMP`, `~$DIBLCA.ASD`, and similar-looking files that usually start with the wavy ~ thing. (Typographically correct people call it a *tilde*.)

✔ To free up wasted disk space, use Windows XP's Disk Cleanup option. Open My Computer from the Start menu, right-click on a disk drive, choose Properties, and click the Disk Cleanup button. It lets you delete bunches of old, unnecessary maintenance files, including temporary files.

The Windows

Windows XP enables you to run several programs at the same time by placing them in *windows*. A window is just a little on-screen box.

You can move the boxes around. You can make them bigger or smaller. You can make them fill your entire screen. You can make them turn into little icons at the bottom of your screen. You can spend hours playing with windows. In fact, most frustrated new Windows XP users do.

✔ You can put as many windows on-screen as you want, peeping at all of them at the same time or just looking into each one individually. This activity appeals to the voyeur in all of us. Remember, though, the more windows you have open, the slower Windows will operate.

✔ For instructions on how to move windows or resize them, head to Chapter 6. To retrieve lost windows from the pile, head immediately to Chapter 7.

The World Wide Web

The World Wide Web, known simply as the Web, is merely a way for sending and receiving pictures, sound, and other information on the Internet network. (See the section "The Internet," earlier in this chapter, or see Chapter 12 if you're *really* interested.)

Part II
Making Windows XP Do Something

The 5th Wave   By Rich Tennant

"Yes, Unicenter has an automated 'Help' function. Why?"

In this part . . .

Windows XP is more fun than cheap tattoos from the bottom of a Cracker Jack box. You can play with its built-in pinball game, play backgammon with unknown opponents through the Internet, and edit your home movies to e-mail to friends.

Unfortunately, some spoilsport friend will eventually mutter the words that bring everything back to Earth: "Let's see Windows XP do something useful, like balance a checkbook or teach the kids to rinse off their plates and put them in the dishwasher."

Toss this eminently practical part at them to quiet 'em down.

Chapter 4

Starting Windows XP

● ●

In This Chapter

▶ Starting Windows XP and logging off

▶ Starting a program

▶ Finding the secret pull-down menus

▶ Loading a file

▶ Putting two programs on the screen

▶ Printing and saving your work

● ●

*M*icrosoft designed Windows XP to link large chains of computers in a corporation. Yet, it's equally suited to run on a single computer in a living room. But whether your computer lives in solitude or mingles with other computers, Windows XP looks and acts pretty much the same, and that's where this chapter comes in.

Here you find a crash course in opening Windows XP, doing some work, and closing down when you're through. You discover how to make Windows XP not only recognize you, but also make you feel at home, as it changes its colors to meet your personal preferences.

This chapter explains where your Windows XP programs live and how to address them properly. You discover how to coax Windows XP into running two or more programs simultaneously without complaining. You find out how to send your work to the printer so you can convince doubting coworkers that you are, indeed, capable of making Windows XP do something useful.

Finally, you discover how to *log off* Windows XP — a required method of bidding your computer adieu until you meet again — if you can get the kids off the computer, that is.

Logging On to Windows XP

If your new PC came with Windows XP already installed (most do), Windows XP probably leaps to your screen automatically when you first turn on the computer. But before you can do anything, Windows XP throws you a fastball with its brilliant blue Welcome screen: Windows wants you to log on, as shown in Figure 4-1.

See, Windows XP allows bunches of people to work on the same computer, yet it keeps everybody's work separate. To do that, it needs to know who's currently sitting in front of the keyboard. The solution? It makes you *log on* — introduce yourself — by clicking your *user name,* as shown in Figure 4-1. A few seconds after you click, Windows XP shows you your desktop, ready for you to make a mess.

When you're through working or just feel like taking a break, log off (explained at the end of this chapter) so somebody else can use the computer. Later, when you log back on, your newly created mess will be waiting for you, just as you left it.

✔ Although the desktop might be a mess, it's your *own* mess. When you come back to the computer, your letters will all be where you saved them. Jerry hasn't accidentally deleted your files or folders while playing Widget Squash. Or, if you left your desktop tidy, it will be just as tidy when you return.

✔ By doling out a separate account to each computer user, Windows XP makes it seem like every person in the house has his or her own computer, set up the way he or she likes it. Jerry's desktop is packed with icons that load his favorite games. Tina's desktop contains Internet links to her favorite quilting and watercolor Web sites. And all of Melissa's favorite MP3 files stay in her own personalized Music folder.

✔ If you're the only person using your computer, Windows XP skips the Welcome screen. There's no need to log in.

✔ Of course, the big question boils down to this: How do you put cute pictures by your user name, like in Figure 4-1? I cover that in detail in Chapter 9.

✔ Don't see a user name listed for you? Then you have three options. If you just bought the computer, look for one named *Owner* or *Administrator,* and use that one. If you're not the owner but you spot the word *Guest,* click it to log on using the computer owner's gracious Guest account. Or, find out who owns the computer — that person probably set herself up as the computer's administrator. Only the almighty administrator can create an account especially for you.

Figure 4-1:
Windows XP
wants all
users to log
on so it
knows
who's
using the
computer at
all times.

It wants me to enter a password!

Windows XP lets bunches of people use the same computer without messing up each other's work. But how do you make sure Josh doesn't read Grace's love letters to Henry Rollins? How can you set up your computer so that nobody accidentally deletes your letters? How can Josh make sure Grace's pink background doesn't replace his spaceships when he logs onto the computer? A password solves some of those problems.

By typing in a secret password when logging on, as shown in Figure 4-2, you enable your computer to recognize *you* and nobody else. If you protect your user name with a password, nobody can access your files (except for the computer's administrator, who can peek into anything — and even wipe out your account).

- ✔ Depending on your network's size and level of security, a password can let you do many things. Sometimes, entering the password merely lets you use your own computer. Other times, it lets you share files on a network of linked computers.

- ✔ Because networks can be notoriously difficult to set up and figure out, most networked offices have a full-time network administrator who tries to make the darn thing work. (That's the person to bug if something goes wrong.)

✔ Windows XP needs at least one person to act as administrator even if your computer isn't connected to other computers. Only an administrator may set up new accounts for new users, install programs, and access all the files on the computer — even those of other users. Head to Chapter 9 if you care about this stuff.

✔ Don't have a password? After you log on, click the lime-green Start button, click Control Panel, and click the User Accounts icon. Click the words *Create a Password* and type in a password that will be easy for you — and nobody else — to remember. Type the password again in the second box, and, in the third box, type a hint that reminds you of your password. Click the Create Password button, and Windows XP will ask for your password the next time you try to log on. (If you're the administrator, you must first choose an account and then select the Create a Password option.)

✔ Have you forgotten your password already? Click the little question mark shown in Figure 4-2 that appears whenever you click your user name. A hint will appear, reminding you of your password. (That's why it's important to type a good hint when creating your password.) And beware — anybody else can read your hint, so make sure it's something that only makes sense to you.

✔ Keep your password short and sweet: the name of your favorite vegetable, for example, or the brand of your dental floss. (See your network administrator if Windows XP doesn't accept your password. He or she can always let you back in.)

✔ Passwords are case-sensitive. That means that the password *caviar* is different from *Caviar.* The computer notices the capital *C,* and considers caviar and Caviar to be two different words.

✔ Actually, sometimes people can peek into files belonging to other user accounts. See, Windows XP's security features require a hard drive to be formatted with *NTFS.* If your hard drive isn't formatted that way — and a user knows precisely where to look, user accounts aren't very secure, and some passwords won't work. You'll find more of this brow-furrowing security detail in Chapter 9.

Figure 4-2:
By using a password, you ensure that nobody else can access your files.

Starting your favorite program with the Start button

When Windows XP first takes over your computer, it turns your screen into a pseudo-desktop: a fancy name for a plate of buttons with labels beneath them. Click a button, and the program assigned to that button hops to the screen in its own little window. Click the Start button in the bottom-left corner of the screen, and you'll have even more buttons to choose from, as shown in Figure 4-3.

Running Windows XP for the first time

Just installed Windows XP or turned on your new computer for the first time? Then you're treated to a few extra Windows XP chores. Depending on how your computer was configured at the shop, some of these forms might vary, but here's a sampler of what you might encounter. (Click Next after filling out each form.)

Regional and Language Options: Windows XP guesses as to your language and location, so it can display the correct words, dialects, currency format, and other information. If you're not using a keyboard to enter text, use the mouse to tell Windows about your device.

Personalize Your Software: Type your name and organization's name.

Your Product Key: Type the number/letter code that's on the CD's case. (Without this number, Windows doesn't work.)

Name Your Computer: Choose a name for your computer, and type it into the box. (This helps people identify your computer on networks.)

Modem Dialing Information: Type your country, area code, and other telephone information.

Date and Time: Windows usually guesses the correct date and time.

Networking Settings: Unless you're a guru, choose Typical Settings.

Next, Windows XP "asks you to spend a few minutes setting up your computer."

Internet Connection: Will your computer connect to the Internet through a network or directly using its attached modem? Click Yes or No and then click the Next button. (I cover this more in Chapter 12.)

Activate Windows: Feel free to activate Windows now. You'll need to within the next 30 days, or Windows won't work anymore.

Registration: If you want junk mail from Microsoft, click Yes. Otherwise click No for this optional item.

Users: Type the names of people who will be using your computer, starting with your own name at the top. Nobody else using it? Then just type your own name and click Next.

If you're confused about any of these items, click the Help button at the screen's bottom.

You're through! And if you've made a mistake with any of these options, you can change them by using the Control Panel, described in Chapter 14.

Figure 4-3:
The Start
button in
Windows XP
hides
dozens of
menus for
starting
programs.

Because the buttons have little pictures on them, they're called *icons*. Icons offer clues to the programs they represent. Click an icon, and its program pops to the screen, ready for work. Click the icon of the stamped envelope, for instance, to launch Outlook Express, a program that lets people send and receive electronic mail on their computers.

Make Windows stop asking me for a password!

Windows asks for your name and password only when it needs to know who's tapping on its keys. And it needs that information for any of these three reasons:

✔ Your computer is part of a network, and your identity determines what goodies you can access.

✔ The computer's owner wants to limit what you can do on the computer.

✔ You share your computer with other people, and each person wants to customize how Windows XP looks and behaves when he or she logs on.

If you're not working on a network, disable the network password request by double-clicking the Control Panel's User Accounts icon and choosing Remove My Password.

Now, Windows XP will never ask for a password again. However, anybody can now log onto the computer using your name and access (or destroy) your files. If you're working in an office setting, this lack of security can get you into some serious trouble. If you've been assigned a password, it's better to simply get used to it.

Click the big blue "e," and Internet Explorer arrives, ready to prowl the Internet. The programs used most often (the list changes as your program usage changes) usually appear below the Internet Explorer and E-mail icons.

To find the majority of your programs, however, click the words All Programs. A menu pops out, listing bunches and bunches of programs. These are programs you haven't used often enough for Windows to turn them into big icons and put them on the Big List below Internet Explorer and E-mail. (Chapter 10 explains how to access those programs in its complete exposé of the Start menu.)

- ✔ The Start button is just a big panel of buttons. When you press one of the buttons by pointing at it and clicking with the mouse, the program assigned to that button heads for the top of the screen and appears in a little window.

- ✔ If you're kind of sketchy about all this mouse *click* and *double-click* stuff, head to Chapter 3. You're not alone.

- ✔ Not sure what an icon does? Hold your mouse button over it, and Windows usually sends a helpful explanatory message or additional menu.

- ✔ The Start button can be customized in bunches of different ways, so yours might look a little different than what you've read here. Chapter 10 shows how to customize your Start button.

Pull-Down Menus

Windows XP, bless its heart, makes an honest effort toward making computing easier. For example, the Start button puts a bunch of options on the screen in front of you. You just choose the one you want, and Windows XP takes it from there.

But if Windows XP put all its options on the screen at the same time, it would look more crowded than a 14-page menu at the Siam Thai restaurant. To avoid resorting to fine print, Windows XP hides some menus in special locations on the screen. When you click the mouse in the right place, more options leap toward you.

For example, begin loading Windows' simple word-processing program, WordPad. If you spot the WordPad icon on the big menu, go ahead and click it. If it's not there, you need to dig a little deeper. Start by clicking the Start button. When the Start menu pops up, click the words All Programs at the screen's bottom. Wham! A new menu appears. Click Accessories from the new menu, and yet another menu appears. Finally, click WordPad to bring it to the screen.

Don't worry if you don't quite understand all this yet — this is a quick run-through. I cover the Start menu in its own chapter, Chapter 10.

See the row of words beginning with File that rests along the top edge of WordPad? You find a row of words across the top of just about every Windows XP program. Move your mouse pointer over the word File and click.

A menu opens from beneath File. This menu is called a *pull-down menu,* if you're interested, and it looks somewhat like what you see in Figure 4-4.

✔ Pull-down menus open from any of those key words along the top of a window. Just click the mouse on the word, and the menu tumbles down like shoeboxes falling off a closet shelf.

✔ To close the menu, click the mouse again, but click it someplace away from the menu.

✔ Different Windows XP programs have different words across the menu bar, but almost all the bars begin with the word File. The File pull-down menu contains file-related options, like Open, Save, Print, and Push Back Cuticles.

✔ You find pull-down menus sprinkled liberally throughout Windows XP.

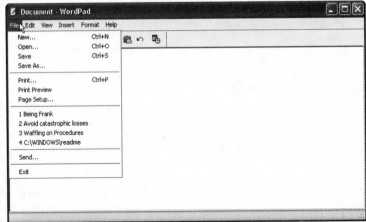

Figure 4-4:
Click a word along the top of any window to reveal a secret pull-down menu.

Loading a file

First, here's the bad news: Loading a file into a Windows XP program can be a mite bit complicated sometimes. Also, *loading* a file means the same thing as *opening* a file.

Now that those trifles have been dispensed with, here's the good news: All Windows XP programs load files in the *exact same way*. So after you know the proper etiquette for one program, you're prepared for all the others!

Here's the scoop: To open a file in any Windows XP program, look for the program's *menu bar,* that row of important-looking words along its top. Because you're after a *file,* click File, as described in the preceding section.

A most-welcome pull-down menu descends from the word File. The menu has a list of important-looking words. Because you're trying to *open* a file, move the mouse to the word Open and click once again.

Yet another box hops onto the screen, as shown in Figure 4-5. You see this box named *Open* appear over and over again in Windows XP.

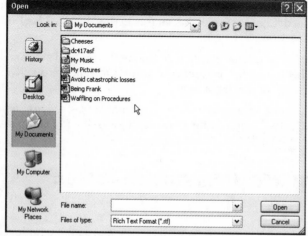

Figure 4-5:
Almost every Windows XP program tosses a box like this at you when you load or save a file.

See the list of filenames inside the box? Point at one of them with the mouse, click the button on the mouse, and that file's name shows up in the box called File Name. Click the Open button, and WordPad opens the file and displays it on the screen.

You've done it! You've loaded a file into a program! Those are the same stone steps you walk across in any Windows XP program, whether it was written by Microsoft or by the teenager down the street. They all work the same way.

✔ Sometimes, you won't immediately spot the file you're after. It's just not listed in that little box. That means that you'll have to do a little spelunking. Just as most people store their underwear and T-shirts in different dresser drawers, most computers store their files in different places called *folders.* (Double-click a folder to see what's stored inside.) If you're having trouble finding a file for your program to open, head for the section on folders in Chapter 11.

- ✔ See the file you want to open? You can speed things up by simply double-clicking the file's name; that action tells Windows XP to load the file immediately.

- ✔ Whenever you open a file and change it, even by an accidental press of the spacebar, Windows XP assumes that you've consciously changed the file for the better. If you try to open another file into that program, Windows XP cautiously asks whether you want to save the changes you've made to the current file. Click the No button unless you do, indeed, want to save that version you've haphazardly changed.

- ✔ The Open box has a bunch of options in it. You can open files that are stored in different folders or on other disk drives. You can also call up files that were created by certain programs, filtering out the ones you don't need. Chapter 5 explains all this in the "Just Tell Me How to Open a File!" section.

Don't know what those little icons along the top and side are supposed to do? Let the mouse pointer rest over them, and a box will appear, announcing their occupations.

- ✔ If you're still a little murky on the concepts of *files, folders, directories,* or *drives,* flip to Chapter 11 for an explanation of the My Computer Program.

Putting two programs on-screen simultaneously

After spending all your money for Windows XP and a computer powerful enough to cart it around, you're not going to be content with only one program on your screen. You want to *fill* the screen with programs, all running in their own little windows.

How do you put a second program on the screen? Well, if you've opened WordPad by clicking its icon in the Start button's Accessories area (that area's listed under the Programs area), you're probably already itching to load Pinball, Windows' electronic pinball game. Simply click the Start button and start moving through the menus, as I describe in the "Starting your favorite program with the Start button" section, earlier in this chapter.

Here goes: Click the Start button, click All Programs, click Games, and click Pinball. Pinball rushes to the screen.

- ✔ This section is intentionally short. When working in Windows XP, you almost always have two or more programs on the screen at the same time. There's nothing really special about it, so there's no need to belabor the point here.

- ✔ If you want to move multiple windows around on the screen, move yourself to Chapter 6.

- ✔ If you've started up Pinball, you're probably wondering where the WordPad window disappeared to. It's now hidden behind the Pinball window. To get it back, check out the information on retrieving lost windows in Chapter 7. (Or, if you see a button called WordPad along the bottom of your screen, click it to put WordPad back in front.)

- ✔ The special part comes when you move information between the two programs, which is explained in Chapter 8. (Moving information between windows is known as *cutting and pasting* in Windows parlance.)

- ✔ To switch between windows, just click them. When you click a window, it immediately becomes the *active* window — the window where all the activity takes place. For more information on switching between windows, switch to Chapter 6.

Printing Your Work

Eventually, you'll want to transfer a copy of your finely honed work to the printed page so that you can pass it around. Printing something from any Windows XP program (or application, or applet, whatever you want to call it) takes only two clicks. Click the word File from along the program's top, and then, when the menu drops down, click Print.

Yet another menu appears, this time asking how you'd like your work to be printed. If you have more than one printer, for example, it's time to choose which one. Do you want *all* the pages printed, or just some? How many copies? Answer the questions and click the Print button. (Or, if you want everything printed in a single copy to the same printer as always, just click the Print button and ignore the questions.)

What you see on your screen is whisked to your printer.

- ✔ If nothing comes out of the printer after a few minutes, try putting paper in your printer and making sure that it's turned on. If it still doesn't work, cautiously tiptoe to Chapter 15.

- ✔ When you print something in Windows XP, you're actually activating yet another program, which sits around and feeds stuff to your printer. You may see the program as a little printer icon in the bottom-right corner of your screen.

- ✔ Many programs, such as WordPad, have little pictures of a printer along their tops. Clicking that printer icon is a quick way of telling the program to shuffle your work to the printer.

Saving Your Work

Anytime you create something in a Windows XP program, be it a picture of a spoon or a letter to *The New York Times* begging for a decent comics page, you'll want to save it to disk.

Saving your work means placing a copy of it onto a disk, either the mysterious hard disk inside your computer, a floppy disk, or a CD.

Luckily, Windows XP makes it easy for you to save your work. Click File from the menu bar along the top of your program. When the secret pull-down menu appears, click Save. Your mouse pointer turns into an hourglass, asking you to hold your horses while Windows XP shuffles your work from the program to your chosen disk for safekeeping.

✔ If you're saving your work for the first time, you see a familiar-looking box: It's the same box you see when opening a file. See how the letters in the File Name box are highlighted? The computer is always paying attention to the highlighted areas, so anything you type appears in that box. Type in a name for the file and press Enter.

✔ If Windows XP throws a box in your face saying something like `The above filename is invalid`, you haven't adhered to the ridiculously strict filename guidelines spelled out in Chapter 11.

✔ Just as files can be loaded from different folders and disk drives, they can be saved to them as well. You can locate different folders, drives, and other storage places by clicking various parts of the Save box. (In fact, the most common storage locations appear as icons along the box's left edge.) All this stuff is explained in the "Just Tell Me How to Open a File!" section of Chapter 5.

Logging Off of Windows XP

Ah! The most pleasant thing you'll do with Windows XP all day could very well be to stop using it. And you do that the same way you started: by using the Start button, that friendly little helper that popped up the first time you started Windows XP. There, along the bottom of the Start menu, are two options: Log Off and Turn Off Computer.

Other Windows XP programs come and go, but the Start button is always on your screen somewhere. (And if it's hiding, hold down Ctrl and press Esc to bring it back from behind the trees.)

Which should you choose? Here's the scoop:

Log Off: Choose this option when you're done working with Windows XP for the time being. Windows then asks if you want to Switch User or Log Off, as shown in Figure 4-6. Which option do you choose?

Figure 4-6:
Under normal circumstances, choose Log Off to save your work and let somebody else use the computer.

If you're *really* through with the computer, choose Log Off. Windows saves your work and your settings, and returns to the Welcome screen for the next user.

If somebody else just wants to borrow the computer for a few minutes, choose Switch User. The Welcome screen appears, but Windows keeps your open programs waiting in the background. When you switch back, everything's just as you left it.

Turn Off Computer: Choose this when nobody else will be using the computer until the next morning. Windows XP saves everything and tells you when it's okay to turn off your computer.

✔ Be sure to shut down Windows XP through its official Shut Down program before turning off your computer. Otherwise, Windows XP can't properly prepare your computer for the event, leading to future troubles.

✔ When you tell Windows XP that you want to quit, it searches through all your open windows to see whether you've saved all your work. If it finds any work you've forgotten to save, it tosses a box your way, letting you click the OK button to save it. Whew!

✔ You don't *have* to shut down Windows XP. In fact, some people leave their computers on all the time. Just be sure to turn off your monitor; those things like to cool down when they're not being used.

Chapter 5

Field Guide to Buttons, Bars, Boxes, Folders, and Files

· ·

In This Chapter

▶ Looking at a typical window

▶ Getting into bars

▶ Changing borders

▶ Getting to know the button family

▶ Disregarding the dopey Control-menu button

▶ Exploring dialog box stuff: Text boxes, drop-down list boxes, list boxes, and other gibberish

▶ Finding out how to open a file

▶ Changing your folder viewing options

▶ Knowing when to click and when to double-click

▶ Knowing when to use the left mouse button and when to use the right mouse button

· ·

A s children, just about all of us played with elevator buttons until our parents told us to knock it off. An elevator gives such an awesome feeling of power: Push a little button, watch the mammoth doors slide shut, and feel the responsive push as the spaceship floor begins to surge upward. . . . What fun!

Part of an elevator's attraction still comes from its simplicity. To stop at the third floor, you merely press the button marked 3. No problems there.

Windows XP takes the elevator button concept to an extreme, unfortunately, and it loses something in the process. First, some of the Windows XP buttons don't even *look* like buttons. Most of the Windows XP buttons have ambiguous little pictures on them rather than clearly marked labels. And the worst part is the Windows XP terminology: The phrase "push the button" becomes "click the scroll bar above or below the scroll box on the vertical scroll bars." Yuck!

When braving your way through Windows XP, don't bother learning all these dorky terms. Instead, treat this chapter as a field guide, something you can grab when you stumble across a confusing new button or box that you've never encountered before. Just page through until you find its picture. Read the description to find out whether that particular creature is deadly or just mildly poisonous. Then read to find out where you're supposed to poke it with the mouse pointer.

You'll get used to the critter after you've clicked it a few times. Just don't bother remembering the scientific name *vertical scroll bar,* and you'll be fine.

A Typical Window

Nobody wants a field guide without pictures, so Figure 5-1 shows a typical window with its most important parts labeled (all 11 of them, unfortunately).

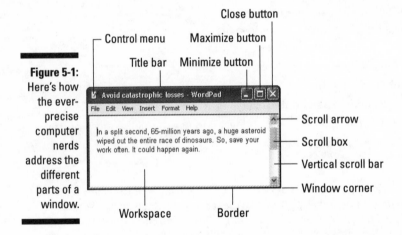

Figure 5-1:
Here's how the ever-precise computer nerds address the different parts of a window.

Just as boxers grimace differently depending on where they've been punched, windows behave differently depending on where they've been clicked. The following sections describe the correct places to click and, if that doesn't work, the best places to punch.

> ✔ Windows XP is full of little weird-shaped buttons, borders, and boxes. You don't have to remember their Latin or Greek etymologies. The important part is just finding out what part you're supposed to click. Then you can start worrying about whether you're supposed to single-click or double-click. (And that little dilemma is explained near the end of this chapter.)

✔ Not sure whether you should single-click or double-click? This trick always works: Click cautiously once. If that doesn't do the trick — the click doesn't prod your program into action, for instance — then double-click by clicking twice in rapid succession.

✔ After you click a few windows a few times, you realize how easy it really is to boss them around. The hard part is finding out everything for the first time, just like when you stalled the car while learning how to use the stick shift.

Bars

Windows XP is filled with bars; perhaps that's why some of its programs seem a bit groggy and hung over. Bars are thick stripes along the edges of a window. You find several different types of bars in Windows XP.

Moving windows with the title bar

The title bar is that topmost strip in any window (see Figure 5-2). It lists the name of the program, as well as the name of any open file. For example, the title bar in Figure 5-2 comes from the Windows XP Notepad. It contains an untitled file because you haven't had a chance to save the file yet. (For example, the file may be full of notes you've jotted down from an energetic phone conversation with Ed McMahon.)

Figure 5-2:
A title bar
lists the
program's
name.

New Text Document - Notepad

Windows XP often chooses the name New Text Document for untitled Notepad files; you choose a more descriptive name for that file when you save it for the first time. That new filename then replaces the admittedly vague New Text Document in the title bar.

✔ In addition to displaying the name of your work, the title bar serves as a *handle* for moving a window around on-screen. Point at the title bar, hold down the mouse button, and move the mouse around. An outline of the window moves as you move the mouse. When you've placed the outline in a convenient spot for working, let go of the mouse button. The window leaps to that new spot and sets up camp.

✔ When you're working on a window, its title bar is *highlighted,* meaning that it's a different color from the title bar of any other open window. By glancing at all the title bars on-screen, you can quickly tell which window is currently being used.

To enlarge a window so that it completely fills the screen, double-click its title bar. The window expands to full size, making it easier to read and covering up everything else on the desktop. Maximized windows can't be moved, however; double-click their title bars once again to return them to window size. Then they can be moved once again.

Bossing around windows with the menu bar

Windows XP has menus *everywhere.* But if menus appeared all at once, everybody would think about deep-fried appetizers rather than computer commands. So Windows XP hides its menus in something called a *menu bar* (see Figure 5-3).

Figure 5-3:
Windows XP
hides
choices in a
menu bar.

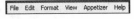

Lying beneath the title bar, the menu bar keeps those little menus hidden behind little words. To reveal secret options associated with those words, click one of those words.

For example, to see the entrees under Edit, click your mouse button on Edit. A secret menu tumbles down from a trap door, as shown in Figure 5-4, presenting all sorts of *edit-related* options.

Keep the following points in mind when using menus:

✔ When you click a word in a menu bar, a menu comes tumbling down. The menu contains options related to that particular key word.

✔ Just as restaurants sometimes run out of specials, a window sometimes isn't capable of offering all its menu items. Any unavailable options are *grayed out,* as the Undo, Cut, Copy, Paste, and Delete options are in Figure 5-4.

✔ If you accidentally click the wrong word, causing the wrong menu to jump down, just sigh complacently. (S-i-i-i-igh.) Then click the word you *really* wanted. The first menu disappears, and the new one appears below the new word.

✔ If you want out of a program's Menu Land completely, click the mouse pointer back down on your work in the window's *workspace* — usually the area where you've been typing stuff.

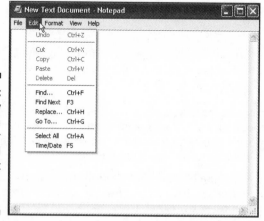

Figure 5-4: Click any word in a menu bar to reveal its secret hidden menu.

If you used earlier versions of Windows, you might miss the underlined *shortcut keys* that appeared in menus. Windows XP doesn't show them automatically. If you miss them, I reveal how to turn them back on in Chapter 18.

Moving inside your window with the scroll bar

The scroll bar, which looks like an elevator shaft, is along the edge of a window (see Figure 5-5). Inside the shaft, a little freight elevator (the *scroll box*) travels up and down as you page through your work. In fact, by glancing at the little elevator, you can tell whether you're near the top, the middle, or the bottom of a document.

For example, if you're looking at stuff near the *top* of a document, the elevator box is near the top of its little shaft. If you're working on the bottom portion of your work, the elevator box dangles near the bottom. You can watch the little box travel up or down as you press the PgUp or PgDn key. (Yes, it's easy to get distracted in Windows XP.)

Figure 5-5:
Scroll bars
enable you
to page
through
everything
that's in a
window.

Here's where the little box in the scroll bar comes into play: By clicking in various places on that scroll bar, you can quickly move around in a document without pressing the PgUp or PgDn key.

✔ Instead of pressing the PgUp key, click in the elevator shaft *above* the little elevator (the *scroll box*). The box jumps up the shaft a little bit, and the document moves up one page, too. Click *below* the scroll box, and your view moves down, just as with the PgDn key.

✔ To move your view up line by line, click the boxed-in arrow (the *scroll arrow*) at the top of the scroll bar. If you hold down the mouse button while the mouse pointer is over that arrow, more and more of your document appears, line by line, as it moves you closer to its top. (Holding down the mouse button while the pointer is on the bottom arrow moves you closer to the bottom, line by line.)

✔ Scroll bars that run along the *bottom* of a window can move your view from side to side rather than up and down. They're handy for viewing spreadsheets that extend off the right side of your screen.

✔ If the scroll bars don't have a little scroll box inside them, then you're already seeing everything on the screen. There's no little elevator to play with. Sniff. Sniff.

✔ Want to move around in a hurry? Then put the mouse pointer on the little elevator box, hold down the mouse button, and *drag* the little elevator box up or down inside the shaft. For example, if you drag the box up toward the top of its shaft and release it, you can view the top of the document. Dragging it and releasing it down low takes you near the end.

✔ Windows XP adds another dimension to some scroll bars: the little elevator's *size*. If the elevator is swollen up so big that it's practically filling the scroll bar, the window is currently displaying practically all the information the file has to offer. But if the elevator is a tiny box in a huge scroll bar, you're only viewing a tiny amount of the information contained in the file. Don't be surprised to see the scroll box change size when you add or remove information from a file.

✔ Clicking or double-clicking the little elevator box itself doesn't do anything, but that doesn't stop most people from trying it anyway.

- ✔ If you don't have a mouse, you can't play on the elevator. To view the top of your document, hold down Ctrl and press Home. To see the bottom, hold down Ctrl and press End. Or press the PgUp or PgDn key to move one page at a time.

Switching windows with the taskbar

Windows XP converts your computer monitor's screen into a desktop. But because your newly computerized desktop is probably only 15 inches wide, all your programs and windows cover each other up like memos tossed onto a spike.

To keep track of the action, Windows XP introduces the taskbar. It usually clings to the bottom of your screen and simply lists what windows are currently open. If you've found the Start button, you've found the taskbar — the Start button lives on the taskbar's left or top end.

- ✔ Whenever you open a window, Windows XP tosses that window's name onto a button on the taskbar. If you open a lot of windows, the taskbar automatically shrinks all its buttons so they'll fit.

- ✔ To switch from one window to another, just click the desired window's name from its button on the taskbar. Wham! That window shoots to the top of the pile.

- ✔ Are all those open windows looking too crowded? Click a blank part of the taskbar with your right mouse button and choose the Minimize All Windows option. All your currently open windows turn into buttons on the taskbar. Or, click the little desktop icon near the Start button. Your desktop is instantly cleared.

- ✔ You can find loads more information about the taskbar — including what to do if it vanishes — in Chapter 10.

Borders

A *border* is that thin edge enclosing a window. Compared with a bar, it's really tiny.

- ✔ You drag borders from side to side to change a window's size. I discuss how to do that in Chapter 6.

- ✔ You can't use a mouse to change a window's size if the window doesn't have a border. A few unruly borders keep the window locked at its current size, no matter how much you fiddle.

- ✔ Except for dragging them, you won't be using borders much.

Undoing what you've just done

Windows XP offers a zillion different ways for you to do the same thing. Here are four ways to access the Undo option, which unspills the milk you've just spilled:

✔ Hold down the Ctrl key and press the Z key. The last mistake you made is reversed, sparing you from further shame.

✔ Hold down the Alt key and press the Backspace key. Nobody but you and the computer know of your now-rectified error.

✔ Click Edit and then click Undo from the menu that falls down. The last command

you made is undone, saving you from any damage.

✔ Press and release the Alt key, press the letter E (from Edit), and then press the letter U (from Undo). Your last bungle is unbungled, reversing any grievous penalties.

Don't bother learning all four methods. For example, if you can remember the Ctrl+Z key combination, you can forget about the menu method or the Alt key method. Best yet, just write Ctrl+Z on the cover of the book. (The publisher's marketing people wouldn't let me put it there.)

The Button Family

Three basic species of buttons flourish throughout the Windows XP environment: command buttons, option buttons, and minimize/maximize buttons. All three species are closely related, and yet they look and act quite differently.

Sending commands with command buttons

Command buttons may be the simplest to figure out — Microsoft labeled them! Command buttons are most commonly found in *dialog boxes,* which are little pop-up forms that Windows XP makes you fill out before it will work for you.

For example, when you ask Windows XP to open a file, it sends out a form in a dialog box. You have to fill out the form, telling Windows XP what file you're after, where it's located, and other equally cumbersome details.

Table 5-1 identifies some of the more common command buttons that you encounter in Windows XP.

Table 5-1	Common Windows XP Command Buttons	
Command Button	*Habitat*	*Description*
OK	Found in nearly every pop-up dialog box	A click on this button says, "I'm done filling out the form, and I'm ready to move on." Windows XP then reads what you've typed into the form and processes your request. (Pressing the Enter key does the same thing as clicking the OK button.)
Cancel	Found in nearly every pop-up dialog box	If you've somehow loused things up when filling out a form, click the Cancel button. The pop-up box disappears, and everything returns to normal. Whew! (The Esc key does the same thing.)
< Back Next > Cancel Finish	Found when you must answer a string of questions as you fill out a form	Boy, would this have come in handy in elementary school! By clicking the Back button, Windows returns you to the previous window so that you can change your answer. Click the Next button to move to the next window's question; click Finish in the final window when you're confident that you've correctly filled out the form.
Setup... Settings... Pizza...	Found less often in pop-up dialog boxes	If you encounter a button with ellipsis dots (. . .) after the word, brace yourself: Clicking that button brings yet another box to the screen. From there, you must choose even more settings, options, or toppings.
Print	Found sprinkled nearly everywhere	Windows XP adopted much of the Internet Web world, where buttons no longer look like buttons. Just about anything can be a button. The clues? When your mouse pointer turns into a little hand, it's hovering over a button. (Little pictures that waver on the screen are telltale signs, too.)

✔ By clicking a command button, you're telling Windows XP to carry out the command that's written on the button. (Luckily, no command buttons are labeled Explode.)

✔ See how the OK button in Table 5-1 has a slightly darker border than the others? That darker border means that the button is highlighted. Anything in Windows XP that's highlighted takes effect as soon as you press the Enter key; you don't *have* to select it.

✔ Instead of scooting your mouse to the Cancel button when you've goofed in a dialog box, just press your Esc key. It does the same thing.

If you've clicked the wrong command button but *haven't yet lifted your finger from the mouse button,* stop! There's still hope. Command buttons take effect only *after* you've lifted your finger from the mouse button. Keep your finger pressed on the button and scoot the mouse pointer away from the button. When the pointer no longer rests on the button, gently lift your finger. Whew! Try *that* trick on any elevator.

Did you stumble across a box that contains a confusing command button or two? Click the question mark in the box's upper-right corner. (If there is a question mark, it will look like the one in the margin.) Then, when you click the confusing command button, a helpful comment appears to explain that button's function in life. Also, try merely resting your mouse pointer over the button. Sometimes, Windows takes pity and sends a helpful caption to explain matters.

Choosing between option buttons

Sometimes, Windows XP gets ornery and forces you to select just a single option. For example, you can elect to *eat* your Brussels sprouts or *not* eat your Brussels sprouts. You can't select both, so Windows XP doesn't let you select both of the options.

Windows XP handles this situation with an *option button.* When you select one option, the little dot hops over to it. If you select the other option, the little dot hops over to it instead. You find option buttons in many dialog boxes. Figure 5-6 shows an example.

Figure 5-6:
When you
select an
option, the
dot hops
to it.

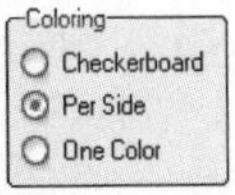

✔ Although Windows XP tempts you with several choices in an option box, it lets you select only one of them. It moves the dot (and little dotted border line) back and forth between the options as your decision wavers. Click the OK button when you've reached a decision. The *dotted* option then takes effect.

✔ If you *can* select more than one option, Windows XP won't present you with option buttons. Instead, it offers the more liberal *check boxes,* which are described in the "Check boxes" section later in this chapter.

✔ Some folks will quickly notice that option buttons are always round. Command buttons, described earlier, are rectangular.

Some old-time computer engineers refer to option buttons as radio buttons, after those push buttons on car radios that switch from station to station, one station at a time.

Changing a window's size with Minimize and Maximize buttons

All the little windows in Windows XP often cover each other up like pages of the morning newspaper on the breakfast island. To restore order, you can separate the windows by using their Minimize/Maximize buttons.

These buttons enable you to enlarge a particular window you want to play with, or shrink all the others so they're out of the way. Here's the scoop.

The Minimize button is one of three buttons in the upper-right corner of almost every window. It looks like that little button in the margin next to this paragraph.

A click on the Minimize button makes its window disappear, although the program lives on. In fact, its little button still lives on the taskbar along the bottom of your screen. (Click the window's taskbar button, described in Chapter 10, to return the window to its normal size.)

✔ Minimizing a window doesn't destroy its contents; it just transforms the window into a little button on the bar that runs along the bottom of the screen.

✔ To make the button turn back into an on-screen window, click the button on the taskbar along the bottom of your screen. The program reverts to a window in the same size and location as before you shrank it.

✔ *Closing* a window and *minimizing* a window are two different things. Closing a window purges the program from the computer's memory. To reopen it, you need to load it from your hard drive again. Turning a window into a taskbar button, by contrast, keeps it handy, loaded into memory, and ready to be used at an instant's notice.

The Maximize button is in the upper-right corner of every window. It looks like the button in the margin.

A click on the Maximize button makes the window swell up something fierce, taking up as much space on-screen as possible.

🖊 If you're frustrated with all those windows that are overlapping each other, click your current window's Maximize button. The window muscles its way to the top, filling the screen like a *real* program.

🖊 Immediately after you maximize a window, its little Maximize button turns into a *Restore button* (described momentarily). The restore button lets you shrink the window back down when you're through giving it the whole playing field.

You don't *have* to click the Maximize button to maximize a window. Just double-click its *title bar,* the thick strip along the window's top bearing its name. That double-click does the same thing as clicking the Maximize button, and the title bar is much easier to aim for.

In the upper-right corner of every maximized window is the Restore button, which looks like the button in the margin. After a window is maximized, clicking this button returns the window to the size it was before you maximized it.

🖊 Restore buttons appear only in windows that fill the entire screen (which is no great loss because you need a Restore button only when the window is maximized).

🖊 To close a window, click the little X in its top-right corner (shown in the margin).

The Useless Control-Menu Button

Just as all houses have circuit breakers, all windows have *Control*-menu buttons, and the buttons look different on each program. However, the buttons always perch in the top-left corner of a window. (Sharp-eyed readers will notice that the Control-menu button is actually a miniature icon representing the program.)

If you click the Control-menu button, a secret hidden menu appears, but it's pretty useless. It just provides methods to manipulate windows using your keyboard in case your mouse should fail. (It contains commands to Move, Minimize, Maximize, Close and a few others.) So ignore it, unless your mouse freezes.

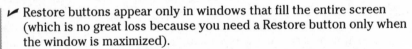

Filling Out Bothersome Forms in Dialog Boxes

Sooner or later, you have to sit down and tell Windows XP something personal — the name of a file to open, for example, or the name of a file to print. To handle this personal chatter, Windows XP sends out a dialog box.

A *dialog box* is merely another little window. But instead of containing a program, it contains a little form or checklist for you to fill out. These forms can have bunches of different parts, which are discussed in the following sections. Don't bother trying to remember the names of the parts, however. It's more important to figure out how they work.

Typing into text boxes

A *text box* works like a fill-in-the-blanks test in history class. You can type anything you want into a text box — words, numbers, passwords, or epithets. For example, Figure 5-7 shows a dialog box that pops up when you want to search for some words or characters in WordPad.

Figure 5-7:
This dialog box from WordPad contains a text box.

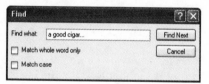

When you type words or characters into this box and press the Enter key, WordPad searches for them. If it finds them, WordPad shows them to you on the page. If it doesn't find them, WordPad sends out a robotic dialog box saying it's finished searching.

✔ Two clues let you know whether a text box is *active* — that is, ready for you to start typing stuff into it: The box's current information is highlighted, or a cursor is blinking inside it. In either case, just start typing the new stuff. (The older, highlighted information disappears as the new stuff replaces it.)

✔ If the text box *isn't* highlighted or there *isn't* a blinking cursor inside it, it's not ready for you to start typing. To announce your presence, click inside it. Then start typing. Or press Tab until the box becomes highlighted or contains a cursor.

✔ If you click inside a text box that already contains words, delete the information with the Delete or Backspace key before you start typing in new information. If the old text is already highlighted, just start typing: Your incoming text will automatically delete the old words. (*Tip:* If the old information isn't highlighted, double-click it; then, the incoming text automatically replaces the old text.)

Choosing options from list boxes

Some boxes don't let you type stuff into them. They already contain information. Boxes containing lists of information are called, appropriately enough, *list boxes.* For example, WordPad brings up a list box if you're inspired enough to want to change its *font* — the way the letters look (see Figure 5-8).

Figure 5-8:
You can select a font from the list box to change the way letters look in WordPad.

✔ See how the Comic Sans MS font is highlighted? It's the currently selected font. Press Enter (or click the OK command button), and WordPad begins using that font when you start typing.

✔ See the scroll bar along the side of the list box? It works just as it does anywhere else: Click the little scroll arrows (or press the up or down arrow) to move the list up or down so you can see any names that don't fit in the box.

✔ Many list boxes have a text box above them. When you click a name in the list box, that name hops into the text box. Sure, you could type the name into the text box yourself, but it wouldn't be nearly as much fun.

✔ When confronted with zillions of names in a list box, type the first letter of the name you're after. Windows XP immediately hops down the list to the first name beginning with that letter.

TIP

When one just isn't enough

Some list boxes, like those in Windows Explorer, let you select a bunch of items simultaneously. Here's how:

✔ To select more than one item, hold down the Ctrl key and click each item you want. Each item stays highlighted.

✔ To select a bunch of adjacent items from a list box, click the first item you want. Then hold down Shift and click the last item you want. Windows XP immediately highlights

the first item, last item, and every item in between. Pretty sneaky, huh?

✔ Finally, when grabbing bunches of icons, try using the "rubber band" trick: Point at an area of the screen next to one icon, and, while holding down the mouse button, move the mouse until you've drawn a lasso around all the icons. After you've highlighted the icons you want, let go of the mouse button, and they remain highlighted. Fun!

Drop-down list boxes

List boxes are convenient, but they take up a great deal of room. So, Windows XP sometimes hides list boxes, just as it hides pull-down menus. When you click in the right place, the list box appears, ready for your perusal.

So, where's the right place? It's that downward-pointing arrow button, just like the one shown next to the box beside the Font option in Figure 5-9. (The mouse pointer is pointing to it.)

Figure 5-9: Click the downward-pointing arrow next to the Font box to make a drop-down list box display available fonts.

(Character Map dialog box screenshot)

Character Map

Font : Times New Roman   Help

Characters to copy :   Select   Copy

☐ Advanced view

U+0021: Exclamation Mark

Figure 5-10 shows the drop-down list box, after being clicked by the mouse.

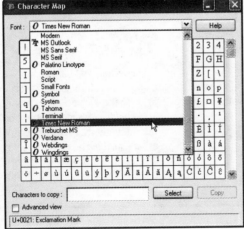

Figure 5-10:
A list box
drops down
to display all
the fonts
that are
available.

✔ Unlike regular list boxes, drop-down list boxes don't have a text box above them. (That thing that *looks* like a text box just shows the currently selected item from the list; you can't type anything in there.)

✔ To scoot around quickly in a long drop-down list box, press the first letter of the item you're after. The first item beginning with that letter is instantly highlighted. You can press the up- or down-arrow key to see the words and phrases nearby.

✔ Another way to scoot around quickly in a drop-down list box is to click the scroll bar to its right. (Scroll bars are discussed earlier in this chapter, if you need a refresher.)

✔ You can choose only *one* item from the list of a drop-down list box.

✔ The program in Figure 5-10 is called Character Map, and it's a handy way for adding characters that don't appear on your keyboard: ½, ¢, and the rest. To play with Character Map, click the Start button and click the All Programs area. Click System Tools from the Accessories area, and click Character Map.

Check boxes

Sometimes you can choose from a whopping number of options in a dialog box. A check box is next to each option, and if you want that option, you click in the box. If you don't want it, you leave the box blank. For example, with the check boxes in the dialog box shown in Figure 5-11, you pick and choose options in FreeCell.

Figure 5-11:
A check
mark
appears in
each check
box that you
choose.

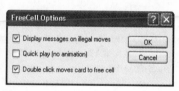

> ✔ By clicking in a check box, you change its setting. Clicking in an empty square turns on that option. If the square already has a check mark in it, a click turns off that option, removing the check mark.

> ✔ You can click next to as many check boxes as you want. With option buttons — those things that look the same but are round — you can select only one option from the pack.

Sliding controls

Rich Microsoft programmers, impressed by track lights and sliding light switches in their luxurious new homes, added sliding controls to Windows XP as well. These virtual light switches are easy to use and don't wear out nearly as quickly as the real ones do. To slide a control in Windows XP — to adjust the volume level, for example — just drag and release the sliding lever, like the one shown in Figure 5-12.

Figure 5-12:
To slide a
lever, point
at it, hold
down the
mouse
button, and
move your
mouse.

Point at the lever with the mouse and, while holding down the mouse button, move the mouse in the direction you want the sliding lever to move. As you move the mouse, the lever moves, too. When you've moved the lever to a comfortable spot, let go of the mouse button, and Windows XP leaves the lever at its new position. That's it.

✔ Some levers slide to the left and right; others move up and down. None of them move diagonally.

✔ To change the volume in Windows XP, click the little speaker near the clock in the desktop's bottom-right corner. A sliding volume control appears, ready to be dragged up or down. If the little speaker near the clock is missing, click the Start button and open the Control Panel. Choose the Sounds, Speech, and Audio Devices option, and select Adjust the System Volume. Finally, click to put a check mark in the box next to the words Place Volume Icon in the Taskbar.

✔ Mouse died and you're frantic to turn down the volume? Press Tab until a little box appears over the sliding lever. Then press your arrow keys in the direction you want the lever to slide. If your keyboard comes with built-in volume control buttons, try those, too (although Windows XP often ignores them until you install their own special drivers; check the discs that came with your PC or keyboard).

Just Tell Me How to Open a File!

Enough with the labels and terms. Forget the buttons and bars. How do you load a file into a program? This section gives you the scoop. You follow these steps every time you load a file into a program. (Chapter 4 contains more general information about loading a program, opening a file, saving the file, and closing the program.)

Opening a file is a *file-related* activity, so start by finding the word File in the window's menu bar (see Figure 5-13).

Figure 5-13:
To open a file, you first choose the word File in the window's menu bar.

Then simply do the following:

1. **Click File to knock down that word's hidden little menu.**

   Figure 5-14 shows the File pull-down menu.

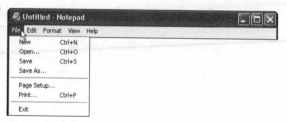

Figure 5-14:
When you
click File,
the File pull-
down menu
appears.

2. **Click Open to bring up the Open dialog box.**

   You can predict that Open will call up a dialog box because of the trailing . . . things beside Open on-screen. (Those . . . things are called an *ellipsis,* or *three dots,* depending on the tightness of your English teacher's hair bun.)

Figure 5-15 shows the Open dialog box that leaps to the front of the screen. A similar dialog box appears when you mess with the File pull-down menu in many programs.

✔ If you find your filename listed in the first list box (in this case, the one listing the Beer Cheese file), you're in luck. Double-click the file's name, and it automatically jumps into the program. Or click the file's name once and click the Open button.

✔ If you don't find the file's name, it's probably in a different folder. Windows XP often lists places to look along the window's left side, as shown in Figure 5-15. Click History to see the names of recently opened files. Click Desktop if the file is located on your desktop. My Documents lets you peek into the My Documents area, a convenient storage space. Head for My Computer to scour the entire computer from the top down, or click My Network Places to scour *other* computers, should you have a network.

✔ Click the little box along the top that is labeled Look In, and Windows XP displays a bunch of other folders to rummage through. Each time you click a different folder, that folder's contents appear in the first list box.

✔ Still can't find the correct folder? Perhaps that file is on a different drive. Click one of the other drive icons listed in the Look In box to search in a different drive. Drive icons are those little gray box things; folder icons, well, look like folders.

✔ Could the file be named something strange? Click the Files of Type drop-down list box to select a different file type. To see *all* the files in a folder, select the All Files (*.*) option. Then all the files in that folder show up.

✔ Don't know what those little icons along the top and sides are supposed to do? Rest your mouse pointer over the one that has you stumped. After a second or so, the increasingly polite Windows XP brings a box of explanatory information to the screen. For example, rest the mouse pointer over the folder with the explosion in its corner, and Windows XP tells you that clicking that icon creates a new folder.

✔ This stuff is incredibly mind numbing, of course, if you've never been exposed to drives, folders, wild cards, or other equally painful computer terms. For a more rigorous explanation of this scary file-management stuff, troop to Chapter 11.

✔ If the file is still lost, make Windows find it. Click the Start menu's Search button and choose the option that describes what you're searching for. (The All File Types option is always a good bet.) Type in the name of your file and choose My Computer in the Look In box. (Chapter 7 offers more information about Search because that chapter is dedicated to helping you find lost things in Windows.)

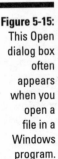

Figure 5-15:
This Open dialog box often appears when you open a file in a Windows program.

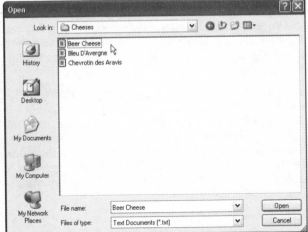

Hey! When Do I Click, and When Do I Double-Click?

That's certainly a legitimate question, but Microsoft only coughs up a vague answer. Microsoft says that you should *click* when you're *selecting* something in Windows XP and you should *double-click* when you're *choosing* something. And even that's not for certain. Huh?

Well, you're *selecting* something when you're *highlighting* it. For example, you may select a check box, an option button, or a filename. You click any of the three to *select* it, and then you look at it to make sure that it looks okay. If you're satisfied with your selection, you click the OK button to complete the job.

To *select* something is to set it up for later use.

When you *choose* something, however, the response is more immediate. Choosing a file immediately loads it into your program. Microsoft's "choose" lingo says, "I'm choosing this file, and I want it now, buster."

You *choose* something you want to have carried out immediately.

✔ All right, this explanation is still vague. So always start off by trying a single-click. If clicking once doesn't do the job, try a double-click. It's usually much safer than double-clicking first and asking questions later.

✔ And even this isn't always true. See, Windows XP can be set up so it chooses files when you perform a single-click *or* a double-click. The software enables you to select a file or program by simply resting your pointer over it and then clicking to prod it into action. That's the way the Internet's World Wide Web works, so Windows XP lets you set it up that way, too.

✔ If you accidentally double-click rather than single-click, it usually doesn't matter. You can usually just close a runaway program with a few clicks. But if something terrible happens, hold down the Ctrl key and press the letter Z. You can usually undo any damage.

✔ Prefer to always single-click instead of double-click? Then choose Folder Options from the Control Panel's Appearance and Themes area, and choose the single-click option: Single-Click to Open an Item (Point to Select). Prefer the traditional double-click way? Then go to the same place and choose the other option: Double-Click to Open an Item (Single-Click to Select).

✔ If Windows XP keeps mistaking your purposeful double-click as two disjointed single-clicks, head for the section in Chapter 14 on tinkering with the Control Panel. Adjusting Windows XP so that it recognizes a double-click when you make one is pretty easy.

When Do I Use the Left Mouse Button, and When Do I Use the Right One?

This one's easy. Always right-click unless you're positive that a single-click will do the trick.

See, when you right-click on an item, Windows XP presents a helpful menu listing all the things you can do with that particular item: Open, Explore, Search, Share, Send to someplace, Cut, Copy, Create Shortcut, Delete, Rename, examine its Properties, or Offer Breakfast Cereal.

Seeing those choices is much handier than when you single-click an item, and Windows assumes you know what you're doing.

For instance, hold down your right mouse button while dragging an item across the desktop. When you release the button, Windows XP brings up a menu, asking you to choose what you want to do with that item. If you drag the item while holding down your left mouse button, Windows XP doesn't ask; it does whatever it wants.

- ✔ The right mouse button is designed more for beginning users or people with bad memories like me. When you're sure you know what you're doing in Windows — if anybody ever does — feel free to left-click instead.

- ✔ Confused about something on the screen? Try clicking it with your right mouse button, just for kicks. The result may be unexpectedly helpful.

Chapter 6

Moving Windows Around

• •

In This Chapter

▶ Moving a window to the top of the pile

▶ Switching from window to window

▶ Moving a window from here to there

▶ Making windows bigger or smaller

• •

Ah, the power of Windows XP. Using separate windows, you can put a spreadsheet, a drawing program, an Internet Web page, and a word processor on-screen *at the same time.*

You can copy a hot-looking graphic from your drawing program and toss it into your memo. You can stick a chunk of your spreadsheet into your memo, too. In the background, the Web can display a constantly running news update. And why not? All four windows can be on-screen *at the same time.*

You have only one problem: With so many windows on-screen at the same time, you can't see anything but a confusing jumble of programs.

This chapter shows how to move those darn windows around on-screen so that you can see at least *one* of them.

Moving a Window to the Top of the Pile

Take a good look at the mixture of windows on-screen. Sometimes you can recognize a tiny portion of the window you're after. If so, you're in luck. Move the mouse pointer until it hovers over that tiny portion of the window and click the mouse button. Shazam! Windows XP immediately brings the clicked-on window to the front of the screen.

That newly enlarged window probably covers up strategic parts of other windows. But at least you'll be able to get some work finished, one window at a time.

- ✔ Windows XP places a lot of windows on-screen simultaneously. But unless you have two heads, you'll probably use just one window at a time, leaving the remaining programs to wait patiently in the background. The window that's on top, ready to be used, is called the *active* window.

- ✔ As soon as you click any part of a window, it becomes the active window. All your subsequent keystrokes and mouse movements will affect that window. (The active window's title bar is a brighter color than all the others.)

- ✔ Some programs can run in the background, even if they're not in the currently active window. Internet Explorer can download a file in the background, for example, and Media Player can play a CD, unconcerned with whether they're the currently active window. Imagine!

Although many windows may be on-screen, you can enter information into only one of them at a time: the active window. To make a window active, click any part of it. It rises to the top, ready to do your bidding. (The Internet and a computer's TV Card can stick information into background windows, but that's not *you* doing it.)

Another way to move to a window is by clicking its name displayed in the Windows XP *taskbar* — that bar that runs along the bottom of your screen. I describe the taskbar in Chapter 10.

Moving a Window from Here to There

Sometimes you want to move a window to a different place on-screen (known in Windows XP parlance as the *desktop*). Maybe part of the window hangs off the edge of the desktop, and you want it centered. Or maybe you want to put two windows on-screen side by side so that you can compare their contents.

In any of those cases, you can move a window by grabbing its *title bar,* that thick bar along its top. Put the mouse pointer over the window's title bar and hold down the mouse button. Now use the title bar as the window's handle. When you move the mouse around, you tug the window along with it.

When you've moved the window to where you want it to stay, release the mouse button to release the window. The window stays put and on top of the pile.

✔ The process of holding down the mouse button while moving the mouse is called *dragging*. When you let go of the mouse button, you're *dropping* what you've dragged.

✔ Sometimes part of a window hangs off the screen's visible edge, making it difficult — if not impossible — to work on it. To move it back onto the center of the screen, grab the window's title bar and hold down the mouse button. When you drag the title bar back toward the center of the screen, you can see the whole window once again.

✔ When positioning two windows next to each other on-screen, you usually need to change their sizes as well as their locations. The very next section tells how to change a window's size. (I also explain how to make Windows line up everything on the screen automatically so you don't have to spend time fiddling around.)

✔ To position windows next to each other quickly and easily, use the Tile or Cascade commands: Right-click on a blank part of the taskbar that runs along the bottom of your desktop. (If the taskbar is full, you can right-click on the little digital clock.) Choose Tile to tile the open windows evenly across the screen, or Cascade to deal them out like cards. I explain this technique more fully in Chapter 7, because it's a handy way to find covered-up windows.

Making a Window Bigger or Smaller

Sometimes, moving the windows around isn't enough. They still cover each other up. Luckily, you don't need any special hardware to make them bigger or smaller. See that thin little border running around the edge of the window? Use the mouse to yank on a window's corner border, and you can change its size.

First, point at the corner with the mouse arrow. When it's positioned over the corner, the arrow turns into a two-headed arrow. Now hold down the mouse button and drag the corner in or out to make the window smaller or bigger. The window expands or contracts as you tug on it with the mouse so you can see what you're doing.

When you're done yanking and the window looks about the right size, let go of the mouse button. As the yoga master says, the window assumes the new position.

Here's the procedure, step by step:

1. **Point the mouse pointer at the edge of the corner.**

   It turns into a two-headed arrow, as shown in Figure 6-1.

Figure 6-1:
The arrow
grows a
second
head, as
shown in
the bottom-
right corner.

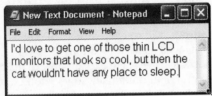

2. **Hold down the mouse button and move the two-headed arrow in or out to make the window bigger or smaller.**

   Figure 6-2 shows how the window becomes smaller as the mouse drags its corner inward.

Figure 6-2:
As you
move the
mouse, the
window's
size
changes to
reflect its
new shape.

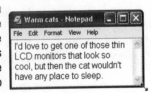

3. **Release the mouse button.**

   The window shapes itself to fit into the border you've just created (see Figure 6-3).

Figure 6-3:
Let go of the mouse button, and the window stays at its new size.

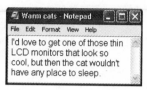

- This procedure may seem vaguely familiar, because it is. You're just *dragging and dropping* the window's corner to a new size. That *drag-and-drop* concept works throughout Windows XP. For example, you can *drag and drop* a title bar to move an entire window to a new location on-screen.

- You can grab a window's side border and move it in or out to make the window fatter or skinnier. You can grab the top or bottom of a window and move it up or down to make the window taller or shorter. But grabbing for a corner is always easiest because then you can make a window fatter, skinnier, taller, or shorter, all with one quick flick of the wrist.

Making a Window Fill the Whole Screen

Sooner or later, you get tired of all this New Age, multiwindow mumbo jumbo. Why can't you just put *one* huge window on-screen? Well, you can.

To make any window grow as big as it can get, double-click its *title bar,* that topmost bar along the top of the window. The window leaps up to fill the screen, covering up all the other windows.

To bring the pumped-up window back to its former size, double-click its title bar once again. The window quickly shrinks, and you can see everything that it was covering up.

- When a window fills the entire screen, it loses its borders. That means that you can no longer change its size by tugging on its title bar or dragging its borders. Those borders just aren't there anymore.

- If you're morally opposed to double-clicking a window's title bar to expand it, you can expand it another way. Click the window's *Maximize button,* the middle-most of the three little boxes in its top-right corner. (It's shown in the margin.) The window hastily fills the entire screen. At the same time, the Maximize button turns into a Restore button; click the Restore button when you want the window to return to its previous size. (Refer to Chapter 5 for more information on the Maximize, Minimize, and Restore buttons.)

Chapter 7

I Can't Find It!

In This Chapter

▶ Finding lost windows

▶ Finding lost files

▶ Finding downloaded files

▶ Finding misplaced snippets of information

▶ Finding lost things on the Internet

Sooner or later, Windows XP gives you that head-scratching feeling. "Golly," you say, as you frantically tug on your mouse cord, "that stuff was *right there* a second ago. Where did it go?"

When Windows XP starts playing hide-and-seek with your information, this chapter tells you where to search and how to make it stop playing foolish games. Then, when you find your Solitaire window, you can get back to work.

Finding Lost Windows on the Desktop

Forget about that huge, 1940s roll-top mahogany desk in the resale shop window. The Windows XP peewee desktop isn't any bigger than the size of your monitor.

In a way, Windows XP works more like a spike memo holder than an actual desktop. Every time you open a new window, you're tossing another piece of information onto the spike. The window on top is relatively easy to see, but what's lying directly underneath it?

If you can see a window's ragged edge protruding from any part of the pile, click it. The window magically rushes to the top of the pile. But what if you can't see *any* part of the window at all? How do you know that it's even on the desktop?

The following two procedures help extricate windows when they're lost from sight.

Plucking a lost window from the Task Manager

Windows' built-in Task Manager keeps a master list of everything that's happening on your screen (even the invisible stuff), making it a prime detective for locating hidden windows.

The Task Manager hides until you call it up by pressing the Magic Key Sequence: Simultaneously press the Ctrl, Alt, and Delete keys. (Most people use two hands for this.) Then the Task Manager appears, as shown in Figure 7-1.

Click the Applications tab, shown in Figure 7-1, and the Task Manager lists all the currently running programs. Your missing window is *somewhere* on the list. When you spot your runaway window, click its name, and click the Switch To button along the Task Manager's bottom.

Your wayward window whisks itself to the forefront.

> ✔ In previous versions, pressing Ctrl, Alt, and Delete simultaneously brought up a wimpy version of Task Manager. Windows XP's more manly version handles bunches more tasks, including some so complicated that they're only discussed in more complicated books.

> ✔ Sometimes you see your missing program listed on the taskbar, and you click its name to dredge it from the depths. But even though the taskbar brings the missing program to the top, you *still* can't find it on your desktop. The program may be hanging off the edge of your desktop. In the next section, I explain how to make Windows reposition *all* your open windows so they're easy to find.

Figure 7-1:
Pressing
Ctrl, Alt,
and Delete
simulta-
neously
brings up
the Task
Manager,
which lists
all open
windows
when you
click the
Applications
tab.

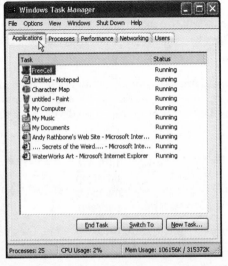

Tiling and cascading windows (The "deal all the windows in front of me" approach)

When you're facing a pile of windows that looks like a pile of dropped playing cards, it's time to turn Windows XP into a personal card dealer. It will gather up all your haphazardly tossed windows and deal them out neatly on the desktop in front of you. That's often an easy way to locate a window buried deep within your pile.

To turn Windows into a card dealer, right-click in the bottom-right corner of your screen. A quick right-click near the clock, for example, brings up the menu shown in Figure 7-2.

Figure 7-2:
Right-click
near the
clock in the
bottom-right
corner of
your screen
to bring up
the Tile or
Cascade
menu.

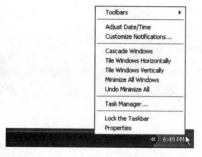

Click the Cascade Windows option, and the taskbar gathers all your open windows and deals them out in front of you, just like in a game of blackjack. (Blackjack fans won't need to glance at Figure 7-3.) Each window's title bar is neatly exposed, ready to be risen from the pile with a quick click of the mouse.

Or, choose Tile Windows Horizontally or Tile Windows Vertically from the Task Manager's Windows menu. Windows XP positions all the windows so that they fit on the screen, as shown in Figure 7-4. They're usually tiny, but hey, at least you can see most of them.

   ✔ If the missing window doesn't appear in the stack of neatly dealt windows, perhaps it's not open on the screen. The Cascade Windows command gathers and deals only the open windows; it leaves the minimized windows resting as buttons along the taskbar on the desktop's bottom. The solution? Retrieve the missing window using the Task Manager *before* cascading the windows across the screen.

   ✔ The Tile Windows Vertically command arranges the windows vertically, like socks hanging from a clothesline. Tile Windows Horizontally arranges the windows horizontally, like a stack of folded sweatshirts. The difference is the most pronounced when you're tiling only a few windows, however.

✔ The high-and-mighty Task Manager, described in the preceding section, also tiles and cascades windows, but with a twist. When it shows you the list of currently open windows, as shown back in Figure 7-1, hold down Ctrl and click the windows you want the command to affect. Then, when you choose Tile or Cascade from the Task Manager's own Windows menu, those commands affect only your selected windows. That lets you position only two important windows side by side when your desktop's crowded with open windows.

✔ If you have only two open windows, the Tile commands arrange them side by side, making it easy for you to compare their contents. The Tile Windows Vertically command places them side by side *vertically,* which makes them useless for comparing text: You can see only the first few words of each sentence. Choose the Tile Windows Horizontally command if you want to see complete sentences.

Figure 7-3:
The taskbar's Cascade command piles all the open windows neatly across the screen. It's a favorite command of blackjack players.

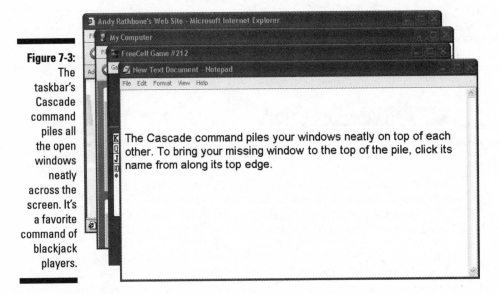

The Cascade command piles your windows neatly on top of each other. To bring your missing window to the top of the pile, click its name from along its top edge.

Finding Lost Files, Folders, Music, Photos, Videos, People, or Computers

Windows XP has gotten much better at finding things. And it should; after all, it's the one who's hiding everything. When one of your files, folders, or just about anything else disappears into the depths of your computer, make Windows XP do the work in getting the darn thing back.

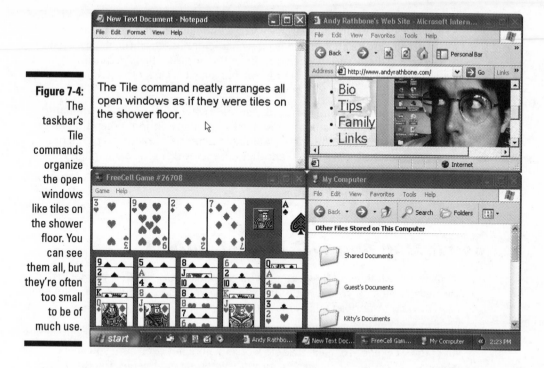

The Tile command neatly arranges all open windows as if they were tiles on the shower floor.

Figure 7-4: The taskbar's Tile commands organize the open windows like tiles on the shower floor. You can see them all, but they're often too small to be of much use.

In almost all cases, the Windows XP Search Companion retrieves your lost goods. To rev it up, click the brilliant green Start button — that button in the screen's bottom-left corner — and click Search from the menu, as shown in Figure 7-5. (I cover the Start button with more detail in Chapter 10.)

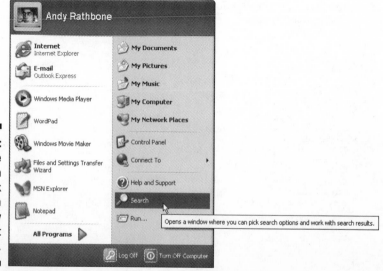

Figure 7-5: Click the Start button and click Search in the window that pops up.

- ✔ When you open the Search Companion for the first time, Windows XP asks whether you'd like to search with or without an "animated character." Cartoon lovers should choose the character option: a little doggy, a gal in a spaceship, a surfing alien, or Merlin the Wizard. The joyful little character subsequently watches your moves, blinking, barking, or twitching when you click. (It doesn't do anything more helpful than that.)

- ✔ When you tire of the barks, blinks, and twitches, turn off the animated character by choosing the Change Preferences option. When that menu appears, choose Without an Animated Screen Character to purge the little goofball. (Or choose another character from the same page.)

- ✔ To do more constructive things than play with your Windows cartoons, check out the next sections.

Finding any lost files or folders

This is it. By following these steps, you can locate *any* file that you've lost somewhere inside your computer. (You can even find that file somebody sent you through America Online, Mom!)

For example, suppose that your file called HYDRATOR INSPECTION disappeared over the weekend. To make matters worse, you're not even sure you spelled the words *Hydrator* or *inspection* correctly when saving the file. You don't even remember what program you used to save your file. Word? WordPad? Notepad? Who knows? All you know is that the hydrator was dirty — so the word *dirty* appears somewhere in the missing file.

The easiest way to find missing files — even those misplaced files that are just "somewhere inside the computer" — is to open the Search Companion from the Start button's menu. Click the Start button, click Search, and the Search Companion appears, as shown in Figure 7-6.

Figure 7-6:
The Windows Search Companion finds files, folders, and other items lost inside your computer.

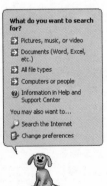

What do you want to search for?
- → Pictures, music, or video
- → Documents (Word, Excel, etc.)
- → All file types
- → Computers or people
- → Information in Help and Support Center

You may also want to...
- Search the Internet
- Change preferences

Because you're not sure what type of file you're looking for, click the words All File Types, and a new window appears, as shown in Figure 7-7.

If you know part of the file's name, enter it in the first box. For instance, you don't know how to spell hydrator, but you remember how to spell inspection. So enter the word **inspection** in the first box. (Or leave it blank if you don't know the file's name.)

In the second box, enter a word that appears in the file. In this case, enter the word **dirty**. The menu will look like the one in Figure 7-7.

Next, you need to tell the computer where to look. Because you don't know where the missing file's hiding, click the downward arrow in the box marked Look In, and choose My Computer. That tells the Search Companion to search your *entire* computer.

Figure 7-7: Enter part of the file's name — if you know it — or just enter a word or phrase appearing in your missing file.

Messed up on any of your choices? Just click the Back button at the bottom of the menu. That takes you back one step to the previous choices, letting you fix your mistake. Or, keep pressing Back until you arrive at the original menu, where you can start over.

When you're satisfied you're made your choices correctly, click the Search button. As the little doggy wags its tail, the Search Companion searches according to your command: It finds and displays any file or folder with a name that contains *inspection,* and that includes the word *dirty* somewhere inside. Figure 7-8 shows the results.

✔ The retrieved file or folder appears on the screen's right side, as shown in Figure 7-8. Double-click the file or folder to open it and begin working. (To translate the computerese information shown beneath the In Folder area — the part that supposedly shows where the file is located — head for Chapter 11.)

✔ Do you remember the time and date you created a missing file or folder? Click the little black arrow next to the words When Was It Modified?, as shown back in Figure 7-7. A new menu appears, letting you narrow down the search to the following times: the past week, the past month, within the last year, don't remember, or on a specific day.

✔ The Search Companion question "When Was It Modified" really means "When Was It Last Saved." That could mean the date you dumped it into your computer, the date you last called it up in a program and changed it somehow, or the date you last changed its name.

✔ For tips on speeding up your searches, check out the sidebar, "Finding files faster."

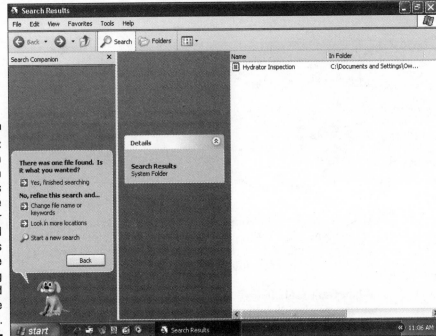

Figure 7-8:
The Search Companion searches the entire computer and retrieves any file containing the word you've designated.

TIP

Finding files faster

The more information you give the Search Companion, the faster it finds your files. Although telling it to search the entire computer for a single file containing a single word is very efficient, it's also excruciatingly slow. The computer must read all of its files from beginning to end. To speed things up, try following some of these tips when possible:

✔ Try to type in at least part of the missing file or folder's name. That keeps the Search Companion from searching through every file.

✔ Remember a folder you stored the file in? Tell the computer to search there. Search Companion will search inside that folder and inside any folders stored inside that folder. Try searching in My Documents before searching My Computer. Many programs automatically save your information in that folder.

✔ Remember when you last saved, created, or edited that file or folder? If you remember that you created it within the past week, for instance, the search becomes faster still.

✔ CD-ROM discs take a _long_ time to search, and when you tell Search Companion to search My Computer, it also searches any CD you've inserted in your drive. Remove CDs before clicking My Computer for searches.

✔ Search for words _least_ likely to turn up in other files. For example, the words _dirty_ and _hydrator_ are more unique than _like, an,_ or _the._ That means they're much more likely to bring up the file you're searching for.

✔ When a search turns up too many files, narrow down your search. Be more precise about when the missing file was created or downloaded, for example, or add a larger portion of its name.

✔ If you have a large hard drive with lots of space, choose Change Preferences from the Search Companion's main menu, and then select With Indexing Service. Your computer then makes an index of your computer's files, speeding up searches dramatically. (Unfortunately, the index can consume quite a bit of room.)

Finding lost pictures, music, or video

When you don't remember much about a file — but gosh darn it, you want to find it anyway — the preceding section shows how to route it out of your computer's innards. But sometimes you know a little bit more about your missing file. You can't find that digital picture you transferred yesterday from the camera, for instance, or that MP3 song you pulled off a CD last week. Perhaps you're missing a short video you downloaded from the Internet.

The Search Companion can easily extract these types of missing files from your computer's digital jowls. Click the lime-green Start button and click Search. When the menu appears, choose the option marked Pictures, Music, or Video.

Yet another menu appears, offering three search options: 1) Pictures and Photos, 2) Music and Sound, or 3) Video. Click in the box next to what you're searching for, and type any part of the file's name in the second box.

Click Search, and the Search Companion finds all the files meeting your specifications.

> ✔ Unfortunately, unless you remember at least a portion of your file's name (which is very difficult to do with digital photos), the over-eager Search Companion will find *all* of your pictures, music, or videos. To increase your odds of a match, click Use More Advanced Options. When that menu appears, add more clues: where your file is located inside your computer, when it was saved, or its approximate size.
>
> ✔ Check out the "Finding files fast" sidebar for more tips on quicker searches.

Finding lost documents

Lost a key Word or Excel document? Search Companion's ready to help out here, too. Because you know it was a Word or Excel document, this search is fairly easy. Click the lime-green Start button, click Search, and click Documents (Word, Excel, etc.).

When the box appears, type in the missing document's name. Click the round button next to the time the file was last changed or saved.

Click Search, and the Search Companion ferrets out your file.

Note: Quick-witted readers will wonder how this search differs from the Find Any File search described earlier in this chapter. Well, Search Companion can tell which program created your files. So it limits its search to Word or Excel files, speeding up the search.

Finding computers or people

Like a teenager who's watched too many sci-fi flicks, Windows XP lumps computers and people in the same category. Neither is all that exciting, unfortunately, but here goes.

Finding computers

The computer search is for people working only on *networks,* mysteriously bundled bunches of computers, covered in Chapter 9. Don't know if you're on a network? Click the Start button, click Search, and choose the Computers or People option. Finally, choose the A Computer on the Network option to begin.

Normally, Windows XP wants you to search for a computer by name. But what if you don't know the computer's name? Here's a trick: Just click the Search button. A list of computers connected to your own computer appears. (If just one computer appears, don't get excited. It's probably just your own.)

Finding people

The people search isn't nearly as exciting as it sounds, even for singles. It only searches for people you've already entered in your Outlook Express address book. Ho hum. There's a little trick, however, but even that's pretty boring: When the Find People box appears, click the downward-pointing arrow next to the words Address Book. That lets you choose between several Internet services that list people's e-mail addresses. None of the services is very complete, and most are loaded with fake names.

Searching the Internet

This one's kind of dumb, too. When you choose the Search Companion's Search the Internet option, a little box pops up for you to type in your question. Then it races over to Internet Explorer, your *Web browser* (covered in Chapter 12), and uses that program to find your answer.

To save time, load Internet Explorer and click the little Search button along the top of its menu. That brings up the Search Companion, too. Because both programs involve Internet Explorer, they're covered in Chapter 12.

When you type in your question, Internet Explorer automatically uses Microsoft's own search program, MSN Search, to find answers. For better results, use Google at www.google.com. Feel free to check out Surfwax (www.surfwax.com), too. Dozens of different search programs, called *search engines,* are available, and everybody has a favorite. To change to your own favorite search engine, choose Change Preferences from the Search program's main menu, and then select Change Internet Search Behavior from the following menu to see the available search engines.

Chapter 8

That "Cut and Paste" Stuff (Moving Around Words, Pictures, and Sounds)

· ·

In This Chapter

▶ Understanding cutting, copying, and pasting

▶ Highlighting what you need

▶ Cutting, copying, deleting, and pasting what you've highlighted

▶ Making the best use of the Clipboard

▶ Putting scraps on the desktop

· ·

*U*ntil Windows came along, PCs had a terrible time sharing anything. Their programs were rigid, egotistical things, with no sense of community. Information created by one program couldn't always be shared with another program. Older versions of programs passed down this selfish system to newer versions, enforcing the segregation with *proprietary file formats* and *compatibility tests.*

To counter this bad trip, Windows programmers created a communal workplace where all the programs could groove together peacefully. In the harmonious tribal village of Windows, programs share their information openly in order to make a more beautiful environment for all.

In the Windows co-op, all the windows can beam their vibes to each other freely, without fear of rejection. Work created by one Windows program is accepted totally and lovingly by any other Windows program. Windows programs treat each other equally, even if one program is wearing some pretty freaky threads or, in some gatherings, *no threads at all.*

This chapter shows you how easily you can move those good vibes from one window to another.

Examining the Cut and Paste Concept (And Copy, Too)

Windows XP took a tip from the kindergartners and made *cut and paste* an integral part of all its programs. Information can be electronically *cut* or *copied* from one window and then *pasted* into another window with little fuss and even less mess.

Just about any part of a window is up for grabs, and the process takes three steps: highlight, cut or copy, and paste. For instance, you might have an exceptionally well-written paragraph in your word processor, or a spreadsheet chart that tracks the value of your Indian-head pennies.

First, *highlight* the desired information. Next, either copy or cut the information from its window. Finally, paste the information into a different window. In fact, after the information has been cut or copied, it lives inside Windows' built-in Clipboard, where it can be pasted into as many windows as you'd like.

The beauty of Windows XP is that with all those windows on-screen at the same time, you can easily grab bits and pieces from any of them and paste all the parts into a new window.

✔ Windows programs are designed to work together, so taking information from one window and putting it into another window is easy. Sticking a map onto your party fliers, for example, is *really* easy.

✔ Cutting and pasting works well for the big stuff, like sticking big charts into memos. But don't overlook it for the small stuff, too. For example, copying someone's name and address from your Address Book program is quicker than typing it by hand at the top of your letter. Or to avoid typographical errors, you can copy an answer from the Windows XP Calculator and paste it into another program.

✔ When somebody e-mails you a Web address, copy and paste it into Internet Explorer. It's much easier than typing it in by hand, and it is less frustrating because you'll know you didn't make any mistakes. It's easy to copy information from the Internet, too.

✔ When you cut or copy information, it lives in a special Windows area called the *Clipboard,* ready to be pasted into other windows. The Clipboard holds only one chunk of information at a time, though. When you cut or copy other information, that information replaces the original information, and it's now ready to be pasted into other windows.

Highlighting the Important Stuff

Before you can grab information from a window, you have to tell Windows XP exactly what parts you want to grab. The easiest way to tell it is to *highlight* the information with a mouse.

You can highlight a single letter, an entire novel, or anything in between. You can highlight pictures of water lilies. You can even highlight files and folders. You can highlight sounds so that you can paste belches into other files.

In most cases, highlighting involves one swift trick with the mouse: Put the mouse arrow or cursor at the beginning of the information you want and hold down the mouse button. Then move the mouse to the end of the information and release the button. That's it! All the stuff lying between where you clicked and released is highlighted. The information usually turns a different color so that you can see what you've grabbed. An example of highlighted text is shown in Figure 8-1.

For delicate work with small text, use the arrow keys to put the cursor at the beginning of the stuff you want to grab. Then hold down Shift and press the arrow keys until the cursor is at the end of what you want to grab. You see the stuff on-screen become highlighted as you move the arrow keys. This trick works with almost every Windows XP program. (If you're after text, hold down Ctrl, too, and the text is highlighted word by word.)

Some programs have a few shortcuts for highlighting parts of their information:

- To highlight a single *word*, point at it with the mouse and double-click. The word turns black, meaning that it's highlighted. (In most word processors, you can hold down the button on its second click, and then, by moving the mouse around, you can quickly highlight additional text word by word.)

- To highlight a single *line* of text, click next to it in the left margin. Keep holding down the mouse button and move the mouse up or down to highlight additional text line by line.

- To highlight a *paragraph*, double-click next to it in the left margin. Keep holding down the mouse button on the second click and move the mouse to highlight additional text paragraph by paragraph.

- To highlight an entire *document*, try clicking three times in rapid succession. If that doesn't work, hold down Ctrl and click anywhere in the left margin. If that doesn't work, hold down Ctrl and press A. So much for consistency in Windows programs.

- To highlight a portion of text in just about any Windows XP program, click at the text's beginning, hold down Shift, and click at the end of the desired text. Everything between those two points becomes highlighted.

✔ To highlight part of a picture or drawing while in Paint, Windows' graphics program, click the little tool button with the dotted lines in a square. (The button is called the Select tool, as Windows XP informs you if you rest your mouse pointer over the tool for a second.) After clicking the Select tool, hold down the mouse button and slide the mouse over the desired part of the picture.

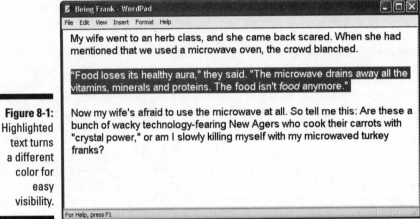

Figure 8-1: Highlighted text turns a different color for easy visibility.

After you've highlighted text, you must either cut it or copy it *immediately*. If you do anything else, like absentmindedly click the mouse someplace else in your document, all your highlighted text reverts to normal, just like Cinderella after midnight.

Highlighted something? To cut or copy it immediately, right-click on it. When the menu pops up, choose Cut or Copy, depending on your needs.

Be careful after you highlight a bunch of text. If you press a key — the spacebar, for example — Windows XP almost always replaces your highlighted text with the character that you type — in this case, a space. To reverse that calamity and bring your highlighted text back to life, hold down Ctrl and press Z. (That's the universal "Undo" command, which works in many programs.)

Cutting, Copying, or Deleting What You Highlighted

After you highlight some information (which I describe in the preceding section, in case you just entered the classroom), you're ready to start playing with it. You can cut it, copy it, or just plain delete it. All three options differ drastically.

TIP

This clever tip bears repeating. After highlighting something, right-click on it. When the menu pops up, choose Cut or Copy, depending on your needs.

Cutting the information

Cutting the highlighted information wipes it off the screen, but it's not *really* gone: Instead, Windows stores the extracted information in a special Windows XP storage tank called the *Clipboard.*

To cut highlighted stuff, right-click on your highlighted text and choose Cut from the pop-up menu, as shown in Figure 8-2. Whoosh! The highlighted text disappears from the window, scoots through the underground tubes of Windows XP, and waits on the Clipboard for further action.

Figure 8-2:
Right-click on information you've highlighted and choose Cut to move the information to Windows' Clipboard, where you can paste it into other windows.

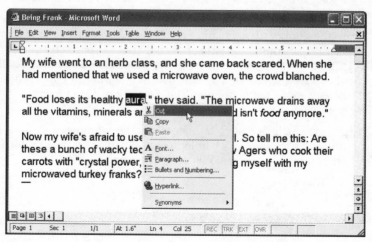

✔ One way to tell whether your Cut command actually worked is to paste the information back into your document. If it appears, you know that the command worked, and you can cut it out again right away. If it doesn't appear, you know that something has gone dreadfully wrong. (For the Paste command, discussed a little later, hold down Ctrl and press V.)

✔ Microsoft's lawyers kicked butt in an old Apple lawsuit, so Windows uses the same cut keys as the Macintosh computer. You can hold down Ctrl and press the letter *X* to cut. (Get it? That's an *X,* as in *you're crossing,* or *X-ing, something out.*)

Copying the information

Compared with cutting, *copying* information is quite anticlimactic. When you cut something, the information disappears from the screen. But when you copy information to the Clipboard, the highlighted information just sits there in the window. In fact, it looks as if nothing has happened. Feel free to repeat the Copy command a few times before giving up and just hoping it worked. (It works.)

To copy highlighted information, right-click on it and choose Copy. Or hold down Ctrl and press C (C for *Copy*). Although nothing seems to happen, that information really does head for the Clipboard.

- ✔ Feel free to cut and paste entire files back and forth in My Computer. When you cut a file, however, the icon is just gray until you paste it. (Making the file disappear would be too scary.) Changed your mind in mid-cut? Press Esc to cancel the cut and turn the icon back to normal.

- ✔ To copy a picture of your entire Windows XP desktop (the *whole screen*) to the Clipboard, press the Print Screen key, which is sometimes labeled PrtScrn or something similar. A snapshot of your screen heads for the Clipboard, ready to be pasted someplace else. Computer nerds call this snapshot a *screen shot.* All the pictures of windows in this book are screen shots. (And, no, the Print Screen key doesn't send anything to your printer.)

- ✔ To copy an image of your currently active window (just one window — nothing surrounding it), hold down Alt while you press Print Screen. The window's picture appears on the Clipboard.

Deleting the information

Deleting the highlighted information just wipes it out. Zap! It simply disappears. To delete highlighted information, just press the Delete or Backspace key.

Unfortunately cutting and deleting look identical on-screen. In fact, the first few times you try to cut something, you feel panicky, thinking that you may have accidentally deleted it instead. (This feeling never really goes away.)

- ✔ If you've accidentally deleted the wrong thing, panic. Then hold down Ctrl and press the letter Z. Your deletion is graciously undone. Any deleted information pops back up on-screen. Whew!

- ✔ Holding down Alt and pressing Backspace also undoes your last mistake (unless you've just said something dumb at a party, in that case, use Ctrl+Z).

Finding out more about cutting, copying, and deleting

Want to know more about cutting, copying, and deleting? Read on (you really should read this stuff).

- Windows XP often puts *toolbars* across the tops of its programs. Figure 8-3 shows the toolbar buttons that stand for cutting, copying, and pasting things.

- If you prefer to use menus, click the word Edit on any program's menu bar. The Cut, Copy, and Paste commands tumble down.

- When you're using the Print Screen key trick to copy a window or the entire screen to the Clipboard (see the preceding section), one important component is left out: The mouse arrow is *not* included in the picture, even if it was in plain sight when you took the picture. (Are you asking yourself how all the little arrows got in this book's pictures? Well, I drew some of 'em in by hand!)

Figure 8-3: Clicking these toolbar buttons cuts, copies, or pastes highlighted information.

Cut

Paste

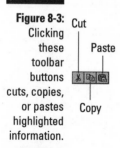

Copy

Pasting Information into Another Window

After you've cut or copied information to the special Windows XP Clipboard storage tank, it's ready for travel. You can *paste* that information into just about any other window.

Pasting is relatively straightforward compared with highlighting, copying, or cutting: Open the destination window, and move the mouse to the spot where you want the stuff to appear. Then right-click the mouse and choose Paste from the pop-up menu. Presto! Anything that's sitting on the Clipboard immediately leaps into that window.

Or, if you want to paste a file onto the desktop, right-click on the desktop and choose Paste. The copied file appears where you've right-clicked.

- ✔ Another way to paste stuff is to hold down Ctrl and press V. That combination does the same thing as Shift+Insert. (It also is the command those funny-looking Macintosh computers use to paste stuff.)

- ✔ You can also choose the Paste command from a window's menu bar. Choose the word Edit and then choose the word Paste. But don't choose the words Paste Special. That command is for the complicated Object Linking and Embedding stuff used only by Windows gurus with weird hats.

- ✔ Some programs have toolbars along their tops. Clicking the Paste button, shown in Figure 8-3, pastes the Clipboard's current contents into your document.

- ✔ The Paste command inserts a *copy* of the information that's sitting on the Clipboard. The information stays on the Clipboard, so you can keep pasting it into other windows if you want. In fact, the Clipboard's contents stay the same until a new Cut or Copy command replaces them with new information.

Leaving Scraps on the Desktop Deliberately

The Clipboard is a handy way to copy information from one place to another, but it has a major limitation: Every time you copy something new to the Clipboard, it replaces what was copied there before. What if you want to copy a *bunch* of things from a document?

If you are cutting and pasting over a real desktop, you can leave little scraps lying everywhere, ready for later use. The same *scraps* concept works with Windows XP: You can move information from window to window, using the desktop as a temporary storage area for your scraps of information.

 For example, suppose that you have some paragraphs in a WordPad or Word document that you want to copy to some other places. Highlight the first paragraph, drag it out of the WordPad window, and drop it onto the desktop. Poof! A small Scrap icon appears on your desktop, just like the one in the margin. See another interesting paragraph? Drag it onto the desktop as well: Another Scrap icon appears.

Eventually, you'll have copies of your report's best paragraphs sitting in little scraps on your desktop. To move any of the scraps into another document, just drag them into that other document's window and let go.

Any remaining, unused scraps can be dumped into the Recycle Bin or simply left on the desktop, adding a nice, comfortable layer of clutter.

To make a scrap, highlight the information you want to move, usually by running the mouse pointer over it while holding down the mouse button. Then point at the highlighted information and, while holding down the mouse button, point at the desktop. Let go of the mouse button, and a scrap containing that information appears on the desktop.

Note: Not all Windows XP applications support scraps. In fact, WordPad is probably the only program in the Windows XP box that makes good use of scraps. Other programs, such as Microsoft Office, let you use scraps, though, so you haven't wasted your time reading about them.

Chapter 9

Sharing It All on the Network

. . . .

In This Chapter

▶ Creating and changing user accounts

▶ Finding other computers on the network

▶ Locating files and folders on other computers

▶ Giving permission to others to look at your files

▶ Adding and using network printers

▶ Buying a network's parts

▶ Installing a network's hardware

▶ Setting up a network

. . . .

*T*hankfully, you only need to bother with this chapter under four conditions:

✔ More than one person will be using your computer, and you'd like to assign a user account to everybody so that they can keep their work separate.

✔ You want to change somebody's user account.

✔ Your computer is connected to other computers on a network, and you need to moves files between them.

✔ You want to set up your own network.

If you don't care about networks or only a few people work on your computer, ignore most of this chapter, thank goodness. Just refer to the first section on user accounts. That explains how to create new user accounts, change their little pictures and passwords, and delete or restrict unruly accounts to keep the wild ones in line.

If you're on a network or want to set one up, stick around for this chapter's second half. That explains how to grab information from other computers, and let other people grab information from your computer. You also find out how to share a printer or Internet connection among several computers.

Finally, if you're working on a larger, more confusing network at work, you find a few tips on how to muddle your way through if the network administrator *still* hasn't returned from the deli down the street.

Fiddling with User Accounts

Everyone who uses Windows XP needs a user account. A user account is like a cocktail party name tag that helps Windows recognize who's sitting at the keyboard. (Chapter 4 explains user accounts in more detail.) Windows XP dishes out three types of user accounts: Administrator, Limited, and Guest.

Who cares? Well, each type of account gets to do different functions on the computer. If the computer were an apartment building, the administrator would be the manager, the limited accounts would be the tenants, and guests would only get to drop by and use the bathroom in the lobby.

In computer lingo that means the administrator controls the entire computer, deciding who gets to use it and what they can do on it. Limited accounts can use most of the computer, but they can't make any big changes to it. And guests, well, they can use the computer, but because the computer doesn't recognize them by name, their actions are tightly restricted.

✔ On a computer running Windows XP Home, the owner usually holds the administrator account. He or she then sets up accounts for other household members, changing their accounts when needed, fixing lost passwords, and if desired, peeking into other users' files. Here's the important part: Only administrators can install software and change the computer's hardware.

✔ In a family, the parents usually hold administrator accounts, the kids usually have limited accounts, and the babysitter logs in using the guest account.

✔ On computers running Windows XP Professional, the administrator holds the same privileges and more. But because Windows XP Professional offers many more security features and settings, its administrator often holds a full-time job in an office setting.

✔ To see what version of Windows XP you're using, Home or Professional, click the lime-green Start button, right-click on My Computer, and choose Properties from the pop-up menu. On the first page — the one beneath the General tab — your version is listed beneath the word *System*.

✔ Administrators should create *limited* accounts for people who use the computer on a regular basis. Windows XP then keeps track of the way each limited account member prefers his or her computer to be set up. After a limited account user logs on, Windows XP displays that person's favorite desktop and background, and remembers his or her favorite Internet Explorer Web sites. Everything looks just the way that user set it up.

- Administrators should create a single *guest* account for people the computer doesn't need to recognize. Guests can't do much more than use the computer as a terminal, much like one in a library. Guests can use the programs, for example, but they can't change any settings, much less install programs or burn CDs. However, guests can still log on to the Internet through a network, cable modem, or DSL connection. (Guest accounts can't access dial-up modems.)

- More than one person can hold an administrator account on a computer. In fact, all the users can hold one, if the computer's owner prefers that. That lets anybody install software and change important computer settings. (It also lets everybody peek into each other's files.)

- When you install Windows XP, the software automatically grants administrator status to every account you create. After the installation is complete, be sure to change these accounts to limited or guest status unless you trust those people to handle your computer wisely.

Changing a user account's picture

Okay, now the important stuff: changing the dorky picture Windows automatically assigns to your user account. When you first create a user account, Windows XP dips into its image bag and randomly assigns to accounts pictures of butterflies, fish, soccer balls, or even more boring images. However, customizing your picture is fairly easy. (It's even easier if you have a digital camera.)

After you log on, click the Start button and choose Control Panel. Click the User Accounts icon and select Change My Picture. (Administrators have to click Change an Account first and then choose the account that needs a new picture.) A new window appears, as shown in Figure 9-1.

If any of the currently shown pictures appeal to you, click a picture and click the Change Picture button. Done! To assign a picture that's not shown, click the Browse for More Pictures button. A new window appears, this time showing the contents of your My Pictures folder. (This folder is where your digital camera stores your pictures.) Click a desired picture from the folder, choose Open, and click Change Picture. That's it!

As shown in Figure 9-2, a picture of my face now replaces the old rubber ducky picture.

- Okay, how did I get the picture of my face? Well, I used my digital camera. What do you do if you don't have a digital camera? You can grab a picture off the Internet. In fact, I grabbed the picture of my face off the Internet at my Web site, www.andyrathbone.com. (I explain how to copy a picture off the Internet in Chapter 12.)

TIP

✔ Don't worry about choosing a picture that's too big or too small. Windows XP automatically shrinks or expands the image to fit the postage-stamp-sized space.

✔ All users can change their pictures — administrators and limited accounts. And pictures are about the only thing that guests are allowed to change.

Figure 9-1:
Choose the Control Panel's User Accounts icon and choose Change My Picture to assign a different picture to your user account.

Figure 9-2:
Use the User Accounts area to assign your own picture to your account.

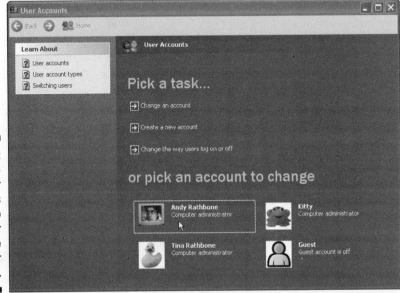

Do you want the Microsoft .NET Passport?

In its ever-expanding push toward computer domination, Microsoft launched an evil concept called the *.NET Passport*. (Soon after installation, Windows XP urgently asks you to sign up for one.) In theory, the Passport sounds great: Give Microsoft a user name and password, and you have a Passport. When you visit any Passport-aware Internet sites, you type in your same Passport name and password. You no longer have to remember different user names and passwords for every place that you visit or shop on the Internet.

In fact, when you move from one Passport-enabled site to another, you don't even need to log on again. With the Passport, your personal data travels with you: name, address, and, if you purchased anything, your credit card number. Microsoft says its .NET Passport enables software, Internet services, and computer gadgetry to work together and share information, making the Internet easier for everyone to use.

Think about it, though. No entity should govern your Internet use — except you. The Microsoft Passport contains your Internet identity. With Passport, Microsoft creates a consumer database that's just too powerful. Microsoft can collect information from any Passport-enabled site you visit, so Microsoft knows the stocks you track in `Investor.com`, the Web pages you view in `MSN.com`, and where you travel through `Expedia.com`. When you move from one Passport-enabled site to another, that information could be shared, too.

In concept, Passport sounds great. When computers are working well, they do great things. But everybody knows how terrible computers can be if something goes wrong. Passport, I'm afraid, offers too much opportunity for things to go wrong. Yes, I occasionally use a Passport account when there's no alternative. But I avoid Passport-enabled sites whenever possible.

Switching quickly between users

Windows XP enables an entire family or small office to share a single computer. Because everybody has a user account, Windows keeps track of everybody's settings. In fact, the same computer acts like five different computers for a family of five.

Best yet, the computer keeps track of everybody's programs while different people use the computer. Mom can be playing chess, and then let Jerry log on to check his e-mail. When Mom logs back on 20 minutes later, her chess game is right where she left it: deciding between the *en passant* pawn move or sacrificing the queen's bishop.

 Switching users is fast and easy. While holding down the Windows key (it's usually between your keyboard's Ctrl and Alt keys), press the letter L. Wham! The Welcome screen pops up, letting another person use the computer for a while.

After you finish using the computer, hold down the Windows key and press the letter L. Wham! The Welcome screen pops up again, letting a different user log on.

- If you don't like the Windows key, use the mouse to switch users: Click the Start button and click Log Off from the bottom of the menu. After the new window appears, click Switch User. The Welcome screen appears.

- Microsoft touts this feature as *Fast User Switching*, or *FUS* in the trade.

- If Fast User Switching doesn't work on your computer, the administrator may have turned it off, a feat described in the next section.

- Choosing Log Off rather than using Fast User Switching is often better, especially for computers without a lot of memory. Programs automatically shut down after users log off the computer, and the computer runs faster for the next user. If you use Fast User Switching, the computer must juggle unsaved settings and open programs, leading to more overhead.

Creating, deleting, or changing a user account

Only administrators may create or delete user accounts. Sorry. If you don't see your name on the Welcome screen, you must log on as a guest. (And some computers don't even offer a guest account. That's up to the administrator, too.)

If you're an administrator (and if you're not, don't bother reading any further), feel free to create a limited user account for everybody who's going to use your computer. That gives them just enough control over the computer to keep them from bugging you all the time, yet it keeps them from accidentally deleting any important files.

 To create, change, or delete a user account, click the Start button, choose the Control Panel, and select User Accounts. A window pops up, as shown in Figure 9-3, that's seen only by administrators. Here's a rundown on the different tasks available.

Change an Account: The most encompassing of the options, this lets you change an account's name, picture, password, or type. (You can upgrade a user's account to administrator if you're tired of handling the computer by yourself, for instance.) Click here to delete an account, as well.

Create a New Account: Click here to create accounts for other computer users. You choose a name and whether the user is to have an administrator or limited account.

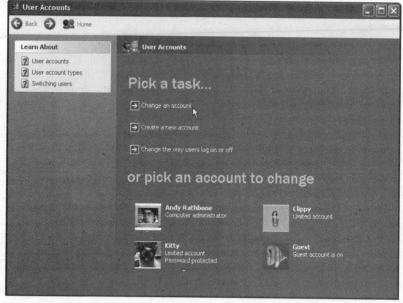

Figure 9-3:
Only administrators can choose the Control Panel's User Accounts icon to change, create, or delete user accounts.

Change the Way Users Log On and Off: This one's a little more complicated, because it brings up two options, described here:

✔ **Use the Welcome Screen:** Normally, people log on by clicking their names on the Welcome screen. Removing the check mark in this box turns off the Welcome screen. Instead, people must type their name and password into little boxes in order to log on. Why? This method is more secure — without the Welcome screen, nobody can tell which people have accounts on the computer. Turning off the Welcome screen also turns off Fast User Switching, described next.

✔ **Use Fast User Switching:** Windows XP usually lets users switch back and forth quickly and easily. When they switch back on, their open programs are just the way they left them. (See the previous section "Switching quickly between users" for more information.) Removing the check mark in this box turns off the Fast User Switching for all users. Instead, they must log off, saving their work in the process, before another user may log on.

Skip the Rest of This Unless You Have or Want a Network

A *network* is just two or more computers that have been connected so that they can share information. But computer networks have more subtleties than nervous high schoolers on their first date.

A password, please

There's not much point to having a user account if you don't have a password. Without one, anybody can click your account on the Welcome screen. Windows will think that person is you and will let him or her delete or snoop through your files.

Administrators, especially, should have passwords, or anybody can log on as an administrator, peek into every user's files, or completely sabotage the computer.

To create or change a password, open User Accounts from the Start menu's Control Panel and choose Create a Password. Make up an easy-to-remember password to type into the first box and then retype the same word into the box below it. (That eliminates the chance of typos.)

In the third box, type in a clue that helps you remember your forgotten password. Make sure the clue only works for you, though. Don't choose "My hair color," for instance. Instead, choose "My cat's favorite food" or "The actor on my favorite TV show." And don't be afraid to change the password every once in a while, too. You can find more about passwords at the beginning of Chapter 4.

Finally, create a Password Reset Disk. That way, if you forget your password, and your hint's not helping you remember it, you can insert your Password Reset Disk as a key. Windows XP will let you in, and all will be joyous. (But if you lose the Password Reset Disk, you have to beg for mercy from the administrator. And be sure to change your password so nobody can use your lost Password Reset Disk to break in.).

For example, how do you tell if a computer is on a network? Who's allowed on the network? Which computers are on the network? Are all parts of Computer A available to Computer B? Should networked computers be allowed to kiss without passwords?

All these technical decisions need to be made beforehand, usually by the network administrator — somebody who often looks as harried as the high school principal at the prom.

Computers aren't the only elements that you can network. You can put printers, modems, CD-ROM drives, some USB-connected drives, CompactFlash card readers, and nearly anything else on a network, as well. No need to buy bunches of stuff for each computer; they can all share.

Windows XP divvies up its attention quite well. It lets all the networked computers share a single Internet connection, for instance, and everybody can be online *at the same time*. Everyone can share a single printer, too. If two people try to print something simultaneously, Windows holds onto the incoming files until the printer is free and ready to deal with them.

Don't know if you're on a network? Click the Start button and choose My Network Places. A window appears, showing any computers connected to your own.

Can I get in trouble for looking into the wrong computer?

Sometimes people *tell* you where to find files and things on your network. They write it on a cheat sheet taped to your computer. If nobody's dropped you a hint, feel free to grab a torch and go spelunking on your own with My Network Places, described in the next section.

If you're worried about getting into trouble, the rule is simple: Windows XP rarely lets you peek into networked areas where you're not supposed to be. In fact, Windows XP is so security conscious that it may keep you from seeing things that you *should* be able to see. (That's when you call on the administrator.)

For instance, if you tried to peek inside a forbidden computer named Clementine, an "access denied" message would appear, as shown in Figure 9-4. No harm done.

- ✔ If you're supposed to be able to read a folder on someone else's computer and you can't, just casually tell the administrator, "Pardon me, bloke, but I don't seem to have permission to access folder X on computer Y. Could you check into that? There's a good chap."

- ✔ If you do accidentally find yourself in a folder where you obviously don't belong — for example, the folder of employee evaluations on your supervisor's computer — that should also be brought to the administrator's attention.

Figure 9-4:
If you try to enter a restricted area on the network, Windows XP politely refuses.

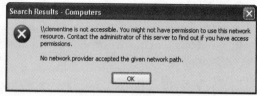

How do I access other networked computers?

The best and fastest way to knock on the doors of other networked computers is to head for the Start button and click My Network Places. A window pops open, such as the one in Figure 9-5, and you might see some folders living on other computers.

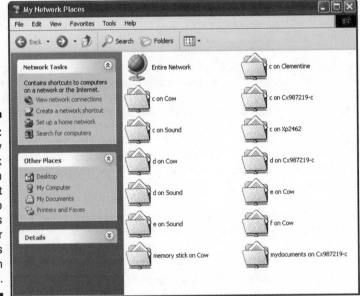

Figure 9-5:
Click My Network Places from the Start button to see folders on other computers that you can access.

Icons for networked folders — folders living on computers connected to yours — look slightly different than icons for your own computer's folders. A sheet of paper sticks out of the top and a little wire runs beneath them. Networked folders work the same, though: Double-click them to see what's inside, just like any other folder.

There's a catch, however: You're only able to poke inside another computer's folder if somebody has decided to *share* it. (Other sections in this chapter show how to share your own folders.)

Sometimes an entire hard disk is shared; for example, other people have permission to come into that computer and stroll around that particular hard disk, pinching peaches and thumping melons. Other times, the sharing involves merely a folder or two. Windows XP, for instance, always makes its Shared Music and Shared Pictures folders available on the network so that everybody can peek at the same photo album and share the same CDs.

✔ Networks being what they are, it's hard to predict what you'll see in your own My Network Places. Just about everybody's network is set up differently. But there's absolutely no rule against looking around. If you're just curious, start spelunking by clicking folders.

✔ To see any currently networked printers, open My Network Places from the Start menu and click Printers and Faxes in the Other Places section along the left side. Icons for networked printers look just like those for regular printers, but with that telltale cable running beneath.

✔ The My Network Places window uses the networked folder icon for just about anything inside. Figure 9-5, for instance, shows a networked floppy drive and a networked Sony Memory Stick; both use a networked folder icon.

Sharing your own computer's stuff with the network

To share a file or folder with your fellow computer users, move the file into your Shared Documents folder, which lives in your My Computer window. (You must move or copy a file into the Shared Documents folder; shortcuts don't always work.)

After you place your file or folder into your Shared Documents folder, it appears in the Shared Documents folder of everybody else using your computer.

As a special perk, administrators can share folders without having to move them into the Shared Documents folder. The trick is to follow these steps:

1. **Right-click on a folder you'd like to share and choose Sharing and Security from the pop-up menu.**

   Open My Computer and right-click on the folder you'd like to share. When the menu appears, select Sharing and Security. A window appears, showing the Properties for that folder. It opens to the Sharing tab, as shown in Figure 9-6.

2. **Click the box marked Share This Folder on the Network.**

   A check mark in that box lets everybody peek at, grab, steal, change, or delete any of the files in that folder. To let visitors look inside the files but not change them, remove the check mark from the box marked Allow Network Users to Change My Files.

3. **Click OK.**

   Now that particular folder and all its contents are available for everybody on the network to share.

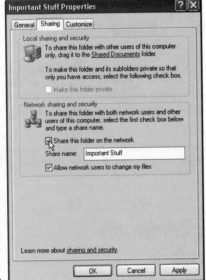

Figure 9-6:
Right-click
on a folder
and choose
Sharing and
Security to
share the
folder on the
network.

✔ Sharing many folders is not a good idea because it gives network visitors too much control over your computer. Even if you trust people, they might accidentally mess something up. To be safest, only share files by placing them in the Shared Document folder.

✔ Inside Shared Documents live two more folders, Shared Music and Shared Pictures. Those two folders are also available to any user. So, if you want to share documents with any user of your computer, store them in the Shared Documents folder. When you make MP3s from your CDs, store them in the Shared Music folder, too, so that everybody can enjoy them.

Sharing a printer on the network

Many households or offices have several computers but only one printer. That creates quite a problem: Who has to keep the printer on *his* desk? The second problem, how everybody can access the same printer, is solved easily: by putting the printer on a network.

If no printer is directly plugged into your computer, you can easily find out what networked printers are available. Click the Start button, choose the Control Panel, and select Printers and Other Hardware. Choose View Installed Printers or Fax Printers. (Or click the Printers and Faxes icon, depending on your setup.)

Windows XP shows you the printers connected to your computer, as shown in Figure 9-7.

Figure 9-7:
The Control
Panel's
Printers
and Faxes
window
shows one
networked
printer
accessible
from this
computer.

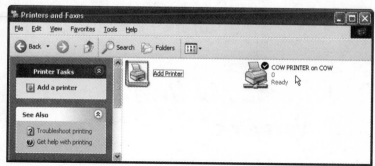

Figure 9-7:
The Control Panel's Printers and Faxes window shows one networked printer accessible from this computer.

To share a printer with the network, follow these steps.

1. **Click the Start button, choose Control Panel, select Printers and Other Hardware, and choose Printers and Faxes.**

   Depending on your setup, you might skip Printers and Other Hardware, because the Printers and Faxes icon will already be showing.

2. **If you see an icon for your computer's printer, right-click on the icon and choose Sharing.**

   No icon for your printer? Move ahead to Step 4.

3. **Click the Share This Printer button, and if desired, type in a name for your printer. Click OK.**

   Any name will do — the make and model works fine. If you're running other versions of Windows on your network, click the Additional Drivers button. Click in the boxes next to the versions used by the other computers and click OK. Click OK to close the window, and you're through.

4. **If there's no icon for your computer's printer, click Add Printer.**

   Fill out the questions Windows XP asks about your printer. If your printer came with an installation disk, use that. Windows XP recognizes many modern printers as soon as you plug them into the USB port. If the printer plugs into a printer port (also called the *LPT* port), you might have to tell Windows the printer's make and model.

   Finally, tell Windows XP to use that printer as the *default* printer if you want Windows XP to use that printer all the time. (This option comes in handy for people who have more than one printer.)

   The new printer's icon now appears in your Printers and Faxes window; you'll also find its name listed in your software programs as an option for printing. Now go back to Step 3 to share the printer with the network.

   That's it. Your computer can send information to any of the printers listed in the window.

If you don't see any printers listed in the Printers and Faxes window, yet you know that one is attached to the network, click the Add Printer icon. This time, though, tell it you're installing a network printer. Windows XP browses for any connected network printers and displays their names.

How Do I Create My Own Computer Network?

If you're trying to set up a lot of computers — more than five or ten — you need a more advanced book: Networks are very scary stuff. But if you're just trying to set up a handful of computers in your home or home office, this information may be all you need.

So without further blabbing, here's a no-fat, step-by-step list of how to set up your own small and inexpensive network to work with Windows XP. The following sections show how to buy the three parts of a network — cables, cards, and a switchbox for connecting the cables. It explains how to install the parts and, finally, how to make Windows XP create a network out of your handiwork.

Buying a network's parts

Today, most networks use Ethernet cable. Some homes come prewired with network jacks in the wall, and people quickly find out what's so weird about Ethernet cable: It looks like plain old phone cable. Ethernet cable's slightly larger connectors won't fit into a phone jack, though, even if you push really hard.

Ethernet cable is known by a wide variety of names, including 10BaseT, 100BaseT, Ethernet RJ-45, TPE (Twisted Pair Ethernet), and 10BT. But when shopping, just ask for network cable that "looks like telephone cord instead of cable-TV cord." When in doubt buy Fast Ethernet or 100BaseT cable.

Next, you need network cards, one for each computer on the network. (Many new computers come with a network card preinstalled, so look in the back of the computer for the giveaway: something that looks like a huge phone jack.)

When you choose a card, keep these factors in mind:

- The card must be an *Ethernet* card with a 10/100 Ethernet connector.

- The card must fit into one of your computer's unused slots.

- The card's box should say that it's Plug and Play and supports Windows XP. If the box doesn't list Windows XP, then Windows 2000 is your next best bet.

Finally, you need a switchbox (or a cheaper but slower hub), where you plug in the cables. The switchbox needs one jack or *port* for every computer's cable, as shown in Figure 9-8.

Only connecting two computers? Then spare the expense of a hub. Feico Nater, this book's Dutch translator, says he merely connects the two computers with a "crossed cable," a special breed of Ethernet cable. A crossed cable connection doesn't require a hub, works just like a network, and costs less.

Without the switchbox, shown in Figure 9-9, the network won't work right. (More complex networks can often link switchboxes, but I'm deliberately leaving the complicated stuff out of this book.)

Here's the shopping list. Drop this onto the copy machine at the office and take it to the computer store.

- One 10BaseT-supporting Ethernet "Plug and Play" card for each computer on the network. (The 100 Mbps or Fast Ethernet cards are ten times as fast, but cost more money.) Make sure the cards are Windows XP or Windows 2000 compatible.

- One switchbox that has enough ports for each computer — plus some extra ports for a few computers that you may want to add at a later time. (Or use a crossed cable if you're only linking two computers.)

- For every computer, buy one network cable that's long enough to reach from the computer to the switchbox.

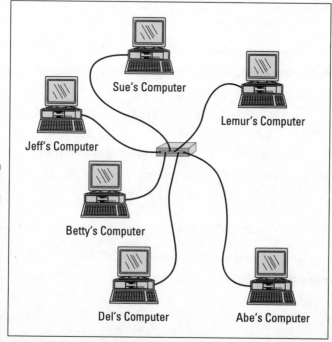

Figure 9-8:
Ethernet cable looks like telephone wire and links computers to a central switchbox.

Sue's Computer

Lemur's Computer

Jeff's Computer

Betty's Computer

Del's Computer

Abe's Computer

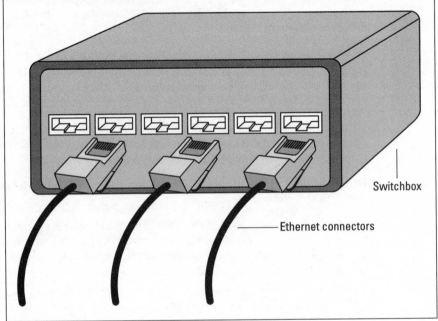

Figure 9-9:
Network
users need
to plug the
cable from
each of their
computers
into a
central
switchbox.

Switchbox

Ethernet connectors

Installing the network's parts

Here's how to install your new network card. Windows XP should automatically recognize the card and embrace it gleefully.

1. **Find your original Windows XP compact disc — you may need it.**

2. **Turn off and unplug all the computers on your soon-to-be network.**

   Turn 'em all off; unplug them as well.

3. **Turn off all the computers' peripherals — printers, monitors, modems, and so on.**

4. **Insert the network cards into their appropriate slots.**

   Remove the computer's case and push the card into the proper type of slot. Make double sure that you're inserting the proper type of card into the proper type of slot — for example, inserting a PCI card into a PCI slot.

   If a card doesn't seem to fit into a slot, don't force it. Different types of cards fit into different types of slots, and you may be trying to push the wrong type of card into the wrong type of slot.

5. **Replace the computers' cases and connect the network cables to the cards.**

6. **Connect the cables between the network cards and the switchbox.**

   Figure 9-9 shows an example of how the cables connect. You may need to route cables under carpets or around doorways. (Most switchboxes have power cords that need to be plugged into a wall outlet as well.)

7. **Turn on the computers and their peripherals.**

   Turn on the computers and their monitors, printers, modems, and whatever else happens to be connected to them.

   ✔ If all goes well, Windows XP wakes up, notices its newly installed network card, and begins installing its appropriate software automatically. Hurrah! Or, if the network card came with an installation disk or CD, double-click the disk's Setup file to install the card.

   ✔ If all doesn't go well, click Windows XP's Start button, choose Control Panel, and double-click the Add Hardware icon. (You may need to click Switch to Classic View to see the icon.) Click the Next button to make Windows try to autodetect the new network card.

Letting the Network Setup Wizard Set Up Your Network

Whoopee! After you've installed the cards, cables, and switchbox, the Windows Network Setup Wizard takes over. First, run the wizard on the computer that connects to the Internet, as described in Chapter 12. (The wizard will let all your networked computers share that connection.)

Now, turn on all your computers, printers, and external modems and then connect your computer to the Internet. Ready? Here's how to summon the wizard to complete the network finalities:

1. **Start the Network Setup Wizard and click the Next button.**

   Click the Start button, choose My Network Places, and choose Set Up a Home or Small Office Network from the Network Tasks area along the left. The Network Setup Wizard rises to the screen, as shown in Figure 9-10, ready for you to click Next.

2. **Read the screen and click Next.**

   The Network Setup Wizard brings your network to life, examining everything connected to it and placing appropriate network icons on your computer. That's why turning everything on is important, as the wizard requests. After you click Next, the wizard looks for your Internet connection.

Figure 9-10:
The
Network
Setup
Wizard
leads you
through the
networking
process.

3. **Tell the wizard about your Internet connection and click Next.**

   Specifically, the wizard needs to know whether your computer connects directly to the Internet, or if it will connect to the Internet through a different computer on the network. Because you're running this wizard on the computer that connects to the Internet, choose the first option.

4. **Choose your Internet connection from the list, if asked, and click Next.**

5. **Type a name and description for your computer and click Next.**

6. **If the settings look correct, click Next.**

   Windows XP lists the settings that it will use and asks for your okay. If you click Next, Windows XP checks out the Internet connection and lets other networked computers share it. It automatically installs a *protective* firewall, described in Chapter 12. And it starts setting up the network. (Give it a few minutes.)

7. **If your network includes Windows 98 or Windows 95 computers, create a Home Networking Setup disk and click Next.**

   If any of your networked computers use those older versions of Windows, create the Network Setup disk by clicking the Create Disk button. (You need a floppy.)

   Ignore this step if you're networking all Windows XP computers. You can insert your Windows XP CD into those computers, choose Perform Additional Tasks, and select Set Up Home or Small Office Networking.

8. **Click Finish.**

   That should do the trick.

   ✔ The wizard does a reasonably good job of casting its spells on your computers. If the computers are all connected correctly and restarted, chances are they'll wake up in bondage with each other. If they don't, try restarting them all again.

✔ Your newly networked Windows XP computers should list currently shared folders in their My Network Places areas. Unless you've shared additional files on your own, you'll probably see a single folder called Shared Documents that contains My Music and My Pictures.

✔ To run the wizard on Windows 95 or 98 computers that aren't running Windows XP, insert your Network Setup disk into the computer you want to network. Open My Computer, double-click your floppy drive, and double-click the file named, `netsetup`. The computer asks a few questions, tweaks itself, and reboots. (Just run the Network Wizard on networked Windows Me computers, if Windows XP didn't already set them up.)

✔ All of your networked computers should now be able to share any shared files, your modem connection, and any printers.

✔ If everything doesn't proceed as merrily as described here, don't worry. Networking *will* work. However, you need to make some more advanced tweaks that I can't describe here or the book would cost too much. Pick up a copy of Curt Simmons's *Windows XP Secrets* published by Wiley Publishing, Inc. (It's around 1,200 pages.)

My user accounts aren't secure!

Some users will find that their computer's Limited and Guest accounts still have the privileges of Administrator accounts. What gives?

It probably boils down to this technicality: Microsoft recommends that a Windows XP computer's hard drive be formatted using the newer, more secure NTFS than the older FAT or FAT32 systems. NTFS enables Windows XP's security measures to take effect. If you're upgrading your computer to Windows XP, select the NTFS option when upgrading.

Unfortunately, some computer manufacturers ship Windows XP preinstalled on a drive that hasn't been formatted with NTFS. That means your user accounts won't be secure. Users can peek into files of other user accounts, if they know where to look. People with Limited and/or Guest accounts can still install programs and delete important files.

To see if your hard drive uses NTFS, open My Computer, right-click your hard drive icon, and choose Properties. If you see the word NTFS

next to the words "File System," you're okay. If you see FAT or FAT32 instead, your computer isn't as secure as you might think.

If this is a problem for you, convert your hard drive to NTFS by using Windows XP's Convert command:

1. **Click Start, point to All Programs, point to Accessories, and then click Command Prompt.**

2. **To convert your C drive, type this at the command prompt:**

   ```
   convert c: /fs:ntfs
   ```

Follow your computer's instructions from here. If Windows XP requests, feel free to let it do the conversion the next time you turn on your computer.

For more detailed information, search for NTFS in Windows Help and Support section, or head to `www.support.microsoft.com` and search for document "Q307881".

Part III
Using Windows XP Applications (And Surfing the Web)

The 5th Wave   By Rich Tennant

"This is amazing. You can stop looking for Derek. According to an MSN search I did, he's hiding behind the dryer in the basement."

In this part . . .

Did you know that

- Rubber bands last longer when refrigerated?
- A human's eyelashes generally fall off after 5 months?
- Windows XP comes with a bunch of free programs that aren't even mentioned on the outside of the box?

This part takes a look at all the stuff you're getting for nothing. Well, for the price on your sales receipt, anyway. It also shows how to get to those darn programs by using the Start button, the desktop, and that little bar along the screen's bottom called the "taskbar."

Finally, it shows how to do the exciting stuff: Surf the Web, download music and videos, and turn your PC into something fun for a change.

Chapter 10

Your Desktop, Start Button, and Taskbar (And *Free* Programs)

In This Chapter

▶ Using the desktop and making shortcuts

▶ Deleting files, folders, programs, and icons

▶ Retrieving deleted items from the Recycle Bin

▶ Using the taskbar and controlling Print Manager

▶ Starting programs, adding programs, and removing programs from the Start button

▶ Making Windows load programs automatically

*I*n the old days of computing, pale technoweenies typed disgustingly long strings of code words into computers to make the computers do something — anything.

With Windows XP, computers reach the age of modern convenience. To start a program, simply click a button. There's a slight complication, however: The buttons no longer *look* like buttons. In fact, some of the buttons are hidden, revealed only by the push of yet another button (if you're lucky enough to stumble upon the right place to push).

To make matters worse, some of the buttons fall off and land on your desktop. (Don't worry; they're *supposed* to do that.) This chapter covers the three main Windows XP buttonmongers: the desktop, the taskbar, and that mother of all buttons — the Start button. Plus, it explains which of the Windows freebie programs are worth the click it takes to load them.

Rolling Objects along the Windows XP Desktop

Usually, nobody thinks of mounting a desktop sideways. Keeping the pencils from rolling off a normal desk is hard enough.

But in Windows XP, your computer monitor's screen is known as the Windows *desktop,* and it's the area where all your work takes place. You can create files and folders right on your new electronic desktop and arrange them all across the screen.

For example, do you need to write a letter asking the neighbor to return the circular saw she borrowed? The following steps show how to put the desktop's functions to immediate use.

Point at just about any Windows XP item and click your right mouse button to see a menu listing the things you're allowed to do with that item.

1. **Right-click on an uncovered area of your desktop.**

   A menu pops up, as shown in Figure 10-1.

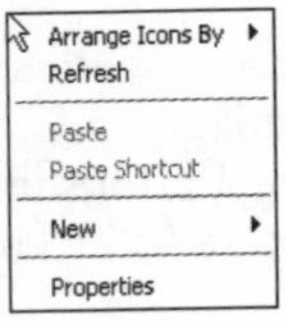

Figure 10-1:
Clicking an empty area of your desktop with your right mouse button brings up a list of helpful options.

| Arrange Icons By ▶ |
| Refresh |
| Paste |
| Paste Shortcut |
| New ▶ |
| Properties |

2. **Point at the word New and click WordPad Document from the menu that appears.**

   Because you're creating something new — a new letter — you should point at the word New. Windows XP lists the new things you can create on the desktop. Choose WordPad Document, as shown in Figure 10-2. Poof! A little WordPad icon appears on the desktop, bearing the vivid name New WordPad Document.

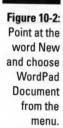

Figure 10-2:
Point at the
word New
and choose
WordPad
Document
from the
menu.

As your computer fills up with programs, your menu choices change, too. In fact, if you install Microsoft Office or Microsoft Word, WordPad is kicked off the menu completely. If you don't see WordPad on the menu, try this alternative approach: Click the Start button and choose Run. When the Run box appears, type **WordPad** into the Open box and then press Enter. WordPad opens automatically, ready for action. Now run ahead to Step 5.

3. Type a name for your letter and press Enter.

When an icon for a new WordPad document appears on the desktop, the first step is to give it a name of up to 255 characters — something like *Polite Circular Saw Request.* As soon as you start typing, your new title replaces the old name of New WordPad Document, as shown in Figure 10-3.

Figure 10-3:
Start typing
to create
the icon's
new name.

Press Enter when you're through typing the name, and WordPad saves the new name. (Occasionally, Windows XP frets about your choice of name; if so, try a different name or skip ahead to Chapter 11 to see why Windows is so finicky about names.)

4. Double-click your newly created WordPad icon to open it.

Double-clicking the new icon calls up WordPad, the word processor, so you can write the letter requesting the return of your circular saw.

5. Write your letter.

Remember, word processors automatically wrap your sentences to the next line for you; don't hit the Enter key when you're nearing the right side of the page.

6. **Click Save from the WordPad File menu to save the letter.**

   If you created the file by right-clicking on the desktop, you've already named the file, and Windows will save it without further ado. If you opened WordPad through the Start menu's Run command, Windows now asks you to choose a name for the file.

7. **Head back to the WordPad File menu and choose Print to send the letter to the printer.**

8. **Close the file by clicking the X in its upper-right corner. To delete it, drag the file to the Recycle Bin.**

   After you finish writing and printing the letter, you can either save it or throw it away. You can simply leave your new WordPad letter icon on your desk. When your desktop gets too cluttered, feel free to move the icon to a new folder, a process covered in excruciating detail in Chapter 11.

   If you want to delete the letter, drag the icon to your Recycle Bin, which I describe in the nearby section "Using the Recycle Bin."

   ✔ Windows XP is designed for you to work right on top of the desktop. From the desktop, you can create new things like files, folders, sounds, and graphics — just about anything. After working with your new file or folder, you can store it or delete it.

   ✔ Are you confused about what something is supposed to do? Right-click on it or simply rest the pointer over the confusing spot. Windows XP often tosses up a menu that lists just about everything you can do with that particular object. This trick works on many icons found on your desktop or throughout your programs.

   ✔ Sometimes Windows XP does something nasty, and everything on your desktop disappears, leaving it completely empty. What gives? To fix the problem, right-click on your desktop and choose Arrange Icons By from the pop-up menu. Then choose Show Desktop Icons from the next menu to make everything reappear with no harm done.

Arranging icons on the desktop

Windows XP offers many — too many, in fact — ways to organize your desktop's icons. If your desktop's icons start to look like an unorganized pile, right-click on a blank area of your desktop. Then choose Arrange Icons By from the menu that appears. Windows arranges the icons along the left edge of the screen, depending on your option. Here's a rundown:

- **Name:** Arrange icons in alphabetical order by the icon's name.

- **Size:** Arrange icons according to the file's size. (Shortcut files stay near the top because they're small.)

- **Type:** Line up icons by the file's type: All WordPad files are grouped together, for instance, as are all shortcuts to Paint files.

- **Modified:** Arrange icons in the order that the shortcut was created or modified.

- **Auto Arrange:** Automatically arrange any new icons in columns along the screen's left side.

- **Align to Grid:** My favorite. Aligns all icons to an invisible grid on the screen to keep them nice and tidy.

- **Show Desktop Icons:** Make sure you keep this option on. If you click here, Windows hides all the icons on your desktop. If you can remember in your frustration, click this option again to toggle your icons back on.

- **Lock Web Items on Desktop:** Chapter 14 shows how to place a Web page onto your desktop as a background. Click here to "lock" that Web page in place.

Using the Recycle Bin

The Recycle Bin, that little oval wastebasket icon on your desktop (shown here in the margin), is supposed to work like a *real* recycle bin. It's something you can fish the Sunday paper out of if somebody pitched the comics section before you had a chance to read it.

If you want to get rid of something in Windows XP — a file or folder, for example — simply drag it to the Recycle Bin. Point at the file or folder's icon with the mouse and, while holding down the left mouse button, point at the Recycle Bin. Let go of the mouse button, and your detritus disappears. Windows XP stuffs it into the Recycle Bin.

But if you want to bypass that cute metaphor, you can delete stuff another way: Right-click on your unwanted file or folder's icon and choose Delete from the menu that pops up. Windows XP asks cautiously if you're *sure* that you want to delete the icon. If you click the Yes button, Windows XP dumps the icon into the Recycle Bin, just as if you'd dragged it there. Whoosh! (If you're not sure, click No, and Windows leaves the file in place.)

So if you like to drag and drop, feel free to drag your garbage to the Recycle Bin and let go. If you prefer the menus, click with your right mouse button and choose Delete. Or, if you like alternative lifestyles, click the unwanted icon with your left mouse button and press your keyboard's Delete key. All three methods toss the file into the Recycle Bin, where you can salvage it later or, eventually, purge it for good.

✔ Want to retrieve something you've deleted? Double-click the Recycle Bin icon, and a window appears, listing deleted items. See the name of your accidentally deleted icon? Right-click on the icon and choose Restore to send it back to the folder from which it was deleted. Or drag the icon to the desktop or any other folder: Point at the icon's name and, while holding down the left mouse button, point at its desired location. Let go of the mouse button, and the Recycle Bin coughs up the deleted item, good as new.

✔ Sometimes, the Recycle Bin can get pretty full. If you're searching fruitlessly for a file you've recently deleted, tell the Recycle Bin to sort the filenames in the order in which they were deleted. Click View, point at Arrange Icons, and choose Date Deleted from the menu that pops out. The Recycle Bin now lists the most recently deleted files at the bottom.

✔ The Recycle Bin icon changes from an empty wastepaper basket to a full one as soon as it's holding a deleted file. You may have to squint a little to notice the pieces of paper sticking out of the trashcan's top.

✔ The Recycle Bin waits until your deleted files consume 10 percent of your computer's hard drive before it begins purging your oldest deleted files to make room for new ones. If you're running out of hard disk space, shrink the bin's size. Right-click on the Recycle Bin and choose Properties from its menu. If you want the Recycle Bin to hang on to more deleted files, increase the percentage. If you're a sure-fingered clicker who seldom makes mistakes, decrease the percentage.

Making a shortcut

Some people like to organize their desktops, putting a pencil sharpener on one corner and a box of Kleenex on the other corner. Other people like their Kleenex box in the top desk drawer. Microsoft knew that one desktop design could never please everybody, so Windows XP lets people customize their desktops to suit individual tastes and needs.

For example, you may find yourself frequently copying files to or from a floppy disk in drive A. Usually, to perform that operation, you click the Start button, click My Computer, and drag your files to the floppy drive icon living in there. But there's a quicker way, and it's called a Windows XP *shortcut*. A shortcut is simply a push button — an icon — that stands for something else.

For example, here's how to put a shortcut for drive A on your desktop:

1. **Click the Start button and then click My Computer.**

   The My Computer folder opens up, showing the icons for your disk drives as well as oft-used folders. (My Computer gets more coverage in Chapter 11.)

2. With your right mouse button, drag the drive A icon to the desktop.

Point at the drive A icon and, while holding down your right mouse button, point at the desktop, as shown in Figure 10-4. Let go of your mouse button. (Check out Chapter 6 if you're not sure how to shrink the My Computer window to make the desktop visible.)

3. Choose Create Shortcut(s) Here from the menu.

Windows XP puts an icon for drive A on your desktop, but it looks a little different from the drive A icon you dragged. Because it's only a shortcut — not the original icon — it has a little arrow in its corner, as shown in the margin.

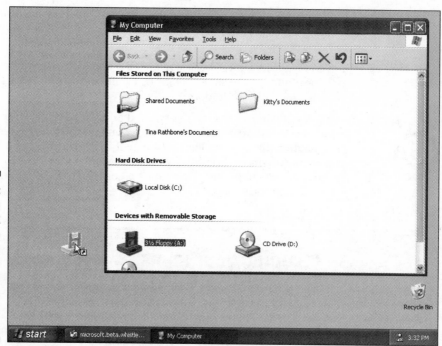

Figure 10-4:
Dragging the drive A icon to the desktop with the right mouse button creates a shortcut.

That's it. Now you won't need to root through any folders to access your floppy drive. The shortcut on your desktop works just as well as the *real* floppy drive icon. To copy or move files to your A drive, just drag them to the newly created shortcut. To see the contents of your floppy disk, double-click the shortcut.

> ✔ Feel free to create desktop shortcuts for your most commonly accessed programs, files, or disk drives. If you're on a network, create shortcuts for networked computers, or just folders on networked computers. Shortcuts are a quick way to make Windows XP easier to use.

✔ Here's a quick trick: Right-click on a disk drive — even your floppy drive — and choose Create Shortcut. Windows will offer to place the shortcut on your desktop. (This trick only works for disk drives, though.)

✔ You can even put a shortcut for your printer onto your desktop. To print a file, drag and drop its icon onto the printer's shortcut.

✔ If your newly dragged icon doesn't have an arrow in its bottom corner, don't let go of the mouse! You might not be making a shortcut. Instead, you've probably dragged the *real* program to your desktop, and other programs may not be able to find it. Press the Esc button with your free hand, and Windows stops what you were doing. (You probably mistakenly held down the *left* mouse button instead of the correct button — the *right* button.)

✔ Have you grown tired of a particular shortcut? Feel free to delete it. Deleting a shortcut has no effect on the original file, folder, or program that it represents.

✔ You can make as many shortcuts as you'd like. You can even make several shortcuts for the same thing. For example, you can put a shortcut for drive A in *all* your folders.

✔ Windows XP shortcuts aren't very good at keeping track of moving files. If you create a shortcut to a file or program and then move that file or program to a different folder, the shortcut won't be able to find that file or program anymore. Windows will panic and try searching for it, but may not be able to find it. Shortcuts, by contrast, can be moved anywhere without problems.

Keeping your icons straight

Don't be confused by a program's icon on your desktop and a program's button on the taskbar along the bottom of your screen. They're two different things. The button at the bottom of the screen stands for a program that has already been loaded into the computer's memory. It's already running, ready for immediate action. The icon on your desktop or in Windows XP Explorer stands for a program that is sitting on the computer's hard disk waiting to be loaded.

If you mistakenly click the icon in Windows Explorer or on the desktop rather than the button on the taskbar at the bottom of the screen, you load a second copy of that program. Two versions of the program are loaded: one running as a window, and the other running as a taskbar button waiting to be turned back into a window.

Running two versions of a program can cause confusion — especially if you start entering stuff into both versions of the same program. You won't know which window has the *right* version! Check out "The Way-Cool Taskbar," later in this chapter, for more taskbar information.

Uh, what's the difference between a shortcut and the actual program?

 An icon for a file, folder, or program looks pretty much like a shortcut, except the shortcut has a little arrow wedged in its lower reaches. And double-clicking a shortcut and double-clicking an icon do pretty much the same thing: start a program or load a file or folder.

But a shortcut is only a servant of sorts. When you double-click the shortcut, it runs over to the program, file, or folder that the shortcut represents and kick-starts that program, file, or folder into action.

You could do the same thing yourself by rummaging through your computer's folders, finding the program, file, or folder you're after, and personally double-clicking its icon to bring it to life. But it's often more convenient to create a shortcut so that you don't have to rummage so much.

✔ If you delete a shortcut — the icon with the little arrow — you're not doing any real harm. You're just firing the servant that fetched things for you, probably creating more work for yourself in the process.

✔ If you accidentally delete a shortcut, you can pull it out of the Recycle Bin, just like anything else that's deleted in Windows XP.

Shutting down Windows XP

Although the big argument used to be about saturated and unsaturated fats, today's generation has found a new source of disagreement: Should a computer be left on all the time or turned off at the end of the day? Both camps have decent arguments, and there's no real answer (except that you should always turn off your monitor when you won't be using it for a half hour or so).

However, if you decide to turn off your computer, don't just head for the off switch. First, tell Windows XP about your plans. To do that, click the Start button, choose the Turn Off Computer command, and ponder the choices Windows XP places on-screen, as shown in Figure 10-5:

Stand By: Save your work before choosing this option; Windows XP doesn't save your work automatically. Instead, it lets your computer doze for a bit to save power, but the computer wakes up at the touch of a button.

Turn Off: Clicking here tells Windows XP to put away all your programs and to make sure that you've saved all your important files. Then it turns off your computer and most of the newer monitors. Poof! Use this option when you're done computing for the day. (If your monitor doesn't turn off automatically, you'll have to push its power button yourself.)

Figure 10-5:
Click
Stand By to
temporarily
put the
computer to
sleep, click
Turn Off to
turn off your
computer, or
click Restart
to make
Windows
XP shut
down and
come back
to life.

Restart: Here, Windows saves your work and prepares your computer to be shut off. However, it then restarts your computer. Use this option when installing new software, changing settings, or trying to stop Windows XP from doing something awfully weird.

Hibernate: Only offered on some computers, this option works much like Shut Down. It saves your work and turns off your computer. However, when turned on again, your computer presents your desktop just as you left it: Open programs and windows appear in the same place. Putting your computer into hibernation mode is not as safe as shutting it down. (Don't see the Hibernate feature? Hold down Shift, and it will replace the Standby button.)

✔ The Hibernate command takes all of your currently open information and writes it to the hard drive in one big chunk. Then, to re-create your desktop, it reads that big chunk and places it back on your desktop.

✔ Don't ever turn off your computer unless you've chosen the Turn Off command from the Start button. Windows XP needs to prepare itself for the shutdown, or it may accidentally eat some of your important information — as well as the information of anybody else using the computer at the time.

✔ Remember, if you're done with the computer but other people might want to use it, just click Log Off from the Start menu: Windows XP saves your work and brings up the Welcome screen, allowing other people to log on and play video games.

The Way-Cool Taskbar

This section introduces one of the handiest tricks in Windows XP, so pull your chair in a little closer. Whenever you run more than one window on the desktop, there's a big problem: Programs and windows tend to cover each other up, making them difficult to locate.

Windows XP's solution is the *taskbar* — a special program that keeps track of all your open programs. Shown in Figure 10-6, the taskbar normally lives along the bottom of your screen, although you can move it to any edge you want. (*Hint:* Just drag the taskbar to any of the screen's four edges. If it doesn't move, right-click on the taskbar and click Lock the Taskbar to remove the check mark by its name.)

Figure 10-6:
The handy taskbar lists your currently running programs and lets you bring them to the forefront by clicking their names.

See how the button for Calculator looks "pushed in" in Figure 10-6? That's because Calculator is the currently active window on the desktop. One or more of your taskbar's buttons always look pushed in unless you close or minimize all the windows on your desktop.

From the taskbar, you can perform powerful magic on your open windows, as described in the following list:

- ✔ To play with a window you see listed on the taskbar, click its name. The window rises to the surface and rests atop any other open windows, ready for action.

- ✔ To close a window listed on the taskbar, right-click on its name and choose Close from the menu that pops up. The program quits, just as if you'd chosen its Exit command from within its own window. (The departing program gives you a chance to save any work before it quits and disappears from the screen.)

✔ Don't see the taskbar? If the taskbar's top edge peeks up along the screen's bottom, grab the visible part with your mouse and drag it toward the center of the screen until the entire taskbar is visible.

Shrinking windows to the taskbar and retrieving them

Windows spawn windows. You start with one window to write a letter to Mother. You open another window to check her address, for example, and then yet another window to see whether you've forgotten any recent birthdays. Before you know it, four more windows are crowded across the desktop.

To combat the clutter, Windows XP provides a simple means of window control: You can transform a window from a screen-cluttering square into a tiny button on the bar — the taskbar — that sits along the bottom of the screen.

 See the three buttons lurking in just about every window's top-right corner? Click the *Minimize button* — the button with the little line in it. Whoosh! The window disappears, represented by its little button on the bar running along the bottom of your screen. Click that button, and your window hops back onto the screen, ready for action.

✔ To make a minimized program on the taskbar revert into a regular, on-screen window, just click its name on the taskbar. Pretty simple, huh?

✔ To shrink an open window so that it's out of the way, click the leftmost of the three buttons in the window's top-right corner. The window *minimizes* itself into a button and lines itself up on the bar along the bottom of the screen.

✔ Each taskbar button shows the name of the program it represents.

✔ When you minimize a window, you neither destroy its contents nor close it. You merely change its shape. It is still loaded into memory, waiting for you to play with it again.

✔ To put the window back where it was, click its button on the taskbar. It hops back up to the same place it was before.

✔ Whenever you load a program by using the Start button or Explorer, that program's name automatically appears on the taskbar. If one of your open windows ever gets lost on your desktop, click its name on the taskbar. The window immediately jumps to the forefront.

TIP

What's the MSN Messenger Service?

With its *MSN Messenger Service,* Microsoft has created a combination doorbell/peephole for the Internet. When a friend logs onto the Internet, your bell rings automatically, and a window pops up, ready for you to bug your friend with a message.

Then, when you get tired of your friends bugging you, you search for a way to turn off the darn thing. (Right-click on the little "people" icon in the bottom-right corner of your screen near the clock, and choose Exit.)

To keep this icon always hidden, check out this chapter's section on customizing the taskbar. You want to click the Customize button, click MSN Messenger Service, and choose Always Hide.

Clicking the taskbar's sensitive areas

Like a crafty card player, the taskbar comes with a few tips and tricks. For one thing, it has the *Start button*. With a click on the Start button, you can launch programs, change settings, find programs, get help, and order takeout food. (Well, forget the food, but you can do all the things mentioned in the Start button section later in this chapter.)

The Start button is only one of the taskbar's tricks; some others are listed in Figure 10-7.

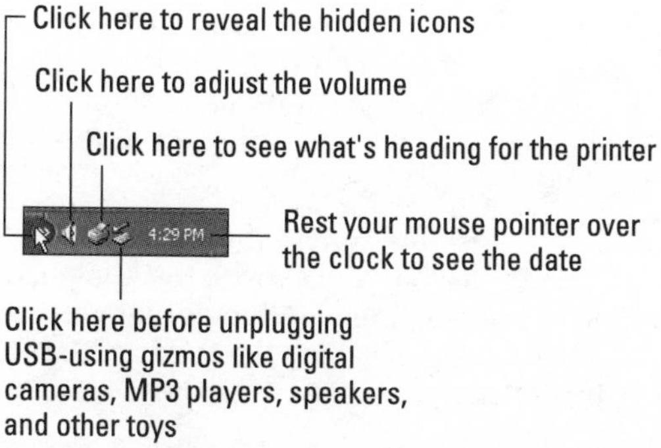

Figure 10-7:
Clicking or double-clicking these areas of the taskbar performs these tasks.

┌─ Click here to reveal the hidden icons

Click here to adjust the volume

Click here to see what's heading for the printer

Rest your mouse pointer over the clock to see the date

Click here before unplugging USB-using gizmos like digital cameras, MP3 players, speakers, and other toys

Hold the mouse pointer over the clock, and Windows XP shows the current day and date. Or if you want to change the time or date, a double-click on the clock summons the Windows XP time/date change program.

Sometimes the taskbar hides things. Click the little double arrows near the clock (refer to Figure 10-7), and a few more icons might slide out. (Check out the "Customizing the taskbar" section for tips and tricks affecting these icons.)

Click the little speaker to adjust the sound card's volume via a sliding control, as shown in Figure 10-8. Or double-click the little speaker to bring up a mixing panel. Mixers let you adjust separate volume levels for your microphone, line inputs, CD and DVD players, and other features. (No speaker icon? Choose Control Panel from the Start menu, open the Sounds and Audio Devices icon, and click in the box marked Place Volume Icon in the Taskbar.)

Figure 10-8:
Clicking
the little
speaker lets
you adjust
the sound
card's
volume.

✔ Other icons often appear next to the clock, depending on what Windows XP is up to. If you're printing, for example, a little printer icon appears there. Laptops often show a battery power-level gauge. As with all the other icons down there, if you double-click the printer or battery gauge, Windows XP brings up information about the printer's or battery's status.

✔ After joining the Internet and activating Windows XP, you can let somebody else play mechanic. Click the icon shown in the margin when it appears next to the clock. Windows XP automatically bellies up to a special Microsoft Web site, analyzes itself, and installs any updated software that may help it run better.

✔ Want to minimize all your desktop's open windows in a hurry? Right-click on a blank part of the taskbar and choose the Minimize All Windows option from the pop-up menu. All the programs keep running, but they're now minimized to icons along the taskbar. To bring them back to the screen, just click their names from the taskbar.

✔ For an even faster way to minimize all your desktop's open windows, click a little icon down by the Start button. As you can see in Figure 10-6 and in the margin, it's a square with blue-tipped corners, a white rectangle in the center, and a little pencil thing resting on top of it all.

✔ To organize your open windows, right-click on a blank part of the taskbar and choose one of the tile commands. Windows XP scoops up all your open windows and lays them back down in neat, orderly squares. (I cover tiling in more detail in Chapter 7.)

Customizing the taskbar

Windows XP brings a whirlwind of new options for the lowly taskbar, letting you play with it in more ways than a strand of spaghetti and a fork. Right-click on a blank part of the taskbar, and a menu appears, as shown in Figure 10-9.

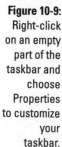

Figure 10-9: Right-click on an empty part of the taskbar and choose Properties to customize your taskbar.

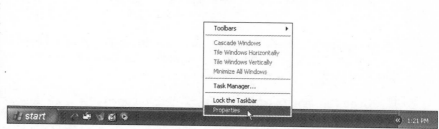

Choose the Properties option, and a new window pops up, as shown in Figure 10-10.

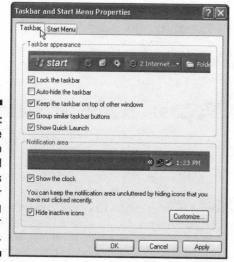

Figure 10-10: Click the Taskbar tab to see all the options available for customizing your taskbar.

Here's what those options mean, and my recommendation for them. (You might need to click the Lock the Taskbar check box to remove its check mark before some of these options will work.)

Lock the Taskbar: Click in this box, and Windows XP "locks" the taskbar in place. You can't drag it to one edge of the window, drag it up to make it bigger, nor drag it down beneath the edge of the screen. Rathbone recommendation: Check this box, but only after you're sure the taskbar is set up the way you like.

Auto-Hide the Taskbar: Some people think the taskbar gets in the way. So, they drag it down below the bottom of the screen. (Try it.) Clicking in this box makes the taskbar automatically hide itself below the screen's bottom. Point the mouse at the screen's bottom, and the taskbar rises automatically from its grave. Rathbone recommendation: Uncheck.

Keep the Taskbar on Top of Other Windows: This option keeps the taskbar always visible, covering up any windows that may be low on the screen. Rathbone recommendation: Check.

Group Similar Taskbar Buttons: When you open lots of windows and programs, the taskbar gets crowded. Windows accommodates the crowd by shrinking the buttons. Unfortunately, that means you can't read the button's names. This option groups similar windows under one button. When things get crowded, Windows groups all your Internet Explorer windows under one Internet Explorer button on the taskbar, for instance, as shown in Figure 10-11.

Figure 10-11:
Choose Group Similar Taskbar Buttons to save space on your taskbar by stacking similar buttons.

Show Quick Launch: Sharp-eyed readers might have noticed tiny icons in some of this book's figures that live next to the taskbar's Start button. What gives? That's the Quick Launch toolbar, and you turn it on by clicking in this box. Try it — the Quick Launch toolbar places itty-bitty icons for Internet Explorer and Media Player next to the Start button for easy access. Just drag program icons to the Quick Launch bar to add them to it. (Drag the icons off to remove them.) Don't like Quick Launch? Then remove it by removing the check mark from this box.

Show the Clock: You want to know when it's time to leave work, don't you? Rathbone recommendation: Check.

Hide Inactive Icons: A new one for Windows XP, this option lets you hide those little icons — like the volume control, printer button, RealPlayer, the desktop cleanup program, and other doodies — that begin hanging out by your clock. Click the Customize button to choose which icons should show up, which should hide, and which should appear only when they're being used. Rathbone recommendation: Click the Customize button and choose Restore Defaults to hide everything except the sound volume. Choose Always Show for that one.

Feel free to experiment with the taskbar, changing its size and position until it looks right for you. It won't break. After you set it up just the way you want, click the Lock the Taskbar box described earlier in this list.

Oh, no! The taskbar looks really weird now!

Your taskbar won't always resemble the familiar entity shown in Figure 10-9 or 10-11. Microsoft lets you customize the taskbar even further, often beyond the point of recognition. To experience this weirdness — or to turn it off, if it's happened to you — right-click on a blank area of the taskbar and click the Toolbars option. A menu pops up, offering several options, each described in the following list:

✔ **Address:** Choose this option, and your taskbar contains a place for quickly typing in Web sites. It's big and bulky, though, so it's rarely used.

✔ **Links:** This option fills the taskbar with links to Internet Web pages. (They're the same ones listed in the Links area of Internet Explorer's Favorites menu. Ho hum.)

✔ **Desktop:** A weird one, this option places the icons from your desktop onto your taskbar.

✔ **Quick Launch:** I like this one. It keeps little icons for these frequently used programs next to your Start button: Internet Explorer, Outlook Express, Media Player, and the

"shrink everything from the desktop" icon. To add your other favorite programs, just drag and drop them onto the Quick Launch toolbar.

✔ **New Toolbar:** This option lets you place any folder's contents onto your taskbar.

Most people don't choose any of these options except Quick Launch, so feel free to do the same unless you like to fiddle with your computer's settings.

Also, you can drag any of these toolbars off the taskbar and onto the desktop. In fact, it's quite distracting if you accidentally drag the Quick Launch toolbar off the taskbar. To replace Quick Launch, right-click on the taskbar, choose Toolbars, and choose Quick Launch. Another replacement Quick Launch appears on the taskbar, in the right place. Close the Quick Launch window that you accidentally dragged onto the desktop, and all is well. (To keep mistakes like these from happening, choose the Lock the Taskbar option described in the "Customizing the taskbar" section.)

Controlling the Printer

Many of the Windows XP features work in the background. You know that they're there *only* when something is wrong and weird messages start flying around. The Windows XP print program is one of those programs.

When you choose the Print command in a program, you may see the little Windows XP printer icon appear at the bottom-right corner of your screen. (Depending on how your computer's set up, you might have to click the little arrows by the clock to see the printer icon.)

Your printer can print only one thing at a time. If you try to print a second memo before the first one is finished, Windows XP jumps in to help. It intercepts all the requests and lines them up in order, just like a harried diner cook.

To check up on what is being sent to the printer, double-click the taskbar's little printer icon, and you see the print program in all its glory: The program lists each of your documents as they wait for their turn at the printer.

- ✔ When the printer is through printing one file, it automatically moves to the second file in the lineup.

- ✔ Changing the order of the files as they're about to be printed is easy. If you have three jobs waiting and you need the third one in a hurry, just drag and drop it so that it's behind the first job. Poof! Windows will print that one next. (The printing order is called a *queue,* pronounced "Q.")

- ✔ To cancel a print job, right-click on the filename you don't like and then choose Cancel Printing from the menu that pops up.

- ✔ If the boss walks by the printer while you're printing your party flier, choose Document from the menu and select Pause Printing from the menu that drops down. The printer stops. After the boss is out of sight, click Pause Printing again to continue.

- ✔ If you're on a network (shudder), you may not be able to change the order in which files are being printed. You may not even be able to pause a file.

- ✔ If your printer is not hooked up, Windows XP will probably try to send your file to the printer anyway. When it doesn't get a response, it sends you a message that your printer isn't ready. Plug the printer in, turn it on, and try again. Or hit Chapter 14 for more printer troubleshooting tips.

The Start Button's Reason to Live

The Start button lives on your taskbar, and it's always ready for action. By using the Start button, you can start programs, adjust the Windows XP settings, find help for sticky situations, or, thankfully, shut down Windows XP and get away from the computer for a while.

The little Start button is so eager to please, in fact, that it starts shooting out menus full of options as soon as you click it. Just click the button once, and the first layer of menus pops out, neatly labeled in Figure 10-12.

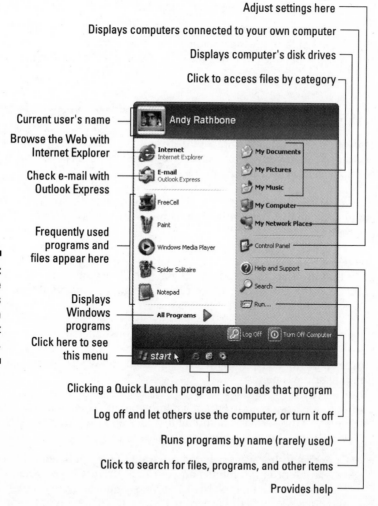

Adjust settings here

Displays computers connected to your own computer

Displays computer's disk drives

Click to access files by category

Current user's name

Browse the Web with Internet Explorer

Check e-mail with Outlook Express

Frequently used programs and files appear here

Figure 10-12: Click the taskbar's Start button to see a list of options.

Displays Windows programs

Click here to see this menu

Clicking a Quick Launch program icon loads that program

Log off and let others use the computer, or turn it off

Runs programs by name (rarely used)

Click to search for files, programs, and other items

Provides help

✔ The Start menu changes as you add programs to your computer. That change means that the Start menu on your friend's computer probably offers slightly different programs than the Start menu on your own computer.

✔ Save your files in your My Documents folder. Save your photos in your My Pictures folder. And save your music in your My Music folder. You can easily access each folder from the Start menu. And each folder is specially designed for its contents. The My Pictures folder automatically shows little thumbnails of all your photos, for instance. By keeping your files organized, you'll have a better chance of finding them again.

✔ See the little arrow by the words All Programs near the bottom left of the Start menu? Click the arrow, and another menu squirts out, listing more programs stored inside your computer.

✔ Windows graciously places your most frequently used programs along the left side of the Start menu. The Start menu in earlier versions of Windows displayed icons for the last ten *documents* you accessed.

Starting a program from the Start button

This one's easy. Click the Start button, and the Start menu pops out of the button's head. If you see an icon for your desired program or file, click it, and Windows loads the program or file.

If your program isn't listed, though, click the words All Programs. Yet another menu pops up, this one listing the names of programs or folders full of programs.

If you see your program listed there, click the name. Wham! Windows XP kicks that program to the screen. If you don't see your program listed, try pointing at the tiny folders listed on the menu. New menus fly out of those folders, listing even more programs.

When you finally spot your program's name, just click it. In fact, you don't have to click until you see the program's name: The Start button opens and closes all the menus automatically, depending on where the mouse arrow is pointing at the time.

✔ Still don't see your program listed by name? Then head for Chapter 7 and find the section on finding lost files and folders. You can tell Windows XP to find your program for you.

✔ There's another way to load a program that's not listed — if you know where the program's living on your hard drive. Choose Run from the Start button menu, type the program's name, and press Enter. If Windows XP finds the program, it runs it. If it can't find the program, though, click the Browse button. Yet another dialog box appears, and this time it lists programs by name. Pick your way through the dialog box until you see your program; then double-click its name and click the OK button to load it.

✔ If you don't know how to pick your way through this particular dialog box, head to the section of Chapter 5 on opening a file. (This particular dialog box rears its head every time you load or save a file or open a program.)

Adding a program's icon to the Start menu

The Windows XP Start button works great — until you're hankering for something that's not listed on its menu. How do you add a favorite program's icon to the Start menu? Windows XP makes it easier than ever.

When you install a program, as described in Chapter 14, the program almost always adds itself to the Start menu automatically. Then it announces its presence to you and to all the other users of the computer, as shown in Figure 10-13.

Figure 10-13:
Most newly installed programs add themselves to the Start menu's All Programs area and announce their presence.

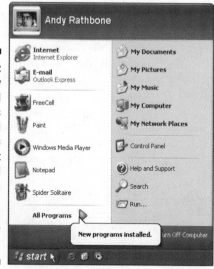

To see the newly installed program, click the words All Programs (located right above the Start button on the Start menu), and a huge menu of additional programs appears. See how the words *Button Studio* are highlighted in Figure 10-14? That's the newly installed program, so Windows XP highlights it and usually places it in alphabetical order on the menu.

Figure 10-14: Click the words All Programs to see the newly installed program — Button Studio, in this case — which appears highlighted and in alphabetical order on the menu.

- ✔ There's another way to add a program to the Start menu. Windows XP adds icons for your five most-frequently used programs to the Start menu's left column. If you come across an icon or shortcut for a program that you'd like to appear there, right-click on the icon. Choose Pin to Start Menu from the menu that appears, and Windows places that icon in the left column of your Start menu.

- ✔ To get rid of unwanted icons from the Start menu's left column, right-click on the icons and choose Remove from This List; they disappear. Remember, though, the icons on the Start menu are just shortcuts. Removing the icon from the list doesn't remove the program from your computer.

- ✔ Here's a dirty little secret: The Start menu isn't really anything special. It's simply one of many folders on your hard drive. In fact, your entire desktop is just a folder, too. Chapter 11 shows how to explore the folders living on your hard drive, so don't be surprised when you discover folders named Desktop and Start Menu on your C drive.

Making Windows start programs automatically

Many people sit down at a computer, turn it on, and go through the same mechanical process of loading their oft-used programs. Believe it or not, Windows XP can automate this computerized task.

The solution is the StartUp folder, found lurking in the Start button's All Programs area. When Windows XP wakes up, it peeks inside that StartUp folder. If it finds a shortcut lurking inside, it grabs that shortcut's program and tosses it onto the screen.

Here's how to determine which programs wake up along with Windows XP and which ones get to sleep in a little:

1. **Right-click on the Start button and choose the Open option.**

   The My Computer program comes to the screen, displaying a Programs folder.

2. **Double-click the folder named Programs.**

   You see shortcuts and folders for most of the programs currently listed in your Start button's All Programs area.

3. **Double-click the folder named StartUp to open it onto your screen.**

4. **Using your right mouse button, drag and drop any programs or files you want to start automatically into the StartUp window.**

   If Windows asks, tell it to turn those programs or files into shortcuts. Then, whenever you start Windows XP from scratch, those programs or files load up right along with it.

   ✔ The items in the StartUp area load themselves only when you log onto Windows after logging off. If you've clicked the Switch Users button instead of the Log Off button, Windows considers you still at work. It launches the StartUp items only after you've logged off and Windows has saved your settings.

   ✔ Do you find yourself using the StartUp area a lot? Make a shortcut that points straight toward it and leave the shortcut on your desktop. Drag and drop a program into the StartUp shortcut, and that program's shortcut will appear in the StartUp area, ready to load itself whenever your computer starts up.

The Start Menu's Free Programs

Windows XP, the fanciest version of Windows yet, comes with oodles of free programs. This makes customers happy and makes the Justice Department members flap their long black robes.

Free software is usually as nice as a free lunch. The Windows problem lies with its menu. Sure, some of its freebie programs control important parts of your computer. But more than 50 additional programs merely buff and polish the details. This extraordinarily long section explains which freebie programs are worthwhile and which ones you can safely ignore.

The Start menu's first-tier programs

These items appear on the Start menu whenever you click the Start button. You'll be using them over and over again, so if you're bored already, just read this part.

 Internet Explorer: Click this button when you're ready to explore the Internet. (I cover Web browsing, e-mail, and other Internet activities in Chapter 12.)

 Outlook Express: This brings up Microsoft's built-in e-mail program. (I also cover it in Chapter 12.)

 My Documents: Always store your documents in this folder so you'll know where to find them later.

 My Pictures: Keep your digital pictures in this folder. Each picture's icon is a tiny thumbnail image of its picture.

 My Music: Store your digital music in here so Media Player can find it more easily.

 My Computer: Open this to see every storage area inside your computer, including your floppy drive, hard disks, CD-ROM drives, digital cameras, and folders shared with other users.

 My Network Places: Is your computer connected to other computers on a network? Click here to see the other computers or folders you're allowed to access.

 Control Panel: Click here to adjust your computer's oodles of confusing settings, all described in Chapter 14.

 Help and Support: Befuddled? Click here for an answer. (Chapter 17 explains the confusing Windows Help system.)

 Search: Missing a file? Click here to find it. (Chapter 7 explains the Windows Search system.)

 Run: Rarely used, this launches a program if you type in its name and location.

 Log Off: Click here either to let somebody else use the computer quickly, or to save your work and let the computer stand idle for others to use it.

 Turn Off Computer: Click this button to restart the computer, turn it off completely, or let it *Standby* — the computer saves everybody's work and "goes to sleep" to save power. (Push the computer's On/Off switch to bring it back to life.)

The Start menu's All Programs area

The Start menu lists quite a few options, but it hides a huge batch of freebie programs in the All Programs area. Open the Start menu, click All Programs near the menu's bottom, and you'll find these freebies on the menu.

 Windows Catalog: Microsoft never has enough of your money. After you've bought Windows, a click here takes to you an Internet page with many more Microsoft products to peruse.

 Windows Update: Microsoft is never happy with Windows. So when it finds a way to make it better — or to keep evil people from breaking into it — it automatically sends a software *patch* to fix it. Click here to grab the fix or set up Windows to grab the fixes automatically.

 Activate Windows: Oh, the horror! When you buy a copy of Windows XP, Microsoft gives you 30 days to activate it. When you click this icon, Windows XP combines its built-in serial number with a "snapshot" of your computer's hardware. Then it dials Microsoft and registers your software with your computer.

 From the moment the software's registered, your copy of Windows XP will work only on the computer it's installed on; it won't work on any other computer. And if you don't activate Windows XP within 30 days, it stops working. Welcome to Windows!

Accessories

By far, the bulk of the Windows XP freebie programs are dumped under the generic menu label *Accessories.* Here are programs that make Windows XP easier to see and hear; they let your computer talk to other computers and the Internet, and they entertain you during slow days. Finally, they let you fiddle with Windows' innards during even slower days.

This section tackles the programs found on the Accessories menu, accessed through the Start button's All Programs button.

Accessibility

Accessibility Wizard creates a customized, easy-to-read version of Windows. It lets you choose your ideal size for fonts, menus, icons, and window borders, making them easier to click. The wizard enables sounds to accompany certain on-screen actions if you're having difficulty seeing the screen.

Magnifier enlarges the mouse pointer's current location, making small buttons and boxes easier to spot.

Narrator reads your on-screen menus, albeit not very audibly.

The **On-Screen Keyboard** draws a keyboard right onto the desktop. Point and click at the letters with the mouse, and you'll never have to type. (Works well for people with broken keyboards.)

Utility Manager helps people with low vision quickly set up computers by using several of the Accessibility options at once.

Communications

Much of this stuff applies to the tech-heads, so don't spend too much time here.

HyperTerminal is a throwback to the old days of telecomputing. Ignore this relic that lets two computers talk over the phone lines.

Network Connections provides techie information about how fast your networked computers send information back and forth. It also lets you connect to networks or other computers across the phone lines or by using a single cable. (It replaces the older Direct Cable Connection option.)

Network Setup Wizard shows how to link two or more computers to share information or even a single modem or printer. It's covered in Chapter 9.

New Connection Wizard walks you through connecting your computer with your Internet service provider (ISP) so you can Web surf like the best of them. It's covered in Chapter 12.

Remote Desktop Connection works like a mini-network, but it lets you run programs on another computer.

Entertainment

Windows XP provides the controls for a complete entertainment center, including your computer's CD player, DVD player, and TV card. Pick up a modem and a bag of microwave popcorn, and a modern young couple's plans are set for the evening. Here's the rundown on the Windows XP stereo cabinet of entertainment goodies.

Sound Recorder merely records up to 60 seconds of sound. Yawn. Most of the time, it's meant to record short messages for embedding into documents or attaching to e-mail. Chances are, you'll never use it.

Volume Control brings up a mixing panel that controls all your sound sources. A CD Player shows up here, as well as general sound (WAV), music (MIDI), or peripherals, such as TV cards or video capture cards (Line-in). Unless you're recording sounds, don't bother with it. Instead, control the volume by clicking the little speaker in the corner of your taskbar. (No little speaker? Then put it there with the Control Panel, as described in Chapter 14.) When the volume control pops up, just slide it up or down to change your volume.

Windows Media Player is hip, it's happening, and it's huge. It can fill your entire screen with '60s-era pulsating lights while playing your favorite tunes from your CDs or MP3 files. Unfortunately, Media Player can't make MP3 files from your CDs, instead opting for Microsoft's competing *WMA* format. It grabs sound and video from the Internet, plays your CDs, and categorizes your sound and video, from CDs to movie trailers to radio station presets to favorite playlists. It's all covered in Chapter 13.

Games

Nothing new here if you've been using Windows Me. Here you find FreeCell, Hearts, Minesweeper, two solitaire games, and some classics like backgammon and checkers for playing over the Internet. Be sure to check out Pinball, though, if you can tear yourself away from the venerable FreeCell.

System Tools

Windows XP comes with several technical programs designed to make the nerd feel at home. Here's a description of what they do so you know which ones to avoid.

Activate Windows does just what is described earlier in this section. You must activate your version of Windows within 30 days, or it stops working. And after it's activated, that copy won't work on any other computer.

Character Map lets you add weird foreign characters, such as *à*, *£*, or even *ß*, into your document. Clicking here brings up a list of foreign characters and symbols, all in your current font. Double-click the character you're after and then click the spot in your document where you'd like that character to appear. Choose Paste from the document's Edit menu, and the new character appears.

Disk Cleanup helps out when you're running out of storage space on your computer. Like the backseat of a car, Windows accumulates junk: files temporarily grabbed from the Internet, deleted files from the Recycle Bin, and other space-wasters. Disk Cleanup automatically gathers these programs and lets you delete them.

Disk Defragmenter organizes your hard drive so it runs faster. See, when a computer reads and writes files to and from a hard drive, it's working like a liquor store stock clerk after a Labor Day weekend. It has to reorganize the store, moving all the misplaced beer cans out of the wine aisles. The same disorganization happens with computer files. When the computer moves files around, it tends to break the files into chunks and spread them across your hard drive. The computer can still find all the pieces, but relocating them takes more time. Disk Defragmenter reorganizes the hard drive, making sure that all the files' pieces are next to each other for quick and easy grabbing.

Files and Settings Transfer Wizard helps out when you finally upgrade to a new computer. It examines your program's settings on your old computer and lets you choose which files you'd like to transfer. The wizard can grab information from older versions of Windows, as well. (The program works fastest and easiest with network cards, second best with a cable-to-cable transfer, third-best by copying information to a CD, and agonizingly slowly with a floppy disk.)

Scheduled Tasks lets Windows XP run programs when you're not around to supervise, whether you're sleeping at night or away from the home computer during the day. The program plans the schedule of your computer's routine, telling it which programs to run, when, and for how long.

System Information, a fix-it tool for the mechanics, compiles vast technical charts about your computer's innards. Chances are, you won't be messing with it.

System Restore is probably the most important item here, so the nearby "System Restore restores your faith in Windows" sidebar covers it in detail.

Address Book

Address Book is used by Outlook Express to send and receive your e-mail. If you ever move up to its more powerful parent program, Outlook, you can move over all your address information by using the Export command from the File menu.

Calculator

Calculator is, well, a calculator. It looks simple enough, and it really is — unless you mistakenly set it for Scientific mode and see some nightmarish logarithmic stuff. To bring the calculator back to normal, choose Standard from the View menu.

For an extra measure of handiness, choose Copy from the File menu. Then click in the window where you want the answer to appear and choose Paste from that window's File menu. That's much easier than retyping a number like 2.449489742783. *Hint:* If the mouse action is too slow, press your keyboard's Num Lock key and punch in numbers with the numeric keypad.

Command Prompt

This remnant lets old-time computer users boss their computers around by typing a command into an ugly text window. Don't bother.

Notepad

Windows comes with two word processors, WordPad and Notepad. WordPad is for the letters you're sprucing up for other people to see. Notepad is for stuff you're going to keep for yourself. It's for typing quick stuff and saving it on the fly.

Unfortunately, Notepad tosses you into instant confusion: All the sentences head right off the edge of the window. To turn those single-line, runaway sentences into normal paragraphs, choose Word Wrap from the Format menu. (After you change this option the first time, strangely enough, Windows XP remembers your preference and uses it each time you use Notepad in the future.)

Notepad doesn't print exactly what you see on-screen. Instead, it prints according to the margins you set in Page Setup from the Format menu. This quirk can lead to unpredictable results.

Paint

Paint creates rudimentary pictures and graphics to stick into other programs. It comes with more than an electronic paintbrush: It has a can of spray paint for that *airbrushed* look, several pencils of different widths, a paint roller for gobbing on a bunch of paint, and an eraser for when things get out of hand.

With such limited capabilities, Paint's better for quick touch-ups than ground-zero creations. Use the View menu's Zoom command and the Airbrush tool to remove spinach caught on somebody's teeth in a digital photo, for instance.

You can copy drawings and pictures from Paint and paste them into just about any other Windows XP program. Paint enables you to add text and numbers to graphics, so you can add street names to maps copied from the Internet, put labels inside drawings, or add the vintage year to your wine labels.

Paint will open and save files in BMP, JPG, GIF, and TIF formats.

Program Compatibility Wizard

If a program seems reluctant to run on Windows XP, the Program Compatibility Wizard does a little coaxing. Fire up the wizard and select the problematic program. The wizard then tricks the program into thinking it's running on an older version of Windows — a version that it's more familiar with.

Synchronize

Some people like to place a Web page on their desktops as a background. The Synchronize option sets up a timetable for how often Windows should automatically update that Web page — once a day, maximum.

(To add a Web page as a background, right-click on your desktop, choose Properties, click the Desktop tab, and choose Customize Desktop. Then click the Web tab and click the New button to add as many Web pages as you want.)

Tour Windows XP

New Windows users might benefit from taking the Windows XP tour — a multimedia extravaganza showing how to use the basic Windows features.

System Restore restores your faith in Windows

When your computer's running well — and you wish it would *always* work that well — open System Restore and click next to the Create a Restore Point option. Windows examines itself and takes a snapshot of its settings. Then, if something awful happens a few days later, you have an out: Head back to the System Restore area and choose Restore My Computer to an Earlier Time. Choose a restore point you saved back when everything was just ducky, and, after Windows restores your pre-disaster settings, your computer will perform swimmingly.

There are a few problems with System Restore, as with anything. When System Restore brings back your earlier, faithful Windows setup, it will most likely leave out any of the programs you've installed since then. You have to reinstall them. Because Windows automatically creates a restore point every day, don't choose a spot further back in time than necessary.

System Restore won't touch any files you've stored in the My Documents folder. It swears it won't touch any of your other data files, either. But to be on the safe side, keep your most favored data in the My Documents folder.

If you use System Restore, use it often. Use it both before and after installing any new program, for instance, or when making any major tweaks to your system settings. That way, System Restore can bring up a reasonably current version of your work.

If you goof and restore something that made your computer function worse than ever, undo the restoration. Call up System Restore and choose Undo My Last Restoration. In fact, don't be afraid to try several restore points when something goes wrong. You can always undo them and try a different one.

Finally, System Restore consumes 12 percent of your hard drive space. To shrink or enlarge that chunk, right-click on My Computer from the Start button, choose Properties, and use the sliding control on the System Restore tab.

Windows Explorer

Windows Explorer provides views of files stored on your computer and lets you copy them from one place to another. I cover this in Chapter 11.

Windows Movie Maker

For years, Windows could only edit words. Eventually, it could edit sounds. Now, Windows XP jumps into the millennium with a program to edit movies from video cameras. It lets you arrange your clips any way you want and add soundtracks or voiceovers. It's cool, it's catchy, it's too complicated to cover in this book, and it requires a special camcorder and a special video camera card. (Check out *Windows Movie Maker For Dummies,* written by Keith Underdahl and published by Hungry Minds, Inc.)

WordPad

Although its icon is fancy, WordPad isn't quite as fancy as some of the more expensive word processors on the market. You can't create tables or multiple columns, like the ones in newspapers or newsletters, nor can you double-space your reports. Ferget the spell checker, too.

But WordPad's great for quick letters, simple reports, and other basic stuff. You can change the fonts around to get reasonably fancy, too. That's because WordPad can handle Windows *TrueType fonts* — that font technology that shapes how characters appear on-screen. You can create an elegant document by using some fancy TrueType fonts and mail it on a disk to somebody else. That person can view your letter in WordPad, and it looks the same as when you created it.

If you've just ditched your typewriter for Windows, remember this: On an electric typewriter, you have to press the Return key at the end of each line or else you start typing off the edge of the paper. Computers avoid that. They automatically drop down a line and continue the sentence. (Hip computer nerds call this phenomenon *word wrap.*)

StartUp

The StartUp folder lists programs that start automatically when Windows XP loads itself for a day's work. It's covered earlier in this chapter, in the section called "Making Windows start programs automatically."

Internet Explorer

Yep, clicking here loads Internet Explorer. But the Start menu's big blue "e" marked *Internet* loads Internet Explorer, too, and it's easier to aim for. Internet Explorer is covered in Chapter 12.

MSN Explorer

Don't have access to the Internet yet? Clicking here brings up Microsoft's own clone of America Online. It collects a monthly fee, connects you to the Internet, and lets you send e-mail. Some love its all-in-one interface. Others say it's nothing new. If you're curious, sign up for a free trial and check it out.

Outlook Express

This icon appears near the Start menu, as well as here. Chapter 12 explains how to set it up.

Remote Assistance

This new option supposedly lets techies log onto your computer and fix it — without coming to your home or office. Don't use it unless you completely trust the other person.

Windows Media Player

Microsoft puts this one in here twice. The Entertainment section holds the description, because that's the first place Microsoft lists it on the menu. See Chapter 13 for more information.

Windows Messenger

Because this icon appears on your taskbar, as well, it's covered in the "What's the MSN Messenger Service?" sidebar, earlier in this chapter. (It lets you send quickie messages to other people signed up for the service.)

My Version of Windows XP Doesn't Have the Right Freebie Programs!

Depending on the buttons you punched when you installed Windows XP, the program installed different varieties of its freebie programs onto your hard drive. Many people won't see all the Start menu programs mentioned in this chapter, for instance. If you feel left out and want some of these freebie programs mentioned earlier, follow these steps:

1. **Double-click the Control Panel's Add or Remove Programs icon.**

   You can load the Control Panel by clicking its Start menu icon.

2. **Click the Add/Remove Windows Components icon.**

   It's the third icon in the left column. The Windows Components Wizard appears, showing the various freebie programs included with Windows XP, as well as the amount of space they need to elbow onto your computer's hard drive.

3. **Click in the little box by the programs or accessories you want to add.**

   Some boxes already have check marks. That means that program or accessory is already installed. Others have gray check marks in the box. That means that some programs in that particular category aren't installed.

   If your Accessories and Utilities area is *grayed out,* for example, not all of your Accessories are installed. Click Accessories and Utilities and click the Details button.

   Windows XP lists the items available in that category so that you can select the ones you want. Again, click the accessory you want and click the Details button again, if it's available.

   Keep selecting items and click Details until you find the program you want to add. Find it? Then click in its empty box to add it.

   (You remove Windows XP accessories the same way, but this time *remove* the check mark from the box next to their names.)

   Click OK until you return to the Windows Components Wizard's opening window.

4. **Click the Next button.**

   Windows XP looks over your check marks to see which, if any, programs should be installed or removed.

5. **Click OK and insert your Windows XP CD if asked.**

   If you've chosen to install anything, Windows XP sometimes copies the necessary files from your CD onto your hard drive. Other times, it copies them from your hard drive.

   A black check mark means that you've already selected all the available programs in that program category. A gray check mark means you've grabbed only some of them. Empty check boxes mean that you aren't using any of those programs.

Chapter 11

That Scary My Computer Program

In This Chapter

▶ Finding out why the My Computer program seems so scary

▶ Looking at folders

▶ Loading a program or file

▶ Deleting and undeleting files, folders, and icons

▶ Copying and moving files, folders, and icons

▶ Copying to a disk

▶ Getting information about files, folders, and icons

▶ Finding files that aren't shown

▶ Working with files, folders, and icons on a network

▶ Formatting new floppy disks

*T*he My Computer program is where people wake up from the easy-to-use computing dream, clutching a pillow in horror. These people bought a computer to simplify their work — to banish that awful filing cabinet with squeaky drawers.

But click the little My Computer icon from the Start menu, and that filing cabinet reappears. Folders, bunches of them, appear. And where did that file go? Unless you understand the basics behind the My Computer program, you might not be able to find your information very easily.

This chapter explains how to use the My Computer program, and, along the way, it dishes out a big enough dose of Windows file management for you to get your work done. Here, you find out the wacky Windows way to create folders, put files inside, and move everything around with a mere mouse.

Why Is the My Computer Program So Frightening?

Windows needs a place to store your programs and files. So, it borrowed the file cabinet metaphor, translated it into light and airy Windows icons, and called it the *My Computer* program. My Computer shows the files and storage areas inside your computer, allowing you to copy or move them, rename them, or delete them.

 Everybody organizes his or her computer differently. Some people don't organize their computers at all. To see how your computer has been organizing your files, click the Start menu and click My Computer (the icon shown in the margin). Your My Computer window probably looks a little different from the one shown in Figure 11-1.

The My Computer program is a big panel of buttons — sort of an extension of your desktop. Here's a brief rundown on what those big icons along My Computer's right side mean. You'll find more detailed explanations throughout this chapter.

Figure 11-1:
The My Computer window displays the files and storage areas inside your computer, allowing you to copy, rename, move, or delete them.

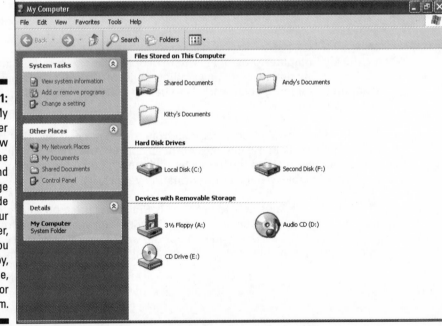

How come I have *two* Music and Pictures folders?

Don't be confused by this bit of confusion. When any users log onto the computer, no matter what type of account they own, they'll find a My Documents folder that contains a My Music and a My Pictures folder. They also find a Shared Documents folder that contains a Shared Music and a Shared Pictures folder. What's the difference? Well, the difference can be embarrassing if you don't understand it.

As described in Chapter 9, Windows XP lets several people share a single computer. When people log onto the computer, Windows XP acts as if they're all using a different computer — each user sees his or her own separate My Documents file, which contains only his or her own files.

However, each user *also* sees a Shared Documents folder inside the My Computer area.

Although everybody has his or her own separate My Documents folder, the Shared Documents folder is the *same folder* for every computer user. If Jeffrey has some great music he wants to share with everybody, he doesn't keep it in his My Music folder. Instead, he stores it in the Shared Documents folder's Shared Music folder. That way he — and everybody else on that computer — can hear the tunes.

To remember this distinction more easily, any folder that has the word *My* in front of its title is a *personal, private* folder. Any folder with the word *Shared* in front of its title can be used by *anybody* on the computer.

And any folder with a little hand beneath its icon can be used by anybody on a computer's network, as described in Chapter 9. Whew!

 Files Stored on This Computer: Windows XP lets many people use the same computer, and everybody's files stay private. However, sometimes everybody wants to share information — letters from relatives, for instance. That's where the Shared Documents folder (shown in the margin) comes in.

The Shared Documents folder contains files and folders accessible to everybody that uses the computer. To share things with other users of your computer, call up My Computer and store the information inside My Computer's Shared Documents folder. (Double-clicking any folder shows its contents.)

Two additional folders live inside the Shared Documents folder: Shared Music and Shared Pictures. Everybody using the computer may also access music and pictures stored in here.

 If you don't want other users to share your information, keep it out of the Shared Documents folder. Instead, store the information in your My Documents folder, accessible from the Start menu. (See the Other Places area listed along My Computer's left side, as shown in Figure 11-1? You can also open your My Documents folder from there by clicking its name.)

Notice two other folders in Figure 11-1, one belonging to Guest and the other to Tina? You see those folders because you're viewing the My Computer area of an administrator's account. As explained in Chapter 9, the administrator can peek inside the files of any other user. So, Figure 11-1 shows the My Documents folders of two other users, Tina and the Guest account. Those folders are called Tina's Documents and Guest's Documents, respectively.

Hard Disk Drives: This one's not too difficult. It lists the hard drives installed on your computer. Double-clicking a folder here shows what's inside, but you rarely find much useful information. In fact, Windows often simply tells you to back off and look for programs on your Start menu, instead. Unlike files and folders, hard drives can't be moved to different areas.

Devices with Removable Storage: This area shows stuff you take in and out of your computer: floppy drives, CD-ROM drives, Iomega Jaz drives, and even MP3 players, if they're Windows XP compatible, like the HipZip's PocketZip player shown in Figure 11-1. (I cover MP3 players in Chapter 13.)

Scanners and Cameras: Digital cameras and scanners often appear down here, depending on their make and model.

Unlike files and folders, Hard Disk Drives, Devices with Removable Storage, and Scanners and Cameras can't be moved to different areas. They're stuck where they live in the My Computer area. To make them more accessible, you can place *shortcuts* to them on your desktop or any other convenient spot, as explained in Chapter 10.

My Computer also includes several boxes along its left side. They serve mainly as shortcuts — pointers — that take you to other areas on your computer. The boxes change according to what you're viewing in My Computer. These choices appear when you first open My Computer, and here's what they mean.

System Tasks: All three items listed here deal with your computer's innards, and each takes you to Windows XP's Control Panel or part of it. Choose any of these to see technical information about your computer; add new programs or remove previously installed ones; or to simply open the Control Panel for you to tweak a plethora of settings.

Other Places: Three of these items, My Network Places, My Documents, and Control Panel, are simply shortcuts to items that appear on your computer's Start menu. I cover My Network Places in Chapter 9, My Documents appears later in this chapter, and the Control Panel's covered in Chapter 14.

I dunno why there's a shortcut to the Shared Documents folder here, because the Shared Documents folder already appears a few inches to the right, as you can see in Figure 11-1.

Details: Finally, something interesting. Click almost any icon in My Computer, and the Details window automatically displays information about that object: the date a file was created, for instance, or how much space it consumes.

Getting the Lowdown on Folders

This stuff is really boring, but if you don't read it, you'll be just as lost as your files.

A *folder* is a storage area on a disk, just like a real folder in a file cabinet. Windows XP divides your computer's hard drives into many folders to separate your many projects. You can work with a spreadsheet, for example, without having all the word-processing files get in the way. Or you can keep all your music in your My Music folder, and your pictures in your My Pictures folder.

Any type of disk can have folders, but hard drives need folders the most because they need a way to organize their thousands of files. By dividing a hard drive into little folder compartments, you can more easily see where everything sits.

Windows' My Computer program lets you probe into different folders and peek at the files you've stuffed inside each one. It's a pretty good organizational scheme, actually. Socks never fall behind a folder and jam the drawer.

Folders used to be called *directories* and *subdirectories*. But some people were getting used to that, so the industry switched to the term *folders*.

- In a way, learning how to deal with files and folders is like learning how to play the piano: Neither is intuitively obvious, and you hit some bad notes with both. Don't be frustrated if you don't seem to be getting the hang of it. Liberace would have hated file management at first, too.

- You can place folders inside other folders to add deeper levels of organization, like adding drawer partitions to sort your socks by color. Each sock color partition is a smaller, more-organized folder of the larger sock-drawer folder.

- Of course, you can ignore folders and keep all your files right on the Windows XP desktop. That's like tossing everything into the backseat of the car and pawing around to find your tissue box a month later. Stuff that you've organized is a lot easier to find.

- If you're eager to create a folder or two (and it's pretty easy), page ahead to this chapter's "Creating a Folder" section.

- Windows creates several folders when it installs itself on your computer. It created a folder to hold its internal engine parts and a folder to hold your programs. Windows creates a My Documents folder for you to store your work. And it creates a My Pictures folder and a My Music folder inside your My Documents folder to keep your pictures and music separate from your other stuff.

✔ Just as manila folders come from trees, computer folders use a *tree metaphor,* shown in Figure 11-2, as they branch out from one main folder to several smaller folders.

Figure 11-2: The structure of folders inside your computer is tree-like, with main folders branching out to smaller folders.

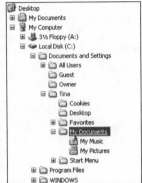

Peering into Your Drives and Folders

Knowing all this folder stuff can impress the people at the computer store. But what counts is knowing how to use the My Computer program to get to a file you want. Never fear. Just read on.

Seeing the files on a disk drive

Like everything else in Windows XP, disk drives are represented by buttons, or icons:

When it's first loaded, Windows' My Computer program shows those icons. See the icon labeled 3½ Floppy (A:)? The icon is a picture of a floppy disk and its disk drive. You see a compact disc floating above drive D: to show that it's a compact disc drive. The hard drive, in the middle, doesn't have anything hovering over it except a nagging suspicion that it will fail horribly at the worst moment.

What's all this path stuff?

Sometimes, Windows XP can't find a file, even if it's sitting right there on the hard drive. You have to tell Windows where the file lives. And to do that, you need to know that file's *path*.

A path is like the file's address. When heading for your house, a letter moves to your country, state, city, street, and finally, hopefully, your apartment or house number. A computer path does the same thing. It starts with the letter of the disk drive and ends with the name of the file. In between, the path lists all the folders the computer must travel through to reach the file.

For example, look at the My Music folder in Figure 11-2. For Windows XP to find a file stored there, it starts from the computer's C: hard drive, travels through the Documents and Settings folder, and then goes through the Tina folder. From there, it goes into the Tina folder's My Documents folder. And only then does it reach the My Music folder.

Take a deep breath. Exhale. Now, in a path, a disk drive letter is referred to as *C:*. The disk drive letter and colon make up the first part of the path. All the other folders are inside the big C: folder, so they're listed after the C: part. Windows separates these nested folders with something called a *backslash*, or \ . The name of the actual file — for example, *Rivers of Babylon* — comes last.

`C:\Documents and Settings\Tina\My Documents\My Music\Rivers of Babylon` is what you get when you put it all together, and that's the official path of the Rivers of Babylon file in Tina's My Music folder.

This stuff can be tricky, so here it is again: The letter for the drive comes first, followed by a colon and a backslash. Then come the names of all the folders, separated by backslashes. Last comes the name of the file (with no backslash after it).

When you click folders, Windows XP puts together the path for you. Thankfully. But whenever you click the Browse button when looking for a file, you're navigating through folders and showing Windows the path to the file.

My Computer also shows information stored in other areas, like MP3 players or digital cameras, as shown in these icons:

Clicking these icons isn't as straightforward as clicking a disk drive icon because cameras and music players can be set up in many different ways. However, clicking these icons usually lets you access their contents and move files back and forth.

> ✔ If you're kinda sketchy on those disk drive things, you probably skipped Chapter 2. Trot back there for a refresher.

✔ Double-click a drive icon in My Computer, and the My Computer window displays the drive's contents. For example, put a disk in drive A and double-click My Computer's drive A icon. After a few gears whirl, My Computer shows what files and folders live on the disk in drive A.

✔ Hold down the Ctrl key while double-clicking a drive icon, and a second My Computer window appears, to show the drive's contents. (You might have to rearrange one window's size to see them both.) So what? Well, a second window comes in handy when you want to move or copy files from one folder or drive to another, as discussed in the "Copying or Moving a File, Folder, or Icon" section of this chapter.

✔ If you click an icon for a CD or floppy drive when no disk is in the drive, Windows XP stops you gently, suggesting that you insert a disk before proceeding further.

✔ Spot an icon called My Network Places? That's a little doorway for peering into other computers linked to your computer — if there are any. You find more network stuff near the end of this chapter and in Chapter 9.

Seeing what's inside folders

 Because folders are really little storage compartments, Windows XP uses a picture of a little folder to stand for each separate place for storing files.

To see what's inside a folder, either in My Computer or on your computer's desktop, just double-click that folder's picture. A new window pops up, showing that folder's contents. Spot a folder inside that folder? Double-click it to see what's inside. Keep clicking until you find what you want or reach a dead end.

 If you mistakenly open the wrong folder, all is not lost. Just back your way out as if you're browsing the Web. Click the lime-green Back arrow at the window's top-left corner. (It's the same arrow that appears in the margin.) That closes the wrong folder and shows you the folder you just left. If you keep clicking the Back arrow, you end up right where you started.

✔ As you keep climbing farther out on a branch and more folders appear, you're moving toward further levels of organization. If you climb back inward, you reach files and folders that have less in common.

✔ Yeah, this stuff is really confusing, but keep one thing in mind: Don't be afraid to double-click, or even single-click, a folder just to see what happens. Clicking folders just changes your viewpoint; nothing dreadful happens, and no tax receipts fall onto the floor. You're just opening and closing file cabinet drawers, harmlessly peeking into folders along the way.

✔ To climb farther out on the branches of folders, keep double-clicking new folders as they appear.

- How do you know which folders contain something and which are empty? Rest your mouse pointer over the folder and wait a few seconds. A small pop-up often displays the folder's size and the names of the folder's first few files. If you're tired of waiting, just double-click the folder and look inside.

- Sometimes, a folder contains too many files or folders to fit in the window. To see more files, click that window's scroll bars. What's a scroll bar? Time to whip out your field guide, Chapter 5.

While mining deep into folders with My Computer, and not finding what you want, here's a quick way to return to any of the folders you've plowed through: See the little downward-pointing black arrow next to the green Back arrow in the window's top-left corner? Click there, and a list drops down to reveal the names of all the folders you've plowed through to reach your current folder. Click any of the listed folders, and Windows XP immediately opens that folder. (Click the History option, by the way, to make Windows display all the Internet sites you've visited in the past few weeks.)

Using a Microsoft IntelliMouse, the kind with the little wheel embedded in the mouse's neck? Point at a long list of files and folders in My Computer and spin the little wheel; the list moves up or down as you spin the wheel, letting you see some files and folders that were off-screen.

Can't find a file or folder? Instead of rummaging through folders, check out the Search command that I describe in Chapter 7. It's the fastest way to find files and folders that were "there just a moment ago."

Loading a Program or File

A *file* is a collection of information on a disk. Files come in two basic types: program files and data files.

Program files contain instructions that tell the computer to do something: balance the national budget or dial up the Internet and display pictures of exotic monkeys.

Data files contain information created with a program, as opposed to computer instructions. If you write a letter to the grocer complaining about his soggy apricots, the letter is a data file.

To open either kind of file in Windows XP, double-click its name. Double-clicking a program file's name brings the program to life on the screen.

Double-clicking a data file tells Windows XP to load the file *and* the program that created it. Then Windows simultaneously brings both the file and the program to the screen.

✔ Depending on how your computer is configured, sometimes a single-click does the trick: Point at the file or program to highlight it and then click it to bring it to life. (If that doesn't bring the file or program to life, try a double-click.)

✔ Windows XP sticks little icons next to filenames so that you know whether they're program or data files. In fact, even folders get their own icons so that you won't confuse them with files. Chapter 20, at the tail end of the book, provides a handy reference for figuring out which icon is which.

✔ Because of some bizarre New School of Computing mandate, any data file that Windows recognizes is called a *document*. A document doesn't have to contain words; it can have pictures of worms or sounds of hungry animals.

Deleting and Undeleting Files, Folders, and Icons

Sooner or later, you'll want to delete a file that's not important anymore — yesterday's lottery picks, for example, or something you've stumbled across that's too embarrassing to save any longer. But suddenly you realize that you've made a mistake and deleted the wrong file! Not to worry, the Windows XP Recycle Bin can probably resurrect that deleted file. The next two sections show how to delete a file and retrieve files you've deleted.

Getting rid of a file or folder

To delete a file or folder, right-click on its name. Then choose Delete from the pop-up menu. This surprisingly simple trick works for files, folders, shortcuts, and just about anything else in Windows.

The Delete option deletes entire folders, as well as any files or folders stuffed inside them. Make sure that you've selected the right folder before you choose Delete.

✔ After you choose Delete, Windows tosses a box in your face, asking whether you're sure. If you are, click the Yes button.

 ✔ Be extra sure that you know what you're doing when deleting any file that has pictures of little gears in its icon. These files are sometimes sensitive hidden files, and the computer wants you to leave them alone. (Other than that, they're not particularly exciting, despite the action-oriented gears.)

✔ As soon as you find out how to delete files, you'll want to read the very next section, "How to undelete a file."

Don't bother reading this hidden technical stuff

Sometimes, programs store information in a data file. They may need to store information about the way the computer is set up, for example. To keep people from thinking that those files are trash and deleting them, Windows hides those files.

You can view the names of these hidden files and folders, however, if you want to play voyeur. Open My Computer and choose Folder Options from the Tools menu. Select the View tab from along the menu's top and click the Show Hidden Files and Folders button under the Hidden Files and Folders option.

Click the OK button, and the formerly hidden files appear alongside the other filenames. Be sure not to delete them, however: The programs that created them will gag, possibly damaging other files. In fact, please click the View tab's Restore Defaults button to hide that stuff again and return the settings to normal.

 Deleting a shortcut from the desktop or any other place just deletes a button that loads a file or program. You can always put the button back on or even create a new one. The program itself is undamaged and still lives inside your computer. Deleting an icon that doesn't have the little shortcut arrow *removes* that file or program from the hard disk and puts it into the Recycle Bin, where it disappears after a few weeks.

How to undelete a file

Sooner or later, your finger will slip, and you'll delete the wrong file. A slip of the finger, the wrong nudge of a mouse, or, if you're in southern California, a small earthquake at the wrong time can make a file disappear.

 Scream! After the tremors subside, double-click the Recycle Bin, and the Recycle Bin window drops down from the heavens, as shown in Figure 11-3.

To restore a file or folder to its former place among the living, right-click on its name in the Recycle Bin and choose Restore from the menu. The file or folder reappears in the place where you deleted it.

You can also drag deleted goodies out of the Recycle Bin window: Use the mouse to point at the name of the file you want to retrieve and, while holding down the mouse button, point at the desktop. Then let go of the mouse button. Windows XP moves the once-deleted file out of the Recycle Bin and places the newly revived file onto your desktop. Feel free to drag the file anywhere you want.

Figure 11-3:
The Recycle
Bin's
Restore
button drops
from the
heavens
to save
the day.

The Recycle Bin chokes under a few circumstances, however, so be careful:

✔ First, you can only restore deleted items within a few weeks of deleting them. If you wait too long, the Recycle Bin eventually sends your files to the trash heap. It can't keep saving your deleted files forever, or your computer would run out of storage space. So, the Recycle Bin waits until its stash of deleted files consumes about 10 percent of your computer's storage space. Translation? That means you probably have a few weeks to retrieve things before the Recycle Bin sends them down the pipes forever.

✔ Second, the Recycle Bin only restores files deleted from your *hard drive*. Sure, that's 99 percent of your files. But that doesn't help when you accidentally delete an important file from a floppy disk, a genuine picture of a UFO on your digital camera, your favorite song from an MP3 player, or a file from the network. The Recycle Bin doesn't save files deleted from those areas. When they're deleted, they're gone for good.

✔ If you delete something from somebody else's computer while using the network, it can never be retrieved. The Recycle Bin only holds items deleted from your own computer, not somebody else's computer. And, for some awful reason, the Recycle Bin on the other person's computer won't save the item, either.

✔ After you restore your file, it's as good as new. Feel free to store it in any other folder for safekeeping.

✔ The Recycle Bin normally holds about 10 percent of your hard drive's space. For example, if your hard drive is 20GB, the Recycle Bin holds onto 2GB of deleted files. After it reaches that limit, it starts deleting the files you deleted the longest time ago to make room for the incoming deleted files. To increase or decrease that percentage, right-click on your desktop's Recycle Bin icon, choose Properties, and adjust the amount on the window that appears.

Copying or Moving a File, Folder, or Icon

To copy or move files to different folders on your hard drive, it's sometimes easiest to use your mouse to *drag* them there. For example, here's how to move a file to a different folder on your desktop. In this case, I'm moving the Traveler file from the Home folder to the Morocco folder.

1. **Move the mouse pointer until it hovers over the file you want to move, and then press and hold down the right mouse button.**

   As you see in Figure 11-4, I've opened the House folder by double-clicking it. Inside is the Traveler file, the one I want to move.

2. **While holding down the right mouse button, use the mouse to point at the folder to which you'd like to move the file.**

   The trick is to hold down the right mouse button the whole time. When you move the mouse, its arrow drags the file along with it. For example, Figure 11-4 shows how the desktop looks when I drag the Traveler file from the House folder to my Morocco folder.

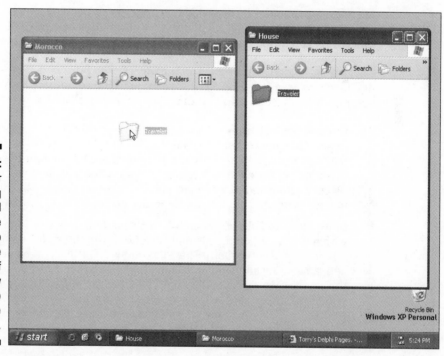

Figure 11-4: The Traveler file is being dragged to the Morocco folder on the left side of the window in order to move the file there.

And what if I *don't* hold down the right mouse button while dragging and dropping?

My Computer does something awfully dumb to confuse people: When you drag a file from one folder to another on the same drive, you *move* the file. When you drag a file from one folder to another on a different drive, you *copy* that file.

I swear I didn't make up these rules. And the process gets more complicated: You can click the file and hold down the Shift key to reverse the rules. That's why it's much easier to simply hold down the right mouse button whenever you drag and drop *anything*.

3. **Release the mouse button and choose Copy, Move, or Create Shortcut from the pop-up menu.**

   When the mouse arrow hovers over the place to which you want to move the file, take your finger off the mouse button and choose Copy, Move, or Create Shortcut from the menu that appears.

Moving a file or folder by dragging it is pretty easy, actually. The hard part comes when you try to put the file and its destination on-screen at the same time, especially when one folder is buried deep within your computer.

That's why Windows offers a few other ways to copy or move files — you don't have to drag and drop icons if you don't want to. Although none of these methods is the best for all situations, they all work well at different times.

- ✔ **Cut and paste:** Right-click on a file or folder and choose Cut or Copy, depending on whether you want to move or copy it. (I cover cutting and pasting extensively in Chapter 8.) Then right-click on your destination folder and choose Paste. It's simple, it always works, and you needn't place the item and its destination on-screen simultaneously. However, moving from one folder to another often takes a few keystrokes.

- ✔ **Copy/Move to Folder commands:** This method only works on items within folders. Click the file and click Edit from the menu along the folder's top. Choose Copy This File or Move This File, and a new window appears, listing all your computer's folders and their locations. Click through the window's folders until you find the destination folder, and Windows carries out the Copy or Move command. This method works well, but only if you know your destination folder's exact location within your computer's pile of folders.

✔ **Windows Explorer:** Described later in this chapter, Windows Explorer presents a My Computer window, but with all your folders lined up along the window's left side. That makes it easier to see both the object and its destination on the same screen. Using Windows Explorer is often the easiest method, but you need to figure out the program, which I describe toward this chapter's end. (For a peek at Windows Explorer, open My Computer and click Folders on the toolbar along the top.)

Always drag icons while holding down the *right* mouse button. Windows XP is then gracious enough to give you a menu of options when you position the icon, and you can choose to move, copy, or create a shortcut. If you hold down the left mouse button, Windows XP sometimes doesn't know whether to copy or move.

✔ To copy or move files to a floppy disk, digital camera, or MP3 player in the My Computer window, hold down the right mouse button while dragging those files to that item's icon.

✔ Don't ever move these folders: My Documents, My Pictures, My Music, Shared Documents, Shared Pictures, or Shared Music. Keep them where they are so they're easy to find.

✔ After you run a program's installation program to put the program on your hard drive, don't ever move the program's folder or files around. An installation program often wedges a program into Windows pretty handily; if you move the program, it may not work anymore, and you'll have to reinstall it. Feel free to move the program's shortcut, though, if it has one.

Selecting More Than One File or Folder

Windows XP lets you grab an armful of files and folders at one swipe; you don't always have to piddle around, dragging one item at a time.

To pluck several files and folders, hold down the Ctrl key when you click the names or icons. Each name or icon stays highlighted when you click the next one.

To gather several files or folders sitting next to each other in a list, click the first one. Then hold down the Shift key as you click the last one. Those two items are highlighted, along with every file and folder sitting between them.

Windows XP lets you *lasso* files and folders as well. Point slightly above the first file or folder you want; then, while holding down the mouse button, point at the last file or folder. The mouse creates an invisible lasso to surround your files. Let go of the mouse button, and the invisible lasso, er, disappears, leaving all the surrounded files highlighted.

✔ You can drag these armfuls of files in the same way that you drag a single file.

✔ You can also simultaneously cut or copy and paste these armfuls into new locations using any of the methods described in the "Copying or Moving a File, Folder, or Icon" section.

✔ You can delete these armfuls of goods, too.

✔ To rename *all* the files at once, right-click the first highlighted file and choose Rename. Rename the first one — choose Hawaii, for instance — and press Enter. Windows XP renames the first file as `"Hawaii"`, and then gives the same name to the other highlighted files, tacking on consecutive numbers: `Hawaii(1)`, `Hawaii(2)`, `Hawaii(3)` and so on.

✔ To quickly select all the files in a folder, choose Select All from the folder's Edit menu. (Or press Ctrl+A.) Here's another nifty trick: To grab all but a few files, press Ctrl+A and, while still holding down Ctrl, click the ones you don't want.

Renaming a File, Folder, or Icon

Sick of a file or folder's name? Then change it. Just right-click on the offending icon and choose Rename from the menu that pops up.

The old filename gets highlighted and then disappears when you start typing the file or folder's new name. Press Enter or click the desktop when you're through, and you're off.

Or you can click the file or folder's name to select it, wait a second, and click the file's name again. Windows XP highlights the old name, ready to replace it with your incoming text. (Some people click the name and press F2; Windows automatically lets you rename the file.)

✔ If you rename a file, only its name changes. The contents are still the same, it's still the same size, and it's still in the same place.

✔ To rename groups of files, select them all, right-click the first one, choose Rename, and type in its new name. When you press Enter, Windows XP renames that file. Then it renames all the other files to the new name, plus a number: cat, cat (1), cat (2), cat (3), and so on. (Please try this on a copy of your original files before experimenting.)

✔ Renaming some folders confuses Windows, however, especially if those folders contain programs. And please don't rename these folders: My Documents, My Pictures, or My Music.

Some icons, like the one for the Recycle Bin, won't let you rename them. How do you know which icons don't let you meddle with their names? Right-click on the icon you want to rename. If you don't see the word *Rename* on the menu, you won't be able to rename the file. Handy button, that right mouse button.

Using Legal Folder Names and Filenames

Windows is pretty picky about what you can and can't name a file or folder. If you stick to plain old letters and numbers, you're fine. But don't try to stick any of the following characters in there:

```
: / \ * | < > ? "
```

If you use any of those characters, Windows XP bounces an error message to the screen, and you have to try again.

These names are illegal:

```
1/2 of my Homework
JOB:2
ONE<TWO
He's no "Gentleman"
```

These names are legal:

```
Half of my Term Paper
JOB2
Two is Bigger than One
A #@$%) Scoundrel
```

- ✔ As long as you remember the characters that you can and can't use for naming files, you'll probably be okay.

- ✔ Using a digital camera, scanner, or MP3 player? Don't use any of those forbidden characters in the file's name, or Windows will freak out when you try to import the file into the My Pictures folder.

- ✔ Like their predecessors, Windows XP programs *brand* files with their own three-letter extensions so that Windows XP knows which program created what file. Normally, Windows XP hides the extensions so that they're not confusing. But if you happen to spot filenames like SAVVY.DOC, README. TXT, and SPONGE.BMP across the hard disk, you'll know that the extensions have been added by the Windows XP programs WordPad, Notepad, and Paint, respectively. Windows XP normally keeps the extensions hidden from view, so you just look at the file's icon for heritage clues.

If you really want to see a filename's extension, choose Folder Options from the folder's Tools menu (or the Control Panel) and then click the View tab. Finally, click the little box next to the line that says Hide File Extensions for Known File Types; that removes the check mark. Then click the Apply button, and the files reveal their extensions. (Click the box again or click the Restore Defaults button to hide the extensions.)

You may see a filename with a weird *tilde* thing in it, such as `WIGWAM~1.TXT`. That's the special way that Windows XP deals with long filenames. Most older programs expect files to have only eight characters; when there's a conflict, Windows XP whittles down a long filename so that those older programs can use those files. When the program's finished, the shorter, weird filename is the file's new name.

Copying a Complete Floppy Disk

To copy files from one disk to another, drag 'em over there, as described a few pages back. To copy an entire floppy disk, however, use the Copy Disk command.

What's the difference? When you're copying files, you're dragging specific filenames. But when you're copying a disk, the Copy Disk command duplicates the disk exactly: It even copies the empty parts! (That's why the process takes longer than just dragging the files over.)

The Copy Disk command has two main limitations:

✔ It can only copy floppy disks that are the same *size* or *capacity*. Just as you can't pour a full can of beer into a shot glass, you can't copy one disk's information onto another disk unless the disks hold the same amount of data.

✔ It only copies removable disks — floppies, Zip drives, Syquest, and things with even more esoteric names.

Here's how to make a copy of a floppy disk or other removable disk:

1. **Put your floppy disk in your disk drive.**

2. **Double-click the My Computer icon.**

3. **Right-click on your floppy disk's icon.**

4. **Choose Copy Disk from the pop-up menu.**

   A box appears, letting you confirm which disk and disk drive you want to use for your copy.

5. **Click the Start button to begin making the copy and follow the helpful directions.**

✔ All this *capacity* and *size* stuff about disks and drives is slowly digested in Chapter 2.

✔ The Copy Disk command can be handy for making backup copies of your favorite programs.

✔ The Copy Disk command completely overwrites the disk that it's copying information to. Don't use a disk containing anything particularly important.

✔ In fact, you should always use the Copy Disk command when making backup copies of programs. Sometimes, programs hide secret files on their floppies; by making a complete copy of the disk with the Copy Disk command, you can be sure that the entire disk gets copied, hidden files and all.

Creating a Folder

To store new information in a file cabinet, you grab a manila folder, scrawl a name across the top, and start stuffing it with information.

To store new information in Windows XP — a new batch of letters to the hospital billing department, for example — you create a new folder, think up a name for the new folder, and start moving or copying files into it.

Here's how to create a new folder in your My Documents area, the home for lots of your user-created junk:

1. **Choose My Documents from the Start menu.**

2. **Right-click inside your My Documents window and choose New.**

   Right-clicking inside your My Documents window causes a menu to shoot out the side. Choose New.

3. **Select Folder from the menu that appears.**

   When a menu squirts out from the word New, choose Folder, as shown in Figure 11-5. Poof! A new folder appears on the desktop, waiting for you to type in a new name.

4. **Type in a new name for the folder.**

   A newly created folder has a highlighted name; when you start typing, Windows XP automatically erases the old name and fills in your new name. Done? Either press Enter or click somewhere away from the name you've just typed.

   If you mess up and want to try again, right-click on the folder, choose Rename, and start over.

✔ To move files into a new folder, drag them there. Or follow the directions in the "Copying or Moving a File, Folder, or Icon" section, earlier in this chapter.

✔ When copying or moving lots of files, select them all at the same time before dragging them. You can chew on this stuff in the "Selecting More Than One File or Folder" section, earlier in this chapter.

✔ Just as with naming files, you can use only certain characters when naming folders. (Stick with plain old letters and numbers, and you'll be fine.)

✔ Shrewd observers noticed that in Figure 11-5 Windows offers to create many more things than just a folder when you click the New button. You follow this same process to create a new Shortcut, WordPad Document, Text Document, or several other things.

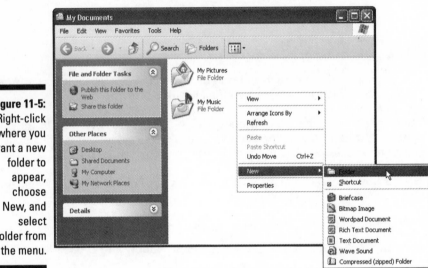

Figure 11-5:
Right-click where you want a new folder to appear, choose New, and select Folder from the menu.

Seeing More Information about Files and Folders

Whenever you create a file or folder, Windows XP scrawls a bunch of secret hidden information on it: its size, the date you created it, and even more trivial stuff. Sometimes it even lets you add your own secret information: lyrics and reviews for your music files and folders, thumbnail pictures to your art folders, and other pertinent information.

To see what Windows XP is calling a file or folder behind your back, right-click on the item and choose Properties from the pop-up menu. Choosing Properties on a Pearl Jam song, for instance, brings up bunches of details, as shown in Figure 11-6.

Windows shows that the file contains a Windows Media Audio (WMA) version of Pearl Jam's song, "Animal." The song is less than 1.5MB in size, and it opens with Windows Media Player. (If you want a different MP3 player to play the song, you can change the application by clicking the Change button.)

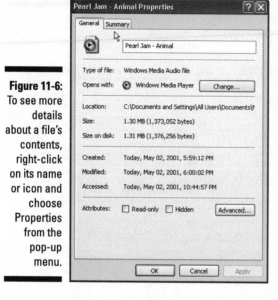

Figure 11-6:
To see more
details
about a file's
contents,
right-click
on its name
or icon and
choose
Properties
from the
pop-up
menu.

Click the Summary tab and choose Advanced for the real fun. As shown in
Figure 11-7, Windows displays the Artist, Album Title, Year, Track Number,
Genre, Duration, and more technical information about how it was encoded.
(I cover this stuff more in Chapter 13.)

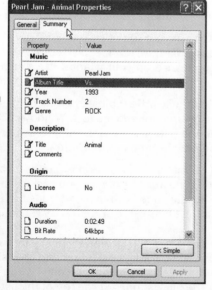

Figure 11-7:
To see even
more details
about a file
or folder's
contents,
click the
Summary
tab of the
Properties
dialog box.

Windows lets you see more information about files as they sit in a folder, too. Choose Details from a folder's View menu, as shown in Figure 11-8. Instead of just displaying icons, Windows displays detailed information about your files.

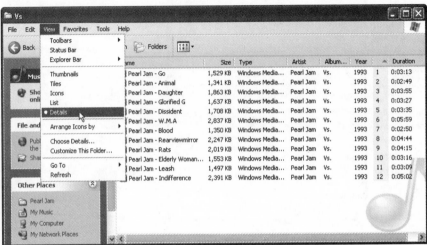

Figure 11-8: Choose Details from a folder's View menu to make the folder display details about its contents.

✔ To change views, click the itty-bitty downward-pointing arrow next to the right-most button on the toolbar, which lives atop most folders. (The button is shown in the margin.) A drop-down menu appears, listing options for arranging icons: Thumbnails, Tiles, Icons, List, and Details. Try them all to see what they do. (Clicking those options merely changes the way the folder displays its contents — it doesn't do any permanent damage.)

✔ Is the menu not living on top of your folder's window? Put it there by choosing Standard Buttons from the View menu's Toolbars option. That little bar of buttons now appears atop your window like a mantel over a fireplace.

✔ If you can't remember what those little toolbar buttons do, rest your mouse pointer over a button and pretend it's lost. Windows XP displays a helpful box summing up the button's mission and, occasionally, places a further explanation along the bottom of the window.

✔ Although some of the additional file information is handy, it can consume a lot of space, limiting the number of files you can see in the window. Displaying only the filename is often a better idea. Then, if you want to see more information about a file or folder, try the following tip.

At first, Windows XP displays filenames sorted alphabetically by name in its My Computer windows. But by right-clicking on a folder and choosing the different sorting methods in the Arrange Icons menu, you display the files in a different order. Windows puts the biggest ones at the top of the list, for example, when you choose Sort by Size. Or you can choose Sort by Type to keep files created by the same application next to each other. Or you can choose Sort by Date to keep the most recent files at the top of the list. Windows offers different sorting options for your music and picture folders.

When the excitement of sorting wears off, try clicking the little buttons at the top of each column — Size, for instance. That sorts the contents appropriately — the largest files at the top, for instance.

What's That Windows Explorer Thing?

Although Windows almost always displays your files and folders in its My Computer program window, another program can help you examine your files and folders. My Computer only shows the contents of a single folder at a time. Windows Explorer, on the other hand, lets you see all your folders at the same time, as shown in Figure 11-9. Best yet, Explorer is easy to load and get rid of.

To load Windows Explorer from My Computer, click the Folders button on the toolbar at the top. A list of folders tacks itself onto My Computer's left side, turning it into Windows Explorer. If you read the beginning of this chapter, where it talks about your folders being organized into a "tree," you'll recognize Windows Explorer's method of displaying files.

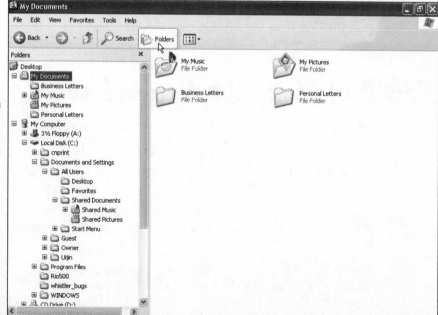

Figure 11-9: Click the Folders button from along a folder's toolbar to add the Windows Explorer program's view of your folders.

See how some folders have tiny plus signs next to them? That means more folders hide inside those folders. Click the plus sign, and the folder opens up, displaying the folders that live inside it. By clicking the plus signs, you can worm your way deeper inside folders.

What's the point? Well, Windows Explorer lets you view one folder's contents on the right side of the window, and all of your folder's names on the left. That makes it easier to move or copy items from one folder to another folder.

To copy a letter from your desktop to your Business Letters folder, for instance, open Windows Explorer and click Desktop on the left to display its contents on the window's right. Right-click on the letter's icon and choose Copy, as described in this chapter's section about copying or moving files.

Find the Business Letters folder among the folders on the window's left side, right-click on that folder, and choose Paste. Windows copies the letter to your Business Letters folder.

- ✔ Some people prefer Windows Explorer's "view it all" method of displaying your computer's contents. Others prefer My Computer. There's no right or wrong way. Try them both and see which you prefer.

- ✔ You can create folders and documents while using the Windows Explorer view, just as you do in My Computer, explained earlier in this chapter. In fact, almost all of the commands and tricks work the same. Windows Explorer works just like My Computer, but with that extra line of folders along its left side.

- ✔ To get rid of the Windows Explorer view — to stop all those folders from showing along the left side — click the Folders button again from the toolbar along the top.

How Do I Make the Network Work?

Windows XP can connect to bunches of other computers through a home network, and, luckily, that makes it pretty easy to grab files from other people's computers. At least it's pretty easy if somebody else has already set up the network. But after the network's running, you'll be running right alongside it. There isn't much new to learn.

See the My Network Places icon on your computer's Start menu (and shown in the margin)? That icon is the key to all the computers currently connected to your computer.

Double-click that icon, and a window appears, as shown in Figure 11-10. Your windows naturally differ because you have different computers. (And the computers probably have different names, too.) Figure 11-10, for instance, shows all the disk drives on other computers that connect to this one through a network.

Figure 11-10:
Double-click
the
desktop's
My Network
Places icon
to see
which
places you
can access
on the
network.

Double-click the folder of the computer that you want to peek inside, and a new window appears, showing the contents of the folder on that computer — even though it might be in another room, in another office, or on another continent.

 To see all the computers currently linked to your computer, click View Workgroup Computers from the Network Tasks menu along the window's left side, as shown in Figure 11-11. Windows XP shows you the names of all the currently available computers.

- ✔ When viewing another computer's files, everything works just like it was on your own computer. Feel free to point and click inside the other computer's folders. To copy files back and forth, just drag and drop them to and from your computer's window to the other computer's window. (Sometimes a computer requires a password, however, so you'll have to ask the computer's owner for permission.)

- ✔ Don't feel guilty when probing the network. You can only access computers that your network administrator has given you access to. You're not really getting away with anything.

- ✔ When you use a network to delete something from another networked computer — or somebody uses the network to delete a file from *your* computer — it's gone. It doesn't go into the Recycle Bin. Be careful, especially because the network administrator can often tell who deleted the file.

- ✔ Windows XP comes with a special Home Networking process to connect your computers with cables. In fact, after you connect them, the computers can share a single modem. Chapter 9 carries much more information about networking.

Who cares about this stuff, anyway?

Windows XP gives each file special switches called *attributes.* Some files offer an advanced button, displaying even more attributes. The computer looks at the way those switches are set before it fiddles with a file. (A check mark means the switch is turned on.) To view a file's attributes, right-click on the file and choose Properties. Here's what you'll probably find.

✔ **Read Only:** Choosing this attribute allows the file to be read, but not deleted or changed in any way.

✔ **Hidden:** Setting this attribute makes the file invisible during normal operations.

By clicking the Advance button, Windows XP presents more switches:

✔ **File Is Ready for Archiving:** Some backup programs look at this one to see if they've backed up that file or not. When backed up, this attribute changes to reflect its new status.

✔ **For Fast Searching:** Normally set to on, this setting tells Windows to let its Indexing Service take note of the file and its contents for faster searching.

✔ **Compress Contents to Save Disk Space:** Only available on computers with special, NTFS drives, this setting lets Windows XP squish the file to save space. That makes the file load more slowly, though.

The Properties box makes it easy — perhaps too easy — to change these attributes. In most cases, you should leave them alone. I just mention them here so that you'll know what computer nerds mean when they tell cranky people, "Boy, somebody must have set your attribute wrong when you got out of bed this morning."

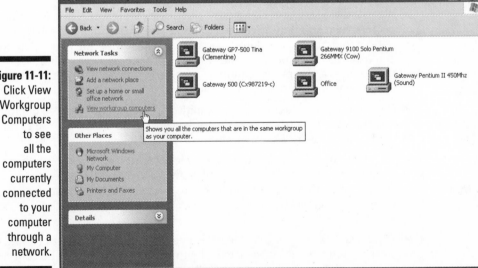

Figure 11-11: Click View Workgroup Computers to see all the computers currently connected to your computer through a network.

Making My Computer and Windows Explorer List Missing Files

Sometimes, Windows XP snoozes and doesn't keep track of what's *really* on a disk. Oh, it does pretty well with the hard drive, and it works pretty well if you're just running Windows programs. But it can't tell when you stick in a new floppy disk, and it sometimes gets confused with networks or when you copy files from one place to another.

If you ever think that the Windows Explorer or My Computer window is holding out on you, tell it to *refresh,* or take a second look at the files it's displaying. You can click View from the menu bar and choose Refresh from the pull-down menu, but a quicker way is to press the F5 key. (It's a function key along the top or left side of the keyboard.) Either way, the program takes a second look at what it's supposed to be showing and updates its lists, if necessary.

Press the F5 key whenever you stick in a different floppy disk and want to see what files are stored on it. Windows XP then updates the screen to show the *new* floppy's files, not the files from the first disk.

Formatting a Disk

Some new floppy disks don't work straight out of the box; your computer burps out an error message if you even try to use them fresh. Floppy disks must be formatted, and unless you paid extra for a box of *preformatted* floppy disks, you must format them yourself.

Some disks on digital cameras and MP3 players must be formatted, as well. Either way, the procedure is pretty much the same:

1. **Place the new disk into your drive.**

2. **In either Windows Explorer or the My Computer window, right-click on the drive's icon and choose Format from the menu.**

3. **Choose the disk's size under Capacity and click Start.**

   Almost all floppy disks are 1.44MB these days, so choose that option if you're not sure.

   Digital cameras and MP3 players use different-sized disks. Luckily, their correct size usually shows up automatically in the Capacity window.

   When you click Start, your disk drive whirs for several minutes, before announcing it's finished.

4. Click the Close button when Windows XP is through.

Then remove the disk and return to Step 1 if you need to format another disk.

✔ Formatting a disk deletes all the information on it forever. It won't be waiting in the Recycle Bin for retrieval. And don't even try to format a hard drive.

✔ Don't get your hopes up: The Quick Format option won't speed things up unless your disk has already been formatted once before.

Chapter 12

Cruising the Web, Sending E-Mail, and Using Newsgroups

In This Chapter

▶ Understanding the Internet and World Wide Web

▶ Understanding differences between the Internet and online services

▶ Knowing how to access the World Wide Web

▶ Using the Microsoft Internet Explorer Web browser

▶ Navigating the World Wide Web

▶ Upgrading with downloaded plug-ins

▶ Sending and receiving e-mail with Outlook Express

▶ Using newsgroups with Outlook Express

*T*he family photo album is disappearing. A friend of mine visited with his family the other day. He brought his new digital camera and took pictures of the vacation.

Each evening, he used the telephone and his laptop to send the camera's pictures to his Web site, and then he tweaked his Web site's settings to create a daily pictorial journal of the day's events. You won't find a black photo album in his closet; he's sharing his life with anyone who cares to look.

Other Web sites go to even greater extremes. A cab driver in New York has a digital camera hooked up to a cellular phone; every few minutes, the camera takes a picture of the bustling streets and automatically sends the photo to the cabby's Web site.

You needn't be as elaborate with your own Web site. In fact, you don't *need* to have a Web site at all. This chapter shows how to peek at all the other sites out there, though, should you get the urge.

What's the Difference between the Internet, the World Wide Web, and a Web Browser?

The *Internet* is a rapidly growing collection of computers linked around the globe through wires and satellites. Millions of people of all ages use these connections to swap information with other computers.

The *World Wide Web* (known as "The Web," to be cool) runs on the Internet to let computers display *Web sites* — interactive software that often resembles magazine pages with pretty pictures.

A *Web browser* lets you flip through a Web site's different pages, just like you flip through the pages of a magazine. Better yet, the Web browser lets you jump from Web site to Web site. You can read newspapers at one site and order books or take-out food at another site.

Internet Explorer, the free browser that comes with Windows XP, makes the Web look like a kiosk in a hotel or airport lobby. Internet Explorer fills your screen with buttons and pictures. But instead of touching the pictures and buttons, like you do at the airport or hotel lobby, you use the mouse to point and click on-screen buttons and links. By doing so, you can view museums, cameras, pizza menus, guitar shops, city maps, and more. (You can also find the right rental car.)

- ✔ Just as a television channel surfer flips from channel to channel, sampling the wares, a Web surfer moves from page to page, sampling the vast and esoteric piles of information.

- ✔ Just about anybody can set up a Web site, but doing so usually involves some programming skills using a language called *HTML* (HyperText Markup Language). Surfing the pages is much easier than building the wave. That's why most people remain Web surfers.

- ✔ Because setting up a customized Web site is fairly easy for programmers, thousands of just plain wacky sites exist. If you're flabbergasted by flying saucers, for example, head for www.fsr.org.uk to read the Flying Saucer Review. Another fellow's well-documented site tests the durability of the pink and white Marshmallow Bunnies sold in drug stores. Head to www.keypad.org/bunnies/ and watch the Laser Exposure Test!

Who Can Use the Internet and World Wide Web?

Gosh, everybody who *doesn't* use the Internet is forced to hear everybody else talk about it at parties and on TV commercials, and read about it in magazines, newspapers, and billboards.

Here are a few of the Internet's most enthusiastic subscribers:

✔ Universities, corporations, government entities, and millions of plain ol' normal folk use the Internet every day. Many users simply send messages back and forth — called *electronic mail* or *e-mail*. Other users swap programs, pictures, or sounds — anything that can be stored as data inside of a computer.

✔ The United States government loves the Internet. The FBI posts pictures of its ten most wanted criminals (www.fbi.gov) for public viewing, for example, and the Internal Revenue Service (www.irs.ustreas.gov/prod/cover.html) lets Internet users make free copies of tax forms 24 hours a day.

✔ Universities love the network, too. Departments can file grant forms more quickly than ever. Worried about the goo coagulating in the center of your bromeliads? The Internet's famed botanical site (www.botany.net) enables researchers to move quickly from 24 Canoe Plants of Ancient Hawaii to the Zoosporic Fungi database.

✔ Many computer companies support their products on the Internet. Visitors to the Web site can leave messages to technicians in hopes that the technicians can figure out why their latest computer doodads aren't working. After posting messages back and forth, callers can often download a software cure or patch to fix the problem.

✔ Artists, spotting a new way to show their work, quickly jumped aboard the Web. Some sites display photos of their watercolors, like the ones shown in Figure 12-1, hoping to snag potential buyers.

✔ Curious about Volkswagen's latest line of cars? Head for the Volkswagen Web site (www.vw.com) and start flipping through the pages of the Volkswagen "point and clickable" brochures. (See Figure 12-2.)

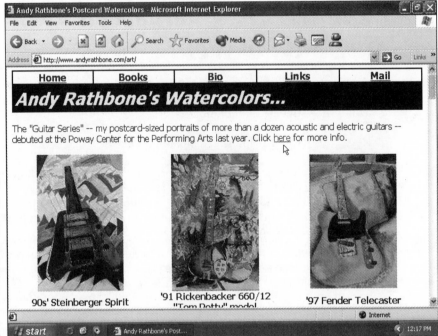

Figure 12-1:
World Wide
Web sites
let you shop
for nearly
everything
— even
watercolor
postcards.

Figure 12-1:
World Wide
Web sites
let you shop
for nearly
everything
— even
watercolor
postcards.

Figure 12-2:
The Web
site for
Volkswagen
features
"point and
clickable"
brochures
for users to
view online
close-ups of
its cars.

What's an ISP, and Do I Need One?

Signals for television channels come wafting through the air to your TV set for free. Unless you're paying for cable or satellite TV, you can watch *Dawson's Creek* simply by turning on the TV.

The Internet ain't free, though. You need to pay for Internet signals, just like you pay for gas and electricity. For the privilege of surfing the Web, you must do business with an *Internet service provider,* known by the hip computing crowd as an *ISP.* You pay the ISP for a password and phone number to dial. When your computer modem dials the number and connects to your ISP's network, you type your password and grab your surfboard: You've entered the Web.

✔ Some ISPs charge for each minute you're connected; others charge a flat fee for unlimited service. The going rate seems to be stabilizing at around $20 a month for unlimited service. Make sure that you find out your rate before hopping aboard, or you may be surprised at the end of the month.

✔ Some ISPs used to let you access the Internet for free, but they went out of business when the bottom fell out of the Internet market in late 2000.

✔ If you're computer-inclined, some ISPs provide hard disk space on their computers so that you can create your *own* Web pages for other Internet members to visit. Show the world pictures of your kids and cats, share your favorite recipes, talk about your favorite car waxes, or swap tips on constructing fishing flies.

✔ ISPs let you connect to the Internet in a variety of ways. The slowest ISPs connect through the phone lines with a modem. Faster still are special DSL lines that some phone companies provide. Some ISPs send their signals through satellites. Some of the fastest connections come from your cable TV company. With the speedy ISPs, your location often determines your options.

What Do I Need to Access the World Wide Web?

A first-timer needs four things to connect to the Web: a computer, Internet browser software, a modem, and an ISP. You already have the computer, and Windows XP comes with an Internet browser called Internet Explorer. And, chances are, your computer already has a modem inside. (If it doesn't, you'll know when you try to set up your ISP, as described in the very next section.)

You can find an ISP listed in your local Yellow Pages under *Computers — Online Services & Internet* or *Telecommunications.* Or ask your local computer dealer for names and numbers. If you're desperate, choose MSN Explorer from the Start button's More Programs area. That lets you sign up for an account run by Microsoft.

- ✔ Blatant Endorsement Department: If you use the Internet a lot, please check with your cable provider to see if it offers cable modem service. No more thumb-twiddling: Pictures, graphics, and animation simply pop onto the screen. I love my Cox Cable service, except when it goes down every month or so.

- ✔ Because techies created the Internet, it's often cumbersome for new users to enter and navigate it. Sometimes, your computer can slip into the Internet just as easily as a crooked politician can. Other times, your computer makes you fill out many forms and enter a lot of numbers before you can access the Internet. Don't be afraid to ask a friend for help the first time you connect to your ISP.

- ✔ Don't be afraid to bug your ISP for help, too. The best ISPs come with technical support lines. A member of the support staff can talk you through the installation process.

- ✔ After you're finally signed up and aboard the Web, though, life rolls along much more easily. The Web is *enormous,* so it contains speedy indexes known as *search engines* that ferret out your favorite goodies. Type in a subject, and the search engine spits out bunches of applicable places to visit.

- ✔ Because Windows XP can run so many programs in the background without being slowed down, forgetting to disconnect your Internet connection is an easy thing to do. If you're being charged by the hour, keep a watchful eye on your Internet browser and make sure that you log off when you no longer need to access the service.

Setting Up Your Internet Account with the Internet Connection Wizard

After you have a computer, a modem, and Windows XP's Internet browser, you need one last thing — an Internet service provider (ISP). And setting up your ISP's account is one of the most terrifying tasks in Windows. (Except for setting up an e-mail account, but that comes later.)

To help you out, Microsoft created the Internet Connection Wizard. After a bit of interrogation, the wizard helps you and your computer connect to your Internet service provider (ISP) so you can Web surf like the best of them.

If your computer connects to the Internet through a network, don't use this wizard. Use the Network Setup Wizard, instead. (Chapter 9 gives you the rundown.)

To transfer your existing Internet account settings from another computer, use the Files and Settings Transfer Wizard. It copies the settings onto a floppy; insert the floppy into your new Windows XP computer, and the wizard automatically installs them.

Here's what you need to get started:

- ✔ **Find an Internet service provider.** This company provides a connection to the Internet. Ask a friend, coworker, or teenager for a recommendation. Don't know which ISP to choose? The Internet Connection Wizard can find one for you that's in your own area.

- ✔ **Get your user name, password, and phone number from your current Internet service provider.** Don't have an ISP? If the wizard finds you a service provider, it dishes out those three items, so grab a pencil and paper.

- ✔ **Find a modem.** Most new computers come with a modem lodged in their innards. To see if one's inside of yours, look for telephone jacks on the back of your computer, near where all the other cables protrude. Make sure a phone cable connects between your computer modem's telephone jack (the jack says *Line,* not *Phone*) and a phone jack in your wall.

Whenever you encounter difficulties in getting your Internet connection "just right," head here and run through the steps in this section. The wizard displays your current settings and allows you to change them.

Modem plugged in? Now you're ready to start the New Connection Wizard by following these steps.

1. **Click the Start button, click More Programs, choose Accessories, select Communications, and load the New Connection Wizard.**

   Or, just choose Internet Explorer from the Start menu. If you haven't set up an Internet account yet, your PC won't be able to connect, so Windows brings up Mr. Wizard automatically.

   On the first screen, the wizard explains that it helps you connect to the Internet or a private network, or set up a home network.

2. **Click Next.**

3. **Choose Connect to the Internet and click Next.**

   Choosing this first option tells Mr. Wizard that yes, you do want to connect to the Internet. (If you want to connect to the Internet through your network, choose Set Up a Home or Small Office Network, and the wizard passes you off to the Network Setup Wizard, instead.)

4. **Choose the second of the three options, as shown in Figure 12-3, and click Next.**

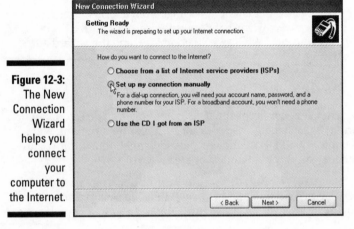

Figure 12-3:
The New
Connection
Wizard
helps you
connect
your
computer to
the Internet.

Here's what the three options mean:

• **Choose from a List of Internet Service Providers (ISPs).**

Choose this option if you don't already have an Internet account and you want to select one from a list provided by Microsoft. If you choose this option, the wizard dials a number to locate Internet service providers in your area and displays their rates and options. The wizard only finds providers with special Microsoft contracts, so it leaves out many providers in your area. (The telephone book is a much better way to find an ISP.)

If you choose a provider with this option, the wizard finishes the rest of the setup work by itself.

• **Set Up My Connection Manually.**

Chances are, you'll end up choosing this option. This lets you set up an Internet account from a previous computer or one at work. It also lets you share a modem on a network. After selecting this, click Next to continue along these steps. You introduce your computer to your existing Internet account by filling out forms and punching buttons.

• **Use the CD I Got from an ISP.**

Many national ISPs offer free CDs for signing up to their service. You would choose this option if you had a CD from America Online, for instance. Choosing this option stops the wizard and lets the ISP's CD take over.

5. **Tell Windows XP how you connect to the Internet and then click Next.**

   The Wizard provides three options:

   - **Connect Using a Dial-up Modem.**

      If your modem plugs into the phone line, choose this option and move to Step 6.

   - **Connect Using a Broadband Connection That Requires a User Name and Password.**

      Broadband connections are the speedy ones provided by cable or DSL modems. Most require a user name and password for access. The connection might seem to be always on, but it's actually logging you on very quickly.

      If you choose this option, you type in a name for your ISP, your user name, and a password to finish the connection.

   - **Connect Using a Broadband Connection That Is Always On.**

      People on a network usually choose this option; the wizard takes over from there.

6. **Type a name for your Internet provider and click Next.**

   Simply type **My Provider** or the name of your provider.

7. **Enter the phone number for your Internet service provider and click Next; then enter your User Name and Password.**

   Your provider should have given you these three things. Call your provider if these three magical tidbits of information aren't in your possession. You need them to proceed.

8. **Click the Finish button.**

   You're done. Windows XP automatically leaps into action and uses your settings to call your Internet provider.

If everything goes correctly, a pop-up message appears with your dial-up modem's connection speed. You're logged on to the Internet. Microsoft tosses its own Web page, The Microsoft Network, onto the Internet Explorer screen, and you're ready to browse. Need a place to go for a quick test? Log on to www.andyrathbone.com and see what happens.

If a cable modem service is available in your area, go for it. Web pages load a zillion times faster. Plus, they come to your house and set everything up for you. (Plus, you won't need to pay for a second phone line while Web surfing.)

Some versions of Windows may not have the New Connection Wizard on the Start menu. To find it, click the Start menu, right-click on the Internet Explorer icon, choose Internet Properties, click the Connections tab, and click the Setup button.

If you have a cable modem or a network, or you spend a lot of time on the Internet, be sure to activate the Windows XP firewall, described later in this chapter.

What Is a Web Browser?

Your Web browser is your Internet surfboard — your transportation to the computers strewn along the Web. Internet Explorer 6 comes free with Windows XP, so many people use it out of convenience. Other people use other companies' browsers, like Netscape Communicator or Opera. People with too much time on their hands switch back and forth between several types of Web browsers.

All browsers work basically the same way. Every Web page comes with a specific address, just like houses do. When you type that address into the browser, the browser takes you there like a veteran cabby — unless you make a typo when you're typing in the address.

To avoid typing laborious addresses (those *www* things), Web browsers allow you to flip through Web pages in a lazy way. Web browsers read *hypertext*, or *Web links*. Web page owners embed addresses of other Web pages into their own Web pages. For example, the Web Museum Network in Paris (`www.sunsite.unc.edu/louvre`) lets you visit museums from Australia to Singapore by simply clicking the museums' names.

Today's Web browsers come with little add-on bits of software for spicing things up. They can handle animated cartoons, voices, sounds, music, scrolling marquees, and other flashy goodies. If you kind of squint — and your computer's powerful enough — it looks like your computer's turning more and more into a TV.

- ✔ If your browser takes you to a boring Web page, there's a quick way to go back to the previous page. Click the big Back button in the top-left corner of Internet Explorer. The dutiful Web browser immediately scurries back to the previous location. (Clicking that big Back button when you're in a folder takes you to the last folder you visited, too.)

- ✔ Almost all Web sites come with *hyperlinks* — highlighted words or buttons that are linked to certain addresses of other computers on the Web. Click the button or highlighted word (usually underlined or a different color), and your Web browser takes you to the Web page with that address. That way you don't have to type in that weird *www* stuff.

- ✔ Many people use their Web sites to display links to certain hobby areas, such as growing vegetables, weaving, or making cigars.

✔ Web site addresses look pretty strange. They usually start with the letters www and end with something even weirder looking, like winespectator.com. Now you know what all of those strange-looking words in parentheses mean throughout this chapter. Other addresses skip the www and use http:// instead. Yes, it's confusing.

✔ Sometimes, clicking a Web address doesn't take you to the page. For example, if a friend e-mails you an address, you may need to type it in by hand. But here's how to avoid any misspellings: Highlight the Web address by holding down your mouse button and sliding the pointer over the address. Then hold down the Ctrl key and press C. (That copies the address.) Now, click in your browser's address box and, while holding down the Ctrl key, press V. By doing so, you paste the address in the address box. Press Enter, and your browser should whisk you off to that new site.

How Do I Navigate the Web with Internet Explorer?

After you've chosen and set up your Internet service provider — either by choosing The Microsoft Network (MSN), America Online (AOL), AT&T WorldNet, Prodigy, or somebody else — you're ready to cruise the Internet.

Although Windows XP makes it easier than ever to hook up with an Internet provider, tweaking the settings can be a drag. First, try using the New Connection Wizard by following the step-by-step process that I outline earlier in this chapter. That cures most of the basic problems.

If you're still having trouble getting your computer set up for the Internet or you need more customized settings, a book like *The Internet For Dummies,* 7th Edition by John R. Levine, Carol Baroudi, and Margaret Levine Young, (published by Hungry Minds, Inc.) may help.

When Internet Explorer comes to the screen for the first time, as shown in Figure 12-4, it shows The Microsoft Network Web page. The next few sections show how to explore the Web to find other goodies.

What's a home page?

Just as your television set always shows a channel when you turn it on, your Web browser automatically displays a certain portion of the Internet.

Figure 12-4:
Click the underlined words —
hyperlinks — in Internet Explorer to head to other Web sites. (Your mouse pointer turns into a hand when it hovers over a hyperlink.)

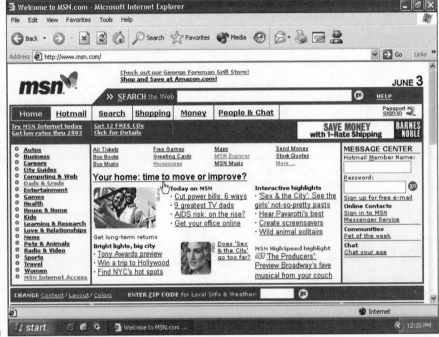

The first Web page you see when a Web browser comes to life is called your *home page*. Your browser's home page is simply the Web page that always appears when the browser is first loaded. It's always the same Web site (although you can change it to be any page you like, as described in the next tip.)

A home page of a *Web site*, however, is a little different. It's like the cover of a magazine that lists the contents. Whenever you jump to a new Web site, you usually jump to the home page of that site.

After you load your own home page, you can move around the Internet, searching for topics by looking in indexes or simply pointing and clicking from topic to topic.

✔ Most Web browsers come with their own home page already configured. After you install Internet Explorer and first log on to the Web, for example, you're whisked away to the Microsoft Network home page (refer to Figure 12-4). A competing company's browser, Netscape Navigator, takes you to the Netscape home page.

✔ You can turn *any* Web site into your home page — the first site that you see when you load your browser. Call up your favorite page in Internet Explorer and choose Internet Options from the Tools menu. Click the General tab (that page usually opens automatically) and click the Use

Current button. (It's the top-left button.) Click OK to save your efforts and return to browsing.

 ✔ To return to your home page quickly while you're connected to the Internet, click the Home button along the top of Internet Explorer.

How do 1 move from Web page to Web page?

Internet Explorer lets you move from page to page in three different ways:

✔ By pointing and clicking a button or link that automatically whisks you away to another page

✔ By typing a complicated string of code words into the Address box of the Web browser and pressing Enter

✔ By clicking the navigation buttons along a browser's menu

The first way is the easiest. Look for *links* — highlighted words or pictures on a page — and click them. See all the underlined words in Figure 12-4? Clicking <u>Your home: time to move or improve?</u> takes you to the Web page where Microsoft's HomeAdvisor section describes remodeling strategies. All the other underlined words on this site are also links; clicking any of them takes you to different pages dealing with that link's particular subject.

The second way is the most difficult. If a friend gives you a napkin with a cool Web page's address written on it, there's nothing to click. You need to type the Web site's address into your browser's address box yourself. That's fairly easy, as long as you don't misspell anything. See the Web site address for Microsoft's page along the top of Figure 12-4? I typed `www.msn.com` into the address box. When I pressed Enter, Internet Explorer scooted me to the Microsoft Network Web page. To head for the Volkswagen Web site, type in **www.vw.com** and press Enter. By pointing and clicking your way to that site's page with pictures of cars, you see the site in Figure 12-2. (You don't need to type in the http:// part, thank goodness.)

Finally, you can maneuver through the Internet by clicking various parts of Internet Explorer itself. Clicking the Favorites button along the top reveals a folder where you can stash buttons leading to your favorite Web sites. Click History from the top-most menu to return to any page that you visited in the past few weeks.

Feel free to explore the Internet by simply clicking the buttons. You really can't get into any trouble; if you get stuck, you can always click the Home button along the top to move back into familiar territory.

✔ The easiest way to start surfing the Internet is to be a button pusher, so remember this bit o' wisdom: Watch how your mouse pointer changes shape as you move it over a Web page. If the pointer changes into a little hand, you're hovering over a button that aches to be pressed.

✔ Web page manufacturers get mighty creative these days, and without the little "hand" pointer, it's often hard to tell where to point and click. Some buttons look like sturdy elevator buttons; others look more like fuzzy dice or vegetables. But when you click a button, the browser takes you to the page relating to that button. Clicking the fuzzy dice may bring up a betting-odds sheet for local casinos, for example.

✔ Pointed and clicked yourself into a dead end? Click the Back button along the top-left corner to head for the last Web page you visited. If you click the Back button enough times, you wind up back at the home page, where you began.

✔ Copying text from the Internet is easy. Slide your mouse pointer over the text while holding down the mouse button, just as if you were in a word processing program. After Internet Explorer highlights the text, right-click on the text and choose Copy from the menu.

How can I revisit my favorite places?

Sooner or later, you'll stumble across a Web page that's indescribably delicious. To make sure that you can find it again later, add it to your favorite pages folder by choosing Add to Favorites from the Favorites menu.

Don't choose the Make Available Offline option. (It tells Windows to automatically download the page's contents once a day, or whenever you press a button.) You probably won't want to change the name, either. Click the Create In button if you want to create a new folder in the Favorites folder for this Web page. (You can always organize your favorites later.) Then click OK to save your efforts.

Whenever you want to return to that page, click the Favorites menu along the top of the screen again, and then click the name of the link you want to revisit.

Librarian-types like to click the Organize Favorites option when the Favorites menu drops down. By doing so, they can create new folders for storing similar links and move related links from folder to folder.

What's an index or search engine?

Just as it is nearly impossible to find a book in a library without a card catalog, it is nearly impossible to find a Web site on the Internet without a good index. Luckily, several exist.

Unfortunately, none exist in Windows XP. Clicking the Search button at the top of the Internet Explorer window brings up Windows' built-in Search function, but that program often stumbles when searching on the Internet. Instead, try this:

1. **Click in the Internet Explorer's address bar, type** www.google.com, **and press Enter.**

   Google, one of the best Internet searching engines, appears.

2. **Type in a few key words describing your interest (cornbread recipes, for instance) and click the Google Search button.**

   In less than a second, Google found 24,200 references to cornbread recipes, as shown in Figure 12-5.

Click any of the sites that Google lists to check out those recipes. Click the Back button to return to Google's search and click a different recipe. Or, right-click on the link and choose Open in New Window. A new copy of Internet Explorer appears, displaying that link, while the other copy keeps displaying your other Google search locations. (That keeps you from losing your place on the search page.)

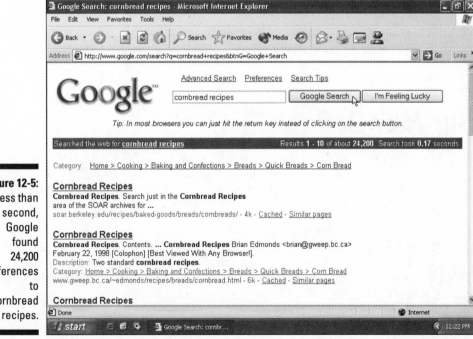

Figure 12-5: In less than a second, Google found 24,200 references to cornbread recipes.

✔ If Google finds Web sites in foreign languages, it often translates them into your own language for you. Or, if you speak a different language, click the Google in Your Language button near the page's bottom. Google uses almost 40 different languages for its menus.

✔ Sometimes Google brings up a Web site that's been updated and no longer lists what you're searching for. If that happens, click the Cached button instead of the site's name. That brings up a snapshot of the Web site as it looked when it contained what you're searching for.

✔ Click the I'm Feeling Lucky button, and Google displays the site most likely to contain what you're after. This option works well when searching for common information.

✔ Although Google is very handy, it's just one way of finding information. The Internet's loaded with other search engines. In fact, Google contains links to several of them at the bottom of its menu. Try clicking AltaVista, Excite, HotBot, Lycos, or Yahoo! to search on those sites.

✔ For many years, computer users have talked to each other on a section of the Internet called *Usenet*. Divided into thousands of discussion areas, Usenet lets people type in questions about nearly every subject, exchanging information, holding discussions, or simply yelling at each other. It's a fantastic source of computer information from real people, without a corporate filter. To search Usenet, click Google Groups (Deja), listed near the bottom of Google's page.

✔ Searches usually come up with hundreds, or even thousands, of hits relating to your subject. If you come up with too many, try again, but be more specific.

But How Do I Do This?

Don't feel bad. The Internet's been around for a while, but this whole Web thing is relatively new and quickly becoming overburdened. It's not supposed to work smoothly yet, and it's not easy to figure out overnight. Here are some of the most common problems and some possible solutions.

The person holding the Administrator account — usually the computer's owner — is the only one who can do many of the changes you read about in this chapter. If a mean message pops up, waving its figure and mumbling about "Administrator restrictions," you're locked out. Better find the computer's owner to proceed.

I can't get it to install!

Installing Internet Explorer isn't all that difficult; the hard part is telling Internet Explorer how to connect to your Internet service provider — the company that's providing the phone connection to the Internet.

Check out the New Connection Wizard, described earlier in this chapter. It displays your current settings and allows you to change them, if needed.

Because ISPs all use slightly different ways to connect, your best bet is to call their tech support number and ask for help. (Be sure to call your Internet service provider, not Microsoft.)

Yeah, connecting to your ISP is a pain, but remember — you only have to connect to the thing once. After Internet Explorer has locked arms with your ISP, you can simply click a button to make it dial up the connection and start surfing.

How do I install the firewall?

Just about everybody's picked up the phone, only to find some recorded voice pushing the latest product. These telemarketers run programs that simply call phone numbers, one after the other, until they find somebody who answers. Computer hackers do the same thing. They run programs that automatically try to break into every computer that's currently connected to the Internet.

If you have a cable modem or other ISP that's constantly connected to the Internet, you're especially vulnerable. See, the Internet assigns your computer a special number whenever it connects. Whenever your modem dials the Internet and connects, your number changes. But if you're constantly connected to the Internet with a cable modem or other 24-hour connection, your number never changes. That makes it easier for hackers to find your computer and, if it's vulnerable, to spread its number around to other hackers.

That's where a *firewall* comes in. Firewall software sits between your computer and the Internet, acting as a door. It lets you decide what software can access your computer, and when. Windows XP comes with a built-in firewall. To install it, follow these steps:

1. **Open the Start menu, right-click on My Network Places, and choose Properties.**

   The Internet is a huge network — it's designed for computers to talk to each other. That's why it's important to make sure that only the friendly computers do the talking.

2. **Right-click on the connection you want to protect, and choose Properties.**

   If you're using a dial-up account, for instance, right-click on that icon. If you're using a network in your home or office, right-click on the Local Area Connection. Either way, choose Properties.

3. **Click the Advanced tab and activate the firewall.**

   Click the box to activate the Windows XP firewall.

   If you're running a network and using the Internet Connection Sharing to let all the networked computers share the modem, the firewall should only be activated on the host computer — the computer that's actually connected to the Internet. It doesn't need to be activated on the client computers — the computers that share the host computer's modem.

I keep getting busy signals!

This problem means that your Internet service provider is probably offering a great deal — unlimited access to the Internet for one low price. Unfortunately, a bargain means that many people are going to be calling at the same time as you, leading to busy signals.

What's the answer? Reassess your priorities. Are you looking to save money or find a reliable connection to the Internet? You may be able to find a better deal with a different provider.

The Web page says it needs [insert name of weird plug-in thing here]!

Computer programmers abandoned their boring old TV sets and turned to their exciting new computers for entertainment. Now, they're trying to turn their computers back into TV sets. They're using fancy programming techniques called Java, Shockwave, RealPlayer, QuickTime, and other goodies to add animation and other gizmos to the Internet.

Programmers are also adding little software tidbits called *plug-ins* that increase your computer's capability to display flashy advertisements along the top of your screen.

What's the problem? New versions of these plug-ins follow the seasons. If your computer says it needs a plug-in or its latest version, click the button on the Web page that takes you to its download area.

Close down all your software (except for the Web browser), download the software, and install it. The next time you open your Web browser, the advertisements will never have looked better.

If you try to view an Internet video and Windows' Media Player wimps out, the video may need software called RealPlayer. Head for `www.real.com` and download RealPlayer Basic. That's the freebie version that lets you view the videos (and sometimes hear radio broadcasts, too.)

How do I copy a picture from the Internet?

As you browse through Web pages and your mouse pointer rests over a photo or other large image, an annoying box of icons appears, as shown in Figure 12-6.

Those little boxes, new to Internet Explorer 6, let you grab the image. Clicking the little disk icon saves the image to your My Pictures folder. Click the Printer to print the image. The little letter e-mails the image through your e-mail program. And clicking the little folder opens your My Pictures folder for browsing.

If you spot a picture on the Internet that you want to use for your "Welcome Screen" picture on your user account, save it to your My Pictures folder. Then use the Control Panel (see Chapter 14) to change your picture to that new picture.

Little boxes keep popping up on the Web pages!

Many cash-hungry Web sites, no longer content with stuffing ads onto their pages, now use "pop-up" ads: Annoying little windows hawking a product. The flying windows often cover up what you're trying to read.

Neither Windows XP nor Internet Explorer include a way to stop those annoying ads, unfortunately, but several third-party programs stop most Web sites from tossing advertisements in your face. The biggest problem? The ad blockers and ad makers constantly battle, trying to bypass each others' efforts.

If you'd like to enter the war against pop-up ads, check out offerings from AdSubtract (`www.adsubtract.com`), Guidescope (`www.guidescope.com`), AdShield (`www.ad-shield.com`), or one of the many others. For best results, always use the most up-to-date version.

Figure 12-6:
A little bar
pops up
when your
mouse
pointer rests
over photos,
allowing you
to save,
print, or
e-mail the
photo.

Managing E-Mail with Outlook Express

Internet Explorer merely flips through the Web pages stuffed onto the Internet, letting you jump from page to page. Outlook Express, on the other hand, uses the Internet as a post office, letting you send letters and files to anybody with an Internet account. Better yet, the recipients of your e-mails don't have to use Outlook Express to view and respond to them: Almost any e-mail program can talk to almost any other one.

Outlook Express is designed to work with an industry-standard Internet service provider that pipes the Internet signal from your computer to the Internet without an online service getting in the way. That's why Outlook Express 6.0, the version included with Windows XP, doesn't work with online services like America Online (AOL). Those online services come with built-in e-mail programs that process mail differently than Outlook Express does. So if you're using America Online, don't bother reading this section. You won't be using Outlook Express 6.0.

The rest of this section guides you through setting up Outlook Express, writing a letter, sending it, and reading the responses.

Setting up Outlook Express 6.0 to send and receive e-mail

In order to set up your e-mail address, also known as an *account,* you need several things from your Internet service provider: your user name, the ISP's phone number, and your password. These are the same items you need to set up your Internet account, as described in the Internet Connection Wizard section earlier in this chapter.

Also, many people have more than one e-mail address — an account from Yahoo! or Hotmail, for instance. Plus, many ISPs offer several e-mail addresses per account. That lets each person in the family have his or her own separate e-mail account. These same steps add additional e-mail addresses to Outlook Express, as well.

1. **Set up your Internet account and open Outlook Express.**

   You need to set up your Internet account *first*, as described earlier in this chapter, or your e-mail won't have any way to connect to the Internet.

    To call up Outlook Express for the first time, open the Start menu and click the Outlook Express icon: an envelope surrounded by twirling blue arrows. Outlook Express pops onto the screen, as shown in Figure 12-7, ready to be set up to send and receive your e-mail.

   Sometimes you won't see the screen in Figure 12-7. You might already have an e-mail account set up, for instance, or you're adding an additional e-mail account. In that case, open Outlook Express and choose Accounts from the Tools menu. Click the Add button and choose Mail. You'll see the window shown in Figure 12-7, ready to add an additional e-mail account.

Figure 12-7:
Type your
own name
into the
Display
Name box.

2. **Type in your name and click Next.**

   This name will appear in the From line of all your e-mail, so most people simply type in their own name, as shown in Figure 12-7. Names like *StarMan* can come back to haunt you.

3. **Type in your e-mail address and click Next.**

   This is your user name, the @ sign, and your ISP, all information that your ISP must provide you. For instance, my user name is *q-a,* and my ISP's name is *home.* So, I type **q-a@home.com** into the E-mail Address box.

   If you're adding another account to Outlook Express, type in the user name for that second account. (You need to either sign up for another e-mail account on your ISP's Web page, or ask your ISP for the user name and password for a second account.)

4. **Choose your server type, and the names for your incoming and out-going mail servers.**

   Here, you need to know what *type* of e-mail account the service uses. It's a weird word like POP3, IMAP, or HTTP. Many ISPs mail you a piece of paper with these handy settings and instructions.

   But if you want to chance it, try these settings, which usually work. Select POP3 in the top box, and type the word **mail** in the Incoming Mail and Outgoing Mail boxes.

5. **Type in your Account Name and Password, and click Next.**

   Your account name is the name on your ISP account — the name you use when setting up your Internet account. Even if you're setting up an additional e-mail account, you'll still type in the same name you use to access the Internet.

   Type in the same password you use to access the Internet, too. If you want to log on automatically without entering your password each time, check the Remember Password box. Check the Secure Password Authentication box only if your Internet provider asks you to.

6. **Click Finish.**

   That's it. You should be able to send and receive e-mail on Outlook Express.

America Online users can't use Outlook Express on their own computers to send e-mail. However, they can still accept e-mail from somebody using Outlook Express or any other e-mail program.

If your copy of Outlook Express doesn't look like the version in this chapter, it's probably configured a little differently. Try this trick: Choose Layout from the View menu and make sure that you've selected Folder Bar, Folder List, Status Bar, and Toolbar. Click the Apply button after you select each one so you can see what that option does to the screen.

Getting ready to send e-mail

The Outlook Express screen consists of three main parts: Folders, where you store your e-mail; Contacts, which displays address book entries; and the work screen, where you choose whether you'll be looking at e-mail or newsgroups. (I talk about newsgroups later in this chapter.)

To send e-mail to a friend or enemy, you need three things:

✔ **A properly configured Outlook Express**

The section before this one describes how to set up Outlook Express to work with e-mail accounts.

✔ **Your friend or enemy's e-mail address**

You need to find out your friend's e-mail address by simply asking him or her. There's no way to guess. It consists of a user name (which isn't always his or her real name), followed by the @ sign, followed by the name of the Internet service provider, be it America Online, Juno, or any of the thousands of other ISPs. The e-mail address of somebody with the user name of Jeff9435 who subscribes to America Online would be `jeff9435@aol.com`.

✔ **Your message**

Here's where the fun part starts: typing your letter. After you type in the e-mail address and the letter, you're ready to send your message along its merry way.

You can find e-mail addresses on business cards, Web sites, and even return addresses: Whenever anybody sends you some e-mail, you can see his or her e-mail address for responding.

If you misspell part of the e-mail address, your message will bounce back to your own mailbox, with a confusing *undeliverable* message attached.

Composing a letter

Ready to send your first letter? After you've set up Outlook Express with your e-mail account, follow these steps to compose your letter and drop it in the electronic mailbox, sending it through virtual space to your friend's electronic mailbox.

1. **Open Outlook Express and click the Create Mail icon from the program's menu.**

   If don't see a Create Mail icon along the top (it looks like the one in the margin), click the File menu, select New, and choose Mail Message.

   A New Message window appears, as shown in Figure 12-8.

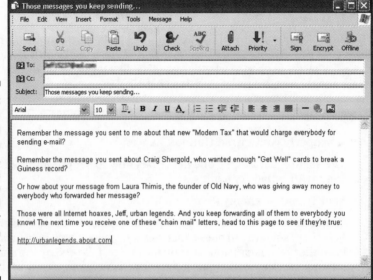

Figure 12-8:
Type an
e-mail
address in
the To box,
type a
descriptive
subject, and
type your
message in
the big box
below.

2. Type your friend's e-mail address into the To box.

Type whatever the person's e-mail happens to be. Or, if you've e-mailed that person previously, click the word *To* next to the address box. A window appears, listing the names of people you've previously e-mailed.

3. Fill in the Subject box.

This one's optional, but it helps your friend know what your e-mail is about so that he or she can choose to respond right away or file it in the "I'll respond when I get around to it" box.

4. Type your message in the large box at the bottom of the window.

Type whatever you want, and for as long as you want. There's very little limit on the size of a text file.

5. Click the Send button in the box's top-left corner.

Whoosh! Outlook Express dials your modem, if it needs to, and whisks your message through the Internet pipelines to your friend's mailbox. Depending on the speed of the Internet connection, mail arrives anywhere within 15 seconds to five days, with a few minutes being the average.

No Send button? Then click File and choose Send Message.

✔ Some people like those big buttons along the top of Outlook Express, like you see in Figure 12-8. If yours are missing and you want 'em back, right-click on a blank part of the Outlook Express menu — an inch to the right of the word Help will do the trick. Choose Toolbar, and the buttons appear. To get rid of 'em, right-click in the same place, but choose Toolbar again to toggle them off.

✔ Not too good of a speler? Then before you send the message, click the spell check button from the icons along the top. Or choose Spelling from the Tools menu. Or press your F7 key. Or grab a dictionary off the shelf. (Pressing F7 is quicker.) If it doesn't work, read the following warning.

Microsoft pulled a dirty trick on the spell checker. Outlook Express borrows the spell checker that comes with Microsoft Word, Microsoft Excel, or Microsoft PowerPoint. If you don't have any of those programs, the spell checker won't work. (That's why the Spelling button is grayed out in Figure 12-8.)

✔ Want to attach a file to your message? After completing Step 4, click the paper clip icon. (Or choose File Attachment from the Insert menu.) Windows XP brings up a box straight out of My Computer. Navigate through the folders to reach the file that you want to send and then double-click its name. When you click the Send button in Step 5 (in the preceding step list), Outlook Express sends your message — and the attached file — to your friend. (Many ISPs balk at sending files larger than about 4MB, though, which includes most MP3 files.)

Reading a received letter

If you keep Outlook Express running 24 hours a day, you'll know when a new letter drops into your mailbox. Most computers make a breezy little sound to notify you of its arrival. You'll also spot a tiny Outlook Express icon sitting in the bottom-right corner of your desktop, right next to the digital clock. Plus, if more than one person uses your PC, the Welcome screen will display how many e-mails each person has received.

To check for any new mail if Outlook Express isn't always running, load the program from the Start menu. When it loads, click the Send/Recv button or click the Tools menu, choose Send and Receive, and then choose Send and Receive All. That sends any outgoing mail you have sitting around and grabs any incoming mail to place in your mailbox.

Follow these steps to read the letters in your mailbox and either respond or file them away into one of Outlook Express' convenient folders.

1. **Open Outlook Express and look at your Inbox.**

   Depending on how Outlook Express is set up, you can do this in several different ways. If you see an opening screen announcing that you have Unread Mail in your Inbox, click the words Unread Mail. If you see folders along the left side of Outlook Express, click the word Inbox. Either way, Outlook Express will show you the messages in your Inbox, and they'll look something like Figure 12-9: All the subjects, called *headers,* will be listed, one by one.

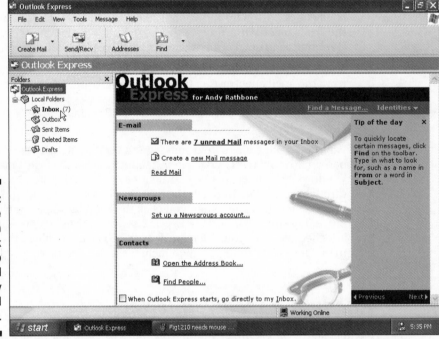

Figure 12-9:
Click the
Inbox in
Outlook
Express to
unveil
your newly
received
messages.

2. **Click any message's subject to read it.**

   The message's contents will then show in the bottom portion of the screen, as shown in Figure 12-10, ready for you to read. Or, to see the entire message in its own window, double-click the subject.

From here, Outlook Express leaves you with many options, each described in the following list.

- ✓ **You can do nothing.** The message stays in your Inbox folder until you delete it.

- ✓ **You can respond to the message.** Click the Reply icon along the top of Outlook Express (or choose Reply to Sender from the Message menu), and a new box appears, ready for you to type in a message. The box is just like the one that appears when you first compose a message, but there's a big difference: This box is preaddressed with the recipient's name and the subject.

- ✓ **You can file the message.** Right-click on the message and choose either Copy to Folder or Move to Folder; then select the desired folder from the pop-up menu. Or, put folders on the left side of the screen so you can drag and drop the message's header to the desired folder: Click the word Inbox, and, when the folders drop down, click the little push pin to keep the folders in place.

✔ **You can print the message.** Click the Print icon along the menu's top, and Outlook Express shoots your message to the printer to make a paper copy.

✔ Outlook Express can be confusing when you drag and drop a message: As you drag the message over to the folders, the little envelope icon turns into a circle with a diagonal line through it. Don't fret. That menacing circle disappears when the mouse rests over a folder that's ready to accept a message.

✔ Outlook Express can handle more-complicated tasks, but these basic steps enable you to send e-mail to and receive e-mail from your friends and congressional leaders.

✔ If you ever receive a message with an attachment that ends in the letters EXE or VBS, *please* delete the message immediately without opening it — even if the message comes from a trusted friend. Those attachments are the easiest way for evil people to send virus and worm programs into computers. After these programs get into your system, they replicate, sending copies of themselves to everybody you know — all your friends — without you knowing what's going on. For complete peace of mind, buy an antivirus program and keep it updated faithfully.

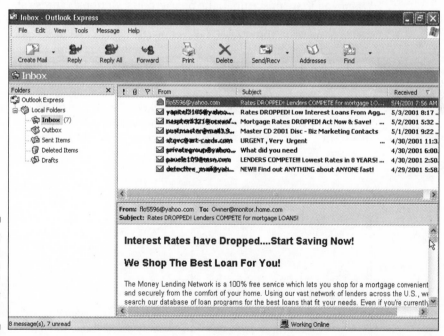

Figure 12-10:
Click a
subject line
to read
that new
message.

What does the News area do?

Thousands of people with similar interests yak it up on the Internet through something called *newsgroups.* Newsgroups work sort of like mail that everybody gets to read.

A newsgroup is also like a public bulletin board. One person posts a message or file, and then everybody can read it and post their own replies, which spawns more replies.

To keep newsgroups on track, they are divided by subject — usually more than 30,000 of them — and Outlook Express can display all the subjects on your screen and let you join in the conversations.

Signing up for a newsgroup account is much easier than setting up an e-mail account. Choose Accounts from the Tools menu, and click the News tab. Click the Add button and choose News from the pop-out menu. Finally, type in your name and e-mail address and type the word **news** when it asks for your News (NNTP) server. Finally, answer Yes when Outlook Express asks if you'd like to download newsgroups for your news account.

When you first subscribe to the newsgroups, Outlook Express searches for names of *all* the newsgroups carried by your Internet service provider and displays them on the screen. Collecting the names and descriptions of thousands of newsgroups takes some time, as shown in Figure 12-11, so play FreeCell for a while. Luckily, Outlook only searches for the newsgroups once and then it remembers them all.

If you receive an error message, or the word **news** doesn't work correctly, it's time to call your Internet Service provider and ask what the heck it calls the newsgroups instead of **news**. It probably uses a slight variation.

Figure 12-11:
Outlook
Express
must track
down
all of the
news-
groups'
names and
descriptions
so that you
can look at
them.

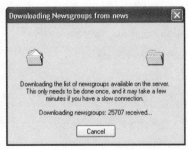

Finding and reading a newsgroup

With many thousands of newsgroups, how can you find the right one? Well, start by making Outlook Express find it for you. For example, here's how to find and subscribe to a newsgroup with discussions on recipes:

1. **Make Outlook Express gather a list of newsgroup names and then choose Read News.**

   Discussed in the preceding section, the searching for newsgroup names must only be conducted once. (Thank goodness, because it can take a l-o-n-g time.) When you choose Read News, a box appears, showing all the available groups. (Well, the first ten or so, starting in alphabetical order.)

2. **Type** recipe **in the Display Newsgroups Which Contain box.**

   That's the word *recipe* — nothing else. As soon as you begin to type, Outlook Express begins weeding out newsgroups that don't contain the letters of the word *recipe*. Eventually, only the newsgroups that deal with recipes remain on your screen.

3. **Look through the findings for something interesting.**

   In this case, a dozen or so newsgroups deal with recipes. Click the scroll bar to the right of the Newsgroup box to view all of the findings.

4. **Subscribe to the newsgroup you want.**

   Click a newsgroup name that looks interesting and then click the Subscribe button to the right. A little icon appears beside the name to let you know that you've subscribed. Subscribe to as many or as few newsgroups as you want.

5. **After subscribing to your chosen newsgroups, click the OK button.**

   Your newly chosen newsgroups now appear at the very bottom of the folders on the left side of the Outlook Express window. (No folders? Click the News button and click the little push pin to lock the folders in place.)

6. **Click one of your recently subscribed names.**

   A list of postings in that particular newsgroup appears on the right side of the screen, as shown in Figure 12-12.

7. **Finally, click one of the postings to see what that person has written about the topic.**

   In Figure 12-12, for example, you click Pork Ribs, and Outlook Express brings up the message in a window, just as if it were an e-mail. (The "Re:" in front of a message means that message is a response to somebody's message about vital gluten.)

That's it; you've subscribed to the wacky world of newsgroups, where you can find people chatting about nearly every subject imaginable — and some unimaginable ones as well.

✔ To respond to a newsgroup post, treat it as if it were e-mail. Click the Reply Group button at the top of the window, type your response, and click the Send button.

✔ Newsgroups are public information, as opposed to e-mail, which is private. Don't say anything on a newsgroup that might hurt your chances for public office. (And don't write anything that you wouldn't want your parents, spouse, boss, or next-door neighbor to read.)

✔ Some of the information on newsgroups deals with very adult-oriented content. Make sure that you know what newsgroups your kids are reading.

✔ Newsgroups can be a valuable source of computer help. If your monitor isn't working correctly, look for a newsgroup dealing with monitor issues. You may even find a newsgroup dealing with your specific brand of monitor. Post your question, and see if anybody has had a similar problem and, best yet, found a solution.

✔ Many people who hang out on newsgroups view themselves as old-timers who resent any encroachment on their territory. Before posting, spend some time *lurking* on a newsgroup to get a taste of its particular flavor and decorum. Read the current posts for a few days to catch the group's flavor before adding your own spice.

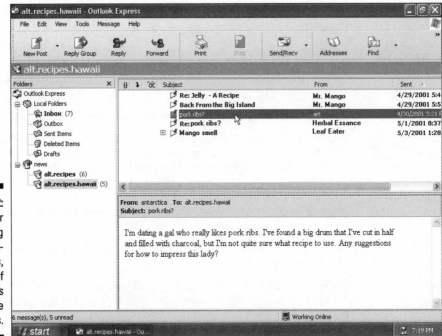

Figure 12-12:
After subscribing to newsgroups, click one of the names to see the postings.

Chapter 13

Sound! Movies! Media Player!

• •

In This Chapter

▶ Figuring out Media Player

▶ Finding music, radio, and movie trailers on the Internet

▶ Finding and cataloging the music on your computer

▶ Playing CDs and DVDs

▶ Playing MP3s, WMAs, and video

▶ Creating WMAs

▶ Making Media Player create MP3s and play DVDs

▶ Moving music to and from MP3 players

▶ Creating CDs

▶ Adding skins to Media Player

▶ Using the My Pictures and My Music folders

▶ Fixing sound and video problems

• •

*F*or years, computers could only cut loose with a rude beep, which they issued to harass confused users who pressed the wrong key. The Windows XP Media Player changes all that, handling fancy videos, Internet radio stations, CDs, DVDs, MP3s, and more. But only if you press the *right* keys.

In fact, the program does so much that figuring out exactly what it's supposed to be doing (and when) is overwhelming. This chapter shows how to do it all, and because there's so much to cover, I'll stop blabbing and start explaining.

Understanding Media Player

Media Player's performance depends entirely upon how much money you paid for your computer — or how much money your computer has absorbed since you first plopped it on your desk.

That's because Media Player is nothing more than a big, fancy package of buttons. Before you can use those buttons to do anything, you need to connect your computer to features, such as speakers, sound cards, CD burners, CD/DVD drives, the Internet, and MP3 players. Pressing the right buttons calls these right things into action and tells the computer what do to with them.

Figure 13-1, which explains some of the zillions of Media Player buttons, shows Media Player while it first loads. (If you get lost amid all those buttons, just rest your mouse pointer over any button, and Windows XP gives you a hint.)

- ✔ You need a sound card and speakers or headphones before you can hear anything. Luckily, most new computers come with preinstalled sound cards; many come with speakers, as well. Another bonus: If your computer doesn't have a sound card, they're cheap and fairly easy to install.

- ✔ A CD-ROM drive is essential for playing CDs or creating WMA (Windows Media Audio) files. You need a Read/Write CD drive, too, so that you can burn CDs of your favorite music. Many new computers come with those included, as well.

- ✔ You need an Internet connection to listen to Internet radio or search the Web for videos or other media content. Faster is better. In fact, most Internet videos look pretty tiny or grainy if you're using a dial-up connection.

- ✔ Windows XP's Media Player uses WMA compatibility to decide whether it will transfer files to a portable MP3 player. If your portable player can't handle WMA files, Media Player probably won't transfer *any* files to it. But if the player handles WMA files along with MP3 files, Media Player can usually transfer both WMA and MP3 files to your player.

- ✔ A newer version of Media Player, Media Player 9 (described at this chapter's end), may be downloaded from the Internet. That version includes fancier features and works on some older Windows versions, as well.

Open files or add to library

Change video size or add skins

Play media

Change options

Find help with Media Player

Toggle Shuffle mode

Toggle Equalizer settings

Show current playing playlist

Maximize

Minimize

Close

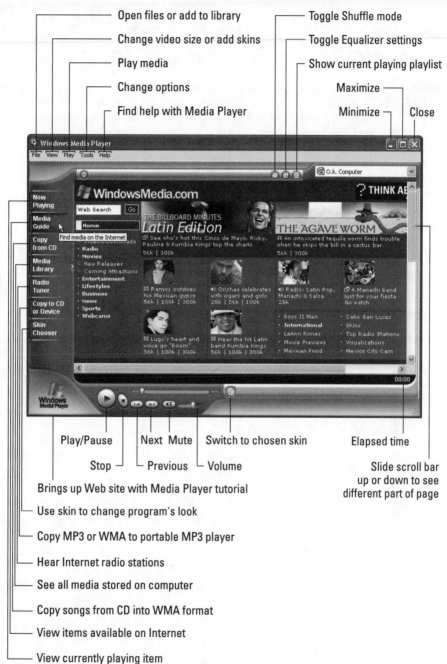

Figure 13-1:
Rest your
mouse over
any button,
and
Windows XP
explains its
purpose.

Play/Pause

Stop

Next Mute

Previous

Volume

Switch to chosen skin

Elapsed time

Slide scroll bar
up or down to see
different part of page

Brings up Web site with Media Player tutorial

Use skin to change program's look

Copy MP3 or WMA to portable MP3 player

Hear Internet radio stations

See all media stored on computer

Copy songs from CD into WMA format

View items available on Internet

View currently playing item

Using Media Guide to Find Videos, Music, and Movie Trailers on the Internet

Media
Guide

Media Player not only plays tunes and videos from your own computer, but it snatches them from the Internet, as well. In fact, if you're online when Media Player's loaded, the program opens to the Media Guide section: a constantly updated Web site also found at www.windowsmedia.com.

The site, shown in Figure 13-1, offers videos, music, and radio, all by clicking various on-screen items. Most of the items along the left menu are obvious — Music, Radio, Movies, Business, News, and Sports. Here are a few of the not-so-obvious ones:

- ✔ **Go:** Click in this box, type in your own musical interest, and Media Guide displays a list of related sites: Band bios and photos, album information, song clips, and other information.

- ✔ **Home:** The home page for WindowsMedia, it offers a variety of media goodies: movie trailers, weird animated shorts from France, radio stations, songs, and other bits of fun.

- ✔ **Entertainment:** Similar to the Home page, this offers news tidbits about trendy television shows, hip movie stars, and pop culture icons.

- ✔ **Lifestyles:** Head here for splashy videos about fancy food, wine, travel, and other bourgeois interests.

- ✔ **Business:** Financial news, money talk, and an emphasis on buying the right technogadgets.

Here's how to start farming the Internet for media goodies — videos, in particular, from the Media Guide section:

1. **Open Media Player and click the Media Guide button along the left.**

   Media Player usually looms large on your Start menu. If Media Player is hiding, click All Programs and choose it from that menu. (Chapter 10 shows how to use the Start Menu's All Programs button, and it explains all the goodies hidden inside there.)

2. **Tell Windows to dial the Internet, if you're not already connected.**

   When connected, Media Player shows the WindowsMedia.com page, shown in Figure 13-1. (Actually, you're just viewing a Web page, the same page you would see if you went to www.windowsmedia.com with Internet Explorer.)

3. **Click an item that interests you.**

The menu items along the left are explained in the preceding bulleted list. Clicking any menu subject — Music, Radio, Movies, Entertainment, Lifestyles, Business, News, Sports, or Webcams — brings up a Web page displaying items relating to that subject.

4. **Click the icon that starts your desired media.**

For instance, if you're interested in watching the Agave Worm video displayed along the top of Figure 13-1, click the Agave Worm picture. Media Player loads the video (which can take some time on slower modems) and plays it on-screen.

Many videos have numbers beneath them, such as 56K | 100K | 300K. Those numbers stand for your modem's connection speed. If you're using a 56K modem, for instance, click the 56K link. The picture quality won't be as good as the higher speeds, but at least it will work. Save the 100K and 300K links for people with DSL, cable, or T1 connections.

- Good news: Even though the video may only update the screen once or twice each second with dial-up modems, the sound usually comes through relatively well.

- You have no Back button on Media Player's menu, making navigation difficult. That means you must remember the keyboard short-cuts for moving back and forward between pages. Hold down Alt and press the left-arrow key to go back a page; hold Alt and press the right-arrow key to go forward.

- Little icons beneath each picture tell you what format the media comes in. The little filmstrip icon, for instance, stands for video. The little speaker means the format is a song or radio station. And two little interlocking windows means clicking there brings up Internet Explorer to feature a different Web site.

- If Media Player's Media Guide area looks and feels cumbersome inside Media Player's restrictive borders, blow it off. Just open Internet Explorer and head for www.windowsmedia.com. You can do the same things there as you can with Media Player.

- Be sure to check out the Coming Attractions section for Movie Trailers. Also, click Videos/Downloads under Music to see videos by dozens of artists.

- Sometimes Media Player takes you to sites where you must register by typing in your name and e-mail address and making up a password. Feel free to type in a fake e-mail address so the sites won't send you junk mail.

Making movies play better

Movies don't always play back smoothly. If the computer and its modem aren't fast enough and expensive enough to keep up the fast pace, the movie looks jerky. The problem is that Media Player skips part of the movie to keep up with the soundtrack. Here are a few tips for smoother sailing when watching movies:

✔ Be sure to use the fastest modem available in your area. Faster computers also process videos faster. Don't be tempted to choose faster download speeds than your modem can handle.

✔ Movies play back at their fastest when they are either full-screen (not contained in a window at all) or in a small window. Hold down Alt and press Enter to toggle a video from full-screen to window mode.

✔ Right-click on a video while it plays to see different size options. Choose Fit to Window to make the video expand and contract as you change the window's size. The percentage signs describe the size of the video. And choose Full Screen to watch the video without Media Player's borders. (Jiggle the mouse, and the controls reappear for volume, pause, and other settings.)

Finding and Playing Internet Radio Stations

Sure, anybody can turn on a $10 radio and flip through the stations. But Windows XP turns your $1,500 PC into a radio that pulls in stations from around the world. These stations arrive through the broadcast waves of the future — the Internet. Internet radio is so much fun that it gets its own button on Media Player's left-hand side.

The following steps show how to track down your favorite types of music through the Internet's radio stations, and assign buttons to them so that they're ready for quick listening.

Radio Tuner

1. **Connect to the Internet, open Media Player, and click the Radio Tuner button.**

   The Radio Tuner window appears, listing featured radio stations as well as allowing you to find your own. Because the Radio Tuner page is also part of the Windows Media Web site (www.windowsmedia.com), these steps may vary slightly.

2. **Click Find More Stations.**

   Click the words, "Find More Stations", seen near the window's top, right corner in Figure 13-2, to bring up a more detailed Search box. Or, type your favorite musical genre in the box.

3. **Choose your categories for searching.**

   Any choice in Step 2 brings you to the search page seen in Figure 13-3. From there, select your favorite musical genre in the first box, and narrow your search by typing some keywords into the Search box. (If desired, find local stations by typing in your zip code.) Click the green arrow next to either box to start searching.

4. **Choose a station within your modem speed's limits.**

   Be sure to click a station broadcasting within the limits of your modem. If you're using a 28K or 56K modem, for instance, don't try to tune in a station broadcasting at 100K. (The modem speeds are listed in the Speed column.)

   Clicking a station's name usually displays options to visit the station's Web site, play its music, or add the station to your list of favorite stations (seen in Figure 13-2) for later return visits.

5. **Choose the Play button.**

   When you click a station's name and see the Play button, click Play to begin listening to the station through Media Player.

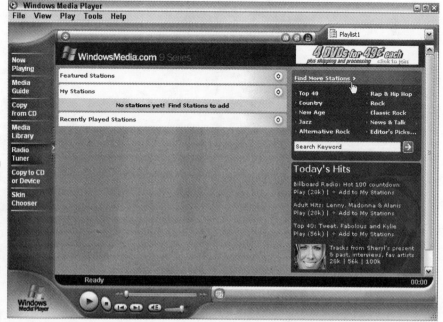

Figure 13-2:
Click the green arrow to start your search for available Internet radio stations.

TIP

Now
Playing

✔ Sometimes selecting a station calls up Internet Explorer, which takes you to that station's Web page; there, you must press a few more buttons before actually hearing the tunes. You need to choose the broadcast rate all over again, for instance; or, if the site broadcasts several stations, you need to select your preferred station again.

✔ Stations broadcasting at higher speeds always sound better than the ones at lower speeds.

✔ To expand your cultural horizons, try choosing stations from different countries, or choose formats you've never tried before. After all, you can hear that same old rock station on your home radio. Taste the Internet for a while.

✔ To see what you're listening to, click the Now Playing button. In many cases, you see a song list, describing the artist, song and album title, and length.

✔ Many Internet radio stations don't just play music, unfortunately. The majority of them sprinkle pop-up ads onto your screen as you listen. This is no big deal if you're microwaving a hot dog across the room, but it's quite annoying if you're trying to surf the Web or play solitaire.

Figure 13-3: Media Player searches for your desired radio station and plays the one you select.

Finding Media on Your Computer and Putting It into the Media Library

After a while, your computer will be filled with music, videos, and radio station call letters. Media Player helps out by cataloging all your computer's media and listing it in a huge card catalog called the Media Library. Whether one of your computer's files just beeps or does a song and dance, Media Player can find it, categorize it, and let you play it quickly and easily. Best yet, Media Player does it all automatically.

 To make Media Player scour your hard drive for songs, sounds, and videos, click Media Player's Tools menu and choose Search for Media Files. After the box appears, leave it searching for All Drives and click Search. (Be sure to remove any CDs from your drives first.) Media Player examines your entire computer, gathering any media files it encounters and placing their locations in the Media Library for easy access.

 To see the results, click the Media Library button, and Media Player displays all your media files, organized by Audio, Video, Playlists, and Radio Tuner Presets.

Here's a breakdown of the categories:

- ✔ **Audio:** Media Player breaks down your audio into four categories. Click All Audio to see *everything* audible: Internet radio stations, CDs, MIDI files, MP3s, and WMAs. Clicking Album groups all your MP3 and WMA files by album. Clicking Artist organizes the songs by a particular artist rather than album. Finally, clicking Genre shows music files separated into categories, such as rock, jazz, or pop.

- ✔ **Video:** Only two categories fall into video. Choose All Clips to see all the movies stored on your hard drive; clicking Author organizes videos by their creators.

- ✔ **Playlists:** To tailor your own personalized daily music background, create a *playlist,* which I describe in the next section. A playlist contains the names and locations of your chosen media, and plays it all back in order — your own Greatest Hits list.

- ✔ **Radio Tuner Presets:** If you've added any Internet radio stations to your My Favorite Stations list, as I describe in the preceding section, they appear here for quick access.

 If you access the Internet a lot to hear or watch stuff, tell Windows Media Player to add the locations of those items to your Media Library, too. Click Tools from the top menu and select Options. Click the Player tab and put a check mark next to Add Items to Media Library When Played under Player Settings.

Creating Playlists

Just about everybody has bought a Greatest Hits album. Media Player lets you create your own, even if you just listen to bagpipe players. You're not limited to selecting music. Media Player lets you add *anything* to your playlist. Media Player lets you place any assortment of items from your Media Library into a playlist for organized listening.

Create your own party soundtrack by mixing radio station streams with MP3 files, favorite videos, and links to Internet movie trailers. To set up and start using a playlist, follow these steps:

1. **Load Media Player and click the Media Library button.**

   The Media Library button is one of the buttons along Media Player's left-hand side. A list of categories appears, looking uncomfortably like the Windows Explorer program. (Actually, it works the same way.)

2. **Click the New Playlist button along Media Player's top.**

   A box appears, asking you to name your new creation.

3. **In the New Playlist box, type a name for your playlist and click the OK button.**

   Type in a name — *Tunes for Toddlers,* for example.

4. **Right-click on files or radio station links, choose Add to Playlist, and select your playlist.**

   Begin browsing through your files, including audio, video, and radio files. To see all possible music files, click All Audio. After you spot something cool, right-click on it and choose Add to Playlist from the pop-up menu.

5. **To play a playlist, click the Media Library button's My Playlists menu and choose your playlist.**

   Your playlist, the one you named in Step 3, contains all your recently selected music and videos. Media Player begins playing it immediately.

Playlists help tame Media Player's button-pushing requirements. Instead of wading through bunches of buttons when trying to hear a tune, choose a different playlist for instant punching during different moods or times of day.

Playing CDs

Just about every CD-ROM drive installed during the past five years plays music CDs as well as reads computer data. A computer with a sound card, speakers, and a CD-ROM drive lets you type to the tunes while you work.

This section shows how to play CDs in your computer. It also explains how Media Player automatically uses the Internet to identify your CD, list the CD's song titles, and even grab a picture of the CD's cover art.

1. **Connect to the Internet.**

   If you're not connected when you insert a new CD, Media Player will still play it, but Media Player won't be able to identify it.

2. **Insert a music CD into your CD-ROM drive tray.**

   Push the tray back in, if required, or push its tray retract button. Media Player jumps to the forefront, switches to its Now Playing window, and starts playing the tunes.

   Keep an eye on the Media Player playlist that currently identifies your CD as Unknown Artist playing Track 1. After a few moments, the names of your CD's songs appear on the playlist on the right, as shown in Figure 13-4.

   While the CD plays, marvel at the swirling visualizations that twitch in time to the tunes.

3. **Control the album's playback by pushing buttons.**

   The control buttons in Media Player's CD player mimic just about every other type of CD player: Play/Pause, Stop, Previous, Next, and Mute. Slide the little bar next to the little speaker icon to change the volume. (Refer to Figure 13-1 for how these buttons work. Or just rest your mouse pointer over the buttons to see what they do.)

Figure 13-4: When connected to the Internet, Media Player recognizes this CD automatically and lists the song titles in the playlist.

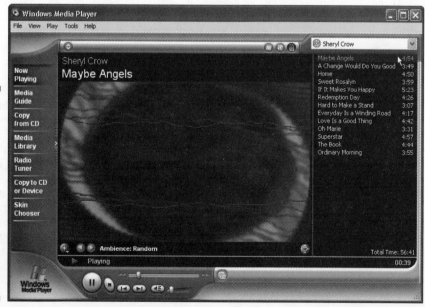

✔ Media Player automatically recognizes the bestsellers and a surprising amount of obscure stuff. Sometimes, however, you need to enter the names yourself: Right-click on a track, choose Edit, and type in the name. After Media Player has identified your CD's title and song names, it remembers them. It doesn't need to connect to the Internet and download them again.

✔ *Visualizations* are those swirling thingies that twitch to the music's beat after you insert a CD. Beneath the swirlies, two little arrows let you choose different types of visualizations. Choose Download Visualizations from the Tools menu to find more. Or right-click on a swirly thing to choose from a menu of swirlies.

✔ Right-click on the swirling visualization and choose Album Art from the pop-up menu. Media Player replaces the swirlies with the CD's art, if it can find it on the Internet.

✔ Play your CDs — or anything else — in random order by choosing Shuffle from the Play menu or clicking the tiny Shuffle button shown in Figure 13-1.

✔ Want to play a CD over and over to see if you get tired of it? Start playing it and choose Repeat from the Play menu. The CD keeps playing until you click the Stop button.

✔ Feel free to tweak the sound to suit your ears. Choose the SRS WOW effects by clicking the little buttons or by choosing from the View menu's Now Playing Tools area. The WOW effect adds a 3-D quality, and TruBass artificially cranks up the bass. For less gimmickry control, choose the Graphic Equalizer. Sculpt the sound yourself or choose from pre-selects including Jazz, Acoustic, Rock, Rap, and more.

Playing DVDs

Microsoft raves about how Media Player plays DVDs. But that's a lie. Windows XP can't play DVDs right out of the box. See, even though you've bought a Windows XP computer, a DVD drive, and a DVD, you need something else: special software called a *decoder.* This bit of software, called a *codec* because it converts one format to another, enables your computer to translate numbers on a disc into videos of galloping horses on the screen.

Unfortunately, Windows XP doesn't come with a DVD codec, so you must pick up one somewhere else. Where? Well, most computers with DVD drives come with DVD playing software — a little box with its own little controls. That software installs its own DVD codec in Windows, and Media Player simply borrows that. But if you don't have DVD playing software, there's nothing to borrow, and Media Player ignores your DVDs.

✔ If you choose Windows Media Player instead of your third-party DVD player to watch DVDs, the controls are pretty much the same as they are for playing CDs (described in the preceding section).

✔ You probably need to update your DVD software so that it will work under Windows XP. Otherwise your DVD software won't work under Media Player, either. Head for the Web site of your DVD player's manufacturer and look for a Windows XP patch or upgrade. If you're lucky, the manufacturer won't charge you for the upgrade. Some companies, however, make you buy a new version.

✔ DVD stands for Digital Video Disc, Digital Versatile Disc, and Dick Van Dyke.

Playing MP3s and WMAs

Windows XP plays MP3 files, the standard for storing music on computers and the Internet. Windows XP also handles Microsoft's competing format, WMA files. (You can create MP3s if you buy Microsoft's "add-on" software described in the sidebar on the next page.) To listen to an MP3 file — whether you downloaded it from the Internet or created it using another program — follow these steps:

1. **Open Media Player.**

   If you don't see its icon on your Start menu or taskbar, click the Start button, choose All Programs, and choose Windows Media Player from that menu.

2. **Choose Open from the File menu.**

   The Open box appears, ready for you to root through your folders for the appropriate file.

3. **Locate your MP3 or WMA file.**

   Open the folder that holds your file.

   Having trouble finding your MP3 file? Then choose Search from the Start menu; choose Pictures, Music, or Video; and click in the Music and Sound box. After you click the Search button, all your MP3 and WMA files appear in the Search window.

4. **Double-click the file that you want to hear.**

   Media Player immediately begins playing the song.

✔ If you've told Media Player to catalog all your media files, as I explain in this chapter's "Finding Media on Your Computer and Putting It into the Media Library" section, click Media Player's Media Library button. Media Player lists your MP3s in the Audio section, sorted by Album, Artist, and Genre.

- Media Player lets you create playlists of your favorite tunes, as I describe in the "Creating Playlists" section, earlier in this chapter. That lets you make a list of what files you'd like to play, and in what order.

- Although Windows Media Player does a decent job of playing MP3 files, the program's just too big and bulky. For a more versatile and slim player, check out Winamp at `www.winamp.com`.

- Blatant plug: For everything you want to know about MP3, check out my book, *MP3 For Dummies,* 2nd Edition, published by Hungry Minds, Inc. Or, if you see a friend's copy, grab it.

What are MP3, WMA, and Mp3PRO?

MP3 ripped open the music industry in a way never seen before. MP3 technology stores music onto a computer as a file that's compressed to about one-tenth of its original size. Yet, the sound stays almost as good as the original CD.

As the public caught on to the implications of MP3, folks began creating MP3 files from their favorite CDs, storing the music onto their computers or portable MP3 players, such as the Rio or Nomad. Many people trade MP3s over the Internet using programs such as BearShare or Newsgroups. The music fans love it. The music industry hates it, saying it results in copyright violations that hurt music sales.

Sensing an opening in the market, Microsoft created its own music compression formula called Windows Media Audio (WMA), which has beat MP3 in a key area. See, MP3 files must be encoded at 128 Kbps for good sound. But WMA can be compressed at 64 Kbps. That makes WMA twice as small, yet it still sounds as good as MP3.

Some people prefer MP3s because of the sound and wide acceptability. Others prefer WMAs because their smaller size makes it easier to stuff more tunes onto a portable player — if the portable player accepts the WMA format.

If you don't click the correct button, however, WMA inserts a special license into the files, making them more difficult to copy: You can't always take WMAs created on one computer and play them on another.

The Windows XP Media Player plays both WMA and MP3 files, yet it only creates WMA files from CDs. By itself, Media Player can't create MP3s.

There's more: The folks who created the MP3 format recently created the newer Mp3PRO format. By tweaking the MP3's sound, they've shrunk the song in half and made it sound as good or better than a standard MP3. Unfortunately, Mp3PRO songs require special Mp3PRO players in order to hear the higher quality. When played through standard MP3 players, Mp3PRO songs sound only half as good as their standard MP3 versions.

MP3 player manufacturers must pay extra to use the Mp3PRO format, however, so only time will tell how well it will be accepted. Feel free to keep an eye on it at `www.thomson-multimedia.com`.

Creating WMAs or MP3s

Media Player lets you copy songs from your CDs onto your computer, but only in the WMA format. That's too bad because MP3 is much more popular and is supported by every portable MP3 player. Microsoft hopes WMA will catch on because of Microsoft's marketing muscle. Plus, WMA files are half the size of MP3 files.

Before you copy files, you must tell Media Player where to store them and what format to use. Choose Options from Media Player's Tools menu and click the Copy Music tab. (Read the sidebar elsewhere in this chapter, "What are MP3, WMA, and Mp3PRO?" to figure out the format you need.)

To save space, I recommend storing your music in your computer's Shared Music folder so that every computer user can hear it: Click the Change button, click My Computer, click Shared Documents, and choose Shared Music. Click OK to save your changes.

Make sure no check mark is in the Protect Content box. Then, you're ready to copy the songs from a CD onto your computer, where you can listen to them, catalog them, or copy them directly to MP3 players and Pocket PCs.

1. **Log onto the Internet.**

   Although not essential, an Internet connection automatically fills in the CD's song titles while Media Player creates your MP3s and WMAs. Using the Internet is a great timesaver and helps avoid embarrassing misspellings.

2. **Load Media Player.**

3. **Insert your audio CD into your computer and click the Stop Play button.**

   Media Player will probably begin playing the songs, but it copies faster if the CD doesn't play.

4. **Click the Copy from CD button.**

   After you click the Copy from CD button, Media Player shows all the CD's song titles, which are all selected.

5. **Remove the check marks from any titles that you don't want to copy.**

6. **Click the Copy Music button.**

   This Copy Music button is the red button near the top, next to the Get Names button. Media Player begins copying the selected song(s) from the CD to your hard drive in your chosen format, as shown in Figure 13-5.

   That's it. Media Player automatically records all the songs onto your hard drive.

Figure 13-5:
Media
Player
creates
WMA files,
but not MP3
files.

Making Media Player create MP3s and play DVDs

Bending to pressure, Microsoft made a last-minute deal with three companies to provide software for Windows Media Player to create MP3s and play DVDs. The catch? The complete package costs between $20 and $30, with separate components (the DVD decoder on its own, for instance) costing less.

The three companies, CyberLink, InterVideo, and RAVISENT, each offer an MP3 Creation Pack for Windows XP and a DVD Decoder Pack for Windows XP. Windows XP users may order and download these new add-on packs from each company's Web site through links inside Windows Media Player.

If you've upgraded to Windows XP from an earlier version of Windows, and your old DVD or MP3 creation software no longer works, using the links to get the add-ons might be your best option.

To create an MP3 after installing the add-on, choose Options from Media Player's Tools menu, click the Copy Music tab, and select MP3 from the File Format area. (MP3 Creation Packs and DVD Decoder Packs usually still work with the newer Media Player 9, described at the end of this chapter, but be sure to visit the site where you purchased them. You might need a free, downloadable upgrade.)

✔ To listen to your newly copied files, click the Media Library button and find your CD listed under the Album section. Click the CD's name, and all the copied songs appear on Media Player's right-hand side.

✔ If you save your music files to your My Music folder, only you can hear them on the computer. Save them to the Shared Music folder so that anyone who uses your computer can access them.

✔ Just like Windows XP doesn't include a codec to play DVD files, it doesn't include a codec for creating MP3 files. The solution? You need third-party MP3 software that includes an MP3 encoder. If Media Player feels that the encoder meets the specifications of Microsoft, it borrows that program's encoder in order to copy MP3s. (Choose Options from the Tools menu and click the Copy Music tab to choose your file format, WMA or MP3.)

Storing Files in Your My Music and Shared Music Folders

When Media Player copies your CD onto your hard drive in WMA format, it stores the songs in your My Music or Shared Music folders, visible in My Computer. But here's the cool part — Media Player sometimes grabs a copy of the CD's cover art and sticks that on the CD's My Computer folder, as shown in Figure 13-6. You need to know a few tricks, though, so read on.

How do I turn off that awful licensing feature?

Everybody but the record industry agrees that the Microsoft licensing feature is awful. Luckily, you have a way to turn it off.

1. **Choose Options from Media Player's Tools menu.**

2. **Click the Copy Music tab.**

3. **Remove any check mark from the box marked Protect Content.**

If no check mark is there, Media Player doesn't embed any license or copy protection in your copied files. Disabling the licensing feature lets you copy your files to any of your computers and portable music devices.

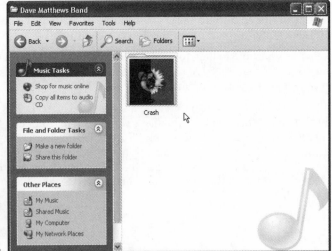

Figure 13-6:
Your My
Music and
Shared
Music
folders
display
a CD's
cover art.

1. **Media Player must be able to download the art, so you need to be connected to the Internet when you copy the files.**

2. **To make sure the art shows, open My Computer and right-click on the folder containing the songs.**

3. **Choose Properties, click the Customize tab, and from the first box, select Music Album (Best for Tracks from One Album). Click OK to return to your folder view.**

4. **Choose View from the folder's menu and select Thumbnails from the drop-down menu.**

5. **If the art doesn't appear on the folder, right-click on the folder again, but this time choose Refresh Thumbnail.**

My Computer stores CDs by artist, with all the artist's CDs stored in separate folders inside that folder. The Artist folder should show small images of the cover art. If it doesn't, follow the same steps for showing the cover art, except choose the option marked Music Artist (Best for Works by One Artist) instead of the Music Album option.

Playing Videos

Windows XP comes with a home video editor that creates small videos for sending along with e-mail. Media Player plays these videos, as well as videos that you may have downloaded from the Internet, including the popular MPG and AVI formats.

(Windows XP doesn't play QuickTime videos, though. For those, you need to download Apple Computer's QuickTime player at `www.apple.com/quicktime`.)

Playing a video file works the same way as playing a WMA file:

1. **Open Media Player.**

2. **Choose Open from the File menu.**

3. **Locate your video file.**

   Open the folder that contains your video file.

4. **Double-click the video file to begin playing it.**

   To make the video fill the screen, hold down Alt and press Enter. (Or choose Full Mode from the View menu.) Beware: Some videos look better full screen than others. Press Alt+Enter to return to normal size.

Moving Music or Video to an MP3 Player or Pocket PC

Start the easy way: Turn off Media Player's WMA licensing features when you copy files from a CD. That way your WMA files will play back on nearly every MP3 player on the market.

Media Player can copy files straight from your Media Library into your MP3 player or Pocket PC. However, it only works that way with some of the newer MP3 players that play both MP3 *and* WMA files. For a list, visit `www.windowsmedia.com`.

Here's how to copy music or video to your MP3 player or Pocket PC:

1. **Connect your device to your computer.**

   Some devices connect through a serial cable; others use a USB or parallel port. Some connect a FlashCard reader to your PC.

2. **Turn on the device.**

   A window usually pops up, asking how Windows should handle your device. Specifically, Windows asks whether it should play the music files on the device, or open the device's contents in a folder so that you can view it. Click Cancel because you don't need either option to copy files using Media Player.

Copy to CD or Device

3. **Click the Copy to CD or Device button.**

Media Player connects with your device. (Press F5 if it has trouble finding your device.) As shown in Figure 13-7, for example, Media Player shows the PocketZip's current contents on the left and your Media Player's songs on the right.

4. **Decide what to copy to your player.**

See the little arrow in Figure 13-7? Click the arrow, and a long list drops down. That's the Music to Copy list, and you can select music by artist, CD title, and Genre. Or choose All Audio from the list to see *all* your available songs.

The songs that you choose appear in the window below. They're all checked, and Media Player keeps a size total so that you know what songs will and won't fit. To uncheck them all, click the little check box next to the word Title. Then you can choose songs separately by clicking in their boxes.

To erase songs on your current player, right-click on their titles and choose Delete from Playlist.

Selected songs that will fit on the player? Time for Step 5.

5. **Click the red Copy Music button near Media Player's upper-right corner.**

Media Player dutifully copies the selected songs into your portable player.

Figure 13-7:
On the left side, choose the songs that you want to copy to your player on the right side.

✔ If you see the message `An Error Occurred`, it probably means you're trying to pack too big of a file onto your player, and there's not enough room. Choose a smaller file and see if that fits in the remaining space.

✔ The quickest way to move files to a player is to buy a CompactFlash card reader and connect it to your computer. Then copy the WMA or MP3 files to the card reader using My Computer. Transfer sessions take seconds instead of minutes.

✔ Media Player also copies videos into Pocket PCs, if you have one of those little goodies. Beware, though: Copying videos can take a *long* time. In fact, unless your music player or Pocket PC connects to your computer with a USB port, the transfer could take 20 minutes or more.

✔ When copying tunes to your portable player or Pocket PC, save space by encoding your WMA files at 64 Kbps. Your files consume half the size of MP3 files and still sound good enough for the streets. To change the rate, choose Options from the Tools menu. Click the Copy Music tab and slide the quality setting bar to the 64 Kbps setting.

✔ WMA handles low encoding rates much better than MP3. That's why a 64 Kbps WMA file sounds much better than an MP3 file at 64 Kbps.

✔ For the latest info on Pocket PCs, head to `www.brighthand.com` or `www.pocketpcpassion.com`.

Burning Your Own CDs

Windows XP lets you burn your music onto writeable CDs in two *very* different ways.

First, it can dump files onto a CD for sheer storage. For instance, you can copy more than 150 MP3 or WMA files onto a single CD. Just open My Computer, right-click on the files, choose Send To, and select your CD drive. Next, open your writeable CD drive in My Computer and choose Write These Files to CD. (In fact, this trick works for any files that you want to copy to a CD, not just music files.)

Second, Windows XP lets you create standard music CDs — CDs containing a dozen or so songs that play back in your home or car CD player. By mixing songs from various albums, you can create your own Greatest Hits CD containing your favorite songs.

To store a dozen or so songs on a CD for playing on your home or car's CD player, follow these instructions. (Actually, they're very much like copying songs to a portable MP3 player, as described in the preceding section.)

1. **Insert your blank CD into your writeable CD drive.**

   When the helpful little message pops up, click Take No Action. Media Player handles the details.

2. **Open Media Player and click Copy to CD or Device.**

   (This button is one of the buttons along the left side of Media Player.) Media Player shows a window split in two. One side displays the files you'd like to copy to the CD; the other side shows the CD. (Both sides are empty because you haven't selected any files, and you're copying to a blank CD.)

3. **Click Media Player's Media Library button.**

   Click an album containing songs that you want to copy to the CD; its songs appear on Media Player's right side.

4. **Right-click on the desired song and choose Copy to Audio CD.**

   Each time you click a song and choose Copy to Audio CD, Media Player immediately shows you the window you see in Step 2, with your currently chosen file on the Music to Copy list. Media Player keeps track of each song's length, listing the total at the list's bottom.

   Why does Media Player care? Because CDs hold only 74 or 80 minutes of music. If you try to stuff too many songs onto the CD, Media Player displays the message Will not fit next to some songs' names.

   To remove songs that won't fit, click the check marked box next to their names.

   After you line up the right amount of songs, move to Step 5.

5. **Click Copy Music.**

   Copy Music is the little red button near the upper-right corner.

   Now it's time to move away from your computer for a while. Windows must convert the files into the proper CD format, and that takes about ten minutes. Then, Windows needs a half hour or so to copy the music onto the CD — and Microsoft warns you not to fiddle with your computer while creating a CD because Media Player could "stop functioning."

✔ Media Player copies to both CD-R and CD-RW discs. Many stereos choke on CD-RW discs, so you're best off with the CD-R discs. I buy 'em in stacks of 50 through Amazon.com.

✔ When storing songs onto your hard drive, Media Player compresses them into WMA format, losing some quality in the process. To let Media Player work with the best-quality recordings when creating CDs, use the highest quality level possible when ripping songs onto your hard drive. (Set the quality level by choosing Options from the Tools menu, clicking the Copy Music tab, and sliding the tab to Best Quality.)

Adding Skins to Media Player

Today's generation wants to play with its toys. So, Microsoft added a whimsical feature to Media Player. The program normally rests on your desktop like a big wet towel, covering everything in its path.

Through skin technology, users can change that ugly wet towel into something much more hip. *Skins* are new interfaces for Media Player that make it less imposing and more friendly.

Here's how to put new clothes on Media Player:

1. **Click the Skin Chooser button.**

   A list of skins appears on the left with the currently highlighted skin displayed on the right.

2. **Choose a skin from the list.**

   More than a dozen skins await the dressing room. Try one on by clicking its name. The preview window shows the skin's appearance, as shown in Figure 13-8.

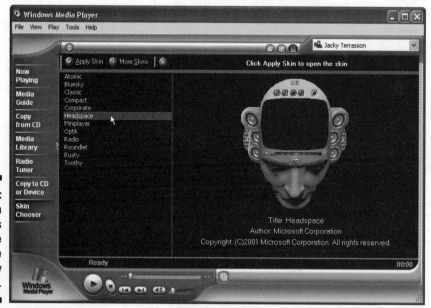

Figure 13-8:
Click a skin to see its appearance in the preview window.

To see even *more* skins, click the More Skins button near the top of the list. That whisks you off to the Microsoft Skins Gallery on the Internet — a collection of user-submitted skins up for the taking.

3. **Click the Apply Skin button.**

   Located near the top of the list, this button dresses Media Player in your newly chosen skin and places it onto the desktop for evaluation, as shown in Figure 13-9.

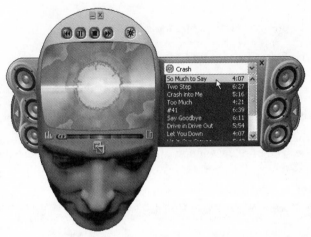

Figure 13-9:
The newly
selected
Media
Player
appears
on-screen.

If you like your new selection, keep it. (And try to figure out the new placement of all the buttons.) If it's not quite up to snuff, repeat Steps 1 through 3.

Choose the Miniplayer skin when listening to music and still working on the computer. A nice small player, it fits into the background nicely. (Miniplayer won't play videos, though.)

Fixing Media Player Muckups

The all-powerful computing world stumbles when trying to act like a simple TV set. Changing a channel on a TV set involves pressing a button. Over the Internet world, users must deal with weird standards, confusing terms (such as *codec*), and computers that shudder under the weight of displaying high-powered Internet sound and graphics.

This section covers the problems you eventually encounter with Media Player.

It just doesn't work!

If Media Player is messing up, check out this list of cheap fixes before grabbing your hair and pulling:

- ✔ **Check the volume on Windows XP.** Click the little speaker in the bottom corner of the taskbar and slide the Volume lever upward. (Make sure that the Mute All box isn't checked, too.) No speaker icon? Open the Start menu's Control Panel; choose Sounds, Speech, and Audio Devices; and click Adjust the System Volume. Finally, click in the box marked Place Volume Icon in the Taskbar.

- ✔ **Check the volume on your sound card.** Some older sound cards have a little rotary knob on the back, and you need to wiggle your fingers through the octopus of cables in the back of the computer to reach the knob. Other cards make you push certain keyboard combinations to control the volume. You may have to pull out the manual for this one. (Try double-clicking the little speaker icon by your digital clock in the bottom corner to see all of your sound card's volume settings.)

- ✔ **Run any Setup or Configuration programs that came with the sound card.** Sometimes these programs can shake loose a problem.

- ✔ **Do you have the proper codecs for DVDs and MP3s?** Windows XP doesn't include codecs for playing DVDs or creating MP3s. You must install a third-party DVD player or MP3 encoder so that Media Player can borrow those codecs.

- ✔ **Are the Windows XP drivers installed correctly for your particular sound card?** Check out the drivers section in Chapter 3.

- ✔ **Did you plug speakers into the sound card?** That sound has to come from somewhere. . . . And is the speaker cord plugged firmly into its jack on the sound card? While you're at it, are those nice desktop speakers plugged in and turned on?

Does it have to be so huge?

Old versions of Media Player simply played media. A thin strip of buttons, the program lived out its name by controlling the playback of CDs, recordings, and occasional videos.

Now, Media Player automatically catalogs tiny details of your media collection and leaves the huge closets of information on the screen. Now, Media Player either consumes the entire screen, or it's an icon at the bottom of your screen. There's not much of an in-between. Try clicking Skin Chooser and choosing the Classic skin for a look at days gone by.

Bizarre Multimedia Words

Here's what some of those weird multimedia buzzwords are supposed to mean. Use caution when murmuring them in crowded elevators.

- **Analog:** Naturally moving elements, such as waves, sounds, and motion — things that computers turn into numbers for storage. (See also *Digital*.)

- **AVI:** Short for Audio Video Interleaved, AVI is video-playing software for IBM-compatible PCs. (It competes with Macintosh's QuickTime movie player, which is winning the battle for the Internet.)

- **CD quality:** The term Windows XP uses for stereo, 16-bit sound recorded at 44 kHz. The cream of the crop, the recording sounds as good as a music CD, but it consumes a lot of hard disk space.

- **Codec:** A way to compress sound or video into a file and then decompress it when playing it back, often in a different format. MP3 and WMA use different codecs, for instance.

- **Copyright:** A legal term establishing ownership rights of a created work. In the case of a song, a copyright can be established for the tune's composer, the lyrics, and the band's performance of the song.

- **Data buffer:** A way to temporarily store information, leading to smoother transfers. Sound or video playing over the Net often requires a buffer. Increasing the buffer leads to better playback but puts more strain on the computer's power.

- **Digital:** Computerized things; collections of numbers to represent pictures, sounds, text, or video. (See also *Analog*.)

- **DSP (Digital Signal Processor):** A bit of computer mechanics for adding echoes, reverb, and other sound benders to a piece of music.

- **Encoding:** Compressing a file. When you create a WMA file, you're encoding a file.

- **FM:** Short for Frequency Modulation, FM is the technology that's used to create instrument sounds from most AdLib-compatible sound cards.

- **Lossy compression:** Compressed files, such as MP3 and WMA, which cut out some of the sound in order to save space.

- **MIDI:** Short for Musical Instrument Digital Interface, but most people try to forget that right away. Pronounced "MID-ee."

- **MP3:** Short for MPEG 3, Layer 1. It's a method of compressing audio files into one-tenth of their normal size while still keeping near CD-quality sound. MP3 stores about one minute of audio in 1MB of space.

- **Playlist:** A list of media files and their locations. Players read the list to find the songs and the order in which they're to be played.

- **Public domain:** Works that may be freely copied and distributed. They enter the public domain after the copyright expires or the copyright holder gives his or her material to the public domain.

- **Radio quality:** The term that Windows XP uses for mono, 8-bit sound recorded at 22 kHz. Basically, it sounds as good as a clear radio station.

- **RealAudio:** Another popular sound format for streaming music over the Internet. Media Player does not support RealAudio, and you must download a separate RealPlayer from www.real.com. (Microsoft is hoping to wipe out RealAudio with WMA.)

- **Sampling:** How closely the computer pays attention to the sound. The higher the sampling rate, the more attention the computer's paying. A higher sampling rate translates to a better sound — and a much bigger file when saved to disk. Most cards sample at 11, 22, or 44 kHz.

- **Skins:** Cosmetic enhancers for a program. Click Media Player's Skin Chooser button to give Media Player a whole new look.

- **Sound module:** A box-like contraption that creates sounds but doesn't have a keyboard: a drum machine, for example.

- **Telephone quality:** A term that Windows XP uses to describe mono sounds recorded at 8-bit, 11 kHz. The recording sounds like a telephone conversation.

- **WAV:** The format that Windows uses to store and play digitally recorded sounds. Pronounced "wave."

- **Weighted keys:** If a synthesizer's keyboard feels like a keyboard on a real piano, it probably has weighted keys — and up to $2,000 more on its price tag.

- **Winamp:** The most popular MP3 player by far, Winamp offers regular updates, easy customization, and great sound. Check it out at www.winamp.com.

- **Windows CE:** A miniature version of Windows that runs on Pocket PCs.

Upgrading to Windows Media Player 9

Windows XP comes bundled with the version of Media Player described in this chapter, but cutting-edge users may want to download a newer version. Dubbed Media Player 9, it's available as a download through Windows Update or the Downloads section of the Microsoft Web site (www.microsoft.com).

Media Player 9, seen in Figure 13-10, looks much like Windows XP's bundled Media Player. Yet Microsoft boasts that it contains over 120 new features. For instance, it supports 5.1 surround sound when watching DVDs and online movies — if your PC supports the format with a compatible sound card, five speakers, and a subwoofer.

Unlike its large predecessor, Media Player 9 shrinks down to a tiny strip on your taskbar, next to the clock. From there, well-placed clicks still control most menus. When you play songs from a playlist, the program can overlap the songs' beginnings and endings for smoother sound.

Built-in playlist editors let you quickly switch between playing your favorite songs, new tunes, songs not played in the last week — nearly anything you can think up.

Like Windows XP's Media Player, Media Player 9 still can't play DVDs or create MP3 files unless you've purchased third-party software. And Media Player 9's Premium Services area makes you pay subscription fees to access special online content.

If you're not satisfied with Windows XP's bundled Media Player or it's not using all of your computer's multimedia features, check out the upgrade. Be prepared to spend some time puzzling through the new menus, however.

Figure 13-10: Windows Media Player 9, a free upgrade, offers more than 120 new features, including surround sound.

Part IV
Help!

The 5th Wave   By Rich Tennant

©RICHTENNANT.COM

Gee, Richard, you'll have to show me where on the toolbar you found an icon labeled "Overkill".

In this part . . .

Windows XP can do hundreds of tasks in dozens of ways. This means that approximately one million things can fail at any given time.

Some problems are easy to fix. For example, one misplaced click on the desktop makes all your icons suddenly vanish. One more click in the right place puts them all back.

Other problems are far more complex, requiring teams of computer surgeons to diagnose, remedy, and bill accordingly.

This part helps you separate the big problems from the little ones. You'll know whether you can fix it yourself with a few clicks and a kick. If your situation's worse, you'll know when it's time to call in the surgeons.

Chapter 14

Customizing Windows XP (Fiddling with the Control Panel)

In This Chapter

▶ Exploring the Control Panel

▶ Customizing the display

▶ Changing colors

▶ Changing video modes

▶ Changing desktop themes

▶ Understanding TrueType fonts

▶ Installing or removing programs

▶ Installing new computer parts

▶ Changing to a different printer

▶ Making Windows XP recognize your double-click

▶ Setting the computer's time and date

*A*fter releasing more than a dozen versions of Windows, the guys and gals at Microsoft have realized that they can't please everybody. Whenever Microsoft added a new feature to its latest release, many Windows users began complaining that they preferred the *old* version.

And the new users? They'd complain that the new version didn't let them do something the way they wanted. No matter how many changes Microsoft made to the software, Microsoft either upset its older users or didn't satisfy the new crop.

So, Microsoft is trying something new with Windows XP. People who prefer the look and feel of old versions can choose the Classic settings: Windows XP immediately behaves like Windows' previous version. To satisfy new users, well, Microsoft has added *hundreds* of different settings for people to set up Windows just the way they like it.

Unfortunately, that creates a new problem. Windows XP contains so many different switches and customizable options that making it work the way you want is harder than ever.

Hundreds of switches and options hide inside the 24 Control Panel icons of Windows. This chapter shows which ones you need and which ones you can avoid. And, if you accidentally flip the wrong switch, this chapter shows how to make everything go back the way it was.

Beware, however: Because these settings affect the computer so drastically, many can only be changed by the computer's owner — the person holding the administrator account.

Finding the Right Control Panel Option

Just like a house's circuit breaker box, the Windows Control Panel holds the switches that control the program's various settings. Flip open the Control Panel from the Start menu, and you can while away an entire workweek adjusting all the various Windows XP options.

But after the Control Panel window pops up, as shown in Figure 14-1, sometimes its little icon switches aren't all visible. Instead, Windows XP groups the icons into categories, often making it difficult to find the right switch.

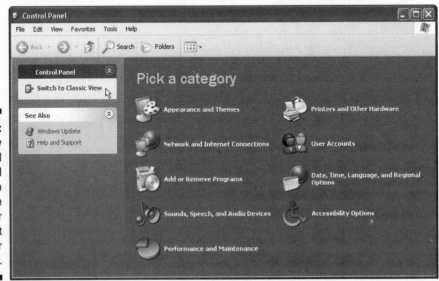

Figure 14-1:
Click any
Control
Panel
category to
change the
settings for
that
particular
subject.

To see all your Control Panel icons, click Switch to Classic View (upper-left corner of Figure 14-1). Voilà! All the Control Panel icons appear, as shown in Figure 14-2. (If you need to make the window larger to see them all, hit Chapter 6 for window-sizing tips.)

Figure 14-2: Classic View shows all available icons in the Control Panel; click Switch to Category View to return to the prettier, categorized view.

Every computer's Control Panel may look slightly different because different people can afford different computer toys. For example, the keyboards on some Gateway computers enable you to control the volume of your DVD player. Those Control Panels include an icon to change that keyboard's special settings. Some laptop owners use high-tech infrared ports to beam information to other laptops. Those Control Panels have a Wireless Link icon. In Table 14-1, I explain the icons you may come across in your copy of Windows XP and why you might need to use them.

I discuss the most important options in more glowing detail later in this chapter.

✔ Don't worry about the Control Panel's overwhelming display of options; chances are that you'll use very few of them.

✔ If the Control Panel's icons don't look like the ones in Figure 14-2, choose Icons from the View menu. To see what the icons do, choose Details from the View menu to see a list of tiny icons followed by descriptions of their purposes.

✔ For an easy way to see what each icon does, rest your mouse pointer over a mysterious icon — without clicking. A reminder appears, explaining the icon's function.

✔ Some third-party programs add additional icons to the Control Panel. Don't be surprised to see icons for Real Player appear in the Classic View, for instance.

✔ Many of the Control Panel's dialog boxes can be reached *without* calling up the Control Panel. Double-click the taskbar's little clock to summon the dialog box for the Date and Time icon, for example. Or right-click on a blank part of your desktop and choose Properties to bring up the dialog box for the Display icon.

Table 14-1	Deciphering the Control Panel Icons	
The Icon	*What It Does*	*When You Should Use It*
	With the Accessibility options, Microsoft performs admirably in making Windows XP accessible to everybody. These options help make the monitor easier to read, add special sonic signals, and make the Customize Windows program's controls work more easily for people with physical limitations.	If you need any of these options, you'll know.
	Installed that new *<insert name of expensive computer gadget here>*? Head for this area to summon the Add Hardware Wizard. This wizard, a helpful piece of advice-counselor software, handles the messy chores of introducing Windows XP to new computer parts.	If Windows doesn't automatically notice your newly installed computer part, start this wizard to introduce them to each other.
	Double-click Add or Remove Programs to make Windows XP install new software or remove software you no longer want. This icon also tells Windows XP to install any software it left out when it installed itself.	Use this icon whenever you want to install new software or delete existing programs.
	Clicking the Administrative Tools icon brings up detailed computer usage statistics that you'll never need to use. If you think you do need it, you're beyond the realm of this book.	Use this icon if you've taken classes in computer sciences or networking. Save this stuff for the computer consultants or technicians.

The Icon	What It Does	When You Should Use It
	Use the Date and Time icon to change your computer's date, time, and time zone settings.	Use this icon to reset the clock or when moving to a new time zone. (That lets Windows XP automatically adjust the clock for daylight saving time.)
	A haven for decorators, the Display icon contains bunches of pre-created backgrounds, colors, fonts, and screen savers to spruce up Windows XP with cool themes.	Best used as a fun time-waster to put off upcoming projects.
	Use the Folder Options icon to change the way Windows displays its folders on the screen and how they behave.	Usually used once or twice, and then ignored.
	With this icon, choose from the basic fonts Windows XP comes with, such as Arial and `Courier`. If you head back to the software store and buy more fonts, install them by double-clicking this icon.	Most programs install and maintain their fonts automatically. *Tip:* Double-clicking a font's name usually shows what its letters look like.
	Windows XP usually spots newly installed joysticks and game pads and installs them automatically. Double-click the Game Controllers icon for help with problems. Also, here's where you calibrate and test your joystick if you're losing.	Avid game players tweak this for every new game.
	When you're ready to join the Internet and surf the World Wide Web, the Internet Options icon is waiting for you. Click this icon to open a Pandora's box of buttons that let you customize the way Windows XP talks through the Internet. (Chapter 12 shows how to point and click your way through the Internet.)	Used rarely, except when setting everything up for the first time. After your Internet access is set up, everything's pretty low-maintenance.

(continued)

Table 14-1 *(continued)*

The Icon	What It Does	When You Should Use It
	Use the Keyboard icon to change how long the keyboard takes to repeat a letter when you hold down a key. Yawn.	Used rarely. Adjust your keyboard's settings once, if necessary, and then forget it.
	Choose among options found in the Mouse icon to make your mouse scoot faster across the screen, change it from right-handed to left-handed, fine-tune your double-click, choose between brands, and change all sorts of mouse-related behaviors.	Used rarely. Dirty mouseballs and rollers — not software settings — cause most mouse problems. But check out this option for fun.
	The Network Connections icon shows your network connections — if you have any — and helps you create them if they don't yet exist.	Used to either create networks or change the settings of existing ones.
	From the Phone and Modem Options icon, add your area code or change it if you're traveling with a laptop. Click the Modem tab to see your modem; double-click the modem's name to change its controls.	Used frequently by laptoppers or people having trouble with their modems. Ignored when everything's working right.
	Windows XP is very power-conscious on new computers and laptops. Use the Power Options icon to automatically turn off the monitor — or the entire computer — when you haven't used it for a while. Choose your Power Schemes setting at the top, and Windows sets the rest of the schemes for you.	Used frequently by laptoppers. Other people make Windows XP turn off their monitors after 30 minutes of inactivity.
	Come here (to the Printers and Faxes icon) to tell Windows XP about your new printer, adjust the settings of a printer or fax modem, or choose which printer (or fax modem) you want Windows XP to use.	Use this option whenever you buy a new printer or permanently change settings on an existing one. (Right-click on a printer icon and choose Properties to change its settings.)

The Icon	What It Does	When You Should Use It
	The Regional and Language Options icon changes the way Windows XP displays and sorts numbers, international currency, the date, and the time according to your country. (If you've simply changed time zones, just double-click the date/time display on the bottom-right corner of the taskbar, a process described later in this chapter.)	Used mostly by laptoppers with frequent-flier cards.
	Windows XP makes an effort to handle those often-troublesome scanners and digital cameras. If Windows doesn't automatically find your scanner or digital camera, try installing those devices here with the Scanners and Cameras icon.	Come here to get pictures from your digital camera and scanner, too, as well as check their connections.
	The Scheduled Tasks icon keeps Windows XP running smoothly because it automatically performs maintenance at certain times.	Ignore it. Windows XP automatically sets things up to run at the right times.
	Use the Sounds and Audio Devices icon not only to change the volume, but also to make Windows XP play different sounds for different events. Click the Sounds tab and try some of the presets in the Sound Scheme box. Sound card owners drop by here to tweak their gear settings, adjust playback/record volumes, fiddle with MIDI instruments, and play with other goodies, such as video capture cards, as well as their CD and DVD players.	Used mostly at homes or small offices where the boss doesn't mind computers that make exploding sounds when they crash.
	Yes, Windows XP can speak to you — if you can understand the little guy. Use the Speech icon to hear Windows read to you.	This text-to-speech translator gives an inkling of what a more professional package can do. It's not very useful, even for blind people.

(continued)

Table 14-1 *(continued)*

The Icon	What It Does	When You Should Use It
	Like racecar mechanics, computer gurus can fiddle around in here for hours. Don't play with the System icon unless a nearby computer guru can serve as Safety Patrol. This is scary stuff.	This area's usage increases with the level of the user's experience.
	Customize your Start button menu, alphabetize its contents, and fiddle with your taskbar by using the Taskbar and Start Menu icon. Windows XP offers an incredible amount of custom-ization options here.	Most people head here to either alphabetize their Start menu or turn off the personalized menus that leave off some options.
	Head for the User Accounts icon to replace Microsoft's little Welcome screen icon with your own picture. Administrators may add or delete accounts here, too.	After you set this up, you probably won't change it much.

Appearance and Themes

 The first category of the Control Panel, Appearance and Themes, controls how Windows XP appears on the screen. Click here to find links to three icons: Display, Folder Options, and Taskbar and Start Menu. Each of these three icons uses different techniques to change how Windows displays infor-mation on the screen.

When you open the Appearance and Themes category, you see several tasks, such as Choose a Screen Saver. Clicking those tasks brings up a shortcut to the correct place to make your change.

Changing the display's background, screen saver, and resolution

 The part of the Control Panel that's used most often is probably the Display icon. Unlike several other switches in the Control Panel, the Display icon doesn't control anything too dangerous. Feel free to fiddle around with all the settings. You can't cause any major harm. If you do want to play, however, be sure that you write down the settings you change. Then you can always return your display to normal if something looks odd.

Changing Windows' desktop background

Windows offers two ways to change the *background* — the picture that covers your desktop or work area. The first comes with the Themes tab of the Display Properties dialog box, seen when you first double-click the Display icon, as shown in Figure 14-3.

Figure 14-3: Choose a pre-configured theme to change how Windows looks, as well as change sounds and icons.

The Display Properties dialog box in Figure 14-3 shows a preview of Windows XP's currently chosen *theme* — a collection of related colors, sounds, icons, and a background that gives Windows a personalized look and feel. Using the Themes tab is a fast, one-click way to change Windows' look: Choose a theme, and Windows XP automatically slips into new clothes.

To see more themes, click the downward-pointing arrow in the Theme box and choose More Themes Online, which enables you to download preconfigured themes from the Internet.

To skip the fancy themes and simply change Windows' background, however, click the Desktop tab and sample some of the listed backgrounds. Click any of the filenames listed for a preview of how your selection would look as a background. Like it? Click Apply to stick the new background to your desktop.

To see other options, click the Browse button and click a file from inside your My Pictures folder to see the new background in the preview window (see Figure 14-4). Like it? Click OK to complete the process and close the Display Properties dialog box.

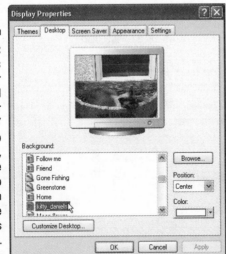

Figure 14-4:
Use pictures
from your
digital
camera for
Windows'
desktop
background,
the
backdrop
beneath
all the
windows
and icons.

Here are some tips for customizing your desktop:

✔ Windows XP looks at an incoming image's size and automatically decides whether it should be *tiled* repeatedly across the screen, *centered* in the middle, or *stretched* to fill the entire screen. To override Windows' choice, set your own preference by selecting it from the Position box.

✔ Background files are BMP or JPG files. Most digital camera images are JPG files. Most background files that come with Windows are BMP files.

✔ Click the Customize Desktop button and choose Web to make Windows XP use a Web site as a background. It's fun for a while, but it eventually gets in the way. If you accidentally click an item on the Web page while aiming for a desktop icon, Internet Explorer pushes itself into the forefront and displays your Web page.

✔ Did you happen to spot an eye-catching picture while Web surfing with Internet Explorer? Right-click on that Web site's picture and choose the Set As Background option. Sneaky Microsoft copies that picture to your desktop and leaves it on the screen as your new background.

Choosing a screen saver

In the dinosaur days of computing, computer monitors were permanently damaged when an oft-used program burned its image onto the screen. The program's faint outlines showed up even after the monitor was turned off.

To prevent this burn-in, people installed a screen saver to jump in when a computer hadn't been used for a while. The screen saver would either blank the screen or fill it with wavy lines to keep the program's display from etching itself into the screen.

Today's monitors don't really have this problem, but people use screen savers anyway — mainly because they look cool.

✔ Windows comes with several screen savers built in. To set one up or change from the default "Windows XP" screen saver, click the Screen Saver tab along the top of the Display Properties dialog box. Then click the downward-pointing arrow in the Screen Saver box. Finally, select the screen saver you want.

✔ Immediately after choosing a screen saver, click the Preview button to see what the screen saver looks like. Wiggle the mouse or press the spacebar to return to Windows XP.

✔ Fiddlers can click Settings for more options — changing colors or animation speed, for instance.

✔ For extra security, select the On Resume, Display Welcome Screen check box. When somebody wants to use the computer again, it starts up at the Welcome screen, where all the accounts can require a password for entry. (I cover this in the "User Accounts" section.)

✔ Click the up or down arrows next to the Wait box to tell the screen saver when to kick in. If you set the option to 5, for example, Windows XP waits until you haven't touched the mouse or keyboard for five minutes before letting the screen saver out of its cage.

✔ To save electricity and extend your monitor's life, click the Power button at the bottom of the Screen Saver tab. Here, you can tell Windows XP to turn off your monitor when you haven't used it for a while. (I cover this topic in Table 14-1.)

Changing Windows' on-screen colors

Feeling blue? You can make Windows XP appear in any color you want by clicking the Appearance tab in the Display Properties dialog box. Although Windows XP comes with very few colors to choose from, switch to Classic style for a variety of different Microsoft-designed color schemes.

Switching to new video modes

Just as Windows XP can print to hundreds of different brands of printers, it can accommodate zillions of different monitors, too. It can even display different video modes on the same monitor.

For example, Windows XP can display different numbers of colors on the screen, or it can shrink the size of everything, packing more information onto the screen. The number of colors and the size of the information on-screen comprise a *video mode,* or *video resolution.*

Some Windows XP programs only work in a specific video mode, and those programs casually ask you to switch to that mode. Huh?

Here's what's happening: Monitors plug into a special place on the back of the computer. That special place is an outlet on a *video card* — the gizmo that translates your computer's language into something you can see on the monitor. That card handles all the video-mode switches. By making the card switch between modes, you can send more or fewer colors to your monitor or pack more or less information onto the screen.

To make a video card switch to a different video mode, click the Settings tab, one of the five tabs along the top of the Control Panel's Display Properties dialog box, as shown in Figure 14-5. (Can't find the Display Properties dialog box? Right-click on a blank part of your desktop and choose Properties from the menu that springs up.)

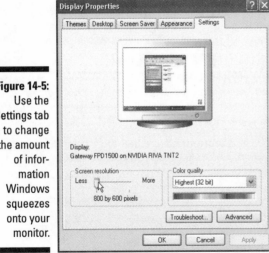

Figure 14-5:
Use the Settings tab to change the amount of information Windows squeezes onto your monitor.

From the Settings tab, select the video mode that you want Windows XP to display on-screen. Click the arrow next to the Color Quality box to change the number of colors Windows XP currently displays; move the slider under Screen Resolution to change the amount of detail Windows can pack onto the screen. Windows XP gives you a chance to back out if you choose a video mode your computer can't handle, thank goodness.

✔ Monitors and cards can display Windows XP in different *resolutions*. The higher the resolution, the more information Windows XP can pack onto the screen (and the smaller the windows become, too). For more information about this monitor/card/resolution stuff, troop over to Chapter 2 and read the section about computer parts that I told you to ignore.

✔ To switch to a higher resolution, use your mouse to slide the little bar in the Screen Resolution area. Then watch how the little preview screen changes. The more you slide the bar to the right, the more information Windows XP can pack onto the screen. Unfortunately, the information also gets smaller. Click the Apply button after you select a new resolution to see it in action.

✔ When Windows XP switches to the new resolution, it usually gives you 15 seconds to click a button saying that you approve of the change. If your card or monitor can't handle the new resolution, you won't be able to see the button on-screen. Then, because you didn't click the button, Windows XP automatically changes back to the original resolution. Whew!

✔ Depending on how you're set up, Windows XP sometimes prefers to restart your computer when changing the amount of colors or resolution. To determine how Windows XP handles your video changes, click the Advanced button on the bottom of the Settings tab.

✔ Want to change the number of colors Windows XP can throw onto the screen? Click the little arrow in the Color Quality box. After the list drops down, select the number of colors you want.

✔ To look at pictures taken with a digital camera, you'll probably want Windows XP to display the highest number of colors as possible. Medium, or 16-bit mode, will display a total of 65,000 colors; Highest, or 32-bit mode, slaps up to 16 million colors on the monitor.

✔ Windows XP works well with two or more monitors simultaneously and can display different video resolutions on each monitor. You need a separate PCI video card to power each monitor, however. See the nearby "Two monitors . . . *at the same time!*" sidebar for more information.

✔ If Windows XP acts goofy with your video card or monitor — or you've recently installed new ones — Windows XP probably needs to be formally introduced to your new equipment before it will talk to it.

Two monitors . . . *at the same time!*

Plug a second video card into your computer, plug in a second monitor, and Windows XP will probably be able to spread its display across both monitors — or even three, if you install yet another card and monitor.

It sounds frivolous, but this new feature can be kind of handy, actually. For instance, you can run your Internet browser on one monitor while keeping your desktop handy for other work. Or

you can spread your work out, making it easy to cut and paste between bunches of open windows.

A few words of caution, however: This two-monitor stuff is relatively new, so not all programs can handle it. Also, TV Viewer cards can only display TV shows on the *primary monitor* — your first monitor. The TV show simply disappears if you try dragging its window to the second monitor.

Making Windows display folders differently

Some people store their folders in a fireproof MacMahon Bros. file cabinet and spread them across a finely polished mahogany desk for viewing. Others spread them across the floor and hope the papers don't fall out. To accommodate different working styles, Windows XP offers several ways of viewing your folders.

 To fiddle with folder settings, choose Control Panel from the Start menu and double-click the Folder Options icon from the Appearances and Themes category. (You can also choose Folder Options from nearly any folder's Tools menu.) Here are the choices thrust upon you in the General tab, as shown in Figure 14-6.

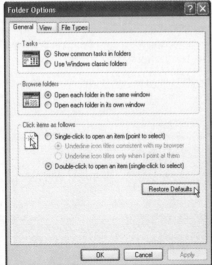

Figure 14-6:
Windows lets you change how you open your folders, how they look inside, and whether you click or double-click to open files.

The Tasks area offers two ways for a folder to display its contents. If you like your folders to display that big blue bar along their left sides, offering quick links to places, such as My Documents, select the Show Common Tasks in Folders option button. To eliminate that bar and give the folder's icons more room, select the Use Windows Classic Folders option button.

The Browse Folders area defines how a folder opens. If you open a folder that's currently inside another folder, should that new folder open in its own new window? Or should its contents merely replace the existing folder's contents, leaving only one open folder on the screen?

Finally, the Click Items As Follows area establishes your mouse click options. Indicate here whether you want to open files with a single click or a double-click.

There is no right or wrong option for any of these. It comes down to your personal style. If you're afraid you're missing something, try each setting to see which one you prefer.

Fiddling with folder options isn't particularly dangerous, but some choices can make Windows XP behave mighty strange. If something terribly weird happens, here's how to return to less-troublesome times. Click the Restore Defaults button on the General tab of the Folder Options dialog box, as shown in Figure 14-6. Your folders and desktop now behave the way they did when Windows XP was first installed.

The View tab of the Folder Options dialog box offers 18 more advanced settings. Unless you understand what the option does, don't select it. And if you select something and everything acts weird, click the Restore Defaults button.

Finally, don't play with the File Types tab of the Folder Options dialog box until you're more familiar with Windows. If you click the wrong setting, Windows won't know how to open your files.

Don't worry if some of these Windows XP options seem rather confusing or pointless. They are.

- ✔ Folder options are aimed at people who *really* like to fiddle with their computers. Chances are that you can avoid using the folder options.

- ✔ If you've been comfortable with Windows 98 or Windows 95, always choose the classic styles. If you're comfortable with Windows XP, leave the default settings. Only choose the other settings if you like to fiddle around with your computer and try new things.

Adjusting your taskbar and Start menu

Clicking the Control Panel's Taskbar and Start Menu icon brings up the same dialog box that I discuss in Chapter 10: the Taskbar and Start Menu Properties dialog box. In that chapter, I explain how to adjust the settings of your taskbar — that long bar along the bottom of your screen.

Feel free to adjust your Start menu here, as well, by clicking the dialog box's Start Menu tab, shown in Figure 14-7. (Right-clicking on your desktop's Start button and choosing Properties brings you to the same page.) Here's how to adjust your Start menu by selecting the options on that page. (Most people don't bother fiddling with them.)

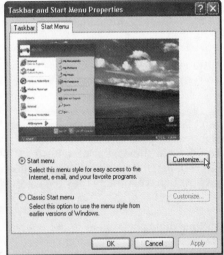

Figure 14-7:
Change the
look and
feel of your
Start menu
and taskbar.

If you're accustomed to earlier versions of Windows, select the Classic Start Menu option button. To stick with the Windows XP look, leave the Start Menu option button selected and click its Customize button to begin tweaking.

Choosing Small Icons doesn't shrink the size of the Start menu, but it lets you pack more icons from recently used programs onto it. In fact, if you choose Small Icons, increase the Number of Programs on Start Menu option below it — small icons leave more room.

Finally, choose whether you want Internet Explorer and Outlook Express to appear on the Start menu.

Click the Advanced button for heavy-duty customizing. For instance, to get rid of that annoying box that pops up whenever you install a new program, remove the check mark by Highlight Newly Installed Programs.

The Start menu doesn't have a Restore Defaults button. If you make any changes, write down what you've done in case you want to go back to the Windows XP "out of the box" look.

Viewing your computer's fonts

Sure, you see the names of the fonts in your word-processing program. But how can you tell what they will look like before choosing one? To find out, open the Control Panel from the Start menu, click Switch to Classic View, and double-click the Fonts icon.

The Fonts dialog box appears, letting you see the names of your installed fonts. From there, you can install additional fonts, as well.

To be on the safe side, don't delete any fonts that come with Windows XP — only delete fonts that you install yourself. Windows programs often borrow Windows XP fonts for menus. If you delete those fonts, your menus mysteriously vanish. And for goodness sake, don't delete any fonts beginning with the letters *MS*. (Don't delete the fonts that have red lettering in their icons, either.)

Double-click any font icon to see what that particular font looks like. For example, if you double-click the Impact font icon, Windows XP brings up an eye chart displaying how that font would look on the printed page, as shown in Figure 14-8. (Click the Print button to see what it really looks like on the printed page.)

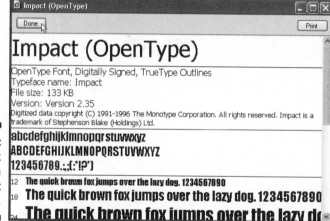

Figure 14-8: Double-click a font icon to see what it looks like.

✔ Icons marked with the letters *TT* are TrueType fonts, so they'll always look the best.

✔ *Note:* You'll probably never need to fiddle with the Fonts icon. Just know that it's there in case you ever want to view your fonts.

Network and Internet Connections

Clicking the Network Connections icon brings up the New Connection Wizard, which helps you connect to the Internet. (I also discuss this topic in Chapter 12, with all the other Internet stuff.) It also brings up the Network Connections window, which lets you set up a small home or office network, or connect to a network at your office. I cover this in Chapter 9 with other network stuff.

If you've already run those wizards, clicking here just shows your network settings, as well as any dial-up connections you've made.

Add or Remove Programs

Windows XP makes it easier than ever to install programs and keep itself up-to-date. Clicking the Add or Remove Programs icon opens the Add or Remove Programs window, shown in Figure 14-9. From there, you can add or remove third-party programs, as well as parts of Windows XP itself.

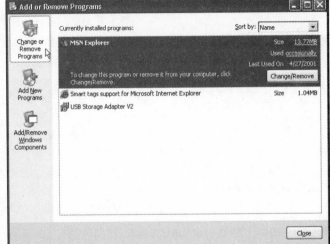

Figure 14-9:
The Add or
Remove
Programs
window tells
you how
often you've
used a
program so
that you
know if it's a
candidate
for removal.

Removing programs

Clicking the Add or Remove Programs category icon opens the Change or Remove Programs area of the Add or Remove Programs window, as shown in Figure 14-9. The window lists your currently installed programs, their size, the last time they were used, and how often they're used.

Click the program you're tired of and then click its Change/Remove button. Windows asks whether you're sure; if you click Yes, it scrapes the program from your computer's innards. Be careful, though, because the program's gone for good unless you kept its installation disc around. The program doesn't go to the Recycle Bin.

Always use the Add or Remove Programs window to uninstall your unwanted programs. Simply deleting their folders won't do the trick. In fact, doing so confuses your computer, and you might see strange error messages.

Installing a new program

When installing a new program, click the Add New Programs button from the Add or Remove Programs window. The window changes to offer two options:

✔ To add a new program, click the CD or Floppy button. Insert the program's CD or first floppy disk and click Next. Windows finds the program's installation program and installs it automatically. If you're installing a program you've downloaded from the Internet, however, Windows will complain that it can't find it. So, in that case, click the Browse button and find your downloaded program's setup program for Windows to install.

✔ To keep Windows up-to-date, click the Windows Update button. Windows connects to the Internet and tells you what your computer needs to keep Windows fresh. Follow the instructions and download any items that Windows recommends as critical.

Programs that live on compact discs often install themselves automatically: Just put them in your disc drive and shut the door.

Adding or removing Windows components

Here's a secret. Windows XP rarely installs itself completely. Windows XP often leaves off a program for sending and receiving faxes, for instance, as well as special programs for laptop users. To see what Windows XP has left off your computer — or to remove some of the features that it has installed — click the Add/Remove Windows Components button from the Add or Remove Programs window.

Windows brings up a window listing all its components. The components with check marks by their names are installed; no check mark means they're left out. If you see components with a gray area, that means some programs in that category are left out; double-click the category to see what's in and what's out.

To add a program, place a mark (click) in its empty check box. To remove one that you've installed, click in its check box — its check mark disappears, as does the program, after you click the Apply button.

Sounds, Speech, and Audio Devices

Looking for the volume control? It's hidden in here, deep in the Control Panel's bowels. You can fix that, however, so hang on. This Control Panel category hides two icons: Sounds and Audio Devices, and Speech. (Yes, Windows can talk to you.) Here's how those icons work.

Changing Windows' volume and playing with its sounds

Strangely enough, Windows XP doesn't provide a quick and easy way to change your computer's volume. Well, it does, but it hides it. Here's a simple way to put the volume control on your desktop, where it's always visible. It just might be the best tip in this book.

Click the Control Panel's Sounds and Audio Devices icon. When the Sounds and Audio Devices Properties dialog box appears, as shown in Figure 14-10, select the Place Volume Icon in the Taskbar check box. Click Apply, and a tiny speaker appears near your clock. (Check out Figure 14-11.)

Figure 14-10: Click the Sounds and Audio Devices icon to change your computer's volume, adjust its speaker setting, and tweak your sound card's settings.

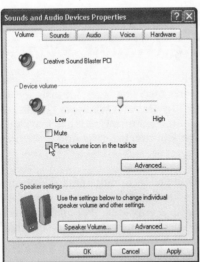

To mute the sound when the phone rings, click the little speaker icon in Figure 14-11 and click the Mute check box. Click the Mute check box again when the long distance company's salespeople hang up, and you're ready to hear your music again.

Figure 14-11: Click the little speaker and slide the bar up or down to change your computer's volume.

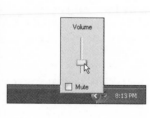

Be sure to click the Advanced button under the Speaker Settings area to tell Windows what type of speakers you're using. I don't know if it changes the sound quality much, but it feels good to know Windows cares about your speakers that much.

Multimedia setup problems

Multimedia gadgetry inevitably brings a multitude of setup problems. There are simply too many file formats and program settings for an easy ride. Although Windows XP does an excellent job of setting up your computer's hardware automatically, the Control Panel's Sounds and Audio Devices Properties dialog box lets techno-fiddlers change some of the settings. Because different computers use different parts, the settings may vary, but here's a general look at what they can do:

✔ **Volume:** Described earlier in this chapter, click here to place the little volume control icon next to your taskbar's clock.

✔ **Sounds:** This area lets you assign different sounds to different events. It's more fun than practical.

✔ **Audio:** This page controls your computer's sound hardware. You decide what device to use to play sounds and what device should record sounds. Unless you're a musician, you'll leave all these settings alone.

✔ **Voice:** Want to sing along to some tunes? Talk to other gamers? Here's where you see whether your sound card can play music and record your voice at the same time. Be sure to click the Test Hardware button before trying anything else.

✔ **Hardware:** Here, Windows XP lists all the multimedia devices attached to your computer. By clicking a device and clicking the Properties button, you can see information about each gadget. You'll rarely use this. Sound and video mavens (especially MP3 fans) like to see what codes they have installed.

After you click the Sounds tab, Windows lets you change the sounds it makes during certain events. Windows lists the Program Events near the bottom of the box and lists the possible sounds directly below them in the Sounds box. To assign a sound, click the event first and then click the sound you want to hear for that event. Click the Preview button (the little black triangle next to the Browse button) to hear the sound.

Windows only lets you assign files stored in its WAV format. You can't use MP3 files, MIDI files, or any other cool sound formats.

Letting Windows talk to you

Click the Speech icon to hear Microsoft Sam. When enabled, Sam reads the information on the screen (not very audibly, unfortunately). Click the Preview Voice button for a kick, however.

Performance and Maintenance

This category contains four icons: Administrative Tools, Power Options, Scheduled Tasks, and System. Chances are that you won't be playing with any of them. But here's a look at what each one does.

Seeing information about your computer

Some people just like to drive their cars. Others like to look under the hood. To peek under the hood of Windows XP, click the System icon. As shown in Figure 14-12, it displays oodles of complete information, more than you'll ever want to know.

The System Properties dialog box lets you tweak bunches of settings. The Hardware tab, for instance, brings up the Add Hardware Wizard. The Device Manager on that page lets you see all of your computer's parts and whether they're working properly. Click the Automatic Updates tab to decide how Windows downloads updates to Windows XP.

Most of this stuff is pretty complicated, however, so don't mess with it unless you're sure of what you're doing. This feature is covered by more-advanced books.

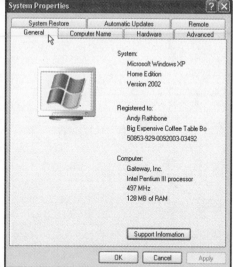

Figure 14-12:
Click the
System icon
to see
information
about your
computer,
Windows
XP, and how
Windows
XP behaves.

Turning on or off visual effects

Windows XP tries to be calm, cool, and collected. Its windows and menus slowly fade in and out, for instance, to make everything look smooth. Sometimes, however, it just looks annoying. To choose between calm and speedy, head for the System icon, click the Advanced tab, and then click Settings under the Performance area.

Choose Adjust for Best Appearance to keep everything smooth. Or choose Adjust for Best Performance to speed up your menus. Or choose Custom and pick your own settings — if you (or anybody else) can figure out what they mean. Don't like the results? Click Let Windows Choose What's Best for My Computer to return to normal.

Freeing up space on your hard disk

Sooner or later, Windows XP will start sending messages complaining about running out of room on your hard disk. Of course, you could always install a larger hard drive. But there's another solution that's less drastic: Use the Free Up Space on My Hard Disk task that pops up when you choose the Control Panel's Performance and Maintenance category.

Or call up My Computer from the Start menu, right-click on your hard drive, and choose Properties. Click the Disk Cleanup button, and Windows calculates how much garbage it can delete, as shown in Figure 14-13.

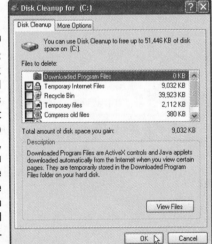

Figure 14-13:
The Disk
Cleanup tool
removes
files that
you no
longer need,
leaving you
more
storage
space on
your hard
disk.

Make sure you select Downloaded Program Files (if any), Temporary Internet Files, Recycle Bin, and Temporary Files. Click OK and then click Yes when Windows asks whether you're sure. Windows erases the files, freeing space in the process.

Rearranging your hard disk to speed it up (defragmenting)

When writing information to your hard disk, Windows isn't the most careful shelf stocker. Sometimes it breaks files apart, stuffing them into nooks and crannies. Unfortunately, Windows then takes longer to retrieve the files. To speed things up, use the Disk Defragmenter: Use the Rearrange Items on My Hard Disk task that pops up when you choose the Control Panel's Performance and Maintenance category.

Or call up My Computer from the Start menu, right-click on your hard drive, and choose Properties. Then click the Tools tab and click the Defragment Now button. After the Disk Defragmenter window appears, click the Analyze button. Windows inspects your computer's hard drive and reports back. If it says your hard drive needs defragmentation, click the Defragment button. If your hard drive's fine, close the window by clicking the little X in its top-right corner.

Feel free to run the Disk Defragmenter every few weeks, especially if your computer seems to be running slowly or you can hear your hard drive making frantic rummaging noises.

Other Performance and Maintenance icons

 The **Administrative Tools** icon is a no-no. Nothing is in there for people who don't like to fiddle with their computers. This icon is only for technicians.

 Although mostly for laptops, **Power Options** also let you set a timer for turning off your monitor, hard disks, and entire computer, if desired, to save power. Choose your current setup from the Power Schemes area and click the OK button. Head here to tell Windows XP how to react after somebody presses the computer's power switch.

 Scheduled Tasks can be left alone. Windows XP lists when it performs certain tasks automatically. They're mostly maintenance jobs that don't need changing.

Printers and Other Hardware

 If you add a new gadget to your computer, be it a mouse, joystick, keyboard, or something deep within its innards, use the Add Hardware icon, listed as a tiny icon on the Printers and Other Hardware window's left side. Windows searches for the newly installed gadget, welcomes it aboard, and makes sure it works correctly (if everything goes according to plan, that is). The rest of the icons in this category mostly adjust items you've already installed.

Adding new hardware

 When you wolf down a sandwich for lunch, you know what you ate. After all, you picked it out at the deli counter, chewed it, swallowed it, and wiped the breadcrumbs away from the corner of your mouth.

But when you add a new part to your computer, the computer is often turned off — Windows XP is asleep. And when you turn the computer back on and Windows XP returns to life, it may not notice the surgical handiwork.

Here's the good news, however: If you simply tell Windows XP to *look* for the new part, it will probably find it. In fact, Windows XP not only spots the new part, but it introduces itself and starts a warm and friendly working relationship using the right settings.

✔ Sometimes Windows XP detects a newly inserted part as soon as you turn on your computer. It occasionally recruits a wizard to help you set it up.

✔ Windows XP is pretty good about identifying various gadgets that people have stuffed inside it, especially if your computer is Plug and Play compatible and you're installing a Plug and Play part. You can find more information about Plug and Play in Chapter 3.

The Control Panel's Add New Hardware icon handles the process of introducing Windows XP to anything you've recently attached to your computer:

1. **Double-click the Control Panel's Add New Hardware icon and click the Next button.**

   The Windows XP Hardware Installation Wizard pops out of a hat, ready to introduce Windows XP to whatever part you've stuffed inside your computer.

2. **Click the Next button.**

   Windows XP looks for any recognizable Plug and Play devices installed in your computer.

Here's where things start getting a little different. Did Windows XP find anything new? If so, click the newly installed part's name from the list, click Finish, and follow the rest of the wizard's instructions.

If the wizard didn't find anything, though, click Add a New Hardware Device from the Installed Hardware List and then click Next, telling Windows to search for additional devices. Follow the instructions to see whether Windows finds the device. If it does, rejoice — and click the device's name for Windows to install it.

If Windows still can't locate your newly installed part, however, you need to contact the manufacturer of your new part and ask for a Windows XP driver.

Fiddling with printers and faxes

Most of the time, your printer works fine. Especially after you turn it *on* and try printing again. In fact, most people will never need to read this section. Even if you're installing a USB printer — one that plugs into your Universal Serial Bus port — you don't need to mess around in here. After you turn on your printer and plug it into your computer's USB port, Windows automatically recognizes it and sets up everything accordingly.

Occasionally, however, you may need to tweak some printer settings, install a new printer, or remove an old one. In any of those instances, start by clicking the Control Panel's Printers and Faxes icon from the Printers and Other Hardware category.

If you're installing a new printer, grab the Windows XP compact disc or floppy disks that came in the box; you'll probably need them during the installation.

Unless instructed otherwise, always choose LPT1: as your printer port.

1. **Click the Add Printer icon.**

   Magic! A Windows XP wizard appears, ready to set up your new printer.

2. **Click Next and follow the wizard's instructions.**

    For example, click to tell Windows whether your printer is physically connected to your computer, or whether it's shared with other computers over a network.

3. **Click Next and follow the wizard's instructions.**

    The Add Printer Wizard box lists the names of printer manufacturers on the left; click the name of your printer's manufacturer. The right side of the box lists the printer models of that manufacturer.

4. **Double-click your printer's name when you see it listed. Windows XP asks you to stick the appropriate set-up disks into a drive, and the drive makes some grinding noises.**

    After a moment, you see the new printer listed in the box.

5. **Click the new printer's icon and select the Set As Default Printer option from the window's File menu.**

    That's it. If you're like most people, your printer will work like a charm.

If you have more than one printer attached to your computer, right-click on the name of your most oft-used printer and select Set As Default Printer from the menu. That choice tells Windows XP to print to that particular printer, unless instructed otherwise.

✔ To remove a printer you no longer use, right-click on its name and then choose Delete from the menu. That printer's name no longer appears as an option when you try to print from a Windows XP–based program.

✔ To share a printer over a network, right-click on its icon and choose Sharing. Select the Share This Printer option and click OK. That printer shows up as an option for all the computers on your network.

✔ You can change printer options from within many programs. Choose File in a program's menu bar and then choose Print Setup or choose Print. From there, you can often access the same box of printer options as you find in the Control Panel. You can also find ways to change elements, such as paper sizes, fonts, and types of graphics.

✔ Check out your printer's installation guide. Some manufacturers prefer that you use their own software and steer clear of the Add Printer Wizard. Unless the printer's manual says not to, install the printer's software before using the Add Printer Wizard. (When you use the Add Printer Wizard, you may find that the new printer has already been set up, so you needn't proceed further.)

✔ Working with printers can be more complicated than trying to retrieve a stray hamster from beneath the kitchen sink. Feel free to use any of the Help buttons in the dialog boxes. Chances are that the Help buttons offer some helpful advice, and many are actually customized for your particular brand of printer. Too bad they can't catch hamsters.

Game controllers

Although Windows XP is based on a business-oriented operating system designed for networking, Microsoft has tried to design it for those who are playing on the network as well.

Because today's joysticks and game pads do much more than let you wiggle a stick and push a button, the Game Controllers icon lets gamers calibrate their fancy game controllers. If you own different controllers for different games, visit here to choose which one to use for which game. If you're constantly losing, click the Troubleshooter button to diagnose and repair any problems.

Scanners and cameras

Windows usually detects scanners and newfangled digital cameras when they're first turned on and plugged into your computer. Other times, scanners and cameras come with their own installation software that places their icons here. Still other cameras need to be formally introduced to Windows — just click the Scanners and Cameras icon and then click the Add an Imaging Device option.

Windows brings up its Installation Wizard that works amazingly like the Add Printers Wizard. Click the manufacturer name on the window's left side and choose the model on the right. Choose the correct COM port if you know where you've plugged in the device; otherwise, choose Automatic Port Detection. If you've turned on your camera or scanner and plugged in its cable correctly, Windows should recognize it and place an icon for it in both your My Computer area and your Control Panel's Scanners and Camera area.

Unfortunately, the installation of cameras and scanners doesn't always work this easily. If yours isn't automatically accepted, use the software that came with your scanner or camera. It should still work — you just won't be able to use Windows XP's built-in software.

To grab the pictures from your installed camera, turn it on and open your My Pictures folder. Choose Get Pictures from Camera or Scanner. Windows recognizes the pictures and displays tiny thumbnail pictures of them across the screen.

To pick and choose among the keepers, hold down Ctrl while clicking the good ones. In fact, because many cameras take such a l-o-o-o-n-g time to download, that trick comes in handy for quick grabs. Save the pictures in your My Pictures folder.

Making Windows XP recognize your double-click

 Clicking twice with a mouse button is called a double-click; most users do a lot of double-clicking in Windows XP. But sometimes you can't click fast enough to satisfy Windows XP. It thinks that your double-clicks are just two single clicks. If you have this problem, head for the Control Panel's Mouse icon that lives in the Printers and Other Hardware category.

Double-clicking the Mouse icon brings up the settings for your mouse, as shown in Figure 14-14. Because different computers come with different brands of mice, the following instructions may not work for you, but you can generally access the same types of options for any mouse. Try pressing F1 for help if an option seems confusing.

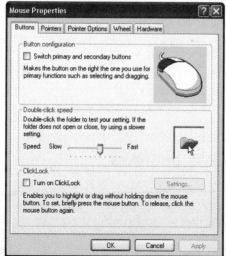

Figure 14-14:
Change your double-click speed.

To check the double-click speed, double-click the box with the little folder. After Windows XP recognizes your double-click, the folder opens. Double-click again, and the folder closes.

Slide the Speed slider bar left toward Slow until Windows XP successfully recognizes your double-click efforts. Click the OK button when you're through, and you're back in business.

- Can't double-click the Mouse icon quickly enough for Windows XP to open the darn thing up? Just click once and poke the Enter key with your finger. Or click once with the right button and choose Open from the menu that shoots out of the Mouse icon's head. Yep, you can do the same thing in Windows XP a lot of different ways.

- If you're left-handed, select the Switch Primary and Secondary Buttons check box (shown along the top of Figure 14-14) and click the Apply button. Then you can hold the mouse in your left hand and still click with your index finger.

- The mouse arrow doesn't have to move at the same speed as the mouse. To make the arrow zip across the screen with just a tiny push, click the Pointer Options tab along the top. Then, in the Pointer Speed box, slide the little box toward the side of the scroll bar marked Fast. To slow down the mouse, allowing for more precise pointing, slide the box toward the Slow side.

- Some brands of mice come with fancier features and their own different settings pages. The Microsoft IntelliMouse, as I describe in Chapter 2, lets you control on-screen action by spinning a wheel embedded in the poor mouse's neck. Laptop users with touch pads and trackballs find their adjustment areas here, too.

- Mouse acting up something fierce? Pointer darting around obstinately like an excited dachshund on a walk? Maybe you need to clean your mouse, a simple maintenance task I describe in Chapter 15.

Phone and modem options

You'll rarely use this phone and modem option unless you're on a laptop and need to enter a different area code. If so, then click the Phone and Modem Options icon, click the Dialing Rules, and click New to add your new location.

If your modem seems to be acting odd, click the Modems tab and click Troubleshoot to see if Windows can figure out what's wrong.

User Accounts

Come here to change the accounts of people you're letting log onto your computer. You can add passwords, create new accounts, add cool pictures to an account on the Welcome screen, and change the way users access Windows. I cover it all in Chapter 9.

Date, Time, Language, and Regional Options

 Designed mainly for laptop users who travel with their computers, this area lets you change your computer's date and time, and add support for other languages. Chances are that you'll fiddle with the icons in this area once and forget it.

Regional and language options

 Taking the laptop to Italy? Head to this icon and choose Italy. Windows automatically sets up Windows to use that country's currency and date formats. You'll find plenty of countries listed.

Setting the computer's date and time

 Many computer users don't bother to set the computer's clock. They just look at their wristwatches to see when it's time to stop working. But they're missing out on an important computing feature: Computers always stamp new files with the current date and time. If the computer doesn't know the correct date, it stamps files with the *wrong* date. Then how can you find the files you created yesterday? Last week? (Also, your e-mails will be sent using your computer's date, possibly confusing their recipients.)

Also, Windows XP sometimes does some funny things to the computer's internal clock, so you may want to reset the date and time if you notice that the computer is living in the past (or prematurely jumping to the future).

To set the computer's time or date, choose the Date and Time icon. A little calendar comes to the screen, where you can click the correct date and time.

Moved to a new time zone? Click the Time Zone tab along the top of the window and select the current time zone from the drop-down list.

Finally, to make Windows grab the time automatically, click the Internet Time tab. On this tab, select the Automatically Synchronize with an Internet Time Server check box.

✔ Windows XP has a Search program, which I describe in Chapter 7, that can locate files by the time and date they were created, modified, or last accessed — but only if you keep your computer's date and time set correctly.

✔ For an even quicker way to change your computer's time or date, double-click the little clock that Windows XP puts on the taskbar that lives along the edge of the screen. Windows XP brings up the Date/Time dialog box, just as if you'd waded through the Control Panel and double-clicked the Date and Time icon.

Chapter 15

The Case of the Broken Window

In This Chapter

▶ Restoring your computer to happier times

▶ Fixing a haggard mouse

▶ Fixing older programs that don't run under Windows XP

▶ Understanding administrator accounts privileges

▶ Getting out of Menu Land, if you're stuck

▶ Keeping Windows up-to-date

▶ Finding vanished desktop icons

▶ Installing a new driver for a new computer gizmo

▶ Installing other parts of Windows XP

▶ Clicking the wrong button and what to do

▶ Fixing a frozen computer

▶ Figuring out why your printer isn't working correctly

▶ Changing double-clicks to single-clicks and vice versa

Sometimes, you just have a sense that something's wrong. The computer makes quiet grumbling noises, or Windows XP starts running more slowly than Congress. Other times, something's obviously wrong. Pressing any key triggers a beeping noise, menus keep shooting at you, or Windows XP greets you with a cheery error message when you first turn it on.

Many of the biggest-looking problems are solved by the smallest-looking solutions. This chapter may be able to point you to the right one.

Restoring Calm with System Restore

It's happened to everybody: Windows works fine until something happens; then it's all over. For instance, you delete a file and Windows begins hitting you up with an ugly error message each time it loads.

Or you install a new program, which promptly disconnects your scanner, digital camera, modem, or all three.

Wouldn't you love to go back in time to when Windows worked right? Thank goodness Windows XP lets you turn back the clock with a few clicks on a program called System Restore.

Every day, Windows stores a "picture" of your computer's settings on your hard disk. If your computer begins acting weird, load up System Restore, click the last day your computer *did* work fine, and System Restore goes back in time to reset your computer to its settings from back when it worked correctly. Whew! Here's how to head back to happier times:

1. **Save any open files, close any loaded programs, and load System Restore.**

   Choose Start, click All Programs, and begin weaving your way through the menus: Choose Accessories, select System Tools, and click System Restore.

2. **Click Restore My Computer to an Earlier Time and then choose Next.**

3. **Click a calendar date when your computer worked well and then choose Next.**

   Yesterday is your best bet. But if the symptoms have been going on for longer, choose a day *before* your computer began having problems.

4. **Make *sure* you've saved any open files and then click Next.**

   Your computer grumbles a bit and then restarts.

   System Restore resets your computer to earlier settings when everything worked fine; you won't lose any work that you've saved.

   If your system is working fine, open System Restore; then, in Step 2, select the System Restore button marked Create a Restore Point. That tells Windows to take a snapshot of its current condition so that you can return to it if things go downhill.

System Restore is completely reversible. If your computer winds up in even *worse* shape, load System Restore and choose a different date.

Before installing a program or any new computer toys, load System Restore and create a restore point in case the installation is a disaster. Name the restore point something descriptive, such as *Before Installing Kitty Dish Webcam.* (That way you know which date to go back to if things go awry.)

You can save many System Restore settings — each one is a snapshot of your computer's configuration.

If you restore your computer to a time before you installed some new hardware or software, those items may not function properly. If they're not working correctly, reinstall them.

My Mouse Doesn't Work Right

Sometimes, the mouse doesn't work at all; other times, the mouse pointer hops across the screen like a flea. Here are a few things to look for:

- ✔ If no mouse arrow is on the screen after you start Windows, make sure that the mouse's tail is plugged snugly into the computer's rump. Then exit and restart Windows XP.

- ✔ If the mouse arrow is on-screen but won't move, Windows may be mistaking your brand of mouse for a different brand. You can make sure that Windows XP recognizes the correct type of mouse by following the steps on adding new hardware, as I describe in Chapter 14.

- ✔ A mouse pointer can jump around on-screen if it's dirty. First, turn the mouse upside-down and clean off any visible dirt stuck to the bottom. Then twist the little round cover until the mouse ball pops out. Wipe off any crud and blow any dust out of the hole. Pull any stray hairs, dust, and goo off the little rollers and stick the ball back inside the mouse. If you wear wool sweaters (or have a cat that sleeps on the mouse pad), you may have to clean the ball every week or so.

- ✔ If the mouse was working fine and now the buttons seem to be reversed, you've probably changed the right- or left-handed button configuration setting in the Control Panel. Double-click the Control Panel's Mouse icon and make sure that the configuration is set up to match your needs. (I cover this in Chapter 14, by the way.)

Making Older Programs Run under Windows XP

Programmers write their programs for specific versions of Windows. Then, when a new version appears, such as Windows XP, some programs feel threatened by their new environment and refuse to work.

If a game or some other program refuses to run under Windows XP, there's hope. Try running the program in Compatibility mode. This trick fools programs into thinking that they're running under their favorite version of Windows, so everything works well.

If you have a problem with a program, right-click its icon and choose Properties. When the Properties window appears, click the Compatibility tab. After checking the program's box or installation disks to see its required version, select that version from the Compatibility mode's drop-down menu, as shown in Figure 15-1.

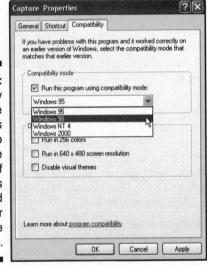

Figure 15-1: Compatibility mode enables you to select the version of Windows required by your incompatible programs.

For more information, as well as a list of compatible programs, select the option Learn More about Program Compatibility (near the bottom of Figure 15-1.)

It Says I Need to Be an Administrator!

You *do* need to be an administrator to perform most of the best stuff on Windows XP. Windows XP is set up so that when different people log onto the computer, they only see their own work. Windows XP saves everybody's individual settings, and it seems like everybody uses a different computer.

Somebody has to be in charge, however, of installing new software, changing network settings, and adding new computer parts. That person is the administrator. Usually the owner has the Administrator account, while other users have Limited accounts or guest accounts.

If you see a message that says you need to be an administrator to do something on the computer, you need to find the computer's owner and ask for help. (If you bug the administrator often enough, he or she might elevate your limited account to an administrator account.) I cover all this stuff in Chapter 9.

I'm Stuck in Menu Land

If your keystrokes don't appear in your work but instead make a bunch of menus shoot out from the top of the window, you're stuck in Menu Land. Somehow, you've pressed and released Alt, an innocent-looking key that's easy to hit accidentally.

If you press and release Alt, Windows turns its attention away from your work and toward the menus along the top of the window.

To get back to work, press and release Alt one more time. Alternatively, press Esc, perhaps twice. One or the other is your ticket out of Menu Land.

Keeping Windows Up-to-Date

Actually, you don't need to worry about keeping Windows up-to-date. Windows updates itself automatically with its Windows Update program — if you have an Internet connection. Every so often, you'll see a little message in the bottom of your screen, such as the one in Figure 15-2.

Figure 15-2:
Click this
message to
download
Windows
updates
for your
computer.

When the message appears, click it. A window appears explaining what Windows wants to install to keep itself current. Tell it Yes, by all means. The update installs on its own, but Windows may want to restart and wake back up, fully up-to-date.

Soon after the administrator first begins using the computer, Windows asks for permission to sign up for the automatic Windows Update program. Say "Yes, please." Windows Update is the best way for Microsoft to fix past mistakes to keep Windows running smoothly.

All My Desktop Icons Vanished

Windows XP does something awfully scary. Normally, when you place a file or shortcut on your desktop, you can see it. But what if all the icons suddenly vanish from your desktop? Well, in its eager desire to please everybody, Windows XP offers an odd option to make your desktop icons invisible.

If you click the desktop with your right mouse button, choose Arrange Icons By, and select Show Desktop Icons, you turn off the normally selected option that keeps your icons visible. The check mark next to that option disappears and with it, all your desktop's icons. Poof!

Sure, your desktop is now completely clean, but it's awfully hard to keep track of your icons if you can't see them. To make them reappear, right-click the desktop, choose Arrange Icons By and then select Show Desktop Icons. That toggles the option back on, and your icons all reappear.

I'm Supposed to Install a New Driver

Windows XP includes *drivers* that automatically recognize most parts when you attach them to your computer. However, sometimes you'll want to install something that's either too new for Windows XP to recognize or too old for it to remember. In that case, Chapter 3 defines drivers and explains how to locate a Windows XP driver for your troublesome new part. (***Hint:*** If you can't locate a Windows XP driver, use that part's "Windows 2000" driver, instead.)

Follow these steps to install a new or updated driver.

   1. **Right-click My Computer from the Start menu and choose Properties.**

   2. **Click the Hardware tab and click the Add Hardware Wizard button.**

The wizard guides you through the steps of installing your new hardware and, if necessary, installing your new driver. My book, *Upgrading and Fixing PCs For Dummies,* 6th Edition, includes a chapter on finding, installing, and troubleshooting Windows XP's drivers.

✔ Not all computer toys work with Windows XP. In fact, some games don't even work with some sound cards, and some software won't work with certain CD-ROM drives. Bring a list of your computer's parts to the store and check them with the requirements listed on the side of a computer toy's box before setting down the cash.

✔ To get a list of your computer's parts, right-click on the Start button's My Computer icon and choose Properties. Click the Hardware tab and the Device Manager button. Click Windows XP at the top of the list, click the Print icon, and click OK. You might not be able to make sense of the detailed computer information, but the folks at the store can decipher the numbers.

✔ The Windows Update program handles many chores for keeping Windows XP up-to-date. Windows Update dials a special place on the Internet and downloads updated information your computer might need.

His Version of Windows XP Has More Programs Than Mine!

Windows XP installs itself differently on different types of computers. As it copies itself over to a hard disk, it brings different files with it. If installed on a laptop, for example, Windows XP brings along programs that help a laptop transfer files and keep track of its battery life.

Computers with smaller hard drives will probably get the minimum files Windows XP needs to run. In Chapter 10, I describe some of the programs and accessories Windows XP comes with. Head to Chapter 14 for instructions on adding or removing programs by using the Start menu's Control Panel.

Windows XP comes with some pretty weird stuff, so don't get carried away and copy *all* of it over — especially stuff that you're not even going to use.

I Clicked the Wrong Button (But Haven't Lifted My Finger Yet)

Clicking the mouse takes two steps: a push and a release. If you click the wrong button on-screen and haven't lifted your finger yet, press the Esc button with your other hand, and then slowly slide the mouse pointer off the button on-screen. Finally, take your finger off the mouse.

The screen button pops back up, and Windows XP pretends nothing happened. Thankfully.

My Computer Is Frozen Up Solid

Every once in a while, Windows just drops the ball and wanders off some-where to sit under a tree. You're left looking at a computer that just looks back. Panicked clicks don't do anything. Pressing every key on the keyboard doesn't do anything — or worse yet, the computer starts to beep at every key press.

When nothing on-screen moves except the mouse pointer, the computer is frozen up solid. Try the following approaches, in the following order, to cor-rect the problem:

 ✔ **Approach 1:** Press Esc twice.

   This action usually doesn't work, but give it a shot anyway.

 ✔ **Approach 2:** Press Ctrl, Alt, and Delete all at the same time.

   If you're lucky, Windows Task Manager appears with the message that you discovered an "unresponsive application." The Task Manager lists the names of currently running programs — including the one that's not responding. Click the name of the program that's causing the mess and then click the End Process button. You lose any unsaved work in it, of course, but you should be used to that. (If you somehow stumbled onto the Ctrl+Alt+Delete combination by accident, press Esc at the unresponsive-application message to return to Windows.)

   If that still doesn't do the trick, try clicking the Task Manager's Shut Down menu and choosing Restart. Your computer should shut down and restart, hopefully returning in a better mood.

 ✔ **Approach 3:** If the preceding approaches don't work, push the com-puter's reset button.

   When the Turn Off Computer box appears, choose Restart.

 ✔ **Approach 4:** If not even the reset button works, turn the computer off and choose Restart from the Turn Off Computer box.

The Printer Isn't Working Right

If the printer's not working right, start with the simplest solution first: Make sure that it's plugged into the wall and turned on. Surprisingly, this step fixes about half the problems with printers. Next, make sure that the printer cable is snugly nestled in the ports on both the printer and the computer. Then check to make sure that it has enough paper — and that the paper isn't jammed in the mechanism.

Then try printing from different programs, such as WordPad and Notepad, to see whether the problem's with the printer, Windows XP, or a particular Windows program. Try printing the document by using different fonts. All these chores help pinpoint the culprit.

Can your printer be out of ink or toner? Sometimes these calamities can stop a printer from working.

For a quick test of a printer, click the Start button, choose Control Panel, and select Printers and Other Hardware. Click Printers and Faxes to see the printers connected to your computer. Right-click on your printer's icon, choose Properties, and click the Print Test Page button. If your printer sends you a nicely printed page, the problem is probably with the software, not the printer.

While still at the Printers and Faxes window, press the F1 key to bring up the Printing Help window. Try the printer's troubleshooting program — Fixing a Printing Problem — to figure out why the printer's goofing off.

My Double-Clicks Are Now Single Clicks!

In an effort to make things easier, Windows XP lets people choose whether a single click or a double click should open a file or folder.

But if you're not satisfied with the click method Windows XP uses, here's how to change it:

1. **Open any folder — the Start menu's My Documents folder will do.**

2. **Choose Folder Options from the Tools menu.**

3. **Choose your click preference in the Click Items as Follows section.**

4. **Click OK to save your preferences.**

Don't like to follow steps? Just click the Restore Defaults button in Folder Options, and Windows brings back double-clicking.

What Is Windows XP Service Pack 1?

Microsoft's programmers constantly tinker with Windows XP, fixing broken spots and plugging security holes. Microsoft releases each new repair as an easy-to-install software *patch,* usually available through Windows Update (found in the Start menu's All Programs area). Eventually, Microsoft combines the patches and releases a *Service Pack.*

Windows XP Service Pack 1 contains all the patches released during Windows XP's first year of operation. Installing Service Pack 1 quickly brings your copy of Windows XP up to date. Feel free to install it.

Service Pack 1's most visible change appears in the Control Panel's Add or Remove Programs area. Microsoft now permits computer vendors to replace Windows' mainstays like Internet Explorer, Media Player, and Windows

Messenger with different programs. Your new computer may use Netscape to browse the Web, for instance, instead of Microsoft's Internet Explorer.

To choose between Microsoft's programs or the substitutes installed by your computer vendor, open the Control Panel's Add or Remove Programs icon and choose the Set Program Access and Defaults icon. The window, seen in Figure 15-2, lets you choose between three options:

- ✓ **Microsoft Windows:** Choose this option to use Microsoft's programs. If your computer isn't using the Windows programs described in this book, this option makes Windows use them.

- ✓ **Non-Microsoft:** Choose this option to hide Microsoft's programs and substitute the alternative programs installed by your computer vendor.

- ✓ **Custom:** Choose here for the most control. You may select which programs you'll use — some of Microsoft's and some of the substitutes installed by your computer vendor.

- ✓ The four Microsoft programs directly affected include your Web browser (Internet Explorer), e-mail program (Outlook Express), media player (Windows Media Player, and instant messenger (Windows Messenger).

- ✓ If you're reasonably satisfied with how your computer handles those four areas, ignore this option. This option exists for people who want their computer to use a different program for some or all of those four tasks.

- ✓ None of these options actually remove Microsoft's programs from your computer. Switching to an alternative program merely hides Microsoft's competing program from the menus.

- ✓ Many computers don't offer any alternative programs. That's because the manufacturer didn't bother to replace Microsoft's with different ones.

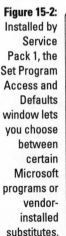

Figure 15-2: Installed by Service Pack 1, the Set Program Access and Defaults window lets you choose between certain Microsoft programs or vendor-installed substitutes.

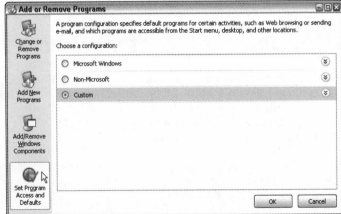

Chapter 16

Figuring Out Those Annoying Pop-Up Messages

. . . .

In This Chapter

▶ Access is denied

▶ Click here to activate now

▶ Error connecting to . . .

▶ Found new hardware

▶ If you remove this file, you will no longer be able to run this program

▶ Missing shortcut

▶ New updates are ready to install

▶ Open with . . .

▶ Privacy alert — saving cookies

▶ Stay current with automatic updates

▶ When you send information to the Internet

▶ You have files waiting to be written to the CD

. . . .

*M*ost people don't have any trouble understanding error messages. A car's pleasant beeping tone means that you've left your keys in the ignition. An electronic stuttering sound from the stereo means that your compact disc has problems.

Things are different with Windows XP, however. The pop-up messages in Windows XP could have been written by a Senate subcommittee, if only they weren't so brief. Are they error messages? Something to rejoice? When Windows XP tosses a message your way, it's usually just a single sentence. Windows XP rarely describes what you did to cause the event and, even worse, hardly ever tells you what to do about it.

Here are some of the phrases that you'll find in the most common messages that Windows XP throws in your face. Look at the title of your confusing error message — Access Is Denied, for instance — then find that title listed alphabetically in this chapter.

In this chapter, I explain what Windows XP is trying to say, why it's saying it, and just what the heck it expects you to do.

Access Is Denied

Figure 16-1:
You must
locate the
computer's
owner and
ask for
permission
to open the
folder or file.

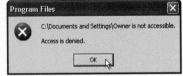

Program Files

C:\Documents and Settings\Owner is not accessible.

Access is denied.

OK

Meaning: You're not allowed to see inside this folder.

Probable cause: The computer's owner hasn't given you permission.

Solutions: Find the administrator for your computer and ask him or her for permission. If you're trying to open a folder on a networked computer, amble over to the person working on that computer and ask him or her to give you permission — if he or she has the authority.

AutoComplete

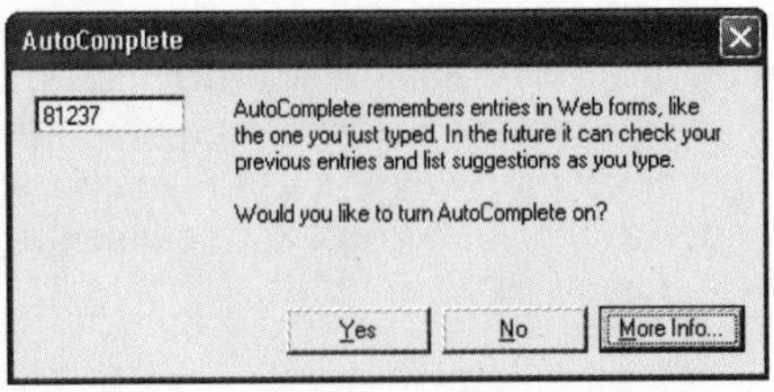

Figure 16-2:
Turn on
Auto-
Complete,
and Internet
Explorer
automa-
tically fills
in words
while you
type them.

AutoComplete

81237

AutoComplete remembers entries in Web forms, like the one you just typed. In the future it can check your previous entries and list suggestions as you type.

Would you like to turn AutoComplete on?

Yes   No   More Info...

Meaning: When turned on, Internet Explorer's AutoComplete guesses what you're about to type and tries to fill it in for you.

Probable cause: Every Windows user is eventually asked to make this decision.

Solutions: Click Yes if you think this feature is handy; click No if you think it's distracting. To turn AutoComplete off later, choose Internet Explorer's Tools menu, choose Internet Options, and click the Advanced tab. Remove the check mark next to the line Use Inline AutoComplete and click OK.

Click Here to Activate Now

Figure 16-3:
If you don't click here to activate Windows, Windows will stop working.

Meaning: If you don't activate Windows by clicking here, Windows will stop working.

Probable cause: The Windows XP new copy-protection scheme requires every user to activate his or her copy so that nobody else — including you — can use that copy on another computer.

Solutions: Click the message and let Windows dial the Internet to activate itself. If you don't have an Internet connection, dial the Activation phone number and talk to the Microsoft people personally.

Connect To . . .

Figure 16-4:
If you
don't have
a password
for this
computer,
you can't
visit.

Meaning: Windows wants to know whether you have permission to enter this area.

Probable cause: You're trying to enter a computer or folder connected to your own computer through a network.

Solutions: Type your password, if you have one. If you don't have one, ask the computer's owner or administrator for a password.

Select the Remember My Password check box, and you won't have to enter the password again. (However, choosing that option allows *anybody* to get into your computer.)

Error Connecting To . . .

Figure 16-5:
Windows is
having
problems
connecting
to your
Internet
service
provider.

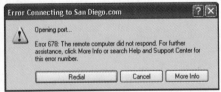

Meaning: Your computer can't currently connect to your Internet service provider (ISP).

Probable cause: If you've connected fine in the past, then your ISP may be turned off temporarily. If this is a constant message, your Internet browser's settings are probably configured incorrectly.

Solutions: Use the New Connection Wizard that I describe in Chapter 12 and check the phone number, user name, and password. If that doesn't work or proves too frustrating, wait a while. Play cards. Sniff flowers in the garden. Paint a watercolor picture of your shoes. Sometimes, an ISP goes down to preserve its users' mental health.

File Name Warning

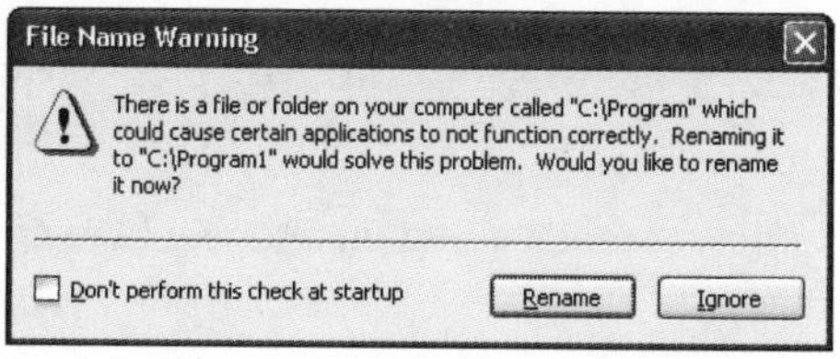

Figure 16-6: Take Windows' suggestion if it complains about a file or folder's name.

Meaning: A newly installed program created a new folder or file, but Windows doesn't approve of the chosen name.

Probable cause: Some programs that weren't written for Windows XP try to install themselves in the wrong place.

Solutions: Take the suggestion that Windows offers you. Windows suggests an alternative name and keeps track of the change, keeping you safe from problems, as well.

Found New Hardware

Figure 16-7:
Windows
recognizes
a newly
added
computer
gadget and
installs it
automa-
tically.

Meaning: Windows recognizes a newly installed computer part and is installing it automatically.

Probable cause: This message usually occurs after you plug devices into your computer's USB port.

Solutions: Relax. Windows knows what's going on and will take charge.

Hiding Your Inactive Notification Icons

Figure 16-8:
Windows
wants to
hide the
little icons
that line up
by your
clock.

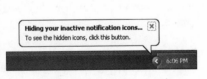

Meaning: Windows wants to hide the little icons that line up by your clock.

Probable cause: Windows likes to keep your desktop tidy. So instead of lining up icons by your clock, it hides them.

Solutions: Click the little arrow by your clock to unveil the icons when you need them. If you want the icons always visible, right-click on a blank part of the taskbar, choose Properties, and click the Customize button at the bottom of the window to decide which icons show and which stay hidden.

If You Remove This File, You Will No Longer Be Able to Run This Program

Figure 16-9:
Use the
Control
Panel's
Add or
Remove
Programs
icon to
delete
program
files; never
delete them
manually.

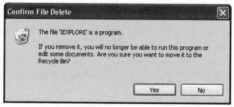

Meaning: You're trying to delete a file needed by one or more programs.

Probable cause: You're clearing off some hard disk space to make room for incoming programs. You may have accidentally tried to delete something you shouldn't have.

Solutions: Click the No button to abort deleting the file. In the future, try to figure out what you're deleting before sending it to the slaughterhouse. Only delete files if you're sure you no longer need them. And above all, remember the following:

Please use the Add or Remove Programs icon in the Control Panel if you're intentionally trying to remove a program. It's the safest way to remove a program. If your program came with its own uninstall program, feel free to use that, as well.

Missing Shortcut

Figure 16-10:
Windows
can't find
what the
shortcut is
supposed to
launch.

Meaning: You clicked a shortcut, but Windows can no longer find the program or file the shortcut leads to.

Probable cause: You've probably either moved or deleted the program and made the shortcut obsolete.

Solutions: If you deleted the program, right-click on the shortcut and choose Delete. If you still want the program, find the program using the search techniques in Chapter 7 and then create a new shortcut for it.

New Programs Installed

Figure 16-11:
Windows
announces
that you've
installed
a new
program and
highlights its
location on
the Start
menu.

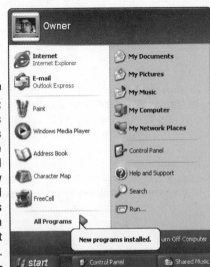

Meaning: Windows is showing you the Start menu location of a newly installed program.

Probable cause: Somebody has installed a program, and until you look at the program's new icon on the Start menu, Windows keeps displaying this message.

Solutions: Either look at the program's icon on the Start menu or disable the message feature: Right-click on the Start button, choose Properties, and click the Customize button. Click the Advanced tab and remove the check mark from Highlight Newly Installed Programs.

New Updates Are Ready to Install

Figure 16-12:
Microsoft is sending you an update to improve Windows or to fix problems.

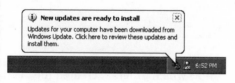

Meaning: Microsoft is sending you an update to improve Windows or to fix a problem.

Probable cause: Microsoft either wants to fix a problem with Windows or add a new feature through Windows' AutoUpdate feature. See "Stay Current with Automatic Updates," later in this chapter.

Solutions: Accept the update. You may need to save your work and let Windows restart to incorporate its changes.

Open With . . .

Figure 16-13:
Windows
doesn't
know what
program
should open
this file.

Meaning: Windows doesn't know which program created the file that you double-clicked, so it displays a list of programs and asks *you* to choose the right one.

Probable cause: Windows XP usually sticks secret hidden codes, known as *file extensions,* onto the ends of filenames. When you double-click a Notepad text file, for instance, Windows XP spots the secret, hidden file extension and uses Notepad to open the file. If Windows doesn't recognize the secret code letters, however, it complains with this error message.

Solutions: This problem's a little rough, so you may have to experiment. If you know what program created that file, choose it from the list of programs. Then select the Always Use the Selected Program to Open This Kind of file check box. Finally, click the OK button, and your problem should be solved. In the future, Windows will always know to open files with this secret code using this program.

Don't have the foggiest idea which program should open that file? Notepad's always a good choice to start with. Choose Notepad, click the OK button, and double-click your mystery file again. If your screen fills with legible text, you're saved! Close Notepad and double-click the mischievous file again. This time, however, select the Always Use This Program to Open This File check box so that Windows XP knows that Notepad should always open that type of file.

Notepad is a safe test, but files missing their file extensions often aren't meant to be opened. Be careful.

Privacy Alert — Saving Cookies

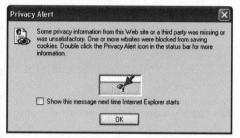

Meaning: The site you're currently visiting didn't meet the privacy settings you created in Internet Explorer, so your browser didn't let the site place a cookie on your computer.

Probable cause: The cookie probably came from an advertising or marketing site. Unless you change the default settings, Internet Explorer allows other, less-invasive cookies.

Solutions: Internet Explorer lets you set your own privacy level while browsing. To see your settings, choose Internet Explorer's Tools menu, select Properties, and click the Privacy tab. If these messages become bothersome or Internet Explorer refuses to open Web sites, move the slider to Medium or Medium Low.

Rename

Figure 16-15:
You are trying to rename a protected folder.

Meaning: This folder belongs to Windows, so you can't mess with it.

Probable cause: You're trying to rename the folder to something else. (Windows displays a similar message if you try to rename a file while it's open.)

Solutions: Give up. Windows simply won't let you rename that folder.

Safe to Remove Hardware

Figure 16-16:
You may now unplug your computer part, probably a USB device.

Meaning: Windows is now prepared for you to unplug your computer part.

Probable cause: You told Windows that you want to unplug your computer part.

Solutions: Feel free to unplug your computer part. Before unplugging a USB part — digital camera, printer, memory card reader, or other goody — you should right-click on its little icon by your clock and choose Stop.

Stay Current with Automatic Updates

Figure 16-17:
Click here to make Windows keep itself up-to-date with the latest fixes.

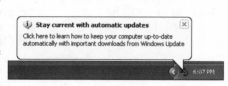

Meaning: Windows wants you to authorize it to download fixes from the Internet.

Probable cause: Windows has been recently installed.

Solutions: Click here and follow the instructions to let Windows update itself. (For more information, see the earlier section "New Updates Are Ready to Install.")

There Are Unused Icons on Your Desktop

Figure 16-18:
Windows offers to remove icons from your desktop.

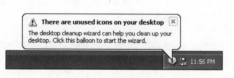

Meaning: In its incessant desire to keep your desktop tidy, Windows keeps track of how often you click the icons on your desktop. It tells you if you haven't clicked some for a while and asks if you want to get rid of them.

Probable cause: Every 60 days, Windows automatically runs its Desktop Cleanup Wizard, which offers to remove the icons you haven't clicked. It moves them to a new desktop folder called Unused Desktop Shortcuts. (You can always retrieve them from there, if desired.)

Solutions: Say No. If you want to keep your desktop tidy, do it yourself so that you can keep track of things. To turn off the feature, right-click on your desktop, choose Properties, and click the Desktop tab. Click the Customize Desktop button and remove the check mark by the Run Desktop Cleanup Wizard Every 60 Days option.

When You Send Information to the Internet

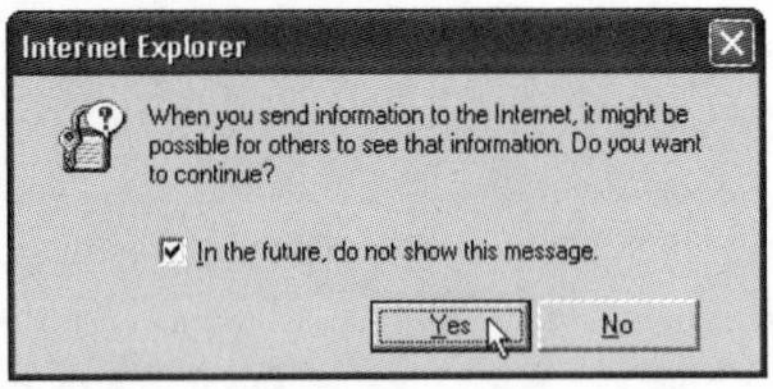

Figure 16-19:
Windows warns you that nothing is completely secure, even the Internet.

Meaning: Windows is warning you that it's possible for people to read information as it's sent through the Internet.

Probable cause: Nothing is secure — not even the Internet. The employees who work at your Internet service provider can read it, for instance. Hackers, too, sometimes run programs to read messages as they travel through the Internet. Even the folks at the FBI can and do monitor e-mail traffic when they feel circumstances warrant it. (Mainly, Microsoft adds this warning so the company is not held liable if somebody reads your e-mail.)

Solutions: Don't worry about it too much. Post office employees, for instance, can read your postcards if they want to. When I worked at a drugstore, one bored gal at the photo counter always peeked into people's photo envelopes. *Nothing's* secure while it moves from one place to another.

The point? If you want something to be *really* secure, send it using a *secure Web site*: A Security Alert window with a padlock icon appears, warning you that you're about to view pages over a secure connection. This means your information is encrypted as it travels the Internet, so it's safe for sending credit card information and other sensitive material.

You Have Files Waiting to Be Written to the CD

Figure 16-20:
You told
Windows to
copy files to
a CD/R disc.

Meaning: Files are waiting to be copied to a CD in your computer's CD recording drive.

Probable cause: You told Windows to copy files to a CD recording drive.

Solutions: Click here to see the files. Or if the balloon disappears too quickly, open My Computer from the Start menu and double-click the CD recording drive to see what Windows wants to copy there. (If you don't want to copy any files listed in this area, feel free to delete the list; the list contains only shortcuts to the files, not the actual files.) To copy the files, insert a writeable CD (not an ordinary CD) into your recording drive and click Write These Files to CD.

Chapter 17

Help on the Windows XP Help System

· ·

In This Chapter

▶ Finding helpful hints quickly

▶ Using the Windows XP Help program

▶ Finding help for a particular problem

▶ Moving around in the Help system

▶ Searching the entire Help system

▶ Using Web Help for Windows XP Help on the Internet

· ·

Sometimes, if you raise your hand in just the right way, Windows XP walks over and offers you some help.

Other times, Windows refuses to give you a straight answer. Instead, it shuffles you to another location: a horrible computerized answering machine sending you from one computerized dead-end to another.

This chapter offers some help on digging the most information from Windows frequently unhelpful Help and Support system.

Get Me Some Help, and Fast!

Don't bother plowing through this whole chapter if you don't need to: Here are the quickest ways to make Windows XP dish out helpful information when you're stumped.

Press F1

When you're confused in Windows XP, press the F1 key or choose Help And Support from the Start button's menu. The F1 key always stands for "Help!" Most of the time, Windows XP checks to see what program you're using and fetches some helpful information about that particular program or your current situation. Other times, pressing F1 brings up Windows huge Help and Support Center, which gets its own section later in this chapter.

Click the right mouse button on the confusing part

Windows XP constantly flings confusing questions onto the screen, expecting you to come up with an answer. If you know where to tackle the program, however, you can often shake loose some helpful chunks of information.

When a particular button, setting, box, or menu item has your creativity stifled, click it with your right mouse button. A What's This? box often appears, as shown in Figure 17-1, letting you know that Windows XP can offer help about that particular area. Click the What's This? box, and Windows XP tosses extra information onto the screen, as shown in Figure 17-2, explaining the confusing area you clicked.

Figure 17-1:
Click a confusing object with the right mouse button to get the hint named *What's This?*

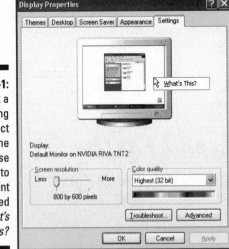

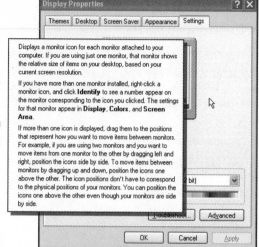

Figure 17-2:
Clicking
the What's
This? button
brings more
information
your way.

When confused about something on-screen, make Windows XP explain it:
Click the confusing item with your right mouse button and click the What's
This? box that pops up.

Choose Help from the main menu

If pressing F1 doesn't get you anywhere, look for the word Help in the menu
along the top of the confusing program. Click Help, and a menu drops down,
usually listing two lines: Help Topics and About. Click Help Topics to make
the Windows XP Help program leap to the screen and bring assistance to
your dilemma. (Clicking About just brings a version number to the screen,
which can be dangerously irritating when you're looking for something a little
more helpful.)

Sending in the Troubleshooters

Sometimes, the Windows XP Help and Support program scores big: It tells
you exactly how to solve your particular problem. Unfortunately, however,
the Help program occasionally says you need to load a *different* program to
solve your problem.

To let Windows XP fix its own problems, follow these steps:

1. **Choose Help And Support from the Start menu.**

2. **Choose Fixing a Problem from the Pick a Help Topic menu.**

   Fixing a Problem is listed at the very bottom, left corner of the Help screen. As you can see in Figure 17-3, it unleashes a torrent of information. Windows offers to help troubleshoot general problems, as well as more specific ones.

3. **Click the subject that troubles you.**

   Click E-mail and Messaging Problems, for example, if your e-mail isn't working correctly, and Windows unveils its Troubleshooter "robots" designed for different problems. Choose the E-mail Troubleshooter if that's your problem, although the troubleshooters for the Internet Explorer and Modem are standing by if needed.

4. **Answer the Troubleshooter's questions.**

   As you answer the questions, shown in Figure 17-4, Windows narrows down your problem until it decides whether it can fix the problem itself, or whether the situation requires outside intervention. (In which case, you need to beg assistance from the computer store or manufacturer, the computer guru at work, or a 12-year-old neighbor.)

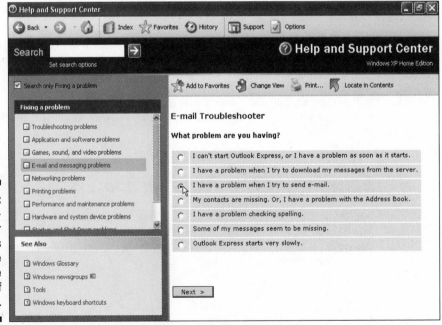

Figure 17-3:
The Trouble-
shooter
programs
help to solve
a wide
variety of
problems.

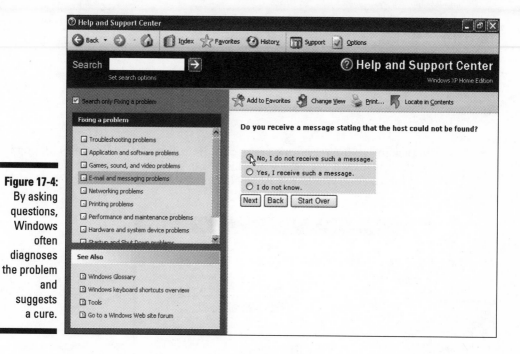

Figure 17-4:
By asking
questions,
Windows
often
diagnoses
the problem
and
suggests
a cure.

Search — letting Windows do the work

When you need an answer in a hurry, let Windows find it for you. Type a few words describing your problem into the Search box at the top of the screen. Click the green arrow next to the box, and Windows lists all the helpful information it can find about your problem. It's quick, it's easy, and it's often the best way to find that tidbit of information you need.

Consulting a Program's Built-In Computer Guru

Almost every Windows program has the word Help in its top menu. Click Help, and the Windows XP built-in computer guru rushes to your aid. For example, click Help in Paint, and you see the menu shown in Figure 17-5.

Figure 17-5:
Click Help
when you
need
"Help!"

To pick the computer guru's brain, click Help Topics, and Windows XP pops up the box shown in Figure 17-6. This box is the table of contents for all the help information Windows XP can offer on the Paint program.

Figure 17-6:
By clicking
the little
books next
to the
subjects,
you can
find the
help you
need.

To see a list of subjects, start by clicking the little book next to the word Paint. Confused about working with color? Then click the little book icon next to that subject, and the book opens to display help on any methods of using color. For example, if you want to know how to apply color with a brush, click the words *Paint with a brush*. The Help program then shows what additional help it can offer, as shown in Figure 17-7.

Confused about a term used in the Help window? If the term is underlined (like drag is in Figure 17-7), click it, and a new window pops up, as shown in Figure 17-8, defining the term.

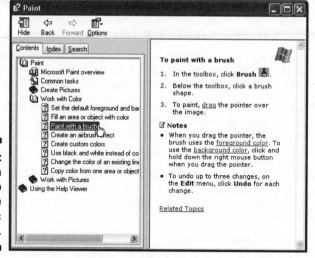

Figure 17-7:
Choose a
topic to
see more
specific
help areas.

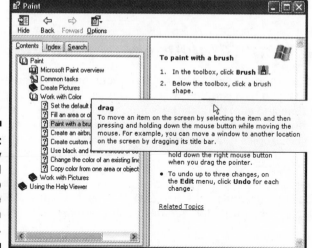

Figure 17-8:
Click any
underlined
terms to
see more
information
about them.

The Windows XP Help system is sometimes a lot of work, forcing you to wade
through increasingly detailed menus to find specific information. Still, using
Help can be much faster than paging through the awkward Windows XP
manual. And it's often much faster than tracking down a pocket-protected
neighbor.

✔ The quickest way to find help in any Windows XP program is to press F1. Windows automatically jumps to the table of contents page for the help information it has for the current program.

✔ Windows XP packs a lot of information into its Help boxes; some of the words usually scroll off the bottom of the window. To see the words, click the scroll bar (which I describe in Chapter 5) or press PgDn.

✔ Sometimes you click the wrong topic, and Windows XP brings up something really dumb. Click the Contents button at the top of the window, and Windows XP scoots back to the contents page. From there, click a different topic to move in a different direction.

✔ If you're impressed with a particularly helpful page, send it to the printer: Click the right mouse button and choose Print from the menu that appears. Windows XP shoots that page to the printer so that you can keep it handy until you lose it.

✔ To grab a Help message and stick it in your own work, highlight the text with your mouse and choose Copy from the menu. Windows then lets you paste the information into other programs. I dunno why anybody would want to do this, but you can do it.

Finding Help for your exact problem

If you don't see your problem listed in the particular table of contents page that you access, you have another way or two to find help (although it takes a little more time and effort). Click the Search tab at the top of any Help window, as shown in Figure 17-9. Type a few words describing your problem and click the List Topics button. Windows XP actively ferrets out anything helpful about your topic.

If Windows matches what you type with an appropriate topic, click the topic that looks the most pertinent and then click the Display button. Windows jumps to the page of information that describes that particular subject the best.

A quicker way to find help is to click the Index tab to see what subjects Windows is willing to explain. The Index tab works just like a book's index — clicking it brings up an alphabetical list of subjects. If you see a subject that even remotely resembles what you're confused about, double-click it. Windows XP brings up that page of Help information.

From there, you can jump around by clicking underlined words and phrases. Sooner or later, you stumble onto the right page of information.

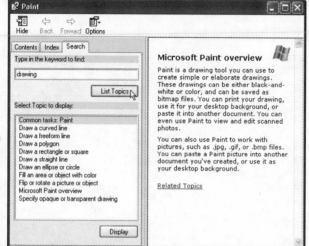

Figure 17-9:
Windows XP
locates any
Help page
dealing with
Drawing.

Windows searches alphabetically and, unfortunately, isn't very smart. So, if you're looking for help on margins, for example, don't type **adding margins** or **changing margins**. Instead, type **margins** so that Windows jumps to the words beginning with *M*.

Using Windows Help and Support Center

Although most Windows programs include an individualized Help program, which you can access by clicking Help from their menus, Windows XP also includes an all-encompassing Help program. It helps with general Windows questions, as well your computer in general. To start using it, choose Help and Support Center from the Start menu. The program rises to the screen, as shown in Figure 17-10.

The program offers help in several ways, each described below.

The Windows Help and Support Center works much like a Web site. To move back one page, click the little green Back arrow in the upper left corner. That arrow helps you out if you've backed into a corner. Just click it to move on to a more helpful page.

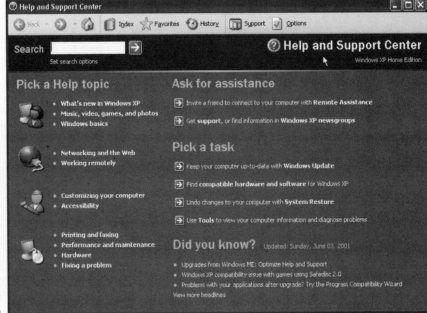

Figure 17-10:
Windows
Help and
Support
Center
offers
assistance
with
Windows
and your
computer.

The Help and Support Center offers assistance in these categories:

✔ **Pick a Help Topic:** Click these to see general information about a topic. Clicking Customizing Your Computer, for example, displays a list of things that you can change about your computer. Choose Your Start Menu from the list, and the Help menu lists how to add items to the Start menu, change the way they open when clicked, or tweak the menu's list of recently used files and documents.

✔ **Ask for Assistance:** Stumped? Here are two ways of bringing in outside help. The Remote Assistance program lets you invite a savvier Windows XP user to connect to your computer through the Internet. When the Geek connects to your computer, he sees your desktop on his screen. He can walk you through problems, offer tutorials, and behave as if he were standing over your shoulder. If you're not into that kind of computer intimacy, try the other options: Click the Support link to get help from Microsoft; Click Windows XP Newsgroups for newsgroup-based help. Or, you can always connect to help sites through the Internet.

✔ **Pick a Task:** Microsoft placed the most commonly used items here. One click enables you to keep your computer up-to-date, find Windows XP–compatible parts for your computer, restore your computer back to a time when it worked well, and run diagnostic tools to view information and test your computer.

✔ **Did You Know?:** Windows XP tosses little updated tips here. You may just get lucky and spot one that's useful.

I forgot that helpful tip!

Found a particularly helpful area? Save it for future reference by clicking the Add to Favorites button near the top of its page. Then, when you click the Favorites button along the top of the Help and Support Center window, that list's name will appear, ready to be displayed after you click it.

If you forget to place that particularly helpful page in your Favorites area, you still have a way to find it. Click the History button next to it. It immediately displays a list of pages you've visited. Hopefully, you'll spot the one you're looking for.

For best results, start your quest for help by glancing at the Pick a Help Topic area. If your troublesome spot is listed here, click it and begin narrowing down the search for pertinent information.

If that doesn't help, use the Search command at the page's top. Type in a key word or two describing your problem and click the green arrow next to the Search box. Typing **e-mail**, for instance, as seen in Figure 17-11, brings up 30 bits of information. Click any of the suggested topics to see if they solve your problem.

Figure 17-11:
Typing **e-mail** into the Search box and clicking the green arrow makes Windows display possible solutions and hints to solve e-mail troubles.

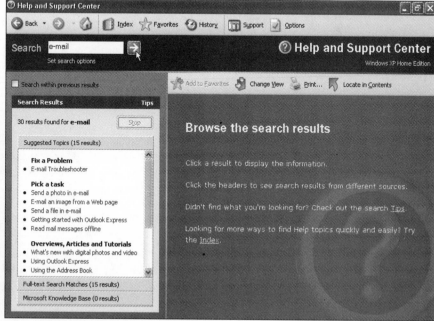

As seen in Figure 17-11, the Search command groups its results in three areas. Suggested Topics, the first and most valuable, lists troubleshooters, step-by-step tutorials, and general information. The Full-text Search Matches area lists any area containing the words you searched for. The last, Microsoft Knowledge Base, shows any results found in a Microsoft-created database listing information about all its products. (Microsoft Knowledge Base requires an Internet connection.)

Part V
The Part of Tens

The 5th Wave   By Rich Tennant

"Well, that's the third one in as many clicks. I'm sure it's just a coincidence, still, don't use the 'Launcher' again until I've had a look at it."

In this part . . .

*E*verybody likes to read top tens in magazines — especially in the grocery store checkout aisle when you're stuck behind someone who's just pulled a rubber band off a thick stack of double coupons and the checker can't find the right validation stamp.

Unlike the reading material at the grocery store, the chapters in this part of the book should be more than time-wasters. You find lists of ways to make Windows XP more efficient — or at least not as hostile. You find tips, tricks, and explanations of Windows XP icons and what they do.

Some lists have more than ten items; others have fewer, but who's counting, besides the guy wading through all those double coupons?

Chapter 18

Ten Exciting New Windows XP Features

- -

In This Chapter

▶ Decorating its folders

▶ Letting somebody fix your computer by calling it up

▶ Copying information to compact discs

▶ Transferring information easily to your new computer

▶ Setting up secure accounts for each user

▶ Keeping from crashing

▶ Stopping Internet hackers with a firewall

▶ Automatically setting the clock

▶ Requiring activation

▶ Making it work like your previous version of Windows

- -

*J*ust bought a new PC? Then you're probably stuck with Windows XP. It almost always comes preinstalled.

Current PC owners have a choice. After reading the Windows XP box in computer stores, they can decide whether or not to upgrade.

To keep you from squinting at the fine print in the computer store, here are the ten most interesting features Windows XP has to offer.

Way Cool Folders

For years, people entered information into their computer using one primary method: They'd type it in. Today, people stuff information inside their computer in bunches of ways: They download it from the Internet, import it from scanners, copy it from their music CDs, and grab it off their digital cameras.

Windows XP has not only kept up by letting you import all this information, but it helps you keep track of where you're putting it. When you insert a CD and copy its songs onto your computer as MP3 or WMA files, as I describe in Chapter 13, Windows not only types in the song titles for you, but it automatically adds a picture of the CD's cover to the folder, as shown in Figure 18-1. They're all in your My Music folder.

Unfortunately, this trick only works when you convert the CD while in Windows. If you dump your MP3 files in from another computer, the art won't appear on the folder. Sniff.

Figure 18-1: When you copy a CD's songs to your computer as MP3 or WMA files, Windows XP automatically places the CD's cover on the folder.

The Harder They Come

Looking for pictures? Store them in your My Pictures folder. Every folder stored in the My Pictures folder places (tiles) four pictures from its contents across its front, making it easier to spot what's inside. After you open the folder, you find thumbnail images of every picture inside. Or, choose Filmstrip from the folder's View menu to see a filmstrip of all your pictures, with the currently selected picture displayed above. (Click a picture to see its properties, as shown in Figure 18-2.)

Figure 18-2:
Windows
XP displays
your photos
in the folder,
making it
much easier
to locate
them.

Remote Assistance

It's late at night, and your computer is acting weird. What did you do wrong?
Luckily, your co-worker's kid across town just got Windows XP, and he's
already mastered it. But his parents won't let him out at night. If only he
could fix your computer for you. . . .

With Windows XP Remote Assistance, he can. If you turn on Remote
Assistance, another person can log onto your computer and control it, just as
if they were sitting in front of it. They can tweak your computer, setting up
what needs to be done, and your computer will run as good as new. (At least,
that's the concept.)

To load Remote Assistant, click the Start button, choose Help and Support,
and choose Remote Assistance. Choose Invite Someone to Help You from the
program's screen, and send a message by using Outlook Express or Microsoft
MSN Messenger. The recipient accepts your request, and he or she sees your
computer's screen on their monitor. You two chat back and forth, typing messages, and the helpful soul moves around your mouse, clicking the right
things, until the situation is fixed.

Expect to see it used by technical support staffs in the future. (And let's hope
the hackers don't figure out how to use it.)

Burning (Writing Information onto) CDs

Windows XP finally caught up with the computers of the day, and it handles the recordable CD drives built in to most new computers. To copy any file or files to a recordable CD drive, right-click on the file or files, choose Send To from the menu that appears, and select Writable CD.

Pop! A little window pops up with the message that you have files waiting to be copied to the CD. Insert a CD into the drive, click the Start button, and choose My Computer. Open your recordable CD with a double-click and select Write These Files to CD to copy them to your CD.

Media Player copies songs to blank CDs as well, letting you create your own "Greatest Hits" packages to play in any standard CD player. It converts MP3s or WMAs back into standard song format, so that you can fit around 10 or 12 songs on the CD, just like normal.

To save your MP3s or WMAs on a CD, use the first method of copying, so that Media Player won't convert the songs into the larger format used by normal CD players.

Files and Settings Transfer Wizard

This little wizard comes in handy as soon as you buy a new computer. How in the world do you transfer all your stuff from the old computer to the new one?

To make Windows XP handle the chores, unleash the wizard from your Start menu's System Tools area. (Click the Start button, choose All Programs, and click Accessories to find System Tools.)

The wizard works the fastest with a networked connection. Tell the wizard what information you want moved: Files, program settings, Internet connection settings, and other pertinent items. Run the wizard on both computers, and it handles the transfer chores, moving things from one computer to the other.

I describe more about the wizard in Chapter 10.

User Accounts

If you're the only person using your computer, you won't care about this. But if your family computer has a line around it like the bathroom of the Brady Bunch, then User Accounts are for you.

Windows XP lets folks have their own User Accounts. They click their name at the Welcome screen and find their own personal folders containing their own information — nobody else's. The screen looks just the way they left it. Windows XP even lets them use their own favorite desktop background.

When everybody has an individual User Account, it's as if everybody has his or her own computer. Windows XP treats everybody differently — they're not all grouped together on the same desktop. If one person changes the menus around, she has only changed the menus on her *own* account. The next person to use the computer finds the same menus he has always used.

I cover User Accounts in Chapter 9.

Increased Stability

If you've been using other versions of Windows, you're probably accustomed to the Blue Screen of Death: The screen turns bright blue, and Windows displays a cryptic message about a Fatal Error in some oddly numbered coordinate. Nobody knows what it means, or why it happened. Everybody knows that it's a Pain in the Butt.

Windows XP throws away the old engine used to run Windows Me, Windows 98, and earlier versions of Windows. Instead, Windows XP uses the more stable engine from Windows 2000 — the version used by businesses requiring a computer that won't crash haphazardly.

Sure, a program will crash every once in a while. But it won't bring down the entire computer. When a program does freeze up, hold down these three keys at the same time: Ctrl, Alt, and Delete. The Windows XP Task Manager pops up, as shown in Figure 18-3, ready to shovel the frozen program out of its memory. Click the naughty program and click the End Task button to whisk it away.

Figure 18-3:
Hold down
Ctrl, Alt,
and Delete
simulta-
neously
to remove
frozen
programs
without
shutting
down
Windows.

Windows XP does something else fun: Turning off the computer's power switch doesn't turn off the computer! It brings up the Turn Off Computer screen, where you can choose Stand By, Turn Off, or Restart.

Built-in Firewall against Internet Hackers

My cable modem is constantly connected to the Internet, so it's no surprise that somebody tries to break into my computer at least a dozen times a day. No, a person isn't sitting at his computer, typing the keyboard, and trying to find a way inside. These people run easy-to-find hacker programs that automatically scan thousands of computers, looking for one that's not secure.

If you're on the Internet, these hackers could be knocking on your door, as well — especially if you run a network or have a cable modem. To keep the bad guys out but let the good ones in, you need a *firewall*, and Windows XP tossed one in the bag. The firewall filters the information that's going into your computer and keeps your computer invisible to the programs that scan for them.

I show how to connect the firewall in Chapter 12.

Automatically Sets Clock

Windows XP automatically sets your computer's clock and keeps it set to the right time — if you tell it to do so. Double-click the little clock in the bottom right corner of your computer, click the Internet Time tab, and click in the box that is labeled Automatically Synchronize With An Internet Time Server. After you're connected to the Internet, your computer checks the time and resets its clock accordingly.

Windows XP Must Be Activated

It's true. Windows XP is copy protected so that you can only install one copy of it on one computer. If you want Windows XP on your laptop, too, you must buy another version of Windows XP. I describe this alarming fact in more detail in Chapter 3.

Making Windows XP Run Like Your Old Version of Windows

Some old-timers don't like Windows XP because it looks, well, different than their older, classic versions of Windows. In its aim to please, Windows XP wears "classic" clothes so that it looks and acts pretty closely to older versions of Windows. Here's how.

- ✔ **Switch to a Classic Start menu:** Right-click the Start menu button, choose Properties, and then choose Classic Start Menu. That replaces XP's huge and rounded Start menu with the straight-edged look of the older versions.

- ✔ **Switch to a Classic Desktop Theme:** Right-click the desktop, choose Properties, and then choose Windows Classic from the Theme drop-down menu. Wham! Now your windows turn from rounded to square, and your rounded chartreuse Start button turns gray and square. Plus, the old familiar icons reappear on the desktop: My Computer, My Documents, My Network Places, and Internet Explorer.

- ✔ **Turn back on the Shortcut keys:** Older versions of Windows had underlined letters in their menus. Instead of clicking the mouse on menu items, you could press Alt and the underlined letter to activate that menu item — a shortcut key, if you will. Although Windows XP leaves them out, here's how to turn them back on: Right-click the Desktop, choose Properties, and click the Appearance tab. Click the Effects button and remove the check mark from the line, Hide Underlined Letters for Keyboard Navigation Until I Press The Alt Key. The underlines all appear, ready for shortcuts.

✔ **Speeding up the menus:** Windows XP sometimes sacrifices speed for looks. Menus fade in and out of place, for instance, looking cool, but slowing down the job. To dump the fashion and bring back the speed, try this: Right-click the My Computer icon, choose Properties, and click the Advanced tab. Click the Settings button in the Performance area and select Adjust For Best Performance. Click OK and enjoy that burst of speed.

Chapter 19

Ten Aggravating Things about Windows XP (And How to Fix Them)

In This Chapter

▶ Changing the volume

▶ Finding out your computer's version of Windows

▶ Wanting to double-click instead of click (or vice versa)!

▶ Reattaching fallen button bars

▶ Keeping track of multiple windows

▶ Finding a missing taskbar

▶ Fixing the Print Screen key

▶ Lining up two windows on the screen

▶ Updating a folder's contents

▶ Understanding why you can't do what an administrator can do

*W*indows XP would be great if only . . . (insert your pet peeve here). If you find yourself thinking (or saying) this frequently, this chapter is for you. This chapter not only lists the most aggravating things about Windows XP, but it also explains how you can fix them.

How Do 1 Change the Volume?

Although Microsoft designed Windows XP to be easier than ever to use, the programmers stubbed their toe when it came to the most important function of all: changing the volume.

What happens if you visit a Web site late at night, only to hear some loud and merry synthesized music? Can you reach through your jumble of wires for the speaker's volume control before the family wakes?

Here's how to put the volume control back where it belongs — right next to the little clock in the bottom right corner of your screen:

1. **Click the Start button, open the Control Panel, and click the Sounds, Speech, and Audio Devices icon.**

2. **Click the Sounds and Audio Devices icon and select the Place Volume Icon in the TaskBar check box.**

   A little speaker then appears next to your clock.

3. **Click OK to close the window.**

   Now, if you need to turn the sound up or down in a hurry, click the little speaker by your clock. A sliding volume control appears, letting you turn the sound up or down by sliding the control up or down. Or, to turn the sound off completely, click the Mute box. Whew!

What Version of Windows Do I Have?

Windows has been sold in more than a dozen flavors since its debut in November 1985. How do you know what version your computer has? Did it *really* come with Windows XP?

Open the Start menu, right-click on My Computer, and choose Properties. Click the General tab, if that page isn't already showing.

Under the word *System*, Windows displays its version and version number.

I Want to Click Instead of Double-Click (Or Vice Versa)!

Slowly but surely, Windows XP is stretching away from your desktop and onto the Internet's World Wide Web, which is a huge, worldwide network of computers stuffed with everything from movie previews to groups of people discussing eggnog recipes.

When accessing the Internet, users click *once* on icons — not twice, the way Windows users have grown accustomed to doing. To see how your computer's currently set up, open any folder and choose Folder Options from the Tools menu.

The last option, titled Click Items as Follows, lets you choose between single-clicking and double-clicking. Select the one you want and click OK to make your change.

When maneuvering through the options listed in the Start menu, you only need to click once, no matter how your mouse is set up: Just click the Start button to bring the Start menu to life. All the other menus contained in the Start menu pop up automatically as the mouse pointer hovers over them. After you spot the program or choice you're after, click it, and the Start menu loads that program or choice.

My Bar Full of Buttons Just Fell Off!

It's happened to the best of us. We reach up to click a button from the row of buttons along the top of a program or on the taskbar at the bottom of the screen, when all of a sudden something awful happens.

The entire row of buttons falls off and appears as a bar or window in the middle of your program. What did you do wrong? Nothing, it turns out. Microsoft figures that some people enjoy the versatility of placing their buttons in the middle of their work. So, Windows lets people drag the button bar off the program and place it someplace else.

To place the button bar back where it started, place the mouse pointer on the bar, hold down your mouse button, and drag the bar back where it belongs. Release the mouse button, and the bar reattaches itself. Or, if that's not working right, try double-clicking the bar. The bar often reattaches itself automatically.

If a toolbar flies off your taskbar, right-click the taskbar and choose Toolbars. Remember which toolbar has a check mark next to it, and then click its name. The toolbar disappears. Right-click the taskbar again, choose Toolbars, and click the name of the same toolbar. After the toolbar reappears, it should resume its rightful position.

Keeping Track of All Those Windows Is Too Hard

You don't *have* to keep track of all those windows. Windows XP does it for you with a secret key combination: Hold the Alt key and press the Tab key, and the little bar appears, displaying the icons for all your open windows. Keep pressing Tab; when Windows highlights the icon of the window you're after, release the keys. The window pops up.

Or, use the taskbar, which I cover in Chapter 10. The taskbar is that long strip along the bottom of your screen. The taskbar lists the name of every window currently open. Click the name of the window you want, and that window hops to the top of the pile.

In Chapter 7, you find more soldiers to enlist in the battle against misplaced windows, files, and programs.

The Taskbar Keeps Disappearing!

The taskbar is a handy Windows XP program that's always running. Usually, the taskbar sits along the bottom of your screen — if you can just find the darn thing. The taskbar sometimes vanishes from the screen. Here are a few ways to bring it back.

If you can only see a slim edge of the taskbar — the rest of it hangs off the edge of the screen, for example — place the mouse pointer on the edge you *can* see. After the mouse pointer turns into a two-headed arrow, hold down your mouse button and move the mouse toward the screen's center to drag the taskbar back into view.

✔ If your taskbar disappears whenever you're not specifically pointing at it, turn off its Auto Hide feature: Click a blank part of the taskbar with your right mouse button and choose Properties from the pop-up menu. When the Taskbar and Start Menu Properties window appears, click in the Auto Hide box until a little check mark disappears. (Or, to turn on the Auto Hide feature, add the check mark.)

✔ While you're in the Taskbar's Properties window, make sure that a check mark appears in the Keep the Taskbar on Top of Other Windows check box. That way, the taskbar always rides visibly on the desktop, making it much easier to spot.

✔ To keep the taskbar locked into place so that it won't move, right-click the taskbar, choose Properties, and select Lock the Taskbar. Remember, though, that before you can make any changes to the taskbar, you must first unlock it.

✔ Running two monitors on Windows XP? Don't forget the taskbar can be on any monitor's edge — that includes the second monitor. Make sure that you point at every edge before giving up.

My Print Screen Key Doesn't Work

Windows XP takes over the Print Screen key (labeled PrtSc, PrtScr, or something even more supernatural on some keyboards). Instead of sending the stuff on the screen to the printer, the Print Screen key sends it to Windows XP's memory, where you can paste it into other windows.

✔ If you hold the Alt key while pressing the Print Screen key, Windows XP sends the current *window* — not the entire screen — to the Clipboard.

✔ If you *really* want a printout of the screen, press the Print Screen button to send a picture of the screen to its memory. Then, open Paint or WordPad, choose Paste from the Edit menu, and print from that program.

Lining Up Two Windows on the Screen Is Too Hard

With all its cut-and-paste stuff, Windows XP makes it easy for you to grab information from one program and slap it into another. With its drag-and-drop stuff, you can grab an address from a database and drag it into a letter in your word processor.

The hard part of Windows XP is lining up two windows on the screen, side by side. That's where you need to call in the taskbar. First, open the two windows and place them anywhere on the screen. Then turn all the other windows into icons (minimize them) by clicking the button with the little line that lives in the top-right corners of those windows.

Now, click a blank area of the taskbar with your right mouse button and then click one of the two Tile commands listed on the menu. The two windows line up on the screen perfectly.

The Folder Lists the Wrong Stuff on My Floppy Disk

Windows sometimes gets confused and doesn't always list the files currently sitting on a disk drive or folder. To prod a program into taking a second look, simply press the F5 key — the *Refresh* key — along the top of your keyboard.

It Won't Let Me Do Something Unless I'm An Administrator!

Windows XP gets really picky about who gets to do what on your computer. The computer's owner gets the Administrator account. Everybody else gets a Limited account. What does that mean? Well, only the administrator can do these things on the computer:

- Install programs and hardware
- Create or change accounts for other users
- Install Plug and Play-type hardware, such as some digital cameras and MP3 players
- Turn off the guest account
- Read everybody else's private files

Most other people have Limited accounts. Those accounts, usually bearing the person's name, are created by the administrator especially for that person. People with limited accounts can do these things:

- Access installed programs
- Change their account's picture and password

Guest accounts are for the babysitter or anybody else you don't intend to let permanently use your computer. Guests can log on to browse the Internet or check e-mail and run installed programs.

Chapter 20

Ten (Or So) Windows XP Icons and What They Do

In This Chapter
▶ What some Windows XP icons look like
▶ What those Windows XP icons do

Windows XP uses different icons to stand for different types of files. That arrangement means that the program is packed with enough icons to befuddle the most experienced iconographer.

Table 20-1 shows pictures of the most common icons built into Windows XP and what the icons are supposed to represent. Double-click the icon to open it or launch it into action.

Table 20-1	Windows XP Icons	
What It Looks Like	*What It Stands For*	*What It Does*
	3½-inch floppy drive	Insert a disk and double-click to see its contents.
	3½-inch floppy drive shared on a network	Almost anybody on the network can access disks inserted into this drive.
	Hard disk	Almost all your files live on this.
	Hard disk shared on a network	Almost anybody on the network can use files on this drive.

(continued)

Table 20-1 *(continued)*

What It Looks Like	What It Stands For	What It Does
	CD-ROM drive	Place a CD in here and double-click to see its contents.
	CD-ROM drive shared on a network	Networked computers can view this drive.
	Audio CD	A music CD is currently inserted in your CD-ROM drive.
	Audio CD on the network	Almost anyone on the network can listen to the CD — but only one at a time.
	Bitmap file	Graphics usually created by Paint.
	Cabinet file	A compressed collection of files that Windows XP usually likes to open by itself.
	Camera	A digital camera, usually attached through the serial, USB, or Firewire port.
	DOS program	A very old-style program.
	Folder	A computerized storage area for files on a disk.
	Help file	This icon contains instructions stored in a special format for the Windows XP Help system.
	Hidden file	The gray, washed-out look means it's a hidden information file; Windows keeps these important system files invisible unless the user flips a secret switch.
	Shortcut to an Internet site	Double-click to make Internet Explorer open that site.

What It Looks Like	What It Stands For	What It Does
	Internet page saved on your computer as an HTML file	When opened by Internet Explorer, these files look just like a Web page — even if you're not connected to the Internet.
	Media	A file containing a movie, sound, MP3 or MIDI song, or almost anything else playable in Media Player.
	Outlook Express Mail	E-mail that's been cut or copied from Outlook Express and pasted to your desktop or another folder.
	Show Desktop	Click this taskbar icon to minimize all your open windows. (To see the icon on your taskbar, right-click the taskbar, choose Toolbars, and select Quick Launch.)
	My Documents	Store the majority of your documents in this folder for safekeeping by creating a separate folder for every project.
	My Music	Store your music in this folder for easy access. (Media Player stores incoming songs here automatically.)
	My Pictures	Store your digital pictures in this folder to see them easily. (Your digital camera stores them here automatically.)
	Recycle Bin	Deleted files end up in the Recycle Bin where they can be grabbed if you change your mind.

(continued)

Table 20-1 *(continued)*

What It Looks Like	What It Stands For	What It Does
	Scrap	Scraps are dabs of information dragged and dropped onto the desktop: a paragraph from WordPad, for example.
	Setup	Double-click here to install a program.
	System file	Technical files for Windows XP to use.
	Technical Text file	Settings information for a computer program or part.
	Text	Usually created by Notepad, these contain text without formatting.
	Word processor file	A file with formatting usually created by either WordPad or Microsoft Word.
	Network workgroup	A collection of computers on a network.
	Zipped file	Files that have been compressed into one. Double-click to see the contents.
	Unrecognizable file	A file Windows XP doesn't think it recognizes.

Chapter 21

Ten Most Frequently Asked Windows Questions

. . . .

In This Chapter

▶ Remembering what things you can do to a file

▶ Choosing between Windows XP Home or Windows XP Professional

▶ Adding a picture of your face to the Welcome screen

▶ Making Windows XP play your DVDs

▶ Making your MP3s sound better

▶ Removing the Welcome screen

▶ Seeing tiny previews of your photos and pictures in a folder

▶ Making Internet Explorer open full-screen instead of in a window

▶ Missing out without the Internet

. . . .

*H*ere they are, all in one place: the most frequently asked questions about Windows XP.

If you don't find your answer here, check out Chapter 19. That chapter shows how to cure the most aggravating facets of Windows, and plenty of people are asking how to do that.

How Do I Remember All the Stuff I Can Do to a File?

Windows lets you do zillions of things to a file in a zillion different ways. How do you remember your options when dealing with a file? By just remembering this one detail:

Right-click on the file. A menu pops up listing all your available options, as shown in Figure 21-1.

Figure 21-1:
Right-click
on a file,
and a menu
lists your
available
options.

Here's a quick explanation of what those options accomplish.

✔ **Open:** This option opens the program that's linked to the file; it then places the file inside the program, ready for playing or editing. See how Open is printed in **bold**? That means it's the default option — it's the one that automatically takes effect if you get lazy and just press Enter or double-click the file.

✔ **Print:** Send the file to the printer by choosing this option.

✔ **Edit:** Select this option to change an item — edit an image, for instance — rather than simply displaying it.

✔ **Open With:** Select this option, and a list appears showing the programs most likely to open that program. Choose one of the programs, and Windows uses that program to open your file. Don't see the right program? Click Choose Program and browse your folders for the right one.

✔ **Send To:** Selecting this option lists several commonly used programs. You can immediately send the program to your floppy drive, compress it into a Zip file, place a shortcut to the file on the desktop, mail it to somebody, store it in your My Documents area, or write it onto a CD.

✔ **Cut:** This option moves the file to your computer's memory, ready to be pasted into another program or area.

✔ **Copy:** This option places a copy of the file to your computer's memory, ready to be pasted somewhere else.

✔ **Create Shortcut:** Click here to create a shortcut in the same folder. Then you can copy the shortcut to a new location.

✔ **Delete:** Poof! Your file's sent to the Recycle Bin.

✔ **Rename:** This option highlights the file's name, ready for you to type in a new name.

✔ **Properties:** Click here to see the file's size, creation date, and even more detailed statistics.

If you drag a file while holding down your right mouse button, a similar menu appears, letting you choose whether you'd like to copy the file, move it, create a shortcut, or cancel your drag.

Should I Upgrade to the Windows XP Home or Professional Version?

Windows XP comes in two versions, Home and Professional. There's not much difference in the way the two versions look or behave.

Part of the difference is mechanical. Windows XP Professional can use two central processing unit (CPU) engines inside your computer, making it run faster and more powerfully.

Much of the remaining difference centers on networking and security. Windows XP Professional includes the features of Windows XP Home, plus it adds a backup program, higher-level of security in networking, multi-language support, and more advanced features.

If you buy XP Home and decide its networking features aren't powerful enough for your needs, feel free to upgrade to XP Professional. That version installs over XP Home without problems. You can't go the other way, though: Windows XP Home can't be installed over Windows XP Professional. You need to free your hard drive of Windows entirely by *formatting* it and then start over with a spotless Windows-free slate.

How Do I Add a Picture of My Face to My User Account?

Tired of the little spaceman or soccer ball Windows XP has added to your User Account photo? Putting your own picture there isn't tough, provided that you have a digital image of yourself stored on your computer.

Don't have a digital image of yourself? Then find a friend with a digital camera, have her snap your picture, and store the picture in your My Pictures folder as a JPG file. Then follow these steps to put that picture on your account.

1. **Click the Start button, choose Control Panel, and select User Accounts.**

2. **Click Change My Picture.**

   If you're the administrator, you might need to click Change an Account, choose an Account, and then choose Change the Picture.

3. **Choose an existing picture or choose Browse for More Pictures.**

   Switch to one of Windows' listed pictures; or, to choose a picture of yourself, choose the Browse option. Your My Pictures folder opens up, showing its contents.

4. **Locate your saved picture, click its name, and click Open.**

   Windows grabs your picture and sticks it on your account. Plus, your picture appears as an option in your list of available pictures for swapping.

   Windows shrinks the entire picture to a thumbnail size to place it onto your account image.

Here are a few more tips for changing your User Account picture:

✔ If you have a digital picture of you within a group, open it with the Windows Paint program, cut out your face, and save the face in your My Pictures folder. When Windows opens that picture, it will grab your face, and not everybody in the picture.

✔ Feel free to grab pictures off the Internet for your User Account, too. If you spot a picture of Bart Simpson on the Web that you'd like to use, right-click it, choose Save Picture As, type a name, and click Save. That automatically saves the picture in your My Pictures folder for later grabbing.

Why Can't Windows XP Play My DVDs?

Many computers today come with CD-ROM drives that can play DVDs as well as CDs. When you insert a CD, Windows Media Player comes up singing tunes. But when you insert a DVD, Windows XP doesn't play the movie. What gives?

There's a catch. Before a computer can read a DVD, it needs a software or hardware *DVD decoder* to translate the numbers on the DVD into sounds and moving pictures on the screen. Some DVD drives have the decoder built-in. But many rely on software. And Windows XP doesn't include that software decoder. So how do you watch the DVD?

Well, you need to install a software DVD player from another company. (Many new computers that include a DVD drive also come with a DVD player.) Windows XP borrows the software decoder from that third-party software and plays the DVD in its own Media Player.

So, even though Microsoft may claim that Windows XP plays DVDs, a key fact is left out: Windows XP plays DVDs *if* you already have DVD-player software installed on your computer.

There's another catch: If you're upgrading your Windows 98 or Windows Me computer to Windows XP, your old DVD software probably won't work on Windows XP. You probably have to upgrade your existing software to Windows XP standards, or buy new Windows XP-compatible DVD software. Bummer.

Why Can't Windows XP Create MP3 Files?

This one's a little sticky, but bear with me. The company that engineered the MP3 file technology charges royalties for its MP3 codes, known as *codecs*. Microsoft didn't include the DVD codecs for playing DVDs, as I discuss in the previous section. And Microsoft left out the MP3 codecs, as well.

So, when you tell Media Player to create digital sound files from your CDs, it lists two options: WMA (Windows Music Audio, Microsoft's sound format), and MP3. However, the MP3 option is grayed out and can't be selected.

Windows XP can create MP3s in the same way that it plays DVDs: It borrows the codec from other software. If you install MP3 creation software that Microsoft approves of, Windows XP borrows that software's codecs, letting you select the MP3 option in Media Player. Then, and only then, will Media Player let you create MP3s.

How Do I Get Rid of the Welcome Screen?

Microsoft added the Welcome screen to make it easier for people to begin using the computer or to switch to other users. The Welcome screen lists the names of all the people who hold accounts on Windows XP. A user clicks his name, enters a password (if necessary), and starts working.

Some people want more security, though, and don't want the account names listed on the Welcome screen. Turning off the screen is easy — if you're the computer's owner or hold an administrator account.

1. **Click the Start button, choose Control Panel, and select User Accounts.**

2. **Select Change the Way Users Log on and Off.**

3. **Remove the check mark by Use the Welcome Screen.**

The simpler Log on to Windows box replaces the Welcome screen where users type in their names and passwords.

The pros: Because there's no Welcome screen with names, nobody knows who uses the computer. If lots of people are using the computer, there's no need to crowd the Welcome screen with a bunch of names. When someone logs off, Windows XP automatically saves any work that was done, as well as the customized settings, leaving the computer ready for the next person.

The cons: Some people prefer the friendly Welcome screen and the convenience of not having to type their name. Doing away with the Welcome screen also does away with the possibility of a fast user switch — where one user can quickly log off so somebody else can borrow the computer for a quick e-mail check.

When waking up from the screen saver, Windows XP normally brings up the Welcome screen, forcing users to log on again. To disable this, right-click on your desktop, choose Properties, and click the Screen Saver tab. Then remove the check mark next to the words, On Resume, Display Welcome Screen.

How Can I See Previews of My Pictures?

Windows XP has made it easier than ever to peek inside your graphics files. Instead of displaying a folder full of bland icons, Windows XP transforms each icon into a thumbnail-sized preview of the file's contents. Best yet, the previews are all done automatically.

That makes it a lot easier to find the picture of Kitty eating the bamboo leaves after you dump 63 cat pictures into the same folder.

Although Windows XP displays the thumbnail view automatically when it spies digital pictures in a folder, keeping your pictures in your My Pictures folder is best. That makes it easier to find them later, and keeps them separate from the pictures stored by other users of your computer.

If you want everybody on the computer to have access to your pictures, store them in the Shared My Pictures folder.

How Can 1 Make All My Web Pages Open in a Full-Screen Window?

Internet Explorer always opens Web windows to the same size as they were when they were last closed. So, open Internet Explorer and double-click its title bar — that strip along the top. That makes it fill the screen. Or simply drag the window's edges until it's the size you want. (In Chapter 6, I explain how to change a window's size.) After Internet Explorer is the size you want, quit the program by clicking the little X in its upper-right corner.

When you restart Internet Explorer, it should always open to its previously set size.

(This trick works for many other programs, too.)

What Will 1 Miss If 1 Don't Use the Internet with Windows XP?

I certainly won't tell anybody. In fact, many people won't notice. Despite the media hype, plenty of people don't use the Internet. Don't get me wrong; I use it an awful lot to look up subjects, such as determining the manufacture dates of potentiometers and finding out whether I should be feeding raw or roasted peanuts to the neighborhood blue jays.

I also read the news, check the weather, and listen to radio stations. Yep, a lot of information is floating around on the Internet, but it's certainly not everybody's top priority.

My point? Rest assured that Windows XP works fine without the Internet plugged in. You can still write letters, make spreadsheets, and create databases. You can participate on networks, including ones run around the office. You can even send faxes through your modem.

However, Windows XP is designed to run exceptionally well with the Internet. So if you don't sign up for an Internet account, you'll miss the extra Internet goodies tossed into Windows XP:

- First, Windows XP needs to be activated during the first 30 days that it's on your computer. Although you can do this by telephone, it only requires a mouse click if you're connected to the Internet.

- Windows Update, a special place on the Internet, automatically dishes out files that help your computer stay up-to-date with new improvements to the Windows software. While you're connected, the Update Wizard peers under your computer's hood and examines the way everything's working. Then the Update Wizard recommends or installs any updates your computer might need.

- Windows XP includes Outlook Express, a freebie program for sending and receiving e-mail — if you have a connection to the Internet.

- The Windows XP program's feature-packed Media Player plays sound and videos through the Internet. Media Player tunes in radio stations from Argentina to Zimbabwe and displays movie trailers, news videos, and TV shows.

- You can download the week's TV program list so that you can always know when your favorite shows are on. (You can even set alarms to go off when *Survivor* or *The Sopranos* begins.)

- Stayed away from the Internet because it was too hard to use? The Windows XP New Connection Wizard makes matters much easier when signing up for Internet service. It automatically handles the software configuration steps necessary for gaining access to the Internet. (The New Connection Wizard can still toss you a few jaw-dropping questions that may send you scurrying to Chapter 12, though.)

Appendix

Glossary

• •

*T*he Windows XP "easy access" Glossary program leaps to the screen in two ways. First, if you spot an unfamiliar word in the Help program — and the word's underlined — click the word, and Windows XP fetches a definition for you.

The second method is more complicated. Choose Help And Support from the Start button, type **Windows Glossary** into the Search box, and click the green arrow. After Windows brings up a list of matching items, click the item labeled "Windows Glossary" to see how Windows defines its most puzzling words.

If Windows isn't particularly handy, feel free to pick up a definition or two right here.

active window: The last window you clicked — the one with a highlighted title bar — is considered active. Any keys that you press affect this window.

Apply: Click this button, and Windows XP immediately applies and saves any changes you made from the current list of options.

background: Formerly known as wallpaper, these graphics, designs, or pictures cover the background of your computer screen. The Windows XP Control Panel lets you choose among different background files.

bitmap: One of many types of graphic files that consist of bunches of little dots on-screen. The Windows XP program called Paint creates, edits, and saves BMP files.

border: The edge of a window; you can move the border in or out to change the window's size.

cache: A storage area where Windows temporarily memorizes recently used files so that they can be retrieved quickly if needed.

case-sensitive: A program that knows the difference between uppercase and lowercase letters. For example, a case-sensitive program considers *Pickle* and *pickle* to be two different words.

Classic style: Like Classic Coke, the Windows Classic style forgoes any fancy Windows XP stylings and makes Windows XP operate like the perpetually crowd-pleasing classic "Windows 95" version released in 1995.

click: To push and release a button on the mouse. Clicking the left mouse button selects something; clicking the right mouse button brings up more information about an item.

Clipboard: A part of Windows XP that keeps track of information that you cut or copied from a program or file. It stores that information so that you can paste it into other programs.

cursor: The little blinking line that shows where the next letter will appear after you start typing.

default: Choosing the default option enables you to avoid making a more-complicated decision. The default option is the one the computer chooses for you after you give up and just press Enter.

defragment: Organizing pieces of files that live on your hard drive so that the drive can access them more easily and quickly.

desktop: The area on your screen where you move windows and icons around. Most people cover the desktop with a background — a pretty picture.

Dial-Up Networking: A way to connect to the Internet through a modem and a telephone line.

directory: A separate folder on a hard disk for storing files. Storing related files in a directory makes them easier to find. Windows XP no longer uses the word directory and prefers the word folder instead.

document: A file containing information, such as text, sound, or graphics. Documents are created or changed from within programs. *See* program.

DOS: Short for *Disk Operating System*, an aging operating system for running programs. Windows XP can still run programs designed for DOS, as well as programs designed for Windows.

double-click: Pushing and releasing the left mouse button twice in rapid succession. (Double-clicking the right mouse button doesn't do anything special.) Left-handed people often switch their mouse buttons for comfort reasons.

download: To copy files onto your computer through phone lines or cables. *See* upload.

drag and drop: A four-step mouse process that moves an object across your desktop. First, point at the object — an icon, a highlighted paragraph, or something similar. Second, press and hold your left mouse button. Third, move the mouse pointer to the location to which you want to move that object. Fourth, release the mouse button. The object is dragged to its new location.

driver: A file letting Windows talk to computer gizmos, such as video cards, sound cards, CD-ROM drives, and other stuff. Windows XP usually requires Windows XP drivers for your computer's parts, or it won't talk to them.

drop: Step four of the drag technique, described in the drag and drop entry. Dropping is merely letting go of the mouse button and letting your object fall onto something else, be it a new window, directory, or area on your desktop.

FAQ: Short for *Frequently Asked Questions*, you usually find these text files on the Internet. Designed to save everyone some time, the files answer questions most frequently asked by new users. For example, the Scanners FAQ explains all about scanners; the Xena FAQ would trace Xena's history, starting with Hercules.

file: A collection of information in a format designed for computer use.

firewall: Specialized hardware or software on a network that keeps unauthorized people from breaking in through the Internet and accessing the network's files. Some firewalls also keep employees from downloading unauthorized material. Windows XP contains a firewall program that sometimes must be activated manually.

folder: An area for storing files to keep them organized (formerly called a directory). Folders can contain other folders for further organization. *See* subfolder.

format: The process of preparing a disk to have files written on it. The disk needs to have "electronic shelves" tacked onto it so that Windows XP can store information on it. Formatting a disk wipes it clean of all previously recorded information.

highlighted: A selected item. Different colors usually appear over a highlighted object to show that it's been singled out for further action.

icon: The little picture that represents an object — a program, file, or command — making it easier to figure out that object's function.

infrared: A special way for computers to communicate through invisible light beams; *infrared ports* (IR ports) are found frequently on laptops, pocket computers, digital cameras, and printers.

Internet: A huge collection of computers linked around the world. The World Wide Web rides atop the Internet along with other computer transactions. You can connect to the Internet's World Wide Web by paying a fee to an Internet Service Provider — much like paying a monthly phone bill.

lasso: Grabbing a bunch of items simultaneously with the mouse. Point at one corner of the items and, while holding down the left mouse button, point at the opposite corner. Releasing the mouse button highlights the items for further action.

maximize: The act of making a window fill the entire screen. You can maximize a window by double-clicking its title bar — that long colored strip across its very top. Or you can click its maximize button — that button with the big square inside, located near the window's upper-right corner. (Double-clicking the title bar again restores the window to its former size.) *See* minimize.

memory: The stuff computers use to store on-the-fly calculations while running.

minimize: The act of shrinking a window down to a tiny icon on the taskbar to get it out of the way temporarily. To minimize a window, click the minimize button — that tiny button with the horizontal bar on it, located near the window's upper-right corner. *See* maximize.

multitasking: Running several different programs simultaneously.

network: Connecting computers so that people can share information without getting up from their desks.

operating system: Software that controls how a computer does its most basic stuff: stores files, talks to printers, runs programs, and performs other gut-level operations. Windows XP is an operating system.

path: A sentence of computerese that tells a computer the precise name and location of a file.

PC card: Used mainly by laptops, PC cards can house modems, memory, network parts, or other handy items. (PC cards used to be called PCMCIA cards.)

PDA: Short for *Personal Digital Assistant*, a PDA is a little computer toy for keeping track of contacts, schedules, and e-mail (and playing Bachman Turner Overdrive tunes).

Plug and Play (PnP): A sprightly phrase used to describe computer parts that Windows XP usually recognizes and installs automatically.

program: Something that enables you to work on the computer. Spreadsheets, word processors, and games are programs. *See* document.

RAM: *Random-Access Memory. See* memory.

scrap: If you highlight some text or graphics from a program, drag the chunk to the desktop, and drop it, you create an official Windows scrap — a file containing a copy of that information. The scrap can be saved or dragged into other programs.

Shortcut: A Windows XP icon that serves as a push button for doing something — loading a file, starting a program, or playing a sound, for example. Shortcuts have little arrows in their bottom corners so that you can tell them apart from the icons that *really* stand for files and programs.

shortcut button: A button in a Help menu that takes you directly to the area that you need to fiddle with.

shortcut key: As opposed to a Shortcut, a shortcut key is an underlined letter in a program's menu that lets you work with the keyboard instead of the mouse. For example, if you see the word Help in a menu, the underlined H means that you can get help by pressing Alt+H. (To see the underlined letters, press the Alt key.)

Start button: A button in the bottom-left corner of your screen that brings up a menu of programs and options. Clicking the Start button brings up the Start menu.

Start menu: A menu of options that appears after the Start button is clicked. From the Start menu, you can load programs, load files, change settings, find programs, find help, or shut down your computer so that you can turn it off.

subfolder: A folder within a folder, used to further organize files. For example, a JUNKFOOD folder may contain subfolders for CHIPS, PEANUTS, and PRETZELS. (Formerly known as a subdirectory.)

SVGA: A popular video standard for displaying information on monitors, SVGA (*SuperVGA*) uses a wide variety of colors and resolutions.

taskbar: The bar along the bottom of the screen that lists all currently running programs and open folders. The Start button lives on one end of the taskbar.

upload: To copy files from your computer to another computer through phone lines or cables. *See* download.

VGA: An aging standard for displaying information on monitors in certain colors and resolutions. VGA is now nearly replaced by SVGA.

virtual: A trendy word to describe computer simulations. Virtual is commonly used to describe elements that *look* real, but aren't really there. For example, when Windows XP uses *virtual memory*, it's using part of the hard drive for memory, not the actual memory chips.

Web browser: Software for maneuvering through the World Wide Web, visiting Web pages, and examining the wares. Windows XP comes with a free Web browser, Internet Explorer.

Web page: Just as televisions contain bunches of different channels, the World Wide Web contains gazillions of different Web pages. These screens full of information can be set up by anyone: The government displays county meeting schedules; corporations project flashy marketing propaganda; publications display online versions of their works; and the Cushmans put up a Family Page with pictures of the baby at Disneyland.

window: An on-screen box that contains information for you to look at or work with. Programs run in windows on your screen.

wizard: Helpful Windows program that takes over the chores of program installation and other computing chores.

World Wide Web: Riding atop the Internet's motley collection of cables, the flashy World Wide Web works as a sort of computerized television, letting you jump from channel to channel by pointing at and clicking the pages. Also known simply as "The Web."

Index

• A •

Access Is Denied (error message), 133, 312
Accessibility options, in Control Panel, 272
Accessibility Wizard, 171
Accessories menu, 171
Activate Windows field, running Windows XP for the first time and, 65
Activate Windows icon, 171
Activate Windows program, 173
Activation feature, 39–40, 347
active text box, 87
active window, 71
adapter cards. See network cards; sound cards; video cards
Add Hardware Wizard, 272
Add New Hardware icon, in Control Panel, 293–294
Add or Remove Programs icon, in Control Panel, 272, 286–287
adding
  programs, 286–287
  Windows components, 287
Add to Favorites option, 222
Address Book, 174
Address option, for taskbar, 163
Adjust for Best Appearance option, 291
Administrative Tools icon, in Control Panel, 272, 293
administrator (Administrator account)
  function of, 64
  logging on to Windows XP and, 62
  need for an, 304–305
  overview of, 126–127
  things that can only be done by, 354
Align to Grid option, 151
Allow Network Users to Change My Files check box, 135
All Programs option, 166
Alt key, 27
  pressing and releasing, 305
AMD Athlon microprocessor, 19
analog, definition of, 264
Any key, 43

Appearance and Themes, in Control Panel, 276–285
arranging icons on the desktop, 150–151
arrows. See pointers
Athlon microprocessor, 19
attachments, messages with, 233, 235
attributes of files, 206
Audio Video Interleaved (AVI), 264
Auto Arrange icons, 151
AutoComplete, 312–313
Auto-Hide the Taskbar option, 162
Automatic Updates, 45
  Stay Current with (pop-up message), 323
automatically starting programs, 168–169
Autoplay, 19
autosave feature, 55
AVI, definition of, 264

• B •

background, desktop
  changing the, 277–278
  overview of, 43
backing up, 40–41
Backspace key, 29
backup programs, 41
backward compatibility of Windows XP, 13
bars. See also toolbars
  menu, 78–79
  scroll, 79–81
  title, 77–78
BMP files, 278
borders of windows, 81
burning CDs, 259–260, 344
buttons
  command, 82–84
  Control-menu, 86
  Minimize and Maximize, 85–86
  option, 84–85
  radio, 85
  Restore, 86
bytes, 49–50
  memory measured in, 51

• C •

cable modem service, 214
cache size, 19
Calculator, 174
cameras, digital, 184, 296
Cancel Printing command, 164
Caps Lock key, 29
cartridge storage units, 41
cascading windows, 105–106
CD quality, definition of, 264
CD-R discs and drives
  backing up to, 41
  overview of, 19
CD-ROM drives
  overview of, 19
  required by Windows XP, 36
CD-ROMs (compact discs) *See also*
    CD-ROMs
  burning, 19
  handling, 22
  labeling, 22
  overview of, 18–19
  write-protected, 21
CD-RW discs, 19
CDs (compact discs). *See also* CD-ROMs
  burning, 259–260, 344
  in My Music folder, 342
  playing, with Media Player, 248–250
central processing unit (CPU), 19.
    See also microprocessor
Character Map program, 173
check boxes, 85, 90–91
choosing, double-clicking for, 94–95
Classic Desktop Theme, 347
Classic Start menu option, 284, 347
cleaning monitors, 25
Click Here to Activate Now (pop-up
    message), 313
clicking (mouse buttons), 23, 41–42.
    See also double-clicking
  selecting something, for, 94–95
  wrong button, the, 307–308
Clipboard, 116, 119
clock, automatically synchronized, 347
closing, a window, 85
codecs, 250, 263–264, 363

colors
  on-screen, changing, 279
  on-screen display of, 28
  themes and, 273, 277
command buttons, 82–84
Command Prompt, 174
communications programs, 172
components of computers
  disks and disk drives, 17–22
  keyboard, 26–30
  microprocessor (CPU), 17, 19
  modems, 30–31
  mouse, 22–25
  ports, 33–34
  printers, 31–32
  required by Windows XP, 35–37
  sound cards, 32–33
  video cards and monitors, 25–26
composing e-mail, 231–232
Compress Contents to Save Disk Space
    attribute, 206
computers. *See also* components of
    computers
  finding, 112–113
  frozen, 308
  IBM compatible (IBM clones), 15–16
  in My Network Places, 204–206
  requirements for Windows XP, 13, 14
  seeing information about your, 290–291
  turning off, 73
Connect To . . . (pop-up message), 314
Control Panel
  Accessibility options in, 272
  Add New Hardware icon in, 293–294
  Add or Remove Programs icon in, 272,
    286–287
  Administrative Tools icon in, 272, 293
  Appearance and Themes icon in, 276–285
  Date and Time icon in, 273
  Display icon in, 273, 276–277
  finding the right option in, 270–276
  Folder Options icon in, 273
  Fonts icon in, 284–285
  Game Controllers icon in, 273, 296
  Internet Options icon in, 273

Keyboard icon in, 274
Mouse icon in, 274, 297–298
Network Connections icon in, 274, 285–286
Phone and Modem Options icon in, 274 298
Power Options icon in, 274
Printers icon in, 274
Regional and Language Options icon in, 275, 299
Scanners and Cameras icon in, 275, 296
Scheduled Tasks icon in, 174, 275, 293
Sounds and Audio Devices icon in, 275, 288–290
Speech icon in, 275, 290
System icon in, 276, 290–291
Taskbar and Start Menu icon in, 276
Control-menu buttons, 86
Copy Disk command, 198–199
Copy This File command, 194
copying
a complete floppy disk, 198–199
files, 193–196
folders, 193–196
information, 120
music or video files, to an MP3 player or Pocket PC, 257–259
pictures, from the Internet, 227
a window or the entire screen, 120, 121
copyright, definition of, 264
CPU (central processing unit), 17, 19
Create a Password option, 64
Create Mail icon, in Outlook Express, 231–232
Create Shortcut option, 194, 360
Ctrl+Alt+Delete key combination, 30
Ctrl key, 28
cursor-control keys, 26–27, 42
cursors, 42
customizing. *See also* Control Panel
desktop, the, 277–281
folder settings, 282–283
fonts, 284–285
taskbar, the, 161–163
taskbar and Start menu, the, 283–284

cutting (and pasting)
concept of, 116
files or folders, 194
highlighted information, 118–119

• D •

data buffer, definition of, 264
data files, 45
definition of, 189
date
changing, 159
setting the computer's, 299–300
on taskbar, 159
Date and Time field, running Windows XP for the first time and, 65
Date and Time icon, in Control Panel, 273
decoder, 250
default printer, 137
defaults (default options), 43
defragmenting your hard disk, 292
Delete key (Del), 29
deleting. *See also* Outlook Express
e-mail attachments that end in EXE or VBS, 235
files, 190–191
files on a networked computer, 205
folders, 190–191
highlighted information, 120
icons, 190–191
into Recycle Bin, 151
shortcuts, 154, 155
user accounts, 130
desktop
arranging icons on, 150–151
changing the background of, 277
copying a picture of the entire, 120
customizing, 277–281
definition of, 43
dragging toolbars to the, 163
leaving scraps on the, 122
right-clicking on an empty area of, 148
desktop background, 43
Desktop option, for taskbar, 163

desktop shortcuts. *See* shortcuts
Details window, in My Computer program, 184
Devices with Removable Storage, in My Computer program, 184
dialog boxes
  command buttons in, 82
  definition of, 29, 87
  filling out forms in, 87–92
digital, definition of, 264
digital cameras, 184, 296
directories. *See* folders
Disk Cleanup option, 57
Disk Cleanup program, 173
Disk Cleanup tool, 291–292
Disk Defragmenter program, 173
Disk Defragmenter tool, 292
disk drives. *See also* CD-ROM drives; floppy disk drives
  backing up, 41
  Iomega, 20
  in a network, 204
  overview of, 19–21
  seeing files on, 186–188
  shortcuts to, 152–154
disks, 17–22. *See also* floppy disks
  do's and don'ts, 22
  labeling, 22
  write-protected, 21–22
display. *See* monitors
Display icon, in Control Panel, 273, 276–277
Display Properties dialog box, 277, 279, 280
documents
  definition of, 190
  finding, 112
  highlighting, 117
dotted options, 85
double-clicking, 44
  adjusting speed of, 297–298
  to choose something, 94–95
  opening files by, 70
  single clicking or, 309, 350–351
  title bar to maximize a window, the, 101
dragging a window's corner to a new size, 101

dragging and dropping, 44–45
  to copy or move files, 193–196
  moving windows by, 98–99
  into Recycle Bin, 151
drivers, 45–46, 306–307
drop-down list boxes, 89–90
DSP (Digital Signal Processor), definition of, 264
DVD decoder, 362–363
DVD drives, 20, 33
DVDs (DVD discs)
  handling, 22
  overview of, 19–20
  playing, with Media Player, 250–251, 254, 362–363

• E •

e-mail. *See* Outlook Express
encoding, definition of, 264
Enter key, 29
entertainment programs, 172
Error Connecting to . . . (pop-up message), 314–315
error messages (pop-up messages), 311–325
Esc key, 28
Ethernet cards, 138–139
Ethernet RJ-45 cable, 138
executing, definition of, 50
exiting programs, 54
extensions, filename, 46, 197

• F •

Fast Ethernet cards, 139
Fast User Switching (FUS), 130–131
Favorites menu, 222
file attachments, 233, 235
File Is Ready for Archiving attribute, 206
File Name Warning (pop-up message), 315
filename extensions, 46, 197
filenames, 46, 55, 198
files
  attributes of, 206
  copying or moving, 193–196

deleting, 190–191
hidden, 190
icons for different types of, 355–358
in Windows Explorer, 203–204
loading (opening), 50, 68–70, 92–94, 189–190
name(s) of, 197
operations that can be performed on, 359–361
on other computers, 205
overview of, 45–46
path of, 187
refreshing lists of, 207
renaming, 196
seeing, with My Computer program, 186–188
seeing more information about, 200–203
selecting more than one, 195–196
sharing, 135
temp, 57
undeleting, 191–192
Files and Settings Transfer Wizard, 173–174, 344
filing, e-mail messages, 234. *See also* Outlook Express
finding. *See also* searching
computers or people, 112–113
files, 106–111
folders, 106–111
lost documents, 112
lost windows on the desktop, 103–106
media, on your computer, 247
newsgroups, 237–238
pictures, music, or video, 111–112
firewall, 225–226, 346
floppy disk drives, 18
required by Windows XP, 36
floppy disks
copying complete, 198–199
do's and don'ts, 22
formatting, 207–208
overview of, 18
preformatted, 207
preformatted or IBM formatted, 18
removing write protection on, 21
write-protected, 21–22

FM (Frequency Modulation), definition of, 264
Folder Options dialog box, 190, 197, 273, 282–283
Folder Options icon, in Control Panel, 273
folders (directories), 185–189, 342
copying or moving, 193–196
creating, 199–200
definition of, 185
deleting, 190–191
hidden, 190
in Windows Explorer, 203–204
name(s) of, 197
networked (shared), 134
opening files and, 69
on other computers, 205
organization of, 186
overview of, 46
refreshing display of, 354
refreshing lists of, 207
renaming, 196
seeing more information about, 200–203
seeing what's inside, 188–189
selecting all files in a folder, 196
selecting more than one, 195–196
settings for displaying, 282–283
sharing, 135–136
F1 key (Help), 328
fonts, 284–285
Fonts dialog box, 285
Fonts icon, in Control Panel, 284–285
For Fast Searching attribute, 206
formatting, floppy disks, 207–208
Found New Hardware (pop-up message), 316
Free Up Space on My Hard Disk task, 291–292
frozen computer, 308
function keys, 26
FUS (Fast User Switching), 130, 131

• G •

Game Controllers icon, in Control Panel, 273, 296
games, 173
gigabytes, 50

Google, 113, 223–224
graphical user interface (GUI), 47
  definition of, 11
graphics modes, 28
grayed out menu items, 78
grid, align icons to, 151
Group Similar Taskbar Buttons
    option, 162
Guest accounts, 62, 126, 127, 354

● *H* ●

hard disk space, definition of, 51
hard disks
  backing up to, 22
  defragmenting, 292
  freeing up space on, 291–292
  in My Computer program, 184
  overview of, 20–21
  required by Windows XP, 35
  shared, 134
hardware. *See also* components of
    computers
  adding new, 293–294
  definition of, 47
headers, of e-mail messages. *See also*
    Outlook Express, 233
Help, right-clicking items to get, 328
Help and Support Center, 335–338
Help and Support system, 327–338
  Index tab, 334–335
  Remote Assistance, 336, 343
  Search box, 331–334
  Troubleshooters, 329–331
  What's This? hint, 328–329
Help menu item, 329
Hibernate option, 156
Hidden attribute, 206
hidden files and folders, 190
Hide Inactive Icons option, 163
Hiding Your Inactive Notification Icons
    (pop-up message), 316–317
highlighted information, cutting, 118–119
highlighting, shortcuts for, 117–118
Highlight Newly Installed Programs
    option, 284
Home Networking Setup disk, 142

home pages, 219–221
hyperlinks (links), 218
HyperTerminal, 172

● *I* ●

IBM compatible computers (IBM clones),
    15–16
IBM computers, 15, 18
icons
  adding to the Start menu, 167
  arranging, on the desktop, 150–151
  copying or moving, 193–195
  definition of, 47–48
  deleting, 190–191
  Hide Inactive Icons option, 163
  in Media Player's Media Guide, 243
  renaming, 196
  running Windows XP for the first time
    and, 66–67
  selecting bunches of, 89
  types of files represented by, 355–358
  vanished, 306
If You Remove This File, You Will No
    Longer Be Able to Run This Program
    (pop-up message), 317
Inbox, in Outlook Express, 233–234.
    See also Outlook Express
indexes of Web sites, 222–223
Insert key (Ins), 29
Insert mode, 29
installing
  Internet Explorer, 225
  new programs, 287
IntelliMouse, Microsoft, 23
Internet, the. *See also* Web, the
  definition of, 210
  not using, 365–366
  overview of, 48–49
  who uses, 211–212
Internet access (Internet connection).
    See also ISPs (Internet service
    providers) *and* modems
  activation of Windows XP and, 40
  networked computers and, 132
  required by Windows XP, 36

requirements for, 213–214
as two-way, 31
Internet account
  Outlook Express and, 229
  setting up an, 214–218
Internet Connection field, running
    Windows XP for the first time and, 65
Internet Connection Wizard, 214–218
Internet Explorer
  AutoComplete, 312–313
  desktop background and, 43
  full-screen windows, 365
  installing, 225
  moving between Web pages in, 221–222
  navigating the Web with, 219–224
  overview of, 210
  Search function in, 223
  on the Start menu, 284
Internet Options icon, in Control Panel, 273
Internet radio stations, in Media Player,
    244–246
Internet service providers. *See* ISPs
Iomega drives, 20
ISPs (Internet service providers)
  busy signals and, 226
  choosing, in Internet Connection
    Wizard, 216
  finding, 214, 215
  overview of, 213
  setting up an account with, 214–218
Itanium microprocessors, 19

● *J* ●

Jaz disks and drives, 20, 41
JPG files, 278

● *K* ●

Keep the Taskbar on Top of Other
    Windows option, 162
Keyboard icon, in Control Panel, 274
keyboards, overview of, 26
keys
  Alt, 28
  Backspace, 29
  Caps Lock, 29

Ctrl, 28
Ctrl+Alt+Delete combination, 30
cursor-control, 26–27
Delete, 29
Enter, 29
Esc, 28
function, 26
Insert (Ins), 29
Num Lock, 28
numeric keypad, 26–27
Pause/Break, 30
PrtScrn/SysRq, 29–30
Scroll Lock, 28, 30
Shift, 28
shortcut, 27
Tab, 29
Windows, 27
kilobytes, 49, 50

● *L* ●

labeling, disks, 22
laptop and notebook computers
  requirements for Windows XP
    Professional, 25
  separate version of Windows XP needed
    for each, 18
  Windows XP Professional as better
    for, 10
lassoing files and folders, 195–196
launching, definition of, 50
LCD monitors, 25
licensing feature, turning off, 255
Limited user account, 126, 130
lines of text, highlighting, 117
links (hyperlinks), 218
Links option, for taskbar, 163
Linux, 47
list boxes
  choosing options from, 88–89
  drop-down, 89–90
  selecting more than one item from, 89
List Topics button, 334
loading programs or files, 189–190
  definition of, 50
Lock the Taskbar option, 162
Lock Web Items on Desktop option, 151

logging off Windows XP, 72–73, 156
  Fast User Switching compared to, 130
logging on to Windows XP, 62
lossy compression, definition of, 264
LPT port, 137
lurking on newsgroups, 238

• M •

Macintosh computers, 18
magnets, floppy disks and, 22
Magnifier, 171
Make Available Offline option, 222
Maximize button, 85–86, 101
Media Guide, 242–243
Media Library, 244–246, 248, 251, 255,
    257, 260
Media Player, 19, 239–265
  adding skins to, 261–262
  burning your own CDs with, 259–260
  creating WMA or MP3 files with,
    253–254
  finding media on your computer
    with, 247
  fixing problems with, 262–263
  Internet radio stations in, 244–246
  Media Guide section of, 242–243
  Media Library in, 244–246, 248, 251, 255,
    257, 260
  movies in, 244
  moving music or video to an MP3 player
    or Pocket PC, 240, 257–259
  overview of, 240–241
  playing CDs with, 248–250
  playing DVDs with, 250–251, 254
  playing MP3s and WMAs with, 240,
    251–252
  playing videos with, 256–257
  playlists in, 247, 248, 252
  size of, 263
  turning off licensing feature in, 255
megabytes, 50
megahertz (MHz), 19
memory
  definition of, 51
  overview of, 51
  required by Windows XP, 35

menu bars, 78
menus
  pull-down, 67–68
  speeding up, 348
microprocessor (CPU), 17, 19
Microsoft IntelliMouse, 23
Microsoft License Pak, 40
MIDI, definition of, 264
Minimize All Windows option, 81, 160
Minimize button, 85–86, 158
minimizing windows
  with Minimize All Windows option,
    81, 160
  with Minimize button, 85
  from taskbar, 160
  to taskbar, 158
Missing Shortcut (pop-up message), 318
Modem Dialing Information field, running
    Windows XP for the first time and, 65
modems
  finding, in your computer, 215
  options, 298
  overview of, 30–31
  required by Windows XP, 36
modes, graphics, 28
modified, arrange icons in the order
    that they were, 151
monitors
  automatically turning off, 274
  cleaning, 26
  definition of, 26
  overview of, 25–26
  pixels on, 28
  required by Windows XP, 36
  resolution of, 28
  screen savers, 278–279
  switching video modes (resolutions),
    279–281
  using two or more, simultaneously, 281
mouse, 22–25
  definition of, 51
  dragging and dropping with, 44–45
  highlighting with, 117
  operating principles of, 22
  optical, 23
  required by Windows XP, 36
  troubleshooting, 303

mouse buttons
  clicking, 23, 41–42, 94–95
  double-clicking, 44, 94–95
  left versus right, 95–96
Mouse icon, in Control Panel, 274, 297
mouse pointer (arrow)
  cursor differentiated from, 42
  function of, 23
  problems with, 303
  shapes of, 23–25
Move This File command, 194
moving
  files, 193–196
  music or video to an MP3 player or
      Pocket PC, 257–259
  the taskbar, 157–158
  windows, to a different place on the
      desktop, 98–99
  windows, with the title bar, 77–78
  windows, to the top of the pile, 97–98
MP3 files
  creating, with Media Player, 253–255, 363
  definition of, 264
  finding, on your computer, 247
  playing, with Media Player, 251–252
  PocketZip disks for, 20
MP3 player, moving music or video to a,
      257–259
Mp3PRO format, 252
MSN Explorer, 177
MSN Messenger Service, 159
MSN Search, 113
multimedia. *See also* Media Player
  setup problems, 289–290
  terms used in, 264–265
multitasking, 52
multiversion license for Windows XP, 40
music. *See also* My Music folder
  finding, 111–112
muting the sound, 288
My Computer program, 181–208
  Details in, 184
  Devices with Removable Storage in, 184
  folders and files in, 185–189
  Hard Disk Drives in, 184
  Other Places in, 184

overview of, 181–182
refreshing lists of files or folders in, 207
Scanners and Cameras in, 184
seeing files with, 186–188
seeing what's inside folders
    with, 188–189
Shared Documents folder in, 135–136,
    143, 183–184, 195, 253
Shared Music folder in, 183
Shared Pictures folder in, 183
System Tasks in, 184
My Documents folder, accessing, from
    Start menu, 166
My Music folder
  accessing, from Start menu, 166
  CD covers in, 342
  storing files in, 255–256
My Network Places, 204
  folders that you can access in, 134
My Pictures folder
  accessing, from Start menu, 166
  display of pictures on, 342, 343
  thumbnail-sized previews in, 364–365

• *N* •

name(s)
  arrange icons by, 151
  of files or folders, 197–198
Name Your Computer field, running
    Windows XP for the first time and, 65
Narrator, 171
.NET Passport, 129
network(s), 131–141. *See also* users (User
    Accounts)
  accessing other networked computers,
      134–135
  creating your own, 138–143
  definition of, 131
  installing parts of, 140–141
  Network Setup Wizard for setting up,
      141–143
  overview of, 32, 52
  parts you need for a, 138–140
network adapter cards, 37
network administrator, 64

network cards, 138–139
  installing, 140–141
Network Connections, 172
Network Connections icon, in Control
    Panel, 274, 285–286
Network Setup disk, 142
Network Setup Wizard, 141–143
Networking Settings field, running
    Windows XP for the first time
    and, 65
New Connection Wizard, 215, 217, 219, 225,
    285, 315, 366
New Programs Installed (pop-up message),
    318–319
New Toolbar option, 163
New Updates Are Ready to Install (pop-up
    message), 319
News (NNTP) server, 236
newsgroups, 236–238
Notepad, 174–175
  in Insert mode, 29
NTFS, 64, 143
Num Lock key, 27
numeric keypad, 26

• O •

older programs, 13, 303–304
On-Screen Keyboard, 172
Open box, options in, 70
Open option, 360
Open with . . . (pop-up message), 320
Open With option, 360
opening, files, 68–70, 92–94
operating system, 10
optical mouse, 23
option buttons, 84–85
options
  default, 43
  dotted, 85
  in list boxes, choosing, 88–89
Organize Favorites option, 222
Other Places, in My Computer
    program, 184
Outlook Express, 228–238
  attachments in, 233, 235
  composing a letter with, 231–233

filing messages in, 234
  getting ready to send e-mail with, 231
  newsgroups in, 236–238
  reading a received letter in, 233–235
  responding to a message in, 234
  setting up an account in, 229–230
  spell checker in, 233
  on the Start menu, 284
Overwrite mode, 29
Owner user account, 62

• P •

Paint program, 175
  highlighting part of a picture or drawing
    in, 118
palmtops and other handheld computers,
    Windows CE for, 18
paragraphs, highlighting, 117
Passport, 129
Password Reset Disk, 132
passwords
  as case-sensitive, 64
  creating, 64
  creating or changing, 132
  disabling the network password
    request, 66
  forgotten, 64
  logging on to Windows XP and, 63–64
  Passport and, 129
  for screen savers, 279
  suggestions for, 64
Paste command, 121, 122
pasting
  into another window, 121–122
  concept of, 116
path of files, 187
Pause Printing command, 164
Pause/Break key, 30
Peerless cartridges, 41
Pentium 3 microprocessors, 19
  required by Windows XP, 35
Pentium 4 microprocessors, 19
people, finding, 113
Personalize Your Software option, running
    Windows XP for the first time and, 65

Phone and Modem Options icon, in Control Panel, 274, 298
pictures
  finding, 111–112
  for user accounts, 127–128, 361–362
pixels, 28
playing
  CDs, 248–250
  DVDs, 250–251, 254
  MP3s and WMAs, 251–252
  videos, 256–257
playlists
  definition of, 264
  in Media Player, 247, 248, 252
Plug and Play, overview of, 53
Plug and Play hardware, Windows XP preferred, 13
plug-ins, 226–227
Pocket PC, moving music or video to a, 240, 257–259
PocketZip disks, 20
pointers (arrows), 53
pop-up messages (error messages), 311–325
  Access Is Denied, 312
  Click Here to Activate Now, 313
  Connect To . . ., 314
  Error Connecting To . . ., 314–315
  File Name Warning, 315
  Found New Hardware, 316
  Hiding Your Inactive Notification Icons, 316–317
  If You Remove This File, You Will No Longer Be Able to Run This Program, 317
  Missing Shortcut, 318
  New Programs Installed, 318
  New Updates Are Ready to Install, 319
  Open with . . ., 320
  Privacy Alert-Saving Cookies, 321
  Rename, 322
  Safe to Remove Hardware, 322
  Stay Current with Automatic Updates, 323
  There Are Unused Icons on Your Desktop, 323–324
  When You Send Information to the Internet, 324–325
  You Have Files Waiting to Be Written to the CD, 325
ports, 33–34
Power Options icon, in Control Panel, 274, 293
preformatted floppy disks, 207
primary monitor, 281
Print Screen key, 120–121, 353
printer icon, on the taskbar, 160, 164
printers
  adding, 294–295
  controlling, 164
  default, 137
  desktop shortcuts to, 154
  overview of, 31–32
  sharing, 136–138
  troubleshooting, 308–309
Printers and Faxes icon, in Control Panel, 274, 294
printing
  messages in Outlook Express, 235
  overview of, 71
Privacy Alert-Saving Cookies (pop-up message), 321
processing speed of CPUs, 19
Program Compatibility Wizard, 175
program files, 45
  definition of, 189
programs. *See also* starting programs
  adding or removing, 286–287
  automatically starting, 168–169
  included with Windows XP, 5, 307
  New Programs Installed (pop-up message), 318–319
  older, 303–304
  putting two programs on-screen simultaneously, 70–71
  quitting or exiting, 54
  running (executing, launching), 50–51
  running two versions of, 154
  shortcuts distinguished from, 155
Properties option, 360
PrtScrn/SysRq key, 29
public domain, definition of, 265
pull-down menus, 67–68

• Q •

Quick Launch toolbar, 162, 163
quitting programs, 54

• R •

radio buttons, 85
radio quality, definition of, 265
radio stations, Internet, in Media Player,
   244–246
Read Only attribute, 206
reading newsgroups, 237–238
RealAudio, 265
Recycle Bin, 151–152
  restoring files from, 191–192
Refresh command, 207
Refresh key (F5), 354
Regional and Language Options icon, in
   Control Panel, 275, 299
  running Windows XP for the first time
   and, 65
Registration, running Windows XP for the
   first time and, 65
Remote Assistance, 177, 343
Remote Desktop Connection, 172
removing
  programs, 286–287
  unwanted icons from Start menu, 168
  Windows components, 287
Rename (pop-up message), 322
Rename option, 360
renaming, files, folders, or icons, 196
reset button, 308
resolution, 28
  video, switching to a different, 279–281
responding
  to e-mail messages, 234
  to newsgroup postings, 238
Restart, 308
Restart option, 156
Restore button, 86
restoring, from Recycle Bin, 152
restoring your computer to an earlier time,
   301–303

right-clicking
  on an empty area of desktop, 148
  purpose of, 42, 95–96
  What's This? hint, 328–329
Run command, on Start button menu, 166
running, definition of, 50

• S •

Safe to Remove Hardware (pop-up
   message), 322
sampling, definition of, 265
Save As command, 55
Save command, 54–55
saving, overview of, 72
ScanDisk program, 55–56
scanners, in My Computer program, 184
Scanners and Cameras icon, in Control
   Panel, 275, 296
Scheduled Tasks icon, in Control Panel,
   174, 275, 293
scraps, 122–123
screen. *See* monitors
screen savers, 278–279
screen shots, 120
scroll arrow, 80
scroll bars, 79–81
scroll box, 79, 80
Scroll Lock key, 28, 30
Search Companion, 107–113
search engines, 113, 214, 222–224
searching. *See also* finding
  Internet, the 113
Select tool, in Paint program, 118
selecting
  clicking mouse buttons for, 94–95
  more than one file or folder, 195–196
Send button, in Outlook Express, 232
Send To option, 360. *See also* Outlook
   Express
Service Pack, 45, 310
Set As Background option, 43, 278
Share This Folder on the Network check
   box, 135
Shared Documents folder, 135–136, 143,
   183–184, 195, 253

Shared Music folder, 136, 183
    storing files in, 255–256
Shared Pictures folder, 136, 183
sharing (shared resources), 134–138
    folders, 135–136
    printers, 136–138
Shift key, 27
shortcut keys, 27
    turning back on, 347–348
shortcuts
    actual programs distinguished from, 155
    deleting, 154–155
    making, 152–154
    missing (pop-up message), 318
    overview of, 56
Show Common Tasks in Folders
        option, 282
Show Desktop Icons option, 151, 306
Show Hidden Files and Folders button, 190
Show Quick Launch option, 162
Show the Clock option, 163
shutting down Windows XP, 155–156
single clicking, 309, 350–351
size
    arrange icons by, 151
    of windows, changing, 85–86, 99–101
skins
    definition of, 265
    for Media Player, 261
sliding controls, 91–92
Small Icons option, 284
smart tags, 227
software, definition of, 47–48
software, included with Windows XP, 5, 307
sound cards, 32–33, 37
    Media Player and, 240
    Media Player problems and, 263
sound module, definition of, 265
Sound Recorder, 172
Sounds and Audio Devices icon, in Control
        Panel, 275, 288–290
speaker icon, on the taskbar, 160
speakers, 289
Speech icon, in Control Panel, 275, 290
speeding up menus, 348
spell checker, in Outlook Express, 233
Stand By option, 155

Start button, 165–168
    functions of, 159, 165
    shortcuts and, 56
    starting a program from, 166–167
    starting programs with, 65, 67
Start menu
    accessing My Documents folder from, 166
    accessing My Music folder from, 166
    accessing My Pictures folder from, 166
    adding a program's icon to the, 167–168
    All Programs option, 166
    Classic, 347
    customizing, 283–284
    free programs on, 169–179
    frequently used programs on, 166
    removing unwanted icons from, 168
starting programs, 50–51
    automatically, 168–169
    with the Start button, 65, 67, 166
starting Windows XP, 61–67
StartUp folder, 169, 177
storing files, in My Music and Shared Music
        folders, 255–256
subdirectories. *See* folders
subfolders, 46
Subject box, in Outlook Express, 232
subscribing to newsgroups, 237
surfing the Internet, 221–222
Surfwax, 113
switchboxes. *See also* network(s),
        installing parts of, 139–141
switching
    task, 52
    between users, 129–130
    video modes (video resolution), 279–281
    windows, by clicking on them, 71
    windows, with the taskbar, 81
Synchronize option, 175
System icon, in Control Panel, 276,
        290–291
System Information program, 174
System Restore program, 174, 176, 301–303
System Tasks, in My Computer
        program, 184
System Tools, 173

• T •

Tab key, 29
  filling out forms and, 42
tape backup units, 41
taskbar, 157–163
  customizing, 161–163, 283–284
  date and time on, 159
  disappearing, 352–353
  moving, 157–158
  overview of, 157
  retrieving windows from, 158
  shrinking windows to the, 158
  switching windows with the, 81
  volume control on, 160
Taskbar and Start Menu icon, in Control
    Panel, 276
Task Manager, locating hidden windows
    with, 104
task switching, 52
telephone quality, definition of, 265
temp files, 57
10BaseT cable, 138–140
text, highlighting, 117–118
text boxes, typing into, 87–88
themes, 276, 277
  Classic Desktop Theme, 347
There Are Unused Icons on Your Desktop
    (pop-up message), 323–324
tilde, in filenames, 57, 198
Tile Windows Horizontally command,
    105, 106
Tile Windows Vertically command,
    105–106
tiling windows, 105–106
time
  changing, 159
  setting the computer's, 299–300
  on taskbar, 159
title bar
  changing a window's size by double-
    clicking the, 101
  moving windows by grabbing its, 77–78,
    98–99
TMP filename extension, 57
To box, in Outlook Express, 232

toolbars
  dragging to the desktop, 163
  falling off, 351
  Quick Launch, 162, 163
touch pad, 23
Tour Windows XP program, 175
TPE (Twisted Pair Ethernet), 138
TrackPoint, 23
turning off the computer, 73
turning off your computer, 155–156
Turn Off option, 155
TV tuner card, 34, 37
Twisted Pair Ethernet (TPE), 138
type, arrange icons by, 151
typing into text boxes, 87–88

• U •

undeleting files, 191–192
undoing, 82
updates, Windows, 305–306
  New Updates Are Ready to Install (pop-up
    message), 319
  Stay Current with Automatic Updates
    (pop-up message), 323
upgrading your computer, Activation
    feature and, 40
USB ports, 37
Use Windows Classic Folders option, 282
Usenet, 224
user names
  logging on to Windows XP and, 62
  Passport and, 129
users (User Accounts), 126–131
  adding a picture of your face to, 127–128,
    361–362
  changing, 130
  creating, 130–131
  deleting, 130
  logging on to Windows XP and, 62
  overview of, 345
  pictures for, 127
  running Windows XP for the first time
    and, 65
  switching quickly between, 129–130
Utility Manager, 172

• *V* •

version of Windows, displaying, 350
video cards
  overview of, 25–26
  required by Windows XP, 36
  switching to a different video mode, 280
  for two or more monitors, 281
video modes (video resolution), switching
    to new, 279–281
videos
  finding, 111–112
  playing, with Media Player, 256–257
visual effects, turning on or off, 291
visualizations, in Media Player, 250
volume
  changing the, 91, 92, 160, 288, 349–350
  Media Player and problems with, 263
volume control, 172, 288

• *W* •

wallpaper, 43
WAV files, definition of, 265
Web, the (World Wide Web). *See also*
    Internet, the
  definition of, 57, 210
  requirements for connecting to, 213–214
Web browsers. *See also* Internet Explorer
  definition of, 210, 218
  overview of, 218–219
Web links. *See* links (hyperlinks)
Web pages
  copying pictures from, 227
  moving between, 221–222
  smart tags on, 227
  Windows XP looks like, 11
Web sites. *See also* Web pages
  home pages of, 219–221
  Passport-enabled, 129
  shortcuts to, 56
webcams, in Media Guide, 242
weighted keys, definition of, 265
Welcome screen
  getting rid of, 363–364
  turning on or off, 131

What's This? hint, 328–329
When You Send Information to the Internet
    (pop-up message), 324–325
Winamp, 265
windows (on-screen elements)
  active, 71
  borders of, 81–82
  changing size of, by dragging the corner
    of a window, 99–101
  changing size of, with Minimize and
    Maximize buttons, 85–86
  definition and functions of, 11
  filling the whole screen, 101
  finding lost windows on the desktop,
    103–106
  keeping track of, 352
  lining up two, 353
  minimizing all, 81
  moving, to a different place on the
    desktop, 98–99
  moving, to the top of the pile, 97–98
  overview of, 57
  parts of, 76
  pasting into other, 121–122
  retrieving, from the taskbar, 158
  shrinking to the taskbar, 158
  switching, by clicking on them, 71
  switching, with the taskbar, 81
  tiling and cascading, 105–106
  typical, 76–77
Windows (operating system), overview
    of, 9–11
Windows Catalog, 171
Windows CE, 16, 265
Windows Explorer
  copying or moving files with, 195
  displaying files and folders with,
    203–204
  refreshing lists of files or folders in, 207
Windows key, 27
Windows Me, Windows XP Home as
    similar to, 10
Windows Media Audio (WMA) files.
    See WMA files
Windows Messenger, 178
Windows Movie Maker, 176

Windows 2000, 10
  Windows XP installed over, 10
Windows Update program, 45, 171, 305–306
Windows XP. *See also* customizing; starting
  activation of, 39–40
  adding or removing components,6, 287, 307
  as backward compatible, 13
  different ways of performing the same computing task, 14
  hardware requirements of, 25, 35–37
  keeping up-to-date, 6, 305–306
  logging off, 72
  memory requirements, 51
  multi-version license for, 40
  older programs and, 13, 303–304
  overview of, 9–10
  reasons for using, 13–14
  running for the first time, 65
  separate copy required for each computer, 37, 39–40
  shutting down, 155–156
  stability of, 345–346
  versions of, 10
Windows XP Home
  choosing between Windows XP Professional and, 361
  as version for homes and small businesses, 10
Windows XP Professional
  administrator in, 126
  choosing between Windows XP Home and, 361
  laptop or notebook computer requirements, 37
  for larger businesses, 10
Windows XP Server edition, 10
WindowsMedia.com, 242–243
WMA files
  creating, 240, 253–254
  playing, with Media Player, 240, 251–252
WordPad
  overview of, 176–177
  starting, 67

WordPad Document, creating a new, 148–150
words, highlighting, 117
World Wide Web (the Web). *See* Web, the
write-protected disks, 21
WYSIWYG (What You See Is What You Get) format, printing in, 32

• Y •

You Have Files Waiting to Be Written to the CD (pop-up message), 325
Your Product Key field, running Windows XP for the first time and, 65

• Z •

Zip drives, 20